T0386260

BEYOND DUTY

BEYOND DUTY

THE REASONS SOME SOLDIERS COMMIT ATROCITIES

WALTER S. ZAPOTOCZNY JR.

FONTHILL

To my wife, Bonnie, whose faith in me never waivers

Fonthill Media Language Policy

Fonthill Media publishes in the international English language market. One language edition is published worldwide. As there are minor differences in spelling and presentation, especially with regard to American English and British English, a policy is necessary to define which form of English to use. The Fonthill Policy is to use the form of English native to the author. Walter S. Zapotoczny Jr. was born and educated in the United States; therefore American English has been adopted in this publication.

Fonthill Media Limited
Fonthill Media LLC
www.fonthillmedia.com
office@fonthillmedia.com

First published in the United Kingdom and the United States of America 2017

British Library Cataloguing in Publication Data:
A catalogue record for this book is available from the British Library

Typeset in 10.5pt on 13pt MinionPro
Printed and bound in England

Preface

The history of warfare is filled with accounts of brutality. The behavior of any human being is, of course, a very complex phenomenon whether in war or in peace. It is the collective behavior of the five groups described in this book that are most disturbing. The Japanese Army's actions in Nanking, China, in 1937 was an unplanned outbreak of inconceivable violence and brutality, while the German *Einsatzgruppen*'s actions in Russia during World War II, by contrast, were in response to an intentional policy of mass murder. The Russian leadership turned a blind eye to the Red Army's rape and murder of German civilians at the close of World War II, and during the Vietnam War, frightened American soldiers massacred women and children in a small village. American guards practiced masochism and abuses of prisoners at a prison in Iraq. While these are different situations in many ways, there are similar factors that allowed most of the soldiers in these groups to abuse or kill men, women, and children in cold blood.

Historians, in large part, have described in great detail the actions of these groups, but they have not adequately dealt with the factors that contributed to those actions. As we examine these factors, we can perhaps predict the actions of future groups given similar circumstances.

The idea for this book sprang from my graduate thesis, which examined the actions of the Japanese Army and the actions of the German *Einsatzgruppen* during World War II. After graduate school, I continued to study these and additional military groups and collect a considerable amount of research material, including court transcripts, witness testimony, official government documents, interviews, and primary and secondary works. This book contains summaries of the research material that has been collected over the years. *Beyond Duty* begins with the examination of the collective behavior of the five military groups representing different combat actions: the Japanese in Nanking, China, in 1937; the German *Einsatzgruppen* in Russia between 1941 and 1943; Russian Army in Germany in 1945;

the Americans at My Lai Massacre in 1968, during the Vietnam War; and the abuse of prisoners by Americans at the Abu Ghraib prison in Iraq in 2004.

After a close analysis of these soldiers, I have identified five principle factors that had the greatest influence, either directly or indirectly, on the many members. Together, the factors supported each other and crystallized into a *modus operandi* that resulted in atrocities and bestial acts on civilians. The soldiers who committed atrocities became violent criminals. They progressed through the stages of 'violentization' outlined by criminologist Lonnie H. Athens. The purpose of this book is to illustrate how the factors described herein enabled some soldiers to progress through Athens' stages to become perpetrators of evil. The reader cannot help but think that the atrocities of these groups were inevitable, given the combination of the factors identified.

CONTENTS

Introduction

The account of humankind's cruelty to fellow humans is a long and regretful tale. For example, on 24 August AD 410, slaves opened Rome's Salarian Gate and the Visigoths poured in and looted for three days. As the barbarians had converted to the Christian sect Arianism, there was only some looting, rape, murder, and damage to buildings.[1] Jerusalem was destroyed by the Mongols in 1244. Egyptian Mamluks managed to stave the Mongol invasion off in 1260, but the invaders razed the city once more later that same year. The sacking of Jerusalem in 1260 left fewer than 2,000 inhabitants in the city. Constantinople City fell to Sultan Mehmed II on 29 May 1453. He allowed the troops to loot the city for three days. Many residents were sold into slavery.[2] Despite the fact that all wars contain horror and suffering, there are degrees of ruthlessness—the worst of which can be categorized as atrocity or even holocaust. During World War II, atrocities were committed by all of the major participants in the conflict. These actions were often covered up or denied.

The Japanese Imperial Army had experienced much harder fighting in the capture of Shanghai than they had anticipated. They outran their supply lines and had to forage for food. After experiencing heavier losses than expected, they felt a great deal of anger towards the Chinese.

On 13 December 1937, Nanking, the capital city of Nationalist China, fell to Japanese troops. Imperial Japanese Army units immediately began committing brutal atrocities against the civilian population. Despite compelling documentary evidence, eyewitness accounts (including some by Japanese soldiers), and photographic evidence, Japanese revisionists continued to reject charges that war crimes and atrocities occurred there. The debate continues as many Japanese find it difficult to accept the past actions of the Imperial Army while some search for the truth. In the History Channel's program entitled 'The Rape of Nanking' in its *History Undercover* series on 22 August 1999, one of the themes presented was an alleged cover-up of the 'Rape of Nanking' for half a century by the Japanese. Yet the heated controversy and debate about the incident in Japan appears to be more than enough to prove that there was no cover-up. Instead, many Japanese scholars and journalists have discussed this issue openly and tried to obtain the truth. Although quite a few of them disagree with the prevailing opinion in the United States and in other Western countries, it is obvious that the expression of disagreement is not necessarily an act of cover-up.[3] Perhaps, many in Japanese society cannot bring themselves to believe that the atrocities actually happened.

The history of Nanking has been altered over time to meet the needs of changing societies in different sociopolitical contexts. While the details and the number of deaths continue to be debated, most historians agree that the Nanking massacre was an atrocity, in which 80,000 or more Chinese civilians and surrendered soldiers were killed and tens of thousands of women raped following the Japanese capture of the city. In Japanese publications seeking to deny or greatly minimize this event, a phrase like 'so-called' is often placed in front of one of the articles describing the events. Some seeking to link the event rhetorically or structurally with the more widely known Holocaust in Europe during the Second World War use the term 'Nanking Holocaust.' The atmosphere of denial and revisionism has made it difficult for historians to determine the causes of the soldiers' actions.

After the German Army invaded Russia on 22 June 1941, the *Einsatzgruppen* (Special Action Group) followed, working to eliminate Jews, Bolsheviks, and sympathizers. In his book *Masters of Death*, Richard Rhodes contributes to the history of the Holocaust by discussing the professional killing squads deployed in Poland and the Soviet Union. Rhodes explains how the Nazis condemned the Jews of Eastern Europe to slaughter by the *Einsatzgruppen*, who went on to execute 1.5 million men, women, and children between 1941 and 1943 by shooting them in killing pits. Rhodes states that these massive crimes have been underestimated or overlooked by Holocaust historians.[4] Like every historical event, the Holocaust evokes certain specific images.

When mentioning the Holocaust, most people think of the concentration camps. They immediately envision emaciated victims in dirty striped uniforms staring incomprehensibly at their liberators or piles of corpses, too numerous to bury individually, bulldozed into mass graves. While those are accurate images, they are merely the product of the systematization of the genocide committed by the Third Reich. The reality of that genocide began not in the camps or in the gas chambers, but with four small groups known as the *Einsatzgruppen*. The *Einsatzgruppen* massacres preceded the invention of the death camps and significantly influenced their development. The *Einsatzgruppen* story offers insight into a fundamental Holocaust question of what made it possible for men, most of them ordinary men, to kill so many people so ruthlessly. While the German Army units also committed atrocities, the *Einsatzgruppen* were motivated by Nazi ideology and racism.[5]

One of the most notable anti-Semitic propaganda movements to develop over the past several decades has been the organized effort to deny or minimize the established history of Nazi genocide against the Jews. The roots of Holocaust denial can be found in the bureaucratic language of Nazi policy itself, which sought to camouflage the genocidal intent of what the Nazis called the 'Final Solution' to the 'Jewish Question,' even as these directives were being carried out.[6] After the war, former Nazis and Nazi sympathizers dismissed the overwhelming proof of the Holocaust established at the Nuremberg trials. Akin to the Japanese story, the atmosphere of denial and revisionism has made it difficult for historians to determine the real causes of the German soldiers' actions.

Similarly, the action of the Russian Army in Germany, during the closing days of World War II, have been cloaked in denial and covered up. Victims were reluctant to tell their stories out of shame. Historians estimate that as many as 2,000,000 women and young girls were raped and many were killed. In her 2006 article for the *Journal of Contemporary History*, Catherine Merridale writes the following:

> There was no shortage of men in the Red Army whose lives had been marked by state violence, whose consciousness was formed in the brutality of civil war. German atrocities on Soviet soil compounded images that had been part of life for 20 years. A kind of wild amorality prevailed along the front, especially among the huge numbers conscripted in the last year of the war. Most of these came from regions that had survived not just German occupation but also the horrors of Soviet invasion back in 1939. These recruits had learned how to survive in an anarchic, brutal world. Many had little reason to love Stalin, let alone his party. But vengeances, and personal survival, were high on their list of private goals.[7]

American soldiers are not immune to cruelty and atrocity. Americans soldiers at My Lai massacred men, women, and children in 1968 during the Vietnam War. The 'Mere Gook Rule' soon developed to rationalize unsoldierly behavior. It was no crime to kill, torture, rob, or maim a Vietnamese because he was a mere gook. One soldier captured the pervasive view: 'They're lost. The trouble is no one sees the Vietnamese as people. They're not people. Therefore, it doesn't matter what you do to them.' The psychiatric report indicated that 1Lt Calley felt he was not killing human beings, but 'rather that … animals with whom one could not speak or reason.' Ironically, 1Lt Calley's Charge Sheet, which expressed our collective values in the form of law, spoke not of the murder of 'people,' 'persons,' or 'human beings,' but of 'oriental human beings.' Racism in Vietnam, along with hatred, fear, and revenge, quickly turned into beatings, torture, rape, and murder. As with other incidents, efforts were made by the government to cover up the crimes.

In April 2004, the world was shocked to see a series of photographs of U.S. military personnel abusing detainees at the Abu Ghraib prison facility in Iraq. Pictures showed prisoners hooded and connected to electrical wires, tied to leashes, stacked naked on the floor, and engaging in simulated sex acts. Some analysts believe that this event marked a turning point in the war, after which Iraqi and world opinion shifted substantially against the United States. The revelations of prisoner abuse were followed by multiple investigations and reports, news stories, and criminal prosecutions. With these actions too, there was a concerted effort by some in the military to cover up the story. Some commentaries on the Abu Ghraib abuses have put nearly exclusive importance on situational factors, such as those found in Philip Zimbardo's 1971 Stanford prison experiment, in which twenty-four male undergraduates were recruited to play the roles of guards and prisoners. Some guards quickly engaged in sadistic behavior, and most prisoners accepted humiliation. The intensity with which students adopted their assigned roles surprised the experimenters and led Zimbardo to stop the experiment before it was completed. Zimbardo attributed the extreme behaviors of the students to the force of the situation in which they were placed, rather than individual deviance. Others have argued that Zimbardo underestimated the ability of individuals to alter situations and that persons are ultimately responsible for their own actions.[8]

The body of academic works that have examined these groups to date has largely focused on the groups' actions and not on the root causes of those actions. Typically, the reasons for these groups' actions are attributed to one or two macro social factors. Lack of discipline or lack of clear instructions or orders are often used to explain these actions. Few studies provide a micro analysis of the factors that had the greatest influence on the soldiers of the military units. For example, in his book *The Creation of Dangerous Violent Criminals*, Lonnie Athens describes his violent-socialization theory. He writes that violence, official or private, is learned through violent experience.[9] In his book *The Nanjing Massacre in History and Historiography*, Joshua Fogel claims the Japanese were taught that their imperial hierarchy lay at the center of the world morality and that the Japanese were superior to all other peoples.[10] Neither of these or other books take into account all of the complex and interwoven factors that influenced the soldiers from the five groups to commit their horrific actions.

Lonnie Athens describes, in great detail, how people who commit heinous acts are created. He developed his conclusions based on interviews with perpetrators. Athens concludes that dangerous, violent criminals progress through several stages of experience—concluding in the act of violence. While Athens' conclusions are certainly plausible as they pertain to individuals, I had several questions. While the above group's actions were for different reasons, are there similar circumstances that caused members of these units to progress through Athens' stages and act so brutally, and can a model be constructed that can be used to predict the actions of future military groups? Not all of the soldiers in these five groups committed violent actions; so, why did some members choose violent actions? Did the five factors examined in this book accelerate the process of becoming violent in some individuals?

Athens proposes that a person's violent actions can be seen as continuous with his past experiences.[11] In other words, if the individual has experienced violence in his past, he may be more prone to commit violence. Perhaps the individuals described in this book were most influenced by the following factors. After a close analysis of these units, five principle factors that had the greatest influence on the members who chose violent actions, either directly or indirectly, on the groups can be identified as indoctrination of the participants; the economic and political conditions that existed in both countries; the characterization of the civilian populace as morally deficient; the tactical military circumstances on the ground; and the living conditions of the soldiers. When the conditions that led to the severity of the group's actions are understood, one can begin to see why some members of these units acted as they did. By understanding the causes of their actions, one can perhaps predict behavior from future army groups given similar circumstances.

The Rape of Nanking by the Japanese Army, December 1937

In November 1948, the IMTFE (International Military Tribunal for the Far East) read its findings to the court. The official narrative of events in Nanking established in this judgment read as follows:

> Japanese soldiers swarmed over the city and committed various atrocities … they were let loose like a barbarian horde to desecrate the city.… Individual soldiers and small groups of two or three roamed over the city murdering, raping, looting and burning. There was no discipline whatsoever.… Organized and wholesale murder of male civilians was conducted with the apparent sanction of the commanders on the pretense that Chinese soldiers had removed their uniforms and were mingling with the population groups of Chinese civilians were formed, bound with their hands behind their backs, and marched outside the walls of the city where they were killed in groups by machine gun fire and with bayonets.[1]

Roughly speaking, there were two phases in the historical event known as the 'Rape of Nanking'. Although one cannot draw a clear demarcation timeline between these two, the mass execution of prisoners, plain clothes soldiers, and those suspected of being so marked the first phase, whereas the delinquent acts of soldiers, such as individually committed murder, robbery, and rape, characterized the second phase. The first category of atrocities happened in a very short time period, most notably during 13 to 16 December 1937, and claimed the lives of men mainly of conscription age. The latter extended through a considerable length of time and affected the entire population in an almost uniform fashion. A Chinese report that lists some individual victims in three separate categories of murder, abduction, and rape signifies this point.

The table, which was attached to one of the reports submitted to the Nationalist Government's Justice Ministry, detailed 104 individual victims of murder, twenty-three rape victims, and 112 abductees who were recorded as missing. A comparison between the 112 abductees and the 104 murder victims reveals some interesting facts. Of the 112 abductees:

1. All but one of those 112 listed as missing were men.
2. Of these 111 men, fifty-one were entered with the dates of their abduction and forty-six of them were taken away from 13 to 16 December.
3. Of the 111 men, sixty-two were recorded with their ages at the time of their disappearance and fifty-five were between fifteen and forty-five years old. These breakdowns strongly suggest that they were mainly the victims of the Japanese army's operation to hunt down former soldiers—an atrocity in the first category.

As for the 104 murder victims:

1. Females accounted for sixteen of the total.
2. Of the thirty-seven male victims whose ages are known, sixteen—less than half of the total—were within the fifteen to forty-five-year-old range and the victims were dispersed almost uniformly throughout all age groups.
3. Although few cases are supplied with precise dates, twenty-one are reported to have happened on 13 December—most likely as a result of combat or semi-combat situations—while the occurrence on other dates was almost equally distributed.

These findings show that these were the victims of the atrocities that affected the entire population over a long period of time—that is, individually committed crimes in the second category. It is appropriate to analyze separately the nature and cause of these two categories of atrocities.[2]

One may define the mass executions conducted more or less systematically by each Japanese unit as a 'massacre,' as many historians and journalists have termed it. This was indeed an atrocity of a monstrous scale, for which the Japanese military leaders were responsible.[3] The most fundamental question is why the Japanese killed the soldiers who had surrendered. One cannot attribute these unlawful acts entirely to the violent end of the siege—a factor that has tended to promote the occurrence of atrocities regardless of the era—because the Japanese accepted the surrender of Chinese soldiers outside the Nanking walls more or less peacefully, while they caught the plain clothes soldiers in the Safety Zone almost without a fight. A traditional interpretation is that the Japanese wanted the horrors to remain as long as possible, to impress on the Chinese the terrible results of resisting Japan.[4] The Japanese military's official order, however, does not include any instruction that would encourage the soldiers to be cruel to the enemy. To the contrary, the CCAA (Central China Area Army) ordained before the entry into Nanking that each unit is required to tighten the discipline further so that the Chinese people, military and civilian alike, will respect the dignified manner of His Majesty's army and become obedient. Accordingly, '…each unit [was] expected never to commit any deed that would disgrace [their] honor.'[5] Moreover, General Matsui met with a local Chinese leader as early as 15 December to discuss the establishment of Chinese civilian authorities in the area. Matsui was also concerned about the local population's fear of the Japanese army and discussed it during the talks.[6] Therefore, one cannot compare the atrocities in Nanking to a calculated policy of genocide like the Nazi Final Solution. One possible explanation is that the Japanese military men's contemptuous attitude toward war prisoners—a view that had been nurtured for decades—affected the Japanese troops' behavior. Actually, the Japanese army incorporated such an attitude into its operation manual. A booklet compiled by the Japanese army's infantry school contains the following passage:

> There will not be so much of a problem even if we execute Chinese soldiers not only because the Chinese census registration is incomplete but also because there are quite a few soldiers of homeless origin whose presences cannot be confirmed easily.[7]

At the same time, the Japanese military's tendency to regard captivity as shameful had pervaded the entire nation by that time. Joseph Clark Grew, U.S. ambassador to Japan, recorded an event that showcased the Japanese attitude toward POWs at the time of the Sino-Japanese War. According to Grew, the Chinese government conveyed to the U.S. Embassy in Tokyo the name of a Japanese soldier who had been captured by Chinese Nationalist troops. That soldier apparently tried to contact the Japanese government to inform his family that he was still alive. The Japanese government, however, replied to Grew that it was not interested in receiving such information and that, as far as his own family was concerned, the man was officially dead. The Japanese authorities added: 'Were he to be recognized as a prisoner of war, shame would be brought upon not only his own family, but also his government and his nation.'[8]

Also, Japanese military leaders at the time seemingly considered the execution of POWs as an extension of military activity instead of a war atrocity. That some official military records openly described POW executions substantiates this view. The killing was, however, not always the Japanese way of solving the prisoner problem. If the Japanese army had a predetermined policy of executing Chinese prisoners, massacres would have happened continuously. To the contrary, when the city of Hangchow fell to the Japanese on 24 December in the same year, a Western news source reported no wholesale executions in Hangchow as marked the Japanese capture of Nanking. The Japanese policy toward war prisoners was inconsistent even on an individual level. Although 16th Division Chief General Kesago Nakajima bluntly stated his policy of not taking prisoners in his diary, he did not necessarily adhere to these words. When Nakajima inspected a Nanking flour milling factory administered by his division's accounting section on 23 December, he encountered about 300 Chinese prisoners working under the supervision of the division's accountant sergeant. Nakajima was surprised to find that the sergeant was completely unarmed while directing those prisoners. Then, he was stunned to see a more incredible scene: the weapons confiscated from these prisoners were not stored in another space but were left within their easy reach. Nakajima scolded the accountant sergeant furiously for such carelessness, but left the factory without ever ordering the execution of the prisoners. Moreover, in his conversations with other ranking SEF (Self Defense Force) generals, he later spoke proudly of that 'brave unarmed sergeant using a large number of prisoners.' In the end, the Japanese military's attitude to POWs alone does not explain sufficiently why Japanese troops in Nanking killed so many POWs.[9]

The criminal acts committed individually in Nanking had multiple characteristics. Except for the fires for which Chinese soldiers hiding in the city were reportedly also responsible, it was the Japanese military that should be held accountable for these incidents. According to Maruyama Masao, a Japanese political scientist, these atrocities, which continued to happen in World War II, were attributable to the nature of Japanese society in which the people transferred the oppression from the upper social class to those in the lower level of the social strata. Maruyama said that the masses who constituted the bulk of the rank-and-file soldiers had no object to which they could transfer oppression, and thus they turned their frustration toward the people in the conquered areas.[10] This analysis, however, does not explain the well-disciplined behavior of the Japanese soldiers in the first Sino-Japanese and Russo-Japanese Wars, when Japan's level of modernization was far less advanced than in the 1930s. Lieutenant Colonel Inada Masazumi, then an officer of the Army Ministry's Military Affairs Division, summarized what he thought made the soldiers so violent:

> The unexpectedly costly battle in Shanghai fostered a sense of vengeance while the complication of the military situation caused the loss of morale and ethic among the troops. These tendencies led to numerous cases of arson, robbery, and physical abuse even during the Shanghai campaign, resulting in the tarnishing of the honorable image of His Majesty's armed services in the eyes of the world. It is a thousand pities that [the Japanese troops] had turned themselves into an oppressive armed horde.[11]

The International Military Tribunal for the Far East, also known as the Tokyo Trials, the Tokyo War Crimes Tribunal, or simply the Tribunal, was convened on 29 April 1946 to try the leaders of the Empire of Japan for war crimes. On 4 November 1948, Tribunal for the Far East issued a judgment. The following is an excerpt from that judgment as it pertains to the Japanese Army's actions in China, leading up to and including their actions in Nanking in 1937:

After carefully examining and considering all the evidence, we find that it is not practicable in a judgment such as this to state fully the mass of oral and documentary evidence presented; for a complete statement of the scale and character of the atrocities, reference must be had to the record of the trial.

The evidence relating to atrocities and other Conventional War Crimes presented before the Tribunal establishes that from the opening of the war in China until the surrender of Japan in August 1945, torture, murder, rape and other cruelties of the most inhumane and barbarous character were freely practiced by the Japanese Army and Navy. During a period of several months, the Tribunal heard evidence, orally or by affidavit, from witnesses who testified in detail to the atrocities committed in all theaters of war on a scale so vast, yet following so common a pattern in all theaters, that only one conclusion is possible—the atrocities were either secretly ordered or willfully permitted by the Japanese Government or individual members thereof and by the leaders of the armed forces.

Before proceeding to a discussion of the circumstances and the conduct of the accused in relation to the question of responsibility for the atrocities, it is necessary to examine the matters charged. In doing so, we will, in some case where it may be convenient, refer to the association, if any, of the accused with the happenings under discussion. In other cases, and generally, as far as it is practicable, circumstances having relevance to the issue of responsibility will be dealt with later.

At the beginning of the Pacific War in December 1941, the Japanese Government did institute a system and an organization for dealing with prisoners of war and civilian internees. Superficially, the system would appear to have been appropriate; however, from beginning to end, the customary and conventional rules of war designed to prevent inhumanity were flagrantly disregarded.

Ruthless killing of prisoners by shooting, decapitation, drowning, and other methods; death marches in which prisoners, including the sick, were forced to march long distances under conditions which not even well–conditioned troops could stand, many of those dropping out being shot or bayoneted by the guards; forced labor in tropical heat without protection from the sun; complete lack of housing and medical supplies, in many cases resulting in thousands of deaths from disease; beatings and torture of all kinds to extract information or confessions or for minor offences; killing without trial of recaptured prisoners after escape and for attempt to escape; killing without trial of captured aviators; and even cannibalism: these are some of the atrocities of which proof was made before the Tribunal.

The extent of the atrocities and the result of the lack of food and medical supplies is exemplified by a comparison of the number of deaths of prisoners of war in the European Theater with the number of deaths in the Pacific Theater. Of United States and United Kingdom forces, 235,473 were taken prisoners by the German and Italian Armies; of these, 9,348, or 4 percent, died in captivity. In the Pacific

Theater, 132,134 prisoners were taken by the Japanese from the United States and United Kingdom forces alone, of whom 35,756, or 27 percent, died in captivity.

From the outbreak of the Mukden Incident until the end of the war, the successive Japanese Governments refused to acknowledge that the hostilities in China constituted a war. They persistently called it an 'Incident.' With this as an excuse, the military authorities persistently asserted that the rules of war did not apply in the conduct of the hostilities.

This war was envisaged by Japan's military leaders as a punitive war, which was being fought to punish the people of China for their refusal to acknowledge the superiority and leadership of the Japanese race and to cooperate with Japan. These military leaders intended to make the war so brutal and savage in all its consequences as to break the will of the Chinese people to resist.

As the Southern movement advanced to cut off aid to *Generalissimo* Chiang Kai-shek, the Chief-of-Staff of the Central China Expeditionary Force, on 24 July 1939, sent an estimate of the situation to War Minister ITAGAKI. In that estimate of the situation, he said: 'The Army Air Force should carry out attacks upon strategic points in the hinterland in order to terrorize the enemy forces and civilians, and so develop among them an anti-war, pacifist tendency. What we expect of offensive operations against the interior is the mental terror they will create among the enemy forces and civilians rather than the material damage inflicted direct upon enemy personnel and equipment. We will wait and see them falling into nervous prostration in an excess of terror and madly starting anti-Chiang and pacifist movements.'

Government and military spokesmen alike from time to time stated that the purpose of the war was to make the Chinese people 'seriously reflect' upon the error of their ways, which in effect meant acceptance of Japanese domination.

HIROTA, in February 1938, speaking in the House of Peers, said 'Japan has been endeavoring to make the Chinese Nationalist Government make reflections, if possible, while chastising their mistaken ideas by armed force...' In the same speech, he said 'Since they were facing Japan with very strong anti-Japanese feeling, we decided on a policy whereby we had to necessarily chastise them.'

HIRANUMA began his 'stimulation of the national morale' by a speech to the Diet on 221 January 1939, in which he said: 'In regard to the China Incident upon which both the Cabinet and the people are concentrating their endeavors, there exists an immutable policy for which Imperial Sanction was obtained by the previous Cabinet. The present Cabinet is of course committed to the same policy. I hope the intention of Japan will be understood by the Chinese so that they may cooperate with us. As for those who fail to understand, we have no other alternative than to exterminate them.'

Before discussing the nature and extent of atrocities committed by the Japanese armed forces, it is desirable to state, very shortly, the system under which such conduct should have been controlled.

Those having authority in the formulation of military policy were the Army and Navy Ministers, the Chiefs of the Army and Navy General Staffs, the Inspector-General of Military Education, the Supreme War Council of Field Marshals and Fleet Admirals, and the War Council. The Army and Navy Ministers administered; the Inspector-General of Military education supervised training; and the Chiefs of the Army and Navy General Staffs directed operations of the armed forces. The two war councils were advisory groups. The Army enjoyed special prerogatives. One of these was the exclusive right to nominate the successor of the War Minister. By the exercise of this power, the Army was able to enforce continued adherence to the policies advocated by it.

In the War Ministry, the policy initiating agency was the Military Affairs Bureau, which after consultation with the army General Staff, other Bureau of the War Ministry, and other departments of the government concerned, announced the policy of the Japanese Military, usually in the form of regulations issued over the signature of the War Minister. This was the Bureau which formed the policy and issued regulations governing the conduct of war in general and the treatment of civilian internees and prisoners of war in particular. Such administration of prisoners of war as there was during the war in China was conducted by this Bureau. Until the opening of hostilities in the Pacific War, the administration of civilian internees and prisoners of war was retained by this Bureau when a special Division was created in the Bureau to perform that function. Three of the accused served as Chiefs of this powerful Military Affairs Bureau; they were KOISO, MUTO, and SATO. KOISO served at the beginning of the war in China, between the dates of 8 January 1930 and 29 February 1932. MUTO served before and after the commencement of the Pacific War; he became Chief of the Bureau on 30 September 1939, and served until 20 April 1942. SATO was employed in the Bureau before the beginning of the Pacific War, having been appointed on 15 July 1938, when MUTO was transferred to command troops in Sumatra, SATO became Chief of the Bureau and served in that capacity from 20 April 1942 to 14 December 1944.

The corresponding Bureau in the Navy Ministry was the Naval Affairs Bureau. The Naval Affairs Bureau formed and promulgated regulations for the Navy and prescribed the policy of the Navy in conducting war at sea, occupied islands and other territory under its jurisdiction, and administered such prisoners of war and civilian internees as came under its power. The accused OKA served as Chief of this Bureau before and during the Pacific War, from 15 October 1940 to 31 July 1944.

In the War Ministry, the Vice-Minister of War was the operating chief of the War Ministry Office and was responsible for coordination of the various Bureau and other agencies under the Ministry. He received reports and suggestions from commanders in the field, advised the War Minister on the affairs under the Ministry and often issued orders and directives. Three of the accused served as

Vice-Minister of War during the period prior to the Pacific War. KOISO served from 29 February 1932 to 8 August 1932. UMEZU occupied the position from 23 March 1936 to 30 May 1938. TOJO became Vice-Minister of War on 30 May 1938, and served until 10 December 1939. KIMURA was Vice-Minister of War before and after the commencement of the Pacific War; he was appointed on 10 April 1941 and served until 11 March 1943.

Lastly, of course, the commanders in the field were responsible for the maintenance of the discipline and the observance of the laws and customs of war by the troops under their command.

The Japanese Delegate at Geneva, in accepting the resolution of the League of Nations of 10 December 1931, setting up the Lytton Commission and imposing a virtual truce, stated that his acceptance was based on the understanding that the resolution would not preclude the Japanese Army from taking action against 'bandits' in Manchuria. It was under this exception to the resolution that the Japanese Military continued hostilities against the Chinese troops in Manchuria. They maintained that no state of war existed between Japan and China; that the conflict was a mere 'incident' to which the laws of war did not apply; and that those Chinese troops who resisted the Japanese Army were not lawful combatants, but were merely 'bandits.' A ruthless campaign for the extermination of these 'bandits' in Manchuria was inaugurated.

Although the main Chinese Army withdrew within the Great Wall at the end of 1931, resistance to the Japanese Army was constantly maintained by widely dispersed units of Chinese volunteers. The Kwantung Army Intelligence Service listed a large number of so-called Chinese route-armies, which in 1932 formed the subdivisions of the volunteer armies. These volunteer armies were active in the areas around Mukden, Haisheng and Yingkow. In August 1932, fighting broke out in the immediate vicinity of Mukden. At the height of the fighting at Mukden on 8 August 1932, Vice-Minister of War KOISO was appointed Chief-of-Staff of the Kwantung Army and also Chief of its Intelligence Service. He served in that capacity until 5 March 1934. On 16 September 1932, the Japanese forces in pursuit of defeated Chinese volunteer units arrived at the towns of Pingtingshan, Chienchinpao and Litsekou in the vicinity of Fushun. The inhabitants of these towns were accused of harboring the volunteers or 'bandits' as they were called by the Japanese. In each town, the Japanese troops assembled people along ditches and forced them to kneel; they then killed these civilians, men, women and children, with machine guns; those who survived the machine-gunning being promptly bayoneted to death. Over 2,700 civilians perished in this massacre, which the Japanese Kwantung Army claimed to be justified under its program of exterminating 'bandits.' Shortly thereafter, KOISO sent to the Vice-Minister of War an 'Outline for Guiding Manchukuo' in which he said: 'Racial struggle between Japanese and Chinese is to be expected. Therefore, we must never hesitate to wield military power in case of necessity.' In this spirit, the practice of massacring or 'punishing' as the Japanese termed it, the inhabitants of cities and towns in retaliation for actual or supposed aid rendered to Chinese troops was applied. This practice continued throughout the China War; the worst example of its being the massacre of the inhabitants of Nanking in December 1937.

Since the Government of Japan officially classified the China War as an 'Incident' and considered Chinese soldiers in Manchuria as 'bandits,' the Army refused to accord to captives taken in the fighting the status and the rights of Prisoners of War. MUTO says that it was officially decided in 1938 to continue to call the war in China and 'Incident' and to continue for that reason to refuse to apply the rules of war to the conflict. TOJO told us the same.

Many of the captured Chinese were tortured, massacred, placed in labor units to work for the Japanese Army, or organized into army units to serve the puppet governments established by Japan in the conquered territory in China. Some of these captives who refused to serve in these armies were transported to Japan to relieve the labor shortage in the munitions industries. At the camp at Akita, on the northwest shore of Honshu Island, 418 Chinese out of a group of 981 so transported to Japan died from starvation, torture or neglect.

Both the League of Nations and the meeting at Brussels of the signatories of the Nine-Power Treaty railed to stop Japan's pursuing this 'punitive' war on China after the outbreak of hostilities at the Marco Polo Bridge in 1937. This policy of Japan to treat the China war as an 'incident' remained unchanged. Even after the establishment of the Imperial General Headquarters, which was considered appropriate only in the case of an 'incident' of such an extent as to require a declaration of war, as suggested by the War Minister at the cabinet meeting held on 19 November 1937, no additional effort was made to enforce the laws of war in the conduct of the hostilities in China. Although the Government and the fighting services were organized on a full wartime basis, the China war was still treated as an 'incident' with the consequent disregard of the rules of war.

As the Central China Expeditionary Force under command of MATSUI approached the city of Nanking in early December 1937, over one-half of its one million inhabitants and all but a few neutrals who remained behind to organize an International Safety Zone, fled from the city. The Chinese Army retreated, leaving approximately 50,000 troops behind to defend the city. As the Japanese forces stormed the South Gate on the night of 12 December 1937, most of the remaining 50,000 troops escaped through the North and West Gates of the city. Nearly all the Chinese soldiers had evacuated the city or had abandoned their arms and uniforms and sought refuge in the International Safety Zone, and all resistance had ceased as the Japanese Army entered the city on the morning of 13 December 1937. The Japanese soldiers swarmed over the city and committed various atrocities. According to one of the eyewitnesses, they were let loose like a barbarian horde to desecrate the city. It was said by eyewitnesses that the city appeared to have fallen into the hands of the Japanese as captured prey, that it had not merely been taken in organized warfare, and that the members of the victorious Japanese Army had set upon the prize to committee unlimited violence. Individual soldiers and small groups of two of three roamed over the city murdering, raping, looting, and burning. There was no discipline whatever. Many soldiers were drunk. Solders went through the streets indiscriminately killing Chinese men, women and children without apparent provocation or excuse until in places the streets and alleys were littered with the bodies of their victims. According to another witness, Chinese were hunted like rabbits, everyone seen to move was shot. At least 12,000 non-combatant Chinese men, women and children met their deaths in these indiscriminate killings during the first two or three days of the Japanese occupation of the city.

There were many cases of rape. Death was a frequently penalty for the slightest resistance on the part of a civtion [*sic*.] or the members of her family who sought to protect her. Even girls of tender years and old women were raped in large numbers throughout the city, and many cases of abnormal and sadistic behaviour in connection with these rapings occurred. Many women were killed after the act and their bodies mutilated. Approximately 20,000 cases of rape occurred within the city during the first month of the occupation.

Japanese soldiers took from the people everything they desired. Soldiers were observed to stop unarmed civilians on the road, search them, and finding nothing of value then to shoot them. Very many residential and commercial properties were entered and looted. Looted stocks were carried away in trucks. After looting shops and warehouses, the Japanese soldiers frequently set fire to them. Taiping Road, the most important shopping street, and block after block of the commercial section of the city were destroyed by fire. Soldiers burned the homes of civilians for no apparent reason. Such burning appeared to follow a prescribed pattern after a few days and continued for six weeks. Approximately one-third of the city was thus destroyed.

Organized and wholesale murder of male civilians was conducted with the apparent sanction of the commanders on the pretense that Chinese soldiers had removed their uniforms and were mingling with the population. Groups of Chinese civilians were formed, bound with their hands behind their backs, and marched outside the walls of the city where they were killed in groups by machine gun fire and with bayonets. More than 20,000 Chinese men of military age are known to have died in this fashion.

The German Government was informed by its representative about 'atrocities and criminal acts not of an individual but of an entire Army, namely, the Japanese,' which Army, later in the Report, was qualified as a 'bestial machinery.'

Those outside the city fared little better than those within. Practically the same situation existed in all the communities within 200 liters (about 66 miles) of Nanking. The population had fled into the countryside in an attempt to escape from the Japanese soldiers. In places they had grouped themselves into fugitive camps. The Japanese captured many of these camps and visited upon the fugitives treatment similar to that accorded the inhabitants of Nanking. Of the civilians who had fled Nanking, over 57,000 were overtaken and interned. These were starved and tortured in captivity until a large number died. Many of the survivors were killed by machine gun fire and by bayoneting.

Large parties of Chinese soldiers laid down their arms and surrendered outside Nanking; within 72 hours after their surrender, they were killed in groups by machine gun fire along the bank of the Yangtze River.

Over 30,000 such prisoners of war were so killed. There was not even pretense of trial of these prisoners so massacred.

Estimates made at a later date indicate that the total number of civilians and prisoners of war murdered in Nanking and its vicinity during the first six weeks of the Japanese occupation was over 200,000. That these estimates are not exaggerated is borne out by the fact that burial societies and other organizations counted more than 155,000 bodies which they buried. They also reported that most of those were bound with their hands tied behind their backs. These figures do not take into account those persons whose bodies were destroyed by burning, or by throwing them into the Yangtze River, or otherwise disposed of by Japanese.

Japanese Embassy officials entered the city of Nanking with the advance elements of the Army; and on 14 December, an official of the Embassy informed the International Committee for the Nanking Safety, one that the 'Army was determined to make it bad for Nanking, but that Embassy officials were going to try to moderate the action.' The Embassy officials also informed the members of the Committee that at the time of the occupation of the city, no more than 17 military policemen were provided by the Army commanders to maintain order within the city. When it transpired that complaints to the Army officials did not have any result, those Japanese embassy officials suggested to the foreign missionaries that the latter should try and get publicity in Japan, so that the Japanese Government would be forced by public opinion to curb the Army.

Dr. Bates testified that the terror was intense for two and one-half to three weeks, and was serious six to seven weeks following the fall of the city.

Smythe, the Secretary of the Int. Committee for the Safety Zone, filed two protests a day for the first six weeks.

MATSUI, who had remained in a rear area until 17 December, made a triumphal entry into the city on that day, and on 18 December held a religious service for the dead, after which he issued a statement in the course of which he said: 'I extend much sympathy to millions of innocent people in the Kiangpei and Chekiang districts, who suffered the evils of war. Now the flag of the rising sun is floating high over Nanking, and the Imperial Way is shining in the southern parts of the Yangtze-Kiang. The dawn of the renaissance of the East is on the verge of offering itself. On this occasion, I hope for reconsideration of the situation by the 400 million people of China.' MATSUI remained in the city for nearly a week.

MUTO, then a colonel, had joined MATSUI's staff on 10 November 1937, and was with MATSUI during the drive on Nanking and participated in the triumphal entry and occupation of the city. Both he and MATSUI admit that they heard of the atrocities being committed in the city during their stay at rear headquarters after the fall of the city. MATSUI admits that he heard that foreign governments were protesting against the commission of these atrocities. No effective action was taken to remedy the situation. Evidence was given before the Tribunal by an eye witness, that while MATSUI was in Nanking on the 19th of December, the business section of the city was in flames. On that day, the witness counted fourteen fires in the principal business street zone. After the entry of MATSUI and MUTO into the city, the situation did not improve for weeks.

Members of the Diplomatic Corps and Press and the Japanese Embassy in Nanking sent out reports detailing the atrocities being committed in and around Nanking. The Japanese Minister-at-Large to China, Ito, Nobofumi, was in Shanghai from September 1937 to February 1938. He received reports from the Japanese Embassy in Nanking and from members of the Diplomatic Corps and Press regarding the conduct of the Japanese troops and sent a résumé of the reports to the Japanese Foreign Minister, HIROTA. These reports, as well as many others giving information of the atrocities committed at Nanking, which were forwarded by members of the Japanese diplomatic officials in China, were forwarded by HIROTA to the War Ministry of which UMEZU was Vice-Minister. They were discussed at Liaison Conferences, which were normally attended by the Prime Minister, War and Navy Ministers, Foreign Minister HIROTA, Finance Minister KAYA, and the Chiefs of the Army and Navy General Staffs.

News reports of the atrocities were widespread. MINAMI, who was serving as Governor-General of Korea at the time, admits that he read these reports in the Press. Following these unfavorable reports and the pressure of public opinion aroused in nations all over the world, the Japanese Government recalled MATSUI and approximately 80 of his officers, but took no action to punish any of them. MATSUI, after his return to Japan on 5 March 1938, was appointed a Cabinet Councilor and 0n 29 April 19490, was decorated by the Japanese Government for 'meritorious services' in the China War. MATSUI, in explaining his recall, says that he was not replaced by HATA because of the atrocities committed by his troops at Nanking, but because he considered his work ended at Nanking and wished to retire from the Army. He was never punished.

The barbarous behavior of the Japanese Army cannot be excused as the acts of a soldiery which had temporarily gotten out of hand when at last a stubbornly defended position had capitulated—rape, arson and murder continued to be committed on a large scale for at least six weeks after the city had been taken and for at least four weeks after MATSUI and MUTO had entered the city.

The new Japanese garrison Commander at Nanking, General Amaya, on 5 February 1938, at the Japanese Embassy in Nanking, made a statement to the foreign diplomatic corps criticizing the attitude of the foreigners who had been sending abroad reports of Japanese atrocities at Nanking and upbraiding them for encouraging anti-Japanese feeling. This statement by Amaya reflected the attitude of the Japanese Military toward foreigners in China, who were hostile to the Japanese policy of waging an unrestrained punitive war against the people of China.[12]

The War was Extended to Canton and Hankow

When Shanghai capitulated on 12 November 1937 and Matsui began his advance on Nanking, the National Government of China, under Generalissimo Chiang Kai-Shek, abandoned its capital city, moved to Chungking (present-day Chongqing) with interim headquarters at Hankow (present-day Hankou), and continued the resistance. After the capture of Nanking of 13 December 1937, the Japanese Government established a puppet government at Peiping.

The program designed to 'pacify' the inhabitants of this occupied area and 'make them rely on the Japanese Army' and force 'self-examination' on the part of the National Government of China, which was adopted at Shanghai and Nanking and proclaimed by Matsui at Nanking, indicated settled policy. In December 1937, at Hsing Tai District on the Peping–Hankow railway, Gendarmes under the command of a Japanese warrant officer seized seven civilians, who were suspected of being Chinese Irregulars, tortured and starved them for three days, then bound them to a tree and bayoneted them to death. Soldiers from this Army had appeared at the village of Tung Wang Chia, in Hopeh Province, earlier in October 1937, and committed murder, rape, and arson, killing twenty-four of the inhabitants and burning about two-thirds of the homes. Another village in the same province known as Wang-Chia-To was visited by a Japanese unit in January 1938 and more than forty of the civilian inhabitants were murdered.

Many of the inhabitants of the area around Shanghai fared no better than those in Nanking and other parts of North China. After the fighting had ceased at Shanghai, observers found around the ashes of farm houses in the suburban areas of Shanghai the bodies of farmers and their families with their hands tied behind them and bayonet wounds in their backs. As Matsui's troops occupied village after village on their march to Nanking, they plundered, murdered, and terrorized the population. Soochow was occupied in November 1937, and a number of residents who had not fled from the advancing troops were murdered.

Hata's troops entered Hankow and occupied the city on 25 October 1938. The next morning, a massacre of prisoners occurred. At the customs wharf, the Japanese soldiers collected several hundred prisoners. They then selected small groups of three or four at a time, marched them to the end of the gangplanks reaching out to deep water, pushed them into the river and shot them. When the Japanese saw that they were being observed from the American gunboats anchored in the river off Hankow, they stopped and adopted a different method. They continued to select small groups, put them into motor launches and took them out in the stream where they threw them in the water and shot them.

It was during the Third Konoye Cabinet that the massacre at the town of Powen, on the Chinese Island of Hainan, occurred. In August 1941, during a punitive operation, a Japanese Naval Unit passed through the town of Powen without opposition. The next day, as a Detachment from that Unit returned to Powen, they found the dead body of a sailor of the Japanese Navy who had apparently been dead for several days. Under the assumption that the sailor had been killed by the residents of Powen, the detachment burned the native houses and the church of the town. They killed the French missionary and twenty-four natives and burned their bodies. This incident is important because the wide circulation given the report of the massacre must have informed the members of the Cabinet and its subordinate officials of the method of warfare continuing to be employed by the Japanese military forces. The Chief-of-Staff of the Japanese occupation forces on Hainan Island made a complete report of this matter to Vice-Minister of War Kimura on 14 October 1941. Kimura at once circulated the report from the information of all concerned to the various bureau of the War Ministry and then sent it to the Foreign Ministry. It received wide circulation both in and out of the Army.

An indication that the ruthless methods of the Japanese Army in waging war continued is revealed by the conduct of a detachment of soldiers from Umezu's Army in Manchukuo in the campaign designed to stifle all resistance to the puppet regime under Emperor Pu Yi. This detachment visited the village of Si-Tu-Ti in Jehol Province one night in August 1941. It captured the village, killed the members of more than 300 families and burned the village to the ground.

Even long after the occupation of Canton and Hankow, the Japanese, while carrying on campaigns into the farther interior, committed large-scale atrocities there. Toward the end of 1941, Japanese troops entered the city of Wei-Yang, in Kwantung Province. They indulged in a massacre of Chinese civilians, bayoneting male and female, old and young, without discrimination. One eyewitness, who survived a bayonet wound in the abdomen, told of the slaughter of more than 600 Chinese civilians by Japanese troops. In July 1944, Japanese troops arrived at the Tai Shan District in the Kwantung Province. They committed arson, robbery, slaughter and numerous other atrocities. As a result thereof, 559 ships were burnt and more than 700 Chinese civilians killed.

From Hankow, the Japanese troops carried on their campaign southward to Changsha. In September 1941, the Japanese troops of the Sixth Division forced more than 200 Chinese prisoners of war to plunder large quantities of rice, wheat, and other commodities. Upon their return, the Japanese soldiers, to conceal these crimes, massacred them by artillery fire. After the Japanese forces had occupied Changsha, they also freely indulged in murder, rape, incendiarism, and many other atrocities throughout the district. Then they drove further down southward to Keilin and Liuchow in Kwangsi Province. During the period of Japanese occupation of Kwelin, they committed all kinds of atrocities such as rape and plunder. They recruited women labor on the pretext of establishing factories. They forced the women thus recruited into prostitution with Japanese troops. Prior to their withdrawal from Kweilin in July 1945, the Japanese troops organized an arson corps and set fire to buildings in the entire business district of Kweilin.

Returning Soldiers told of Atrocities Committed by them

After the occupation of Hankow, Japanese soldiers returning from China told stories of the army's misdeeds in China and displayed loot that they had taken. This conduct on the part of the soldiers returning to Japan apparently became so general that the War Ministry under Itagaki, in an effort to avoid unfavorable criticism at home and abroad, issued special orders to the commanders in the field to instruct returning officers and men upon the proper conduct to be followed by them upon reaching Japan. These special orders were prepared in the military Service Section of the Military Service Bureau of the War Ministry, classified as 'Top Secret' and issued by Itagaki's Vice-Minister of War in February 1939. They were transmitted by the Vice-Chief of the Army General Staff to the Japanese Army Commanders in China. These secret orders detailed the objectionable conduct of returning soldiers that was to be corrected. It was complained that the soldiers told stories of atrocities committed by them on Chinese soldiers and civilians; seven of the stories commonly heard are cited below:

> One company commander unofficially gave instructions for raping as follows: 'In order that we will not have problems, either pay them money or kill them in some obscure place after you have finished.'
>
> 'If the army men who participated in the war were investigated individually, they would probably all be guilty of murder, robbery or rape.'
>
> 'The thing I like best during the battle is plundering. In the front lines the superiors turn a blind eye to plundering and there were some who plundered to their heart's content.'
>
> 'At … we captured a family of four. We played with the daughter as we would with a harlot. But as the parents insisted that the daughter be returned to them we killed them. We played with the daughter as before until the unit's departure and then killed her.'
>
> 'In the half year of battle, about the only things I learned are raped and burglary.'
>
> 'The plundering by our army in the battle area is beyond imagination.'
>
> 'The Prisoners taken from the Chinese Army were sometimes lined up in one line and killed to test the efficiency of the machine-gun.'

Concerning loot brought back to Japan by returning soldiers, it was noted that some commanders distributed among the men license cards authorized by the stamp of the unit commander permitting the soldiers to transport their loot to Japan. These orders stated:

> Not only does the improper talk of the returned officers and men become the cause of rumors, but also impairs the trust of the people in the Army, disrupts the unity of the people supporting the Army, etc. I repeat the order again to make the control of instruction even more strict and consequently glorify the meritorious deeds, raise the Japanese Army's military reputation and insure that nothing will impair the accomplishment of the object of the Holy War.

For additional descriptions of the Japanese war crimes from the International Military Tribunal for the Far East, see Appendix I.

Indoctrination and Training of the Japanese Military

During the Asia-Pacific War, the Japanese were widely regarded as the most fearsome light infantrymen in the field—highly disciplined, devoted to their duty, and ready to fight to the bitter end rather than surrender. This reputation was a product of social influence as well as army training. By the 1930s, Japanese society was imbued with militarism. Many schools gave military instruction to young students. For example, local elementary schools taught boys military drills using wooden guns. The greatest honor, they would tell the young pupils, is to come back dead. There were also army apprentice schools, which took young people directly from school ages of fourteen to fifteen. Military instruction was even offered in colleges.[13]

Schools were molding a new Japanese citizen—stoic, brutal, and obedient. Young boys had been taught to use wooden guns, while older boys had been taught how to use real guns. Even at primary schools, it was part of the curriculum for the teachers to principally teach boys a very strong hatred towards the Chinese. School textbooks were filled with military propaganda in order to prepare the Japanese boys for what was to come. The lives of Japanese males seemed to be an ongoing preparation for a war against the Chinese. Many of the teachers were military officers, where militaristic views were forcefully taught and projected. The schooling system taught the boys obedience and brutality. Telling evidence is given by Hakudo Nagatomi, who was brought up in Korea, which was at the time under Japanese colonial rule:

> I was taught of Japanese racial superiority, and the need for Japan to control Asia according to the teachings of the emperor. I was taught to despise other Asians. These teachings had the desired effect when Nagatomi participated willingly in

the barbarism at Nanking. On my first day in China, back in 1937, I proved my courage by beheading twenty Chinese civilians. It is very hard to say this, but the truth of the matter is that I felt proud of Japan.[14]

As early as 1886, military training and lectures had been instituted in the elementary, secondary, and normal schools of Japan, and after the First Sino-Japanese War of 1894–1895, regular Army officers had conducted the training. After the 1914–18 war, little attention was paid to the matter for some years; but from 1922 onwards, the War Ministry detailed officers to supervise the teaching. During 1925 and thereafter, the War and Education Ministries worked in conjunction to ensure that male students received training. On 23 April 1925, it was ordained that military officers of active service status should be stationed in schools. They would, by agreement between the War and Education Ministries, be posted to teachers' training institutions, to all types of public and government schools, and, upon request, to private schools. They would be under the supervision and orders of the school authorities, but they themselves remained the servants of the War Ministry, which was given the right to inspect the actual conditions of training in the schools. A year later, in September 1926, the War Ministry organized an inspectorate that was required to furnish reports upon the work being carried out.[15]

The samurai warrior class dominated the government and cultural life of Japan during seven centuries of military dictatorship until this class was abolished in 1869, following the restoration of Emperor Meiji as supreme leader of Japan in 1868. The samurai warrior lived by a code called *bushido* that required unquestioning loyalty and obedience to his feudal lord, strict self-discipline, and fearlessness in battle. It was dishonorable for a samurai to be taken alive by an enemy, and samurai were expected to commit suicide rather than surrender. The code of *bushido*, as practiced by the samurai, encouraged compassion for a defeated enemy and did not sanction the murder of babies by samurai warriors or the rape and murder of women.

The values and attitudes incorporated in *bushido* did not die with the formal abolition of the samurai class because the emperor's key advisers were samurai themselves. After the restoration of the emperor, *bushido* was adapted as an ethical code for the whole population, with the emperor replacing the feudal lord as the object of loyalty, obedience, and sacrifice. The samurai code of *bushido* was also adapted to educational philosophy. The new education required that children be taught reverence for and unquestioning loyalty to Emperor Meiji and, of course, to his imperial government. The curriculum followed the authoritarian Prussian education model and was designed to foster national unification, loyalty to superiors, obedience to authority, and patriotism.

Emperor Meiji's samurai advisers saw the emperor as a logical focal point for achieving national unity. To this end, they decided to re-establish and revitalize the ancient Shinto religion with its gods and goddesses as the official state religion of Japan. Three tenets of Shinto were especially relevant to the aims of the emperor's advisers. Shinto held the emperor to be divine because he was deemed to be a descendent of the sun goddess Amaterasu. This provided justification for requiring the emperor to be worshipped and obeyed. The second tenet held that Japan was not just a populated geographical feature in the Pacific Ocean, but a land and people created by the sun goddess, and, accordingly, specially favoured by the ancient gods. Finally, Japan was possessed of a divine mission to extend its rule and enlightenment to less fortunate races.

Shinto was strongly nationalist and racist in character. Combined with the traditional militarism of the samurai warrior class, it was a dangerous cocktail with a strong potential for encouraging fanaticism and support for war as a means to secure what were perceived by the emperor's advisers to be Japan's national interests.[16]

In April 1926, the Education Ministry created a new teaching organization designed to cater for youths of seventeen to twenty-one years of age, who had received no formal schooling. The course, which was of four years' duration, included subjects of general and vocational value; but one half of the total hours of instruction were specifically set aside for military training. In the month of their foundation, provision was made by the War Ministry for inspection of the military drills carried out at these youth schools.

By 1927, military training was compulsory throughout the whole school system; from 1925 to 1930, the amount of school time devoted to this type of instruction was steadily increased. In universities, classes in military subjects were obligatory from 1925; however, the obligation was not strictly enforced at first. Actual military training remained upon a voluntary basis, but, as university students who attended both classes and parades were subsequently exempted from two out of three years of compulsory military service, there was a strong inducement to secure attendance.

Shortly before the Mukden Incident occurred, students were taught that Manchuria was Japan's lifeline, upon the control of which depended the establishment of a stable economic order. With the outbreak of war in Manchuria in 1931, lingering opposition to the military training programme was lost in the new spirit of ultra-nationalism that the military teaching inspired. From 1931 onwards, the military instructors, though nominally subordinate to the school and university authorities, achieved an increasing measure of independence and domination.[17]

As militarists and extreme nationalists increasingly dominated Japan's Imperial government during the 1930s, this extremism was reflected in Japan's foreign policy, education, and military culture. The Imperial Japanese military purported to follow the samurai code of *bushido* after the restoration of the emperor in 1868, but the code that they followed was a perversion of *bushido*. For the Imperial Japanese military, *bushido* meant dedication of their lives to the emperor—defeat was viewed as shameful, surrender was dishonorable, those who surrendered were worthy only of contempt, and compassion for defeated enemies (male or female, the elderly, or tiny children) was weakness. The last view was definitely not part of the traditional samurai code of *bushido*. This perversion of *bushido* was used to justify countless instances of rape and the murder of prisoners of war, women, and even tiny children in countries conquered by the Imperial Japanese military.[18]

In the 1930s, Japanese military recruits began to be subjected to intensive indoctrination in the tenets of *bushido* and Shinto. A culture of extreme brutality was also encouraged within the military itself. If a Japanese colonel was displeased with one of his majors, it would not be unusual for the colonel to strike the offending major a blow across the face to reinforce his reprimand. The major chastised in this way would be expected to strike one of his captains who had incurred his displeasure. This brutality would be passed down the line from the Japanese officers to their own enlisted men, who would then be expected to beat each other up. At the end of this chain of brutality were the men perceived by the Japanese to be the lowest of the low, their enlisted Koreans and Taiwanese, who received the worst beatings. The disgruntled Korean and Taiwanese camp guards had no one but the prisoners of war to beat up, and they were viewed by many prisoners as being the most brutal of their guards. The apparent aim of this indoctrination and brutality was to produce fanatics who would sacrifice their lives without hesitation for the emperor. It was also calculated to produce brutal and racist soldiers.

Although they did not understand that it was normal behavior in the Japanese military, one of the few bright moments in the bleak lives of Allied prisoners of war was the sight of their Japanese guards beating up each other instead of them. Doctor Frank Mills, an Australian prisoner at Sandakan, Malaysia, tells how much the prisoners enjoyed watching this sight:

> I have seen funny occasions when the NCO beat up the young soldier, the lieutenant beat up the NCO, the captain beat up the lieutenant—it went right to the top, beating each other up quite publicly. We used to applaud it. They took no notice. It was some of the only fun we got when the Japs started to beat themselves up.[19]

After Japan invaded China in 1937, Japanese troops were encouraged by their officers to embark on an orgy of murder, rape, and looting that shocked the civilized world. The depravity of the Japanese troops is not surprising having regard to their being taught that Chinese were '*chancorro*,' or sub–human, and that the killing of Chinese was of no greater significance than the killing of vermin.[20]

The culture of fanaticism and extreme brutality encouraged in the Japanese military between 1930 and 1945 was calculated to produce troops with the emotional coldness of psychopaths. Add instilled contempt for other races and one can begin to understand how easy it was for the Japanese Imperial military to commit the atrocities that shocked the civilized world. It appears unlikely that the products of such an appalling military culture would be able to behave any differently when Japan's military aggression was extended to the Pacific and South-East Asia in 1941.

After the military operations in Manchuria had subsided, time devoted to military subjects decreased a little, but it received a new impetus in 1936, when Hirohito's government was in power. The training consisted of drilling, physical culture, and war games. The textbooks used in the schools dealt with Japanese military history and were designed to foster enthusiasm for the fighting services among the students.

The military wanted well-trained new Japanese citizens, and capitalized on the discipline learnt at school by continuing the abuse. 'I do not beat you because I hate you. I beat you because I care for you' was almost a mantra used by officers in order for their charges to become immune to violence and killing civilians. While some draftees died in the brutality of the training, the majority became hardened soldiers for the army to make best use of. This was exemplified by the well-known and numerous kamikaze attacks (particularly towards the end of World War II), in which Japanese pilots were trained to fly their planes directly into American ships. The Japanese military were noted for their easy readiness to sacrifice their lives, in order to save or bring honor to the emperor.[21]

A Japanese soldier, Azuma, was stunned at the reluctance of the Chinese army to fight back to the Japanese army. This man who came from such a strict military culture found it incomprehensible that the Chinese would rather be captured than to fight an enemy to his death. His automatic impulse was to dehumanize the prisoners by comparing them to insects and animals.

There are certain laws that all soldiers must abide by in time of war (which were further codified in the Geneva Convention of 1949), yet obviously the Japanese did not. For example, the rape of women is certainly not permissible, but rape remained so deeply embedded in Japanese military culture and superstition that no one took the rules seriously. Iris Chang asserts that a widespread belief among the Japanese military was that raping virgins would make the Japanese stronger for battle. The military policy forbade rape, thus encouraging the Japanese to kill their victims after they had had their way with them.[22]

Conscription made all males between the ages of fifteen to forty-five liable for military service. The usual call up age was around nineteen years of age and the minimum height requirement was 5 feet. The average Japanese soldier stood 5 feet 3 inches tall, and soldiers ranged in age from eighteen to forty. Before 1933, only 15 percent of draftees received orders to report to the army. During the war in China, however, more and more soldiers were needed. By the early stage of the Pacific War, the ratio had reached 60 percent, and by war's end, it had climbed to 90 percent. Conscripts were liable for service straight after call up, after passing eyesight and hearing tests. Those that failed to meet the requirements on these tests were put into a reserve category for service. Grade 'C' recruits, the lowest level, were placed in the Second National Army, a Japanese equivalent to the U.S. National Guards, whose responsibility included homeland service.

Once in the army, a soldier's training emphasized obedience and loyalty over skilled weapon handling. New soldiers were often lined up for officers to slap them in the face or punch them or beat them with belts—sometimes until blood poured down their faces. During his training, any lack of discipline was punished by his superiors in the form of beatings. By the time he joined his regiment, it was clear to a soldier that it was in his interest to blindly obey orders.

Once in the field, the Japanese soldier was supposed to have three meals a day, mainly of rice supplemented with fish, meat, vegetables, and fruit. He slept on a mat on the ground. Often, however, the Japanese army was faced by supply shortages, and the soldiers more often than not had to fend for themselves. Medical care was very basic, if not nonexistent, and the sick or dying were often left on their own. Malaria, dysentery, cholera, and beriberi took many lives. Given this training, it is perhaps no surprise that attacks often took the form of frontal assaults with fixed bayonets. The Japanese soldier took positions by pure force rather than tactical or technical sophistication and most fought until death. With death for the emperor came everlasting glory, whereas being taken prisoner was to be less than human.[23]

According to the 1944 United States War Department Handbook on Japanese Military Forces, in Japan, military indoctrination began from infancy. Formal regimentation and training begin at about the age of eight years, when, beginning with the third year of primary school, all boys were given semi-military training by their teachers. Those going on to middle school, higher school, college, or university received military training under Regular Army officers. In peacetime, this amounted to two or more hours per week, with four to six days of annual maneuvers. Those who took up employment after finishing primary school received considerable military training at youth schools set up for their particular benefit by the Government. Aviation training in schools, particularly in the use of gliders, had recently received much emphasis. Numerous courses of purely military nature were added to the curriculum in order to turn the middle schools into a training camp for cadets, and the universities and higher schools into military academies for reserves.[24]

Throughout the course of training, special attention was given to the inculcation of morale or spiritual instruction. The *Imperial Rescript to Soldiers*, issued by the Emperor Meiji on 4 January 1882, was frequently read to the men, and the five principles of military ethics—loyalty, courtesy, courage, truthfulness, and frugality— were much emphasized. Japanese infantry training was a gradual toughening-up process that grew in intensity, until, finally, long marches with full equipment and stiff endurance tests were used to produce ability to withstand hunger and fatigue for long periods.

The individual Japanese soldier's whole outlook and attitude to life was naturally influenced by his home life, his schooling, his particular social environment (with its innumerable repressing conventions), and his military training. In the Japanese social system, individualism had no place. Children were taught that, as members of the family, they must obey their parents implicitly and, forgetting their own selfish desires, help each and every one of the family at all times. This system of obedience and loyalty was extended to the community and Japanese life as a whole; it permeated upward from the family unit through neighborhood associations, schools, factories, and other larger organizations, until the whole Japanese nation was finally imbued with the spirit of self-sacrifice, obedience, and loyalty to the emperor himself.

Superimposed on this community structure was the indoctrination of ancestor worship and of the divine origin of the emperor and the Japanese race. Since the restoration of the Imperial rule in 1868, the Japanese Government laid much stress on the divine origin of the race and its titular head, and had amplified this teaching by describing Japan's warlike ventures as divine missions. Famous examples of heroism and military feats in Japan's history were extolled on stage and screen, in literature, and on the radio—hero worship was encouraged. Regimentation of the Japanese national life by government authorities, with their numerous and all-embracing regulations, had been a feature for many centuries.

Throughout his military training, the Japanese soldier was not allowed to forget all he had been taught in the home, school, or factory. It was drummed into him again and again while his military training proceeded by repeated lectures from unit commanders, given under the guise of spiritual training. The object of all this concentrated spiritual training was to imbue the Japanese soldier with a spirit that could endure and even be spurred onto further endeavors when the hardships of warfare were encountered. Yet even though his officers appeared to have an ardor that might be called fanaticism, the private soldier was characterized more by blind and unquestioning subservience to authority. The determination of the Japanese soldier to fight to the last or commit suicide rather than be taken prisoner (displayed in the early stages of the war) may have been prompted partly by fear of the treatment he may receive at the hands of his captors. More likely, it was motivated by the disgrace that he realized would be brought on his family should he fall into the enemy's hands.[25]

Due to his training and background, the Japanese soldier was generally well-disciplined and very amenable to law and order. With firm leadership, the discipline to which he had been accustomed in Japan could be, and usually was, maintained in the field and in territories under Japanese occupation. Elated with success in war and imbued with the idea of Japanese racial superiority, the Japanese soldier was apt to adopt a superior attitude towards conquered people and to forget the strict instructions given him during military training. Numerous instances of breaches of the military laws have occurred, and evidence shows that crimes of rape, plundering, drunkenness, and robbery have been committed. Cases of soldiers deserting their posts or mutilating themselves in order to avoid taking part in combat are not unknown, and a few cases of insubordination and desertion also have been reported.

The Japanese soldier in civilian life was a subservient unit in the Japanese family system, and individualism was discouraged. In the army, his position was similar.

Army training and the Japanese social system placed emphasis on teamwork rather than on individual enterprise. As a member of a squad, platoon, or company, the Japanese soldier meticulously performed duties allotted to him; he was an efficient cog in the machine and would carry out instructions to the letter.

Military training inevitably involves a certain degree of controlled brutality. This element was unusually severe in the case of Japanese army personnel, the idea being presumably to toughen the soldiers in various ways. For the Japanese, Athens' violent socialization process was perhaps even more severe than that of the *Einsatzgruppen*. In the brutalization stage, authority figures constantly used violence to force the Japanese recruit to submit to their authority. The novice witnessed those around him being violently subjugated. The Japanese soldier was instructed on how to conduct himself when confronted with conflict. He learned that he had an inescapable personal responsibility to physically attack people who provoked him.[26]

In the early months of the Pacific War (early 1942), for example, British and American forces were repeatedly surprised by the speed with which Japanese soldiers covered ground on foot or on bicycles. Japan's early victories gave rise to the myth of superhuman Japanese soldiers who did not feel the pain or strain of ordinary humans. They did feel these pains and strains, but the severity of their training enabled them to accomplish seemingly amazing feats. They became known for their brutal treatment of prisoners of war and the civilian population.[27]

Economic and Political Conditions in Japan

To understand the origins of the behavior of the Japanese, we must look not only to the time immediately preceding the Japanese invasion of China, but also to the nineteenth century and before. Japanese society and values were over 1,000 years old, where social hierarchy was very important. The Lords of the islands would employ private armies to go into frequent battle with each other. By medieval times, these armies had become the Japanese samurai warrior class, where the way of the warrior, *bushido*, was the code of conduct. *Bushido* dictated that the greatest honor a warrior could ever achieve was to die in the line of duty in the process of serving his lords. So strict was this code of conduct that anyone who failed to meet the high standards of the military service felt it their moral duty to perform *hara-kiri*, where the warrior commits suicide by disemboweling himself in front of witnesses without flinching.

From the twelfth century on, the powerful military commanders, the shoguns, offered the Emperor protection with this strict military service, and over time they became the real source of power. The protection of the Emperor by the samurai under the shoguns was named the code of the samurai. Although the samurai comprised only some 2 percent of the population, the code was engraved deeply into the Japanese culture and psyche, and gradually became the model of honorable behavior among all men.[28]

The Meiji Restoration of 1868 had seen an almost unbelievably rapid modernization undertaking—of education, infrastructure, engineering and science, and militarization. This modernization resulted in the downfall of the shogunate and the disempowerment of the samurai. Partly as a concession to the samurai, the Japanese Government instituted an aggressive foreign policy in Korea and Manchuria in mainland China. In 1904–05, Japan's power, authority, and self-confidence reached new heights with Japan's defeat of Russia over territorial ambitions in Manchuria.[29]

Following the cessation of hostilities in World War I, the prosperity of the nineteenth century was succeeded by a depression in the 1920s—industrial production slowed down and the international depression of 1929 further reduced demand. The population and unemployment were increasing while food supplies diminished. Japan was under pressure to do something during this depression. Some influential political groups argued that the Japanese must conquer new territory in order to avoid more mass starvation. People spoke of the spacious territories of other countries, and were envious of China and different country's vast land resources. The military propagandist Sadao Araki asked why Japan should accept 142,270 square miles to feed 60 million people, while countries like Australia and Canada have more than 3 million square miles to feed 6.5 million people each. This argument was remarkably similar to Nazi Germany's quest for *Lebensraum* (living space) as a pretext for aggressive expansion.[30]

As well as providing new territory for agricultural exploitation, Japan's prestige and influence would be enhanced by such territorial acquisitions, a matter of some influence for the nationalists. China, weak militarily, seemed like the perfect target. The Japanese knew that the Chinese army was in the process of reorganization and build-up, and were therefore aware of the importance of acting quickly. Education in particular had 'reached the point where schooling and preparation for war had become almost interchangeable.'[31]

'The crumbling of autocracy in Europe after World War I, followed by the tide of democracy, socialism, and communism, had had dramatic impact on the young people of Japan,' writes John Toland in *The Rising Sun: The Decline and Fall of the Japanese Empire, 1936–1945*. They cried for change as political parties emerged and a universal manhood suffrage bill was enacted in 1924. The population explosion that accompanied Japan's westernization added to the confusion. Hokkaido, Honshu, Kyushu, and Shikoku (her four main islands, comprising an area scarcely the size of California) already burst with 80 million people. The national economy could not absorb a population increase of almost 1 million a year. Farmers, who were close to starvation following the plunge of produce prices, began to organize in protest for the first time in Japanese history. Hundreds of thousands of city workers were thrown out of work. Out of all this came a wave of left-wing parties and unions.[32] These movements were counteracted by nationalist organizations that combined a program of socialism with imperialism. One of the most popular leaders of the nationalist organizations was Ikki Kita. His words appealed to all who yearned for reform:

> Seven hundred million brethren in India and China cannot gain their independence without our protection and leadership. The history of East and West is a record of the unification of feudal states after an era of civil wars. The only possible international peace, which will come after the present age on international wars, must be a feudal peace. This will be achieved through the emergence of the strongest country, which will dominate all other nations of the works.[33]

By 1928, many felt that Manchuria was only one answer to poverty in Japan. It could be transformed from a wilderness into a civilized, prosperous area, alleviating unemployment at home and providing an outlet for the overpopulated homeland.[34]

Japanese troops had been stationed in the Peking area ever since the Boxer Rebellion in 1900, but only had the right to station troops along railroads and to engage in mining, farming, and business activities. Alarmed that Japan might take a piece of China for their own, Russia appropriated Liaotung, but lost it in 1904 when the Japanese recaptured it and other Manchuria territory. Japan was in possession of the railroads built by the Russians in southern Manchuria. Japan poured a billion dollars into the region, inspiring Japanese, Chinese, and Korean traders and settlers to flood into the area. Japan began to envision Manchuria free of Chinese warlord rule. In the summer of 1931, they were ready to take Manchuria away from the Chinese by force. They took most of the area and set up a puppet government.[35]

Tensions between the Empire of Japan and China had been inflamed since the Invasion of Manchuria in 1931 and the creation of the nominally independent state of Manchukuo with Puyi, the last monarch of the Qing Dynasty, as its sovereign. Although the Kuomintang Government of China refused to recognize Manchukuo, a truce had been negotiated in 1931. However, by the end of 1932, the Japanese Army invaded Rehe Province and annexed it to Manchukuo in 1933. Per the He-Umezu Agreement on 9 June 1935, China recognized the Japanese occupation of eastern Hebei and Chahar provinces. Later that year, Japan established the East Hebei Autonomous Council. As a result, at the start of 1937, all the areas north, east, and west of Beijing were controlled by Japan.[36]

The Marco Polo Bridge, located outside of the walled town of Wanping to the southwest of Peking was the choke point on the Pinghan Railway, and guarded the only passage linking Peking to Kuomintang-controlled areas in the south. Prior to July 1937, the Japanese military had repeatedly demanded the withdrawal of the Chinese forces stationed in this area and had attempted to purchase land to build an airfield. The Chinese refused as Japanese control of the bridge and Wanping town would completely isolate Peking. On the night of 7 July 1937, at the ancient stone bridge, an incident ensued that became known as the Marco Polo Bridge Incident.[37]

A Japanese company stationed near the landmark was holding night maneuvers about a mile from a large Chinese unit. Just as a bugle signaled the end of the operation, bullets came whistling from the Chinese lines. There was a single Japanese casualty—one man missing. A second company was sent to the bridge along with a staff officer who began arranging a truce when a second fusillade poured into the two Japanese companies. The Japanese counterattacked and it was not until the next morning that both sides agreed to withdraw. Just as the Japanese were pulling out, they again were fired upon and the fighting resumed. The Japanese launched a punitive expedition against Chinese troops that led to war with China.[38] In his book *New History of the World*, J. M. Roberts writes the following:

> When Japan's wartime economic boom finally ended, hard times and social problems followed even before the onset of the world economic depression. By 1931, half of Japan's factories were idle. The position of the Japanese peasant deteriorated as millions were ruined and many had to sell their daughters into prostitution in order to survive. The political consequences were soon marked by the intensification of national extremism. The collapse of European colonial markets and the entrenchment of what remained of them behind new tariff barriers had a shattering effect. Japanese exports of manufactures were down by two–thirds, making Japan's export outlets on the Asian mainland critical. Anything that seemed to threaten Japan's markets provoked intense irritation.[39]

Characterization of the Chinese Population

The 1920s drew down the curtain on Japan's golden era of prosperity. When the end of World War I halted the previously insatiable demand for military products, Japanese munitions factories were shut down and thousands of laborers were thrown out of work. China, enraged by the Versailles decision to grant Japan the German rights and concessions in the Shantung Peninsula, organized widespread boycotts of Japanese goods. These developments hurt the Japanese economy still further and gave rise to the popular belief that Japan had become the victim on an international conspiracy.[40]

If expansion was the manifest destiny of nineteenth-century Western nations, then China was twentieth-century Japan's manifest destiny. Ideologically, Japanese were taught that their imperial hierarchy lay at the center of the world morality and that the Japanese were superior to all other peoples. As part of this philosophy, China was made the focus of contempt. Initially, some Japanese intellectuals used China in order to develop a more confident Japanese identity. Japanese teachers instilled hatred and contempt for the Chinese people in boys, preparing them psychologically for a future invasion of the Chinese mainland. In *The Rape of Nanking*, Iris Chang tells the story about an incident in a school in the 1930s, where a boy started crying while dissecting a frog. His teacher slammed his knuckles against the boy's head and yelled, 'Why are you crying about one lousy frog? When you grow up you'll have to kill one hundred, two hundred chinks!'[41]

Anti-Chinese attitudes spread in Japan as the popular voices of journalists and politicians condemned China as backward and encouraged Japanese expansion into Chinese territory. By the 1930s, Japanese school textbooks taught students to believe in Japan's superior position in Asia, to view China as a civilization in decline, and to consider Chinese people morally deficient. This view permeated the Japanese military, leading to racial slurs and contempt. Soldiers were told that expansion into China was Japan's destiny and that heroic behavior brought victory and death. The overall atmosphere of the Japanese military life created soldiers who followed orders, ignored personal feelings, and treated anyone beneath them with the same contempt that they experienced themselves.[42]

Even as they were engaged in a struggle with the Chinese Communist Party, the Chinese National People's Party and Chinese nationalism had done well with Russia's help to this point and was beginning to reassert itself in Manchuria. The Japanese presence in Manchuria went back to 1905 and the theater was critical to them. At first, the Chinese acquiesced, but in the 1920s, they began to question Japanese presence, with support from the Russians, who foresaw danger from the Japanese pushing their influence towards Inner Mongolia. There had been armed conflict in 1928 when the Japanese had tried to prevent the Nationalist Chinese soldiers from operating against warlords in north China, whom they found it convenient to patronize.[43]

In 1929, the Chinese came into conflict with the Russians over control of the railway that ran across Manchuria and was the most direct route to Vladivostok. This conflict impressed the Japanese with the new vigor of Chinese power. At this time, the effective power in Manchuria rested with the commanders of the Japanese forces there. In 1931, those commanders organized an incident near Mukden, which they used as an excuse for taking over the whole province. There followed the setting up of a new puppet state, Manchukuo. Assassinations in Tokyo led to the establishment of a government much more under military influence that expanded the quarrel with China. In 1932, the Japanese replied to a Chinese boycott of their goods by landing forces at Shanghai. In the following year, they came across the Great Wall to impose a peace, which left Japan dominating a part of historic China and trying unsuccessfully to organize a secessionist north China.[44]

By 1937, Japan was engaged in a full-scale war with China that they continued to call 'The China Incident.' 'Crush the Chinese in three months and they will sue for peace,' War Minister Sugiyama predicted. As city after city fell, patriotic fervor swept through Japan, but almost the entire Western world condemned Japan's aggression. On 5 October 1937, President Franklin D. Roosevelt made a forceful speech in Chicago condemning all aggressors and equating the Japanese, by inference, with the Nazis and Fascists:

When an epidemic of physical disease starts to spread, the community approves and joins in a quarantine of the patients in order to protect the health of the community. We are adopting such measures as will minimize our risk of involvement, but we cannot have complete protection in a world of disorder in which confidence and security have broken down.[45]

Japanese reaction was quick and bitter. 'Japan is expanding,' said Yosuke Matsuoka, a Japanese diplomat, 'And what country in its expansion era has failed to be trying to its neighbors.'[46]

From the beginning of the armed conflict in July 1937, the Japanese Government and its supporters, including the mass media, stressed that Chinese Nationalists had planned and initiated armed struggle. According to the official view, Japan had been seeking peace in Asia, only to be dragged into an unwanted military conflict with China. Prime Minister Konoe Fumimaro's decision to dispatch additional forces to China received enthusiastic support from the large national newspapers. In an article in *Asahi Shimbun* (Morning Sun Newspaper) entitled 'Obviously Planned anti-Japanese Armed Conflict; Firmly Decided to Dispatch to Northern China; Determined Statement by the Government to China and Other Countries,' the editor used boldface to emphasize that this incident was no doubt an anti-Japanese armed conflict. He went on to say that the incident was carefully planned by China, and the Japanese government sincerely hopes that the Chinese side will immediately reflect on its attitude and that peaceful negotiations will be instituted in order not to worsen the circumstance. The media stressed that the Chinese soldiers and guerrillas were recklessly killing innocent Japanese civilians as well as combatants. Japanese casualties inflicted by unlawful Chinese shootings at the Marco Polo Bridge and other places were widely reported in the newspapers.

When approximately 3,000 Chinese troops in Tongzhou attacked Japanese forces as well as civilians, killing some 200 Japanese and Korean residents, the Japanese war correspondents described the event in detail and expressed outrage. *Asahi*, for example, detailed Chinese looting and destruction in the Japanese community as well as the stabbing and killing of women, children, and infants. In another article on the same page, the *Asahi* correspondent Tanaka, who had met survivors of the incident, described his feelings of unprecedented fury and declared that 29 July must not be forgotten.[47]

The Tactical Situation in China

Chinese nationalism had won notable successes in the 1920s and showed no signs of retreat. This began to threaten the long-established Japanese presence in Manchuria. Manchuria was critical theatre to the Japanese, whose presence there went back to 1905. After 1905, the Japanese invested heavily in Manchuria. At first, the Chinese acquiesced to the Japanese, but in the 1920s, they began to question Japan pushing their influence towards Inner Mongolia.[48] Japan saw no other course but to launch an attack on the Chinese government. Japan's expectations of a quick victory over China were shattered when the Battle for Shanghai stretched on for several months before that city finally fell in November 1937.

The battle was significant in that it effectively destroyed Japan's goal of conquering China in three months, and signified the beginning of an all-out war, not just some incidents between the two countries. The battle lasted three months and involved nearly 1 million troops, and it was divided into three stages. The first stage lasted from 13 August to 11 September, during which the Chinese army defended the city against the Japanese who were landing at the shores of Shanghai; the second stage lasted from 12 September to 4 November, during which the two armies involved in a bloody house-to-house battle in an attempt to gain control of the city; and the last stage, lasting from 5 November to end of the month, involved the retreat of the Chinese army by flanking Japanese. In the battle, approximately 200,000 died on both sides.[49]

When Shanghai finally fell in November, military planners and leaders turned their eyes to the Chinese capital, Nanking, with the goal of retribution. Commanders pushed their units toward Nanking, quickly outpacing supply lines and telling their men to survive on what they could scavenge. Soldiers robbed villages they passed through and Chinese they came across. Peasants were forced to carry equipment and goods for the Japanese troops. Villages were razed in order to efficiently end any threat of resistance. Brutalities were excused in the name of war and of capturing Nanking. Conquering the capital grew in importance with each new atrocity. The Japanese knew that their job was to kill the enemy, and the barely acceptable conditions of the frontline warfare grew worse, thereby amplifying the animal natures of these soldiers as they marched toward Nanking. To further encourage their men, officers promised women and plunder. When the soldiers reached Nanking, their expectations of revenge, sex, and goods combined with the heightened desire to make an example of Nanking and prove Japan's dominance.

The imperial troops advanced toward Nanking, the capital city of Chiang Kai-shek's Nationalist government, with heightened aggression, raiding small villages and razing entire cities to the ground. Japanese soldiers keyed-up by the heavy fighting in Shanghai and the losses of their own men were ripe for some outlet of the pressure that had built up within them. The Japanese army's march to Nanking created multiple factors that made the subsequent atrocities in Nanking highly likely. These were the combination of several factors, both old and new.

First, the near robbery-like requisitioning by Japanese soldiers caused the breakdown of their discipline. Quite a few cases of murder and rape recorded in private diaries were its natural consequence. In this respect, the Japanese troops degenerated into a pre-modern army living off the land to support themselves. Lack of logistical preparation for the Nanking campaign due to the typical decision-making process in the Japanese military—local command dragging the central authority—was its major cause.

Second, strong anti-Japanese feeling among the Chinese population in the region and the frequent encounters by Japanese troops with straggling and plainclothes soldiers led to the killing of prisoners of war as well as ordinary civilians. Japanese soldiers conducted such ruthless killing because they were highly sensitive to and scared of the plainclothes soldiers. In this respect, the Japanese were fighting a new type of war against the 'inner front' as the German soldiers had done in Belgium in World War I.

Third, both sides resorted to burning for their own strategic or tactical purposes. The Chinese conducted a 'scorched-earth' policy and burned huge areas to deny the advancing Japanese troops supplies—a campaign of destruction in line with their own tradition. Japanese soldiers frequently burned houses and villages to deprive Chinese irregulars or plainclothes soldiers of their staging bases. Other cases were attributable to the breakdown of discipline such as Japanese soldiers' carelessness or the sadistic pleasure they found in seeing houses in flames. John Rabe writes in his diary *Good Men on Nanking*:

> The Japanese march through the city in groups of ten to twenty soldiers and looted the shops. If I had not seen it with my own eyes I would not have believed it. They smashed open windows and doors and took whatever they liked, allegedly because they were short of rations. I watched with my own eyes as they looted the cafe of our German baker Herr Kiessling. Hempel's hotel was broken into as well, as was almost every shop on Chung Shang and Taiping Road. Some Japanese soldiers dragged their booty away in crates, others requisitioned rickshaws to transport their stolen goods to safety.[50]

Confronted by spreading rumors and increasing body counts, some Westerners in Nanking assumed the Chinese exaggerated family losses to get more relief supplies. By spring, burial stories presented death numbers far beyond initial estimates. Westerners reacted with mistrust. This disbelief was rooted in the feeling that a modern people such as the Japanese could not act in such uncivilized ways. Westerners in Nanking actually expected the Japanese to bring a normalcy back to war-torn China.[51]

Living Conditions of the Japanese Soldier in China

In August 1937, the Japanese troops found themselves at a major standstill as they encountered stern resistance by the Chinese main forces in Shanghai, while the Japanese Government clung to the hope that the Chinese forces could be easily subdued. House-to-house fighting broke out, bombs detonated in the war-shattered city, and naval gunfire backed up the infantry units. Both sides continuously reinforced their troops in order to make up their losses.[52] The war in Shanghai was indeed a decisive battle that caused both sides exorbitant damages, left them with a deep-rooted loathing for each other, and begot vengeance. A sergeant from the Andaman Detachment of Japan's 11th Division, for instance, described what he saw when the unit made a landing at Wusong on 3 September. His postwar memoirs partly stated the following:

> I crawled up onto the embankment at Wusong and beheld the sight of perdition. It was brutal. A bloodbath in the battlefield of Ashura [a demon who is eternally fighting] couldn't have been merciless like this. As far as my eyes could see, there was corpse after corpse on top of the embankment, heaps of which covered the entire ground. The bodies of thousands of soldiers were all piled up in a jumble just like blue-fin tuna in a market. A nauseating stench of death assailed my nostrils. This was what had become of the officers and men of the 3rd Division from Nagoya.... They must have been mowed down the moment they landed. These soldiers must have died without knowing what was happening to them. Due to the decay of the internal organs, all the bodies were in ferment and swollen up, and the soft parts of the bodies had gushed out by pressure, such as the eyeballs bulging five or six centimeters out of their faces.[53]

In addition to a severe weakness in its logistics operations, Japanese forces in China faced the constant threat of guerilla attacks. These attacks often came from the Chinese armies, but Chinese organizations of various kinds also resisted the Japanese presence. The fierce battle in Shanghai ended in mid-November, when a successful landing of Japan's 10th Army at Hangzhou Bay in the south and of the 16th Division at Baimaokou in the north threatened the Chinese forces' flank and forced them to withdraw to the west. The General Staff Headquarters in Tokyo, which had been concerned about the exhausted troops and their declining military discipline, decided not to expand the war front any further. However, on 19 November, the 10th Army led by Lieutenant General Yanagawa Heisuke cabled to the Headquarters, 'The group [the 10th Army] commanded [its troops] to put on a spurt in pursuit of the retreating Chinese to Nanking.'[54]

Contrary to the Japanese military's intention to seek a decisive battle in northern China, Chiang Kai-shek tried to avoid such a showdown in that theater so as to concentrate his military effort in Shanghai. Subsequently, the Chinese troop concentration and the Japanese initial strategy of maintaining a defensive posture in the Shanghai area resulted in stalemated positional warfare in that area. Historians and observers generally dwell on the more advanced equipment used by the Japanese as compared with the relatively outdated weapons with which the Chinese equipped themselves at the Battle of Shanghai. The Japanese troops, however, had their own problems. Although they had more artillery, they did not have sufficient or reliable ammunition.

Foot soldiers often complained that many of their hand grenades did not explode. One company commander referred to such a defective weapon as 'the leftover of the Russo-Japanese War.' As a result, a ranking officer of the General Staff who inspected the Shanghai front concluded in his report that the Japanese army's equipment for close-range fighting was inferior to that of the Chinese troops in terms of both quality and quantity. One soldier of the 19th Mountain Artillery Regiment also said, 'The enemy's machine guns, firing almost without interruption, make our infantry charge nearly impossible.' In the static battle of attrition, the Japanese losses amounted to 9,115 killed and 31,257 wounded by the end of the Shanghai campaign in early November 1937. Heavy casualties caused bitter resentment at home. After the Chinese defense in and around Shanghai crumbled, the ranking Japanese generals wished to pursue the enemy to Nanking.[55]

The Japanese attacked Shanghai and began bombing Nanking in August 1937, with the expectation that all of China would fall in a matter of months. Instead, the siege of Shanghai required four months of bloody fighting. This angered the Japanese high command and the frontline soldiers who had watched their comrades die at the hands of the despised Chinese.[56]

The 10th Japanese Army started its full-scale advance to Nanking on 3 December. This hastily planned and executed military campaign caused considerable confusion and even contradiction in the conduct of front-line troops. Since the Japanese decided on the Nanking campaign without adequate prior planning or logistical arrangement, they could not supply the advancing troops sufficiently. Apparently, the Japanese depended mainly on water transportation for sending materials forward. Major Kisaki Hisashi, a staff officer of the 16th Division, said in his diary: 'Supply columns have not arrived yet. Beyond Tanyang, there is no river route. Moreover, motor vehicles could not run due to the conditions of the road.' When some troops could not obtain necessary food and other materials, these items were sometimes supplied by air drops. In most cases, however, the Japanese army had to live off the land. Even General Matsui apparently hoped to procure a substantial amount of food in the enemy's territory. Although he worried about the supply situation in his diary on 20 November, he quickly added, 'We need not be concerned about the victuals despite the lack of supply because rice is plentiful in the areas where the troops are operating.'

The Army leadership set forth the same principle in its official guideline for the Nanking campaign—that is, it would give a logistical priority to ammunition, rather than food. An U.S. military attaché's report underlined this supply policy. According to Major Harry I. T. Creswell, acting U.S. Military Attaché to China, the Japanese army used horse-drawn carts as a major means of transportation and loaded most of the carts with ammunition and only a few with rations for the men and forage for the animals.

The forced march from Shanghai to Nanking made the Japanese dependent on robbery-like requisition for their food provisions and caused a constant food shortage. One can easily imagine how difficult it might be for troops, who had trouble feeding themselves, to allot food to POWs. According to Major Sakakibara Kazue, an SEF staff officer, the SEF made available one food ration for POWs out of every five rations given to the Japanese soldiers. Provisions were so scarce that the prisoners interned within the city walls suffered from hunger. Hanekura Shoro, who was a squad commander of the 16th Division's engineer regiment, noted a rumor that the hunger was so acute that some prisoners had even committed suicide by hanging themselves. Hanekura also witnessed a dismal scene:

> One day I saw some prisoners carrying rice (about three tons) transported by a cargo truck up to the gate of a POW camp. Some punched holes on hemp bags and put some grains in to their mouth on the spot while others scattered rice on the ground on purpose to scoop it up with sand. The prisoner shit each other to take away the rice. The scene was like a living hell.[57]

The Japanese Central China Area Army held a number of army reserves who had wives and families back home. When the prolonged Battle of Shanghai was finally over, those exhausted soldiers were hoping to go home. When ordered to advance westward instead of crossing the Sea of Japan, the Imperial Army soldiers began wreaking their inflamed animosities on Chinese soldiers and civilians throughout their march to Nanking, which, according to many historians, was a prelude to the massive atrocities that would later take place in Nanking. In his memoirs, journalist Matsumoto Shigeharu, the Shanghai bureau chief of Domei News Agency, recalled a circulating rumor among his colleagues: 'The reason that the 10th Army is advancing to Nanking quite rapidly is due to the tacit consent among the officers and men that they could loot and rape as they wish.'[58]

2

Actions of the German *Einsatzgruppen* between 1941 and 1943

Like every historical event, the Holocaust evokes certain specific images. When mentioning the Holocaust, most people think of the concentration camps. They immediately envision emaciated victims in dirty striped uniforms staring incomprehensibly at their liberators or piles of corpses, too numerous to bury individually, bulldozed into mass graves. While those are accurate images, they are merely the product of the systematization of the genocide committed by the Third Reich. The reality of that genocide began not in the camps or in the gas chambers, but with four small groups of murderers known as the *Einsatzgruppen*. Formed by Heinrich Himmler (*Reichsführer*-SS) and Reinhard Heydrich (head of the Reich Security Main Office (RSHA)), they operated in the territories captured by the German armies with the cooperation of German army units Wehrmacht and local militias.[1] By the spring of 1943, when the Germans began their retreat from Soviet territory, the *Einsatzgruppen* had murdered 1.25 million Jews and hundreds of thousands of Polish, Lithuanian, Latvian, Estonian, and Soviet nationals, including prisoners of war.[2]

Einsatzgruppen (Operational Squads of the Security Service and the Security Police) was the task force of mobile killing units that operated in German-occupied territories during World War II. The fundamental structure of the *Einsatzgruppen* was in place during the Anschluss (the incorporation of Austria into the Reich in March 1938). These were intelligence units of the police accompanying the invading army. They reappeared in the invasion of Czechoslovakia in March 1939, and of Poland, on 1 September that year. In the invasions of Austria and Czechoslovakia, the task of the *Einsatzgruppen* was to act as mobile offices of the *Sicherheitsdienst* (SD) (Security Service) and the *Sipo* (Security Police), which consisted of the Gestapo (Secret State Police) and the Kripo (Criminal Police) until these organizations established their permanent offices. The *Einsatzgruppen* were immediately behind the advancing military units and assumed responsibility for the security of the political regime. In the Sudetenland, the *Einsatzgruppen*, in close cooperation with the advancing military forces, lost no time in uncovering and imprisoning the 'Marxist traitors' and other enemies of the state in the liberated areas.[3]

In spring 1941, in contemplation of the coming assault upon the Soviet Union, the *Einsatzgruppen* were created as military units, but not to fight as soldiers. They were organized for murder. In *Masters of Death*, Richard Rhodes describes how early in May 1941, the men who had been chosen as candidates for the Eastern Front *Einsatzgruppen* were assembled in the training school of the German border guards in Pretzsch (a town on the Elbe River, northeast of Leipzig), in the Saxony region.[4] They were not told what their assignment would be, but the commonalities offered a clue. Many of them had served in the *Schutzstaffel* (SS) (Protective Squadron) detachments in Poland and preference was given to men who spoke Russian. Large contingents from the Berlin-Charlottenburg SS leadership school, as well as Gestapo and *Kriminal polizei*, were also assigned there. Some of them were passed on gratefully by their home regiments because they were considered too wild.

The commanders of the *Einsatzgruppen* and the commanders of the *Sonderkommando* and *Einsatzkommandos* (sub-units of the *Einsatzgruppen*) were chosen by Himmler and Heydrich from a list compiled by the RSHA. Most of the handpicked leaders were lawyers. A few were physicians or educators and most had earned doctoral degrees. A reserve battalion of the regular *Ordnungspolizei* (Order Police) completed the Pretzsch roster. In addition to Sipo and SS officers, a support staff of drivers, translators, radio operators, and clerks was also assembled. They later came from all over Germany, though most were members of the SS.[5]

Many of the candidates assembled were former members of the Hitler *Jugend* (Hitler Youth). The Hitler Youth went on separate vacation camps for boys and girls where they were indoctrinated in the ways of National Socialism. Hitler Youth members attended rallies, held regular weekly meetings with their youth counselors, who were ardent Nazis. They participated in songfests, gym tournaments, shooting matches, sports events, and street collections. The Hitler Youth was, for the most part, intended to provide preliminary military training and make boys combat ready. Most SS recruits were training in the Hitler Youth to think of themselves as pure blooded Germans and true Aryans.

The training that SS recruits received before their arrival in Pretzsch prepared them very well for the new mission of the *Einsatzgruppen*. The SS was to be the living embodiment of the Nazi doctrine of the superiority of Nordic blood, and of the Nazi conception of a master race. SS candidates were thoroughly examined and checked. They were asked for the political reputation record of their parents, brothers, and sisters, the record of their ancestry as far back as 1750, their physical examination, and any records from the Hitler Youth. Further, they were asked for a record of hereditary health showing that no hereditary disease exists in their parents and in their family. Last, but perhaps most important, was a certification from the race commission.[6] This examining commission was composed of SS leaders, anthropologists, and physicians.

The very process of selection and acceptance gave the new member a sense of superiority. Only pureblooded Germans in good health could become a member. He must have been of excellent character, had no criminal record, and been well versed in all National Socialist doctrines. The members had to be ready and willing tools, prepared to carry out tasks of any nature, however distasteful. Absolute obedience was therefore the necessary foundation stone of the SS.

Obedience had to be unconditional. It corresponded to the conviction that the National Socialist ideology must reign supreme. Every SS man was prepared, therefore, to carry out blindly every order that was issued by the Führer. The SS troops were also taught a view of the past based on racial struggle and *Lebensraum* (Living Space). The past provided a sense of continuity and showed the recruit that the Jews and Slavs had always been the enemies of Germany. This meant that the need for living space and a solution to the Jewish question was deemed inevitable. The SS soldiers, as well as the other men who arrived in Pretzsch, had also been exposed to the ideas of Euthanasia.[7]

The T-4 Euthanasia Program was established in the fall of 1939 in order to maintain the supposed purity (eugenics) of the so-called Aryan race by systematically killing children and adults born with physical deformities or suffering from mental illness. It put much emphasis on the survival of the fittest and argued that genetic selection should be practiced deliberately. This included the breeding of a racial elite and the extermination of racially inferior or damaging groups. Slavs, Gypsies, and Africans were considered racially inferior to a supposed race of German Aryans—a race that the Nazi ideologues believed to be weakened by what they called the Jewish cancer. This propaganda added to the overall state of mind of the soldiers assembled in Pretzsch and contributed to their special motivation.[8]

The course of training given by the *Einsatzgruppen* at Pretzsch consisted of lectures and speeches on their new and special functions. There were a number of briefings about the aims and activities of the *Einsatzgruppen* in the Nazi-occupied territories of the Soviet Union. At a briefing, which probably took place shortly before 22 June 1941, high-level SS and Police chiefs met in the office of the Chief of Order Police General Kurt Daluege. As Heydrich was unable to attend, he sent them a memorandum specifying who was to be eliminated:

All the following are to be executed: Officials of the Comintern, together with professional Communist politicians in general, top and medium level officials and radical lower level officials of the Party, Central committee and district and sub-district committees. In addition, peoples' commissars, Jews in Party and State employment, and other radical elements, saboteurs, propagandists, snipers, assassins, inciters, etc., insofar as they are, of special importance for the further economic reconstruction of the Occupied Territories. The principal targets of execution by the *Einsatzgruppen* will be political functionaries, Jews mistakenly released from POW camps, Jewish sadists and avengers, and Jews in general.[9]

The mission of the soldiers in Pretzsch was thoroughly understood, from the highest-ranking leader of a *gruppe* down to the lowest SS man.

On 22 June 1941, Germany invaded Soviet Russia. The *Einsatzgruppen*, already alerted, fell in behind the marching columns of the Wehrmacht as an integral part of the machine constructed for swift and total war. Within a space of three days, the training grounds in Saxony were empty and all *Einsatzgruppen* had entered upon the performance of their various missions.

The Wehrmacht rapidly overran vast territory in the early months of the invasion of the Soviet Union. *Einsatzgruppe* 'A' started out from East Prussia, and its units rapidly spread out across Lithuania, Latvia, and Estonia. *Einsatzgruppe* 'B' had Warsaw as its starting point; some of its units passed through Vilna and Grodno on the way to Minsk, where they arrived on 5 July 1941.[10] Other units belonging to *Einsatzgruppe* 'B' passed through Brest-Litovsk, Slonim, Baranovichi, and Minsk, and from there proceeded to southern Belorussia—Mogilev, Bobruisk, and Gomel, advancing as far as Briansk, Kursk, Orel, and Tula. Along their route, in all the places through which they passed, they murdered masses of people— Jews, Gypsies, Communist activists, and prisoners of war. *Einsatzgruppe* 'C' made its way from Upper Silesia to the western Ukraine, by way of Krakow. Two of its units, *Einsatzkommandos* 5 and 6, went to Lvov, where they organized a pogrom (from Russian: 'погром' meaning 'wreaking of havoc') against the Jews with the participation of Ukrainian nationalists. *Sonderkommando* 4b organized the mass murders at Ternopol and Zolochev, and then continued on its way to the east.

On 29 and 30 September, *Sonderkommando* 4a, commanded by Paul Blobel, perpetrated the mass slaughter of 34,000 Kiev Jews at Babi Yar. *Einsatzgruppe* 'D' was attached to the Eleventh Army. During its advance, it carried out massacres in the southern Ukraine (Nikolayev and Kherson), in the Crimea (Simferopol, Sevastopol, Feodosiya, and other places), and in the Krasnodar and Stavropol districts (Maykop, Novorossisk, Armavir, and Piatigorsk). Jewish prisoners of war were separated from the rest and put to death at an early stage, in the advance transit camps.

Einsatzgruppen men were told of Joseph Stalin's order of 3 July 1941, calling on the entire Soviet civilian population to conduct a campaign of terror, sabotage, and guerrilla warfare against the Germans. The soldiers knew that Jews were especially active in this campaign as numerous Jewish historians have proudly acknowledged.[11] This news added to their motivation.

As the *Einsatzgruppen* moved east, political functionaries were shot where found. Prisoners of war who fell in the category of opponents of National Socialism were handed by the Wehrmacht to the *Einsatzgruppen* and killed. These swift methods were also applied in disposing of Jews, Gypsies, and persons falling under that vague denomination—undesirables. The *Einsatzgruppen* first promoted pogroms by inciting already existing anti-Semitism and age-old grievances against the Jews by the local population. Many were killed by the locals as the *Einsatzgruppen* assisted and watched. However, the number of humans marked for slaughter was too large to be disposed of by casual assassination. Their very numbers demanded that they were killed *en masse*.[12]

The methods of extermination varied little. Mass shooting, the most common means of slaughter, was described with classic simplicity by Herman Graebe, a German civilian, before the International Military Tribunal. Graebe was in charge of a building firm in the Ukraine:

> I walked around the mound, and found myself confronted by a tremendous grave. People were closely wedged together and lying on top of each other so that their heads were visible. Nearly all had blood running over their shoulders from their heads. Some of the people shot were still moving. Some were lifting their arms and turning their heads to show that they were still alive. The pit was already ⅔ full. I estimated that it contained about 1,000 people. I looked for the man who did the shooting. He was an SS man, who sat at the edge of the narrow end of the pit, his feet dangling into the pit. He had a Tommy gun on his knees and was smoking a cigarette. The people, completely naked, went down some steps, which were cut in the clay wall of the pit and clambered over the heads of the people lying there, to the place to which the SS man directed them. They lay down in front of the dead or injured people; some caressed those who were still alive and spoke to them in a low voice. Then I heard a series of shots. I looked into the pit and saw that the bodies were twitching or the heads lying already motionless on top of the bodies that lay before them. Blood was running from their necks. I was surprised that I was not ordered away, but I saw that there were two or three postmen in uniform nearby. The next batch was approaching already. They went down into the pit, lined themselves up against the previous victims, and were shot. When I walked back around the mound, I noticed another truckload of people, which had just arrived. This time it included sick and infirm persons. Old, very thin women appeared. Naked people held her up. The woman appeared to be paralyzed. The naked people carried the woman around the mound. I left and drove in my car back to Dubno. On the morning of the next day, when I again visited the site, I saw about 30 naked people lying near the pit—about 30 to 50 meters away from it. Some of them were still alive; they looked straight in front of them with a fixed stare and seemed to notice neither the chilliness of the morning nor the workers of my firm who stood around. A girl of about 20 spoke to me and asked me to give her clothes, and help her escape. At that moment, we heard a fast car approach and I noticed that it was an SS detail. I moved away to my site. Ten minutes later, we heard shots from the vicinity of the pit. The Jews still alive had been ordered to throw the corpses into the pit; then they had themselves to lie down in this to be shot in the neck.[13]

The method that the *Einsatzgruppen* employed was to shoot their victims in ravines, abandoned quarries, mines, anti-tank ditches, or huge trenches that had been dug for this purpose. The brutality of many of the SS men is illustrated in a description of a typical Russian village. Hearing of the approach of a murder commando, the Jews of the village has gone into hiding. When the commando reached the village, the only person whom the SS men saw in the street was a woman with a baby in her arms. She refused to tell them where the Jews were hidden. One of the men snatched the baby from her, gripped it by the legs, and smashed its head against a door. An SS man recalled: 'It went off with a bang.' Beside her, the women gave away the hiding place. The *Einsatzgruppen* performed their murderous work in broad daylight and in the presence of the local population. Only when the Germans began their retreat was an effort made to erase the traces of their crimes. This was the job of *Sonderkommando* to open the mass graves, disinter the corpses, cremate them, and spread the ashes over the fields and streams.[14]

The killing by shooting, especially of women and children, had a devastating effect on many of the *Einsatzgruppen* member's mental state, which even heavy drinking of hard liquor (of which they were given a generous supply) could not suppress. A few committed suicide and some asked for transfer to other units. Units began experimenting with methods that would ease the burden on the shooters. Some units experimented with using quick lime (calcium hydroxide). Used in the trenches between the layers of bodies, it was thought that if the victims were made to lie down on top of each other, quick lime could be spread over them and then water could be added. The calcium hydroxide reacted with the water and actually boiled away the flesh of the victims. This method proved too grotesque, since the victims were still alive when the water was added, and it was discontinued. Other experiments such as alternating victims with wood in piles then burning the piles was attempted but found to be too time consuming.

After trying to dynamite the victims and burn those alive in their homes and barns proved unproductive, the RSHA, in Berlin, began to look for an alternative method of execution in August 1941. It was found in the form of gas vans (heavy trucks with hermetically sealed vans into which the truck's exhaust fumes were piped). Within a short time, these trucks were supplied to all the *Einsatzgruppen*. The carbon monoxide from the car's exhaust would be channeled into the sealed cabin, in which the victims stood. The gassing process took between fifteen and thirty minutes. During this time, the van was driven from the loading site to prepared graves. The shootings continued, augmented with the gas vans. The gas vans lead to the construction of the gas chambers at the concentration camps.[15] With the construction of the camps with gassing facilities, the *Einsatzgruppen* would soon be out of the business of killing Jews. From the beginning of 1942 onward, the *Einsatzgruppen* increasingly turned to fighting Soviet partisans.

In *German Anti-Partisan Warfare in Europe, 1939–1945*, Colin Heaton describes how the SS was dispatched to handle the partisan/guerrilla threat in a unique way. *Generalfeldmarschall* Wilhelm Keitel ordered decrees allowing for the seizure or property and the execution without trial of all persons suspected of compromising

German security in the occupied zones. Various SS units created their own counterinsurgency teams that were usually comprised of company sized elements numbering approximately 200 men. These units were motorized, well-armed, and would be rushed rapidly to an area of suspected partisan activity.[16]

Clearly, the *Einsatzgruppen* record is one of brutality and devastation. They were indoctrinated to view Jews, Slavs, partisans, and Bolsheviks as threats to the German people. They viewed these peoples as sub-human. Through indoctrination and training, they developed a special motivation to conduct violence. This special motivation not only enabled them to kill, it also enabled them to carry out cruel and bestial acts on their victims.[17]

Trials of War Criminals before the Nuernberg Military Tribunals began in October 1946 and lasted two and a half years, producing more than 300,000 pages of testimony and evidence. Part of the trials included the crimes committed by the *Einsatzgruppen*. The following is an excerpt from Volume IV of the proceedings:

Count One—Crimes Against Humanity

1. Between May 1941 and July 1943 all of the defendants herein committed crimes against humanity, as defined in Article II of Control Council Law No. 10, in that they were principals in, accessories to, ordered, abetted, took a consenting part in, were connected with plans and enterprises involving, and were members of organizations or groups connected with, atrocities and offenses, including but not limited to, persecutions on political, racial, and religious grounds, murder, extermination, imprisonment, and other inhumane acts committed against civilian populations, including German nationals and nationals of other countries.

2. The acts, conduct, plans, and enterprises charged in paragraph 1 of this count were carried out as part of a systematic program of genocide, aimed at the destruction of foreign nations and ethnic groups by murderous extermination.

3. Beginning in May 1941, on the orders of Himmler, special task forces called 'Einsatzgruppen' were formed from the personnel of the SS, the SD, the Gestapo, and other police units. The primary purpose of these groups was to accompany the German Army into the eastern territories, and exterminate Jews, gypsies, Soviet officials, and other elements of the civilian population regarded as racially 'inferior' or 'politically undesirable.'

4. Initially four *Einsatzgruppen* were formed, each of which supervised the operation of a number of subordinate units called 'Einsatzkommandos' or 'Sonderkommandos.' Some *Einsatzgruppen* had, in addition, other units for special purposes. Each *Einsatzgruppe*, together with its subordinate units consisted of about 500 to 800 persons. *Einsatzgruppe* 'A', operating mainly in the Baltic region, included *Sonderkommandos* 1a and 1b and *Einsatzkommandos* 2 and 3. *Einsatzgruppe* 'B', operating mainly in the area towards Moscow, included *Sonderkommandos* 7a and 7b, *Einsatzkommandos* 8 and 9, and special units named *Vorkommando* Moscow (also known as *Sonderkommando* 7c) and Trupp

Smolensk. *Einsatzgruppe* 'C', operating mainly in the area towards Kiev, included *Sonderkommandos* 4a and 4b and *Einsatzkommandos* 5 and 6. *Einsatzgruppe* 'D', operating mainly in the area of southern Russia, included *Sonderkommandos* 10a and 10b and *Einsatzkommandos* 11a, 11b, and 12.

5. All of the defendants herein, as officers or staff members of one or more *Einsatzgruppen* or their subordinate units, committed murders, atrocities, and other Inhumane acts as more specifically set forth in paragraphs 6 to 9, inclusive, of this count.

6. *Einsatzgruppe* 'A' and the units under its command committed murders and other crimes which included, but were not limited to, the following:

(A) During the period 22 June 1941 to 15 October 1941 in Lithuania, Latvia, Estonia, and White Ruthenia, *Einsatzgruppe* 'A' murdered 118,430 Jews and 3,398 Communists.

(B) On or about 4 July 1941 in the city of Riga, *Sonderkommando* 1a and *Einsatzkommando* 2, together with auxiliary police under their command, carried out pogroms in which all synagogues were destroyed and 400 Jews were murdered.

(C) During October 1941 in Estonia, *Einsatzkommando* 1a, together with Estonian units under their command, committed murders pursuant to a program for the extermination of all Jewish males over sixteen except doctors and Jewish elders.

(D) During the period 7 November 1941 to 11 November 1941 in Minsk, *Sonderkommando* 1b murdered 6,624 Jews.

(E) During the period 22 June 1941 to 16 January 1942 in its operational areas, *Einsatzkommando* 2 murdered 33,970 persons.

(F) On 30 November 1941 in Riga, 20 men of *Einsatzkommando* 2 participated in the murder of 10,600 Jews.

(G) During the period 22 June 1941 to 19 September 1941 in Lithuania, *Einsatzkommando* 3 murdered 46,692 persons.

(H) During the period 22 June 1941 to 10 August 1941 in the area of Kovno [Kaunas] and Riga, *Einsatzgruppe* 'A' murdered 29,000 persons.

(I) During the period 2 October 1941 to 10 October 1941 in the vicinity of Krasnogvardeysk, *Einsatzgruppe* 'A' murdered 260 persons.

(J) During the period 15 October 1941 to 23 October 1941 in the vicinity of Krasnogvardeysk, *Einsatzgruppe* 'A' murdered 156 persons.

(K) During the period 24 October 1941 to 5 November 1941 in the vicinity of Krasnogvardeysk, *Einsatzgruppe* 'A' murdered 118 persons.

(L) On 20 November 1941 in the vicinity of Krasnogvardeysk, *Einsatzgruppe* 'A' murdered 855 persons.

(M) In about December 1941 in the ghetto in Vitebsk, units of *Einsatzgruppe* 'A' murdered 4,090 Jews.

(N) On 22 December 1941 in Vilnyus [Vilna], units of *Einsatzgruppe* 'A' murdered 402 persons including 385 Jews.

(O) On 1 February 1942 in Loknya, units of *Einsatzgruppe* 'A' murdered the 38 gypsies and Jews remaining there.

(P) On 2 and 3 March 1942 in Minsk, units of *Einsatzgruppe* 'A' murdered 3,412 Jews.

(Q) On 2 and 3 March 1942 in Baranovichi, units of *Einsatz–V gruppe* 'A' murdered 2,007 Jews.

(R) On 17 March 1942 in Ilya, east of Vileika, units of *Einsatzgruppe* 'A' murdered 520 Jews.

(S) On or about 7 April 1942 in Kovno and Olita, Lithuania, units of *Einsatzgruppe* 'A' murdered 44 persons.

(T) During the period 10 April 1942 to 24 April 1942 in Latvia, units of *Einsatzgruppe* 'A' murdered 1,272 persons, including 983 Jews, 204 Communists and 71 gypsies.

7. *Einsatzgruppe* 'B' and the units under its command committed murders and other crimes which included, but were not limited to, the following:

(A) In about July 1941 in the city of Minsk, units of *Einsatzgruppe* 'B' murdered 1,050 Jews and liquidated political officials, 'Asiatics' and others.

(B) During the period 22 June 1941 to 14 November 1941 in the vicinity of Minsk and Smolensk, *Einsatzgruppe* 'B' murdered more than 45,467 persons.

(C) On 15 October 1941 in Mogilev, units of *Einsatzgruppe* 'B' murdered 83 'Asiatics.'

(D) On 19 October 1941 in Mogilev, units of *Einsatzgruppe* 'B' participated in the murder of 3,726 Jews.

(E) On 23 October 1941 in the vicinity of Mogilev, units of *Einsatzgruppe* 'B' murdered 279 Jews.

(F) During the period 22 June 1941 to 14 November 1941 in its operational areas, *Sonderkommando* 7a murdered 1,517 persons.

(G) In September or October 1941 in Sadrudubs, *Sonderkommando* 7a murdered 272 Jews.

(H) During the period 6 March 1942 to 30 March 1942 in the vicinity of Klintsy, *Sonderkommando* 7a murdered 1,585 Jews and 45 gypsies.

(I) During the period 22 June 1941 to 14 November 1941 in its operational areas, *Sonderkommando* 7b murdered 1,822 persons.

(J) During the period from September to October 1941 in Rechitsa, White Rrithenia, *Sonderkommando* 7b murdered 216 Jews.

(K) During the period 6 March 1942 to 30 March 1942 in the vicinity of Bryansk, *Sonderkommando* 7b murdered 82 persons, including 27 Jews. (L) During the period 22 June 1941 to 14 November 1941 in its operational areas, *Einsatzkommando* 8 murdered 28,219 persons.

(M) In September or October 1941 in the area of Shklov, *Einsatzkommando* 8 murdered 627 Jews and 812 other persons.

(N) In September or October 1941 in Mogilev, *Einsatzkommando* 8 participated in the murder of 113 Jews.

(O) In September or October 1941 in Krupka, *Einsatzkommando* 8 murdered 912 Jews.

(P) In September or October 1941 in Sholopaniche, *Einsatzkommando* 8 murdered 822 Jews.

(Q) During the period 6 March 1942 to 30 March 1942 in the vicinity of Mogilev, *Einsatzkommando* 8 murdered 1,609 persons, including 1,551 Jews and 33 gypsies.

(R) On 8 October 1941 in the ghetto of Vitebsk, *Einsatzkommando* 9 began murdering Jews and by 25 October 1941, 3,000 Jews had been executed.

(S) During the period 6 March 1942 to 30 March 1942 in the vicinity of Vitebsk, *Einsatzkommando* 9 murdered 273 persons, including 170 Jews.

(T) During the period 22 June 1941 to 14 November 1941 in its (operational areas, the group staff of *Einsatzgruppe* 'B' and the *Vorkommando* Moscow murdered 2,457 persons.

(U) During the period 22 June 1941 to 20 August 1941 in the vicinity of Smolensk, the group staff of *Einsatzgruppe* 'B' and the *Vorkommando* Moscow murdered 144 persons.

(V) In September or October 1941 in Tatarsk, the group staff of *Einsatzgruppe* 'B' and the *Vorkommando* Moscow murdered all male Jews.

(W) During the period 6 March to 30 March 1942 in the vicinity of Roslavl, *Vorkommando* Moscow murdered 52 persons.

(X) During the period 6 March 1942 to 30 March 1942 in the vicinity of Smolensk, Trupp Smolensk murdered 60 persons, including 18 Jews.

8. *Einsatzgruppe* 'C' and the units under its command committed. Murders and other crimes which included, but were not limited to, the following:

(A) During the period 22 June 1941 to 3 November 1941 in the vicinity of Zhitomir, Novo Ukrainka and Kiev, *Einsatzgruppe* 'C' murdered more than 75,000 Jews.

(B) On 19 September 1941 in Zhitomir, *Einsatzgruppe* 'C' murdered 3,145 Jews and confiscated their clothing and valuables.

(C) During the period 22 June 1941 to 29 July 1941 in the vicinity of Zhitomir, *Sonderkommando* 4a murdered 2,531 persons.

(D) During the period 22 June 1941 to 12 October 1941 in its operational areas, *Sonderkommando* 4a murdered more than 51,000 persons.

(E) During the period from 27 June to 29 June 1941 in the vicinity of Sokal and Lutsk, *Sonderkommando* 4a murdered 300 Jews and 317 Communists.

(F) In July or August 1941 in Fastov, *Sonderkommando* 4a murdered all the JeW8 between the ages of 12 and 60.

(G) In September or October 1941 in the vicinity of Vyrna and Dederev, *Sonderkommando* 4a murdered 32 gypsies.

(H) On 29 and 30 September 1941 in Kiev, *Einsatzkommando* 4a, together with the group staff and police units, murdered 33,771 Jews and confiscated their clothing and valuables.

(I) On 8 October 1941 in Jagotin, *Sonderkommando* 4a murdered 125 Jews.

(J) On 23 November 1941 in Poltava, *Sonderkommando* 4a murdered 1,538 Jews.

(K) In about July 1941 in Tarnopol, *Sonderkommando* 4b murdered 180 Jews.

(L) During the period from 13 September to 26 September 1941 in the vicinity of Kremenchug, *Sonderkommando* 4b murdered 125 Jews and 103 political officials.

(M) During the period 4 October 1941 to 10 October 1941 in Poltava, *Sonderkommando* 4b murdered 186 persons.

(N) From about 11 October 1941 to 30 October 1941 in the vicinity of Poltava, *Sonderkommando* 4b murdered 595 persons.

(O) During the period 14 January 1942 to 12 February 1942 in the vicinity of Kiev, *Sonderkommando* 4b murdered 861 persons, including 139 Jews and 649 political officials.

(P) During the period from February 1942 to March 1942 in the vicinity of Artemovsk, *Sonderkommando* 4b murdered 1,317 persons, including 1,224 Jews and 63 'political activists.'

(Q) During the period from 22 June 1941 to 10 November 1941 in its operational areas, *Einsatzkommando* 5 murdered 29,644 persons.

(R) During July or August 1941 in Berdichev, *Einsatzkommando* 5 murdered 74 Jews.

(S) During the period 7 September 1941 to 5 October 1941 in the vicinity of Berdichev, *Einsatzkommando* 5 murdered 8,800 Jews and 207 political officials.

(T) On 22 and 23 September 1941 in Uman, *Einsatzkommando* 5 murdered 1,412 Jews.

(U) During the period 20 October 1941 to 26 October 1941 in the vicinity of Kiev, *Einsatzkommando* 5 murdered 4,372 Jews and 36 political officials.

(V) During the period from 23 November 1941 to 30 November 1941 in the vicinity of Rovno, *Einsatzkommando* 5 murdered 2,615 Jews and 64 political officials.

(W) During the period from 12 January 1942 to 24 January 1942 in the vicinity of Kiev, *Einsatzkommando* 5 murdered about 8,000 Jews and 104 political officials.

(X) During the period from 24 November 1941 to 30 November 1941 in the vicinity of Dnepropetrovsk, *Einsatzkommando* 6 murdered 226 Jews and 19 political officials.

(Y) From about 10 January 1942 to 6 February 1942 in the vicinity of Stalino, *Einsatzkommando* 6 murdered about 149 Jews and 173 political officials.

(Z) In about February 1942 in the vicinity of Stalino, *Einsatzkommando* 6 murdered 493 persons, including 80 'political activists' and 369 Jews.

9. *Einsatzgruppe* 'D' and the units under its command committed murders and other crimes which included, but were not limited to, the following:

(A) During the period from 22 June 1941 to July 1943, *Einsatzgruppe* 'D', in the area of southern Russia, murdered more than 90,000 persons.

(B) On 15 July 1941 in the vicinity of Beltsy, *Sonderkommando* 10a murdered 45 persons, including the Council of Jewish Elders.

(C) In July 1941 in the vicinity of Chernovitsy, *Sonderkommando* 10b murdered 16 Communists and 682 Jews.

(D) During the period 22 June 1941 to 7 August 1941 in the vicinity of Kichinev, *Einsatzkommando* 11a murdered 551 Jews.

(E) In about July 1941 in Tighina, *Einsatzkommando* 11b murdered 151 Jew.

(F) In about December 1941 in the vicinity of Simferopol, *Einsatzkommando* 11b murdered over 700 persons.

(G) During the period from 22 June 1941 to 23 August 1941 in Babchinzy, *Einsatzkommando* 12 murdered 94 Jews.

(H) During the period 15 July 1941 to 30 July 1941 in the vicinity of Khotin, *Einsatzgruppe* 'D' murdered 150 Jews and Communists.

(I) During the period 19 August 1941 to 15 September 1941 in the vicinity of Nikolayev, *Einsatzgruppe* 'D' murdered 8,890 Jews and Communists.

(J) During the period 16 September 1941 to 30 September 1941 in the vicinity of Nikolayev and Kherson, *Einsatzgruppe* 'D' murdered 22,467 Jews.

(K) During the period 1 October 1941 to 15 October 1941 in the area east of the Dnepr, *Einsatzgruppe* 'D' murdered 4,891 Jews and 46 Communists.

(L) During the period 15 January 1942 to 31 January 1942 within its operational areas, *Einsatzgruppe* 'D' murdered 3,601 persons, including 3,286 Jews and 152 Communists.

(M) During the period 1 February 1942 to 15 February 1942 within its operational areas, *Einsatzgruppe* 'D' murdered 1,451 persons, including 920 Jews and 468 Communists.

(N) During the period 16 February 1942 to 28 February 1942 within its operational areas, *Einsatzgruppe* 'D' murdered 1,515 persons, including 729 Jews, 271 Communists and 421 gypsies and other persons.

(O) During the period 1 March 1942 to 15 March 1942 within its operational areas, *Einsatzgruppe* 'D' murdered 2,010 persons, including 678 Jews, 359 Communists, and 810 gypsies and other persons.

(P) During the period 15 March 1942 to 30 March 1942 within its operational areas, *Einsatzgruppe* 'D' murdered 1,501 persons, including 588 Jews, 405 Communists, and 261 gypsies and other persons. 10. The acts and conduct of the defendants set forth in this count were committed unlawfully, willfully, and knowingly and constitute violations of the law of nations, international conventions, general principles of criminal law as derived from the criminal law of all civilized nations, the internal penal laws of the countries in which such crimes were committed, and Article II of Control Council Law No. 10.

Count Two—War Crimes.

10. Between 22 June 1941 and July 1943 all of the defendants herein committed war crimes as defined in Article II of Control Council Law No. 10, in that they were principals in, accessories to, ordered, abetted, took a consenting part in,

were connected with plans and enterprises involving, and were members of organizations or groups connected with, atrocities and offenses against persons and property constituting violations of the laws or customs of war, including, but not limited to, murder and ill-treatment of prisoners of war and civilian populations of countries and territories under the belligerent occupation of, or otherwise controlled by Germany, and wanton destruction and devastation not justified by military necessity. The particulars concerning these crimes are set forth in paragraphs 6 to 9, inclusive, of count one of this indictment and are incorporated herein by reference.

11. The acts and conduct of the defendants set forth in this count were committed unlawfully, willfully; and knowingly and constitute violations of international conventions, particularly of Articles 43 and 46 of the Regulations of the Hague Convention No. IV, 1907, the Prisoner-of-War Convention (Geneva, 1929), the laws and customs of war, the general principles of criminal law as derived from the criminal laws of all civilized nations, the internal penal laws of the countries in which such crimes were committed, and Article II of Control Council Law No. 10.

Count Three—Membership in Criminal Organizations.

12. All the defendants herein are charged with membership, subsequent to 1 September 1939, in organizations declared to be criminal by the International Military Tribunal and paragraph 1 (d) of Article II of Control Council Law No. 10.

(A) All the defendants were members of the *Schutzstaffeln der Nationalsozialistischen Deutschen Arbeiterpartei* (commonly known as the 'SS').

(B) The defendants Ohlendorf, Jost, Naumann, Rasch, Six, Blobel, Blume, Sandberger, Seibert, Steimle, Biberstein, Braune, Haensch, Ott, Strauch, Haussmann, Klingelhoefer, Fendler, von Radetzky, Schubert, and Graf were members of offices (Aemter) III, VI, and VII of the Reich Security Main Office (*Reichssicherheitshauptamt*—RSHA) constituting the Reich Security Service of the Reich Leader-SS (*Reichssicherheitsdienst des Reichsführer*-SS), commonly known as the 'SD'.

(C) The defendants Rasch, Schulz, Blume, Braune, Biberstein, Nosske, and Ruehl were members of Amt IV of the *Reichssicherheitshauptamt*—RSHA constituting the Secret State Police (*Geheime Staatspolizei*), commonly known as the 'Gestapo'. Wherefore, this indictment is filed with the Secretary General of the Military Tribunals and the charges herein made against the above–named defendants are hereby presented to the Military Tribunals.[18]

Indoctrination and Training of the German Army

Systematic universal military training in modern times is an invention of the Germans and has been developed to its highest degree of refinement by them. It grew out of the mass armies that were necessary to overthrow Napoleon and was introduced by a Prussian law of 3 September 1814 as a part of the far-reaching army reforms initiated by Scharnhorst and his colleagues to cope with the new forms of warfare. From its meager roots as a mercenary force of Brandenburg during the Thirty Years' War, the Prussian Army evolved into a formidable force by the time it became the German Army of World War II. Harsh military discipline had a long tradition in Germany. SS training, as Himmler organized it, was known for its brutality. Even ordinary police training before the war was brutalizing. This was in keeping in the Prussian tradition. The Nazis prepared for war by a system of military training and indoctrination that began with children of high-school age. The training system was directed by the old professional army: it depended on effort, thoroughness, and the application of old and tested principles to the means of modern warfare. As an observer remarked, the Germans believed that by hard work and hard training they would save blood later.

The Nazi government from the start was dedicated to the purpose of a war of conquest; from 1934, the Party controlled and directed every aspect of German life to this aim. German military leaders had followed Carl von Clausewitz's principles for years, but only under the Nazi regime could his key concept of total war be realized: the principle that every agency and every individual of a nation must be used in the effort of war. Nothing is more revealing of Nazi plans and methods than the application of this principle in a very broad program of military training. The goal of this program was a large and highly trained army, but the shaping of this army was not left to the two years of actual military training for conscripts. From the age of fourteen, boys were to receive a preparation for military service that would cover much of the basic training ordinarily given recruits.[19]

At the age of ten, German boys were brought into the Nazi scheme as members of the *Jung Volk* (Young Folk) organization, and received their first taste of official indoctrination. Real shaping for the army began at fourteen, when they entered the Hitler Youth. In 1939, the Storm Trooper section of the Nazi party took charge of the Hitler Youth, and after the start of war, boys aged sixteen to eighteen were compelled to take six months of regular pre-military work. The aim was to provide the army with the largest possible reserve of mentally, physically, and militarily trained young men. The training included infantry fundamentals, care and use of weapons, and signaling. When German youths, at nineteen, were inducted for military service, most of them had already had the equivalent of basic military training, were in excellent physical condition, and had been indoctrinated both with Nazi ideology and military attitudes.[20]

The importance of physical condition was fully recognized in German training doctrine. One of the services of the Hitler Youth (with its emphasis on sports) and the Labor Service was to furnish the army with recruits who were fully conditioned and toughened. The training period was thereby shortened and made more effective.

A U.S. observer saw an infantry battalion on maneuvers in January 1940. Troops lay patiently in 4 inches of snow, waiting their orders, for over an hour. Many men had no gloves. This difficult period seemed to have no effect on their performance later. Other observers of a German division in field exercises before the outbreak of war reported that fitness and endurance were made a fetish by both officers and men. For training purposes, officers often went twenty-four hours without food. Troops carried heavy loads of mortars, machine guns, and other equipment as far as 1,200 yards in fast rushes of 50 yards. Just before the exercises, one engineer battalion had marched 85 miles through mountains in three days.

Good physical condition has been a basis for the notable march achievement of German infantry. Despite all the mechanization of modern armies, German doctrine foresaw the possibility that motorized personnel might lose their equipment and would therefore have to move rapidly on foot. In some cases, German troops, under the prolonged strain of combat operations, have covered 30 to 40 miles a day for several days, and German sources claim a march of 44 miles in twenty-four hours during the Polish campaign.[21]

Many members of the *Einsatzgruppen* came from the *Waffen*-SS, the Order Police, or from other branches; most were volunteers. In *Masters of Death*, Richard Rhodes describes how early in May 1941, the men who had been chosen as candidates for the Eastern Front *Einsatzgruppen* were assembled in the training school of the German border guards in Pretzsch (a town on the Elbe River, northeast of Leipzig), in the Saxony region.[22] They were not told what their assignment would be, but the commonalities offered a clue. Many of them had served in the SS detachments in Poland and preference was given to men who spoke Russian. Large contingents from the Berlin-Charlottenburg-SS leadership school, as well as the Gestapo and *Kriminalpolizei* were also assigned there. Rhodes writes:

> Assignment to Pretzsch emptied the SS leadership school in Berlin-Charlottenburg and depleted the professional examination course of an SS criminal division. It drew from the lower and middle-ranking officers of the Security Police, some of them passed on gratefully by their home regiments because they were considered too wild.[23]

The indoctrination into Nazi ideas that the recruits had received, no matter where they came from, prepared them very well for the new mission of the *Einsatzgruppen*. According to Telford Taylor in *The Anatomy of the Nuremberg Trials*, there were approximately 600 to 1,000 men in each *Einsatzgruppe*, although many were support staff. The active members of the *Einsatzgruppen* were drawn from various military and non-military organizations of the Third Reich. The bulk of the members were drawn from the *Waffen*-SS, the military arm of the SS. In *Einsatzgruppen* 'A', for example, the breakdown of active members was as follows:

Waffen-SS	340
Gestapo (Secret State Police)	89
SD (Security Service)	35
Order Police	133
Kripo (Criminal Investigation Agency)	41
TOTAL	638[24]

The SS was to be the living embodiment of the Nazi doctrine of the superiority of Nordic blood and of the Nazi conception of a master race. SS candidates were thoroughly examined and checked. They were asked for the political reputation record of their parents, brothers and sisters, the record of their ancestry as far back as 1750. Their physical examination and any records from the Hitler Youth were examined. Further, they were asked for a record of hereditary health showing that no hereditary disease exists in their parents and in their family.[25] The members had to be ready and willing to carry out tasks of any nature, however distasteful. Absolute obedience was therefore the necessary foundation stone of the SS.[26]

Obedience had to be unconditional. It corresponded to the conviction that the National Socialist ideology must reign supreme. Every man was prepared, therefore, to carry out blindly every order that was issued by Hitler. The *Einsatzgruppen* troops were also taught a view of the past based on racial struggle and *Lebensraum* (living space). The past provided a sense of continuity and showed the recruit that the Jews and Slavs had always been the enemies of Germany. This meant that the need for living space and a solution to the Jewish question was deemed inevitable. The men who joined the *Einsatzgruppen* had been exposed to the ideas of euthanasia.[27]

Clearly, the *Einsatzgruppen* record is one of brutality and devastation. They were indoctrinated to view Jews, Slavs, partisans, and Bolsheviks as threats to the German people. They viewed these people as sub-human. Through coaching, they developed a special motivation to conduct violence. This indoctrination not only enabled them to kill, it also contributed to their ability to carry out cruel and bestial acts on their victims.[28]

With the outbreak of the war in Europe and the march of Nazi armies over the continent, the SS and the *Einsatzgruppen* participated in 'solving' the Jewish question in all the countries of Europe. The solution was nothing short of extermination. The SS carried out the policies and beliefs of Hitler: the extermination of the Jews. The selection criteria of SS membership and their training largely explain their motivation and commitment to this systematic extermination. The fundamental principle of selection and membership in the SS was what Heinrich Himmler, their leader, called that of 'Blood and Elite.'

The SS were indoctrinated into the beliefs of Adolf Hitler. Hitler developed his anti-Semitism by placing his desire to remove the Jews in the context of a wider theory of the struggle between races for living space. In Hitler's view, the Jews, lacking a state of their own, were parasites trying to destroy those states, which had been established by superior races. He referred to the Jews as a plague, an epidemic, germ carriers, a harmful bacillus, a cancer, and as maggots. In his writings and speeches, Hitler blamed the situation of Germany at the end of the World War I on an international Jewish conspiracy. His basic wish throughout had been by one means or another to remove the Jews from German soil. The SS were developed to be the master race who would occupy German soil.

The new formations of young SS captivated public imagination. Clad in smart black uniforms, the SS attracted more and more young men. Many young people, looking for work and a sense of belonging, joined. They were taught why they were fighting and what kind of Germany was being resurrected before their very eyes. The new recruits were shown how Germany was being morally united through class reconciliation and physically united through the return of the lost German homelands. They were made aware of their kinship with all the other Germans living in foreign lands—in Poland, Russia, the Sudetenland, and other parts of Europe— and were taught that Jews were sub-human—to blame for most of Germany's ills and a scourge on society. These were the principles, which were publicly reiterated, repeatedly, so that the newest recruit was thoroughly steeped in them. They totally believed in Hitler's views. Indoctrination of the organization in principles of racial hatred was not enough. The members had to be ready and willing tools, prepared to carry out tasks of any nature, however distasteful, illegal, or inhuman. Absolute obedience was the necessary second foundation stone of the SS. Every SS man was prepared, therefore, to carry out blindly every order which was issued by Hitler or which was given by his superior, irrespective of the heaviest sacrifices involved.[29] Their political indoctrination, training, and commitment to the Hitler made them willing participants in the extermination of Jews.

Economic and Political Conditions in Germany

The Paris Peace Conference opened on 12 January 1919. Meetings were held at various locations in and around Paris until 20 January 1920. Leaders of thirty-two states, representing about 75 percent of the world's population, attended. However, negotiations were dominated by the five major powers responsible for defeating the Central Powers: the United States, Britain, France, Italy, and Japan. Important figures in these negotiations included Georges Clemenceau (France), David Lloyd George (Britain), Vittorio Orlando (Italy), and Woodrow Wilson (United States). The Treaty of Versailles was one of the products of the conference. The Germans believed that the treaty would be based on President Wilson's Fourteen Points, which offered a framework for a just peace, and the hopes that any future international tension would be prevented. The Germans believed the Fourteen Points would have resulted in drastically less devastation to Germany if used in the treaty. Yet the Big Four were determined to punish Germany for the war, and so they did.[30]

The treaty held Germany solely responsible for World War I. They were forced to pay reparations totaling 132,000,000,000 in gold marks, they lost one-eighth of land, all of its colonies, all overseas financial assets, a new map of Europe was carved out of Germany, and the German military was basically non-existent. The German people believed they were being ruthlessly punished for a war they did not start, but had to fight.[31] The main terms of the Treaty of Versailles were as follows:

1. The surrender of all German colonies as League of Nations mandates.
2. The return of Alsace-Lorraine to France.
3. Cession of Eupen–Malmedy to Belgium, Memel to Lithuania, the Hultschin district to Czechoslovakia, Poznania, parts of East Prussia and Upper Silesia to Poland.
4. Danzig to become a free city.
5. Voting to be held in northern Schleswig to settle the Danish-German frontier.
6. Occupation and special status for the Saar under French control.
7. Demilitarization and a fifteen-year occupation of the Rhineland.
8. German reparations of £6,600 million.
9. A ban on the union of Germany and Austria.
10. An acceptance of Germany's guilt in causing the war.
11. Provision for the trial of the former Kaiser and other war leaders.
12. Limitation of Germany's army to 100,000 men with no conscription, no tanks, no heavy artillery, no poison-gas supplies, no aircraft and no airships.
13. The limitation of the German Navy to vessels under 100,000 tons, with no submarines.

Germany signed the Treaty of Versailles under protest. The United States Congress refused to ratify the treaty. Many people in France and Britain were angry that there was no trial of the Kaiser or the other war leaders.[38] The treaty devastated Germany politically and economically.

The German people suffered extreme economic hardships after World War I. The hyperinflation of 1923 reached such heights that housewives literally used the valueless German currency to kindle fires. By mid-1923, workers were being paid as often as three times a day. Their wives would meet them, take the money, and rush to the shops to exchange it for goods. However, by this time, more and more often, shops were empty. Storekeepers could not obtain goods nor do business fast enough to protect their cash receipts. Farmers refused to bring produce into the city in return for worthless paper. Food riots broke out. Parties of workers marched into the countryside to dig up vegetables and to loot the farms. Businesses started to close down and unemployment suddenly soared. The economy was collapsing.[32]

The extreme poverty of the time caused hardship in rural communities among farmers. Traditionally, much of the village life was filled with community and people helping one another. Yet the harder it became financially, the more the communities began to break down. National Socialism was able to appeal to these fragmented communities with notions of blood, land, and national unity. In Germany, 600,000 of the 4 million white-collar workers had lost their jobs by 1931. Graduating students could not find work or had to resort to jobs they regarded as insecure or demeaning. Figures of 6 million overall unemployed in Germany were statistics of stark misery and despair. Families were disrupted as men felt powerless at their inability to provide for their families. Women and children were disgusted at authority figures whose authority was now hollow. In some cases, wives and mothers found it easier to gain jobs in a low-wage economy than their husbands.[33]

As a result of the hardships, many Germans were desperate to find a new leader to get them out of the Great Depression, which they blamed on the extravagant reparations they had to pay to the Allies. They found this leader in Adolf Hitler. Hitler believed Germany had given up too easily to the Allies. He thought Germany still had a chance to win the war because there had been no fighting on German soil. He encouraged many Germans' feelings of being betrayed by their own government and therefore thought they had no obligation to follow the treaty. This group became the Nazis, who felt they had more fighting to do and the Treaty of Versailles fueled their anger. It created aggressive resentment and nationalism in Germany. There was a lot of increasing hostility towards the Allied nations.[34]

Leaders like Hitler saw this treaty as something that weakened the great empire he was striving for. He did not sign it and he was not about to follow it. However, because of this treaty, he was able to conquer and manipulate people by justifying his actions on the unfairness of it. This lead to the emergence of the National Socialist Party in Germany.[35]

The rise of the Nazi Party was achieved over an incredibly short period of time. From abject failure at the Munich Putsch and the imprisonment of Hitler to the election of Hitler as chancellor took only ten years. This turnaround was due to a number of changes and policies implemented by the party within a very short period of time. The failure of the Putsch led Hitler to realize that the only way he would achieve power was through democratic, legal means. As soon as the Putsch was over, Hitler set about reorganizing the party to enable such a turnaround in the party's fortunes. The party played on historic fears and complaints with great effect. Hitler was well aware of German animosity towards the Treaty of Versailles. He used this for political gain, blaming the Jews, often a scapegoat in European history, for many of the woes of the '20s, and he promised to tear up the terms of the hated treaty. While other groups also made similar claims, Hitler's party achieved a higher level of credibility among the German public by putting some of their rhetoric into action. The *Sturmabteilung* (SA) was deployed to break up communist meetings, which won the approval of a very nervous middle class. He made promises to farmers about the quality of life and a guarantee of earnings. Ex-soldiers were won over by the militaristic images that Hitler used. His promise of tearing up the

Treaty of Versailles and restoring the forces to their previous size won acclaim from many former servicemen.[36]

Even while in prison, Hitler's aims and objectives proved to be fruitful. *Mein Kampf*, written while behind bars, became a bestseller. It publicized the Nazi ideology and, as it was clearly a statement of intent with regards to Germany's greatness, it was recognized as being an ideal. This contained his basic ideas, including that Aryans were superior and they should control the world. He believed the only way to accomplish this would be to have a dictator ruling. Racial awareness would also be important with their hatred for all other 'inferior' races, especially Jews. No class or other distinctions in German society mattered. Another of Hitler's major ideas was *Lebensraum*. Hitler argued that Germany needed large amounts of territory to expand, which meant conquering territory and expelling or killing the local populations. Once out of prison, Hitler was able to play on the popularity of these ideals through speeches, and he was famed for the power and effectiveness of his rhetoric.[37]

The Wall Street Crash of 1929 provided the spark that allowed the Nazis to gain support. All of a sudden, the support of the Americans and the aid plans were withdrawn, Germany was again isolated and the economy was in crisis. The rise in unemployment and a renewed fear of a Communist uprising gave Hitler's messages a new importance. People were again interested in the views of this extremist party. In a land where the government was struggling to control the economy, any alternative that appeared to be willing and able to combat the problems, through whatever means, was seen in a very positive light. Hitler wasted no time in consolidating his position as chancellor. Once in power, the use of propaganda, the radio, posters, and film shows by the Nazis was groundbreaking. It captured the imagination of a disillusioned population and gave them fresh hope. An image had been created of a powerful party with strong leadership.[28] Hitler and his National Socialist movement offered something for everyone at a time when German politicians were failing to control the economy.

Once the Nazi Party had taken power, or rather gained control of the Reichstag, Hitler made moves to gain control of the institutions that ran Germany on a day-to-day basis. This was achieved in a number of ways. Following his election as chancellor, Hitler was in a position where he was the nominal leader of the Weimar Republic, but he did not have the majority necessary to implement his political program. To do as he wanted, he required such a majority; he needed the opposition to be silenced.[38]

A fire in the Reichstag buildings provided him with the ideal opportunity to take the initiative. The fire was publicly blamed upon the Communists, and 4,000 communist party members were consequently arrested and sent to concentration camps around Germany. In one stroke, Hitler had annihilated the most potent threat to his leadership. This was followed, very quickly, by the Enabling Act. This measure allowed Hitler the right to rule without consultation of the Reichstag (German

Parliament) or the president. It was in effect a decree of a state of emergency. The result was the banning of all opposition parties, censorship of broadcasts and publications, and a rapid replacement of Government officials who were deemed to be unsympathetic towards Nazi policy. Such swift actions left the Nazi Party with little political opposition, certainly no legalized opposition.[39]

Hitler now had a one party state and control of most means of communication: the Nazi propaganda machine could begin its work. Even so, Hitler was not entirely certain of his position. The party itself was not united behind his vision of National Socialism. On the Night of the Long Knives, this situation was rectified. Hitler asserted that Rohm, the leader of the SA, had plotted to overthrow him, and 400 members of the organization were rounded up and killed. This brutal action secured the loyalty of the Armed forces, who had previously been wary of the SA's influence. Hitler was now in control of both his party and the Government, with a mandate to fix the economy.[40]

Characterization of the Jews, Poles, Lithuanians, and Russians

Jewish communities existed continuously in Europe for over 2,000 years. Their social and religious distinctiveness made them persistent targets for persecution. The emergence of Christianity as the dominant religion in Europe intensified the persecution of Jews. Since both the religious and political life of Europe became organized around the Christian faith, Jews were seen as outcasts—the deniers and 'killers' of Christ. For millions of European Christians, for over 1,600 years, the hatred and persecution of Jews was religiously sanctioned. Anti-Semitism intensified during the nineteenth- and twentieth-century industrialization of Europe as Jews participated more directly in European economic and social life. By the time the Nazis came to power in Germany, the patterns of economic, social, and personal persecution of European Jews were well established.[41]

The Germans viewed the Eastern Jews with particular disdain. Throughout the nineteenth century and into the twentieth, a four-tiered social structure existed in Eastern Europe. It consisted of Poles, Ukrainians, Ethnic Germans, and Jews. The Jews were considered by the others as last in the social order. Prejudice towards the Jews became deeply rooted. Hitler accused the Eastern Jews with sympathies for Marxism and made the case that the Jews stood in the way of Germany becoming a great nation again.[42]

The seeds of genocide were successfully sown by Christian Europe and the Nazis against the Jews, giving rise to the Holocaust. Nazi racial anti-Semitism and propaganda amplified and manipulated these patterns, ultimately adding the deadly tenet that all Jews must be eliminated.

On 30 January 1933, Adolf Hitler, leader of the Nazi Party, was named chancellor by President Paul von Hindenburg after the Nazi party won a significant percentage of the vote in the elections of 1932. The Nazi Party had taken advantage of the political unrest in Germany to gain an electoral foothold. The Nazis incited clashes with the communists, who many feared, disrupted the government with demonstrations, and conducted a vicious propaganda campaign against its political opponents—the weak Weimar government and the Jews, whom the Nazis blamed for Germany's ills. A major tool of the Nazi propaganda assault was the weekly Nazi newspaper *Der Stürmer* (*The Attacker*). At the bottom of the front page of each issue, in bold letters, the paper proclaimed, 'The Jews are our misfortune!' *Der Stürmer* also regularly featured cartoons of Jews in which they were caricatured as hooked-nosed and ape-like. The influence of the newspaper was far-reaching.[43]

The use of laws to discriminate against Jews began on 24 March 1933, when the Reichstag passed the Enabling Act giving the new chancellor, Adolf Hitler, and the Nazi Party dictatorial powers. The Reichstag's action gave the government power to govern and legislate by decree, thereby providing the Nazis a cloak of legality with which to cover their official actions. The biological premises of Nazi anti-Semitism prescribed a specific approach to anti-Jewish legislation. It would have been reasonable to predict in 1932 that the first anti-Jewish laws of a Nazi regime would be designed to halt the process of biological assimilation. Therefore, it is not surprising that the first concrete proposals for anti-Jewish legislation were aimed at de-assimilating the Jews from Germany. However, the set of four laws promulgated in April 1933 had little to do with what Nazi ideology proclaimed to be the heart of the Jewish question. Rather than comprising a frontal attack upon the blood aspects of assimilation, they were directed against the Jewish professionals who had been the object of party terrorism. The first two laws, both decreed on 7 April, were aimed at the civil servants and legal profession. Two more laws, one affecting Jewish doctors practicing within the National Health Service, the other affecting Jewish teachers and students, went into effect on 22 April and 25 April respectively.[44]

The April Laws were followed on 14 July by a Denaturalization Law, which allowed the Reich government to revoke the citizenship of people it considered undesirable. Three further pieces of legislation affecting the Jews came into effect in 1933. On 29 September, a 'Hereditary Farm Law' excluded Jews from owning farmland or engaging in agriculture. The remaining pieces of legislation in 1933 dealt a major blow to Germany's Jews. The first law established chambers of culture within the Propaganda Ministry, to regulate the film, theater, music, fine arts, literature, broadcasting, and the press. The law establishing the Chambers of Culture contained no Aryan clause. None was necessary. Joseph Goebbels, Minister of Propaganda, had been granted authority to refuse admission of undesirable to any of the chambers. The second, a more specific law dealing with journalists, was effected on 4 October. Its provisions were similar to the ones that established the chambers of culture. None of these laws though, were sufficient in defining the Jew.[45]

During 1934, very few official measures of any public significance were taken against the Jew. Legislative action against the Jews was renewed on a very subdued scale in May 1935 with the announcement of a new Military Service Law. The new law reinforced general conscription. Its effect upon Jews centered on the question of who was eligible for military service. Aryan ancestry was made an absolute perquisite for entry into the services. Although it reintroduced the Aryan paragraph for the first time since 1933, it still represented no progress in defining the Jew. The courts and Nazi party members were confused and looked to the Reich Interior Ministry for guidance. The final and most complete attempt to arrive at a definition of the Jew began in September 1935, with the announcement of the most anti-Jewish legislation to date at the Nuremburg Party Rally. The first law, The Law for the Protection of German Blood and German Honor, prohibited marriages and extra-marital intercourse between 'Jews' (the name was now officially used in place of 'non-Aryans') and 'Germans'. It also prohibited the employment of 'German' females under forty-five in Jewish households. The second law, The Reich Citizenship Law, stripped Jews of their German citizenship and introduced a new distinction between 'Reich citizens' and 'nationals'. The laws created the racial categories of German Jew, half-Jew (Jewish Mischlinge first degree), and quarter-Jew (Jewish Mischlinge second degree), each with its own regulations. The Nuremberg Laws by their general nature formalized the unofficial and particular measures taken against Jews up to 1935. The Nazi leaders made a point of stressing the consistency of this legislation with the Party program, which demanded that Jews should be deprived of their rights as citizens.[46]

With a police infrastructure in place, opponents of the Nazis were terrorized, beaten, or sent to one of the concentration camps the Germans built to incarcerate them. By the end of 1934, Hitler was in absolute control of Germany, and his campaign against the Jews in full swing. The Nazis claimed the Jews corrupted pure German culture with their 'foreign' and 'mongrel' influence. They portrayed the Jews as evil and cowardly, and Germans as hardworking, courageous, and honest.[54] The Nazis claimed that the Jews—who were heavily represented in finance, commerce, the press, literature, theater, and the arts—had weakened Germany's economy and culture. The massive government-supported propaganda machine created a racial anti-Semitism, which was different from the longstanding anti-Semitic tradition of the Christian churches. The superior race was the 'Aryans', the Germans. The word Aryan derived from the study of linguistics, which started in the eighteenth century and, at some point, determined that the Indo-Germanic (also known as Aryan) languages were superior in their structures, variety, and vocabulary to the Semitic languages that had evolved in the Near East. This judgment led to a certain conjecture about the character of the peoples who spoke these languages. The conclusion was that the Aryan peoples were likewise superior to the Semitic ones. The Nazis then combined their racial theories with the evolutionary theories of Charles Darwin to justify their treatment of the Jews. The Germans, as the strongest and fittest, were destined to rule, while the weak and racially adulterated Jews were doomed to extinction.[47]

On 20 January 1942, several top officials of the German government met to officially coordinate the military and civilian administrative branches of the Nazi system to organize a system of mass murder of the Jews. This meeting, called the Wannsee Conference, marked the beginning of the full-scale, comprehensive extermination operation of the Jews and laid the foundations for its organization, which started immediately after the conference ended.[48]

The results of the *Einsatzgruppen* help in understanding the magnitude of their deeds. They averaged over 1,350 murders per day, seven days a week, for more than 100 weeks. That is over 337 murders per average day by each group of 600-1,000 men during the two-year period. All these thousands of men, women, and children had first to be selected, brought together, held in restraint, and transported to a place of death. They had to be counted, stripped of possessions, shot or gassed, and buried. In addition, burial did not end the job, for all of the possessions taken from the dead have to be salvaged, crated, and shipped to the Reich. Finally, books were kept to cover these transactions. Details of all these things had to be recorded and reported.[49]

Contrary to the views of some authors, anti-Semitism alone was not responsible for the Holocaust. Other social, cultural, and psychological factors existed in Germany when Hitler came to power and combined with anti-Semitism to make the Holocaust possible. They are the tradition of obedience to authority; conformity to group norms; deliberate training for acceptance of violence against Jews; and the practical experience with mass murder gained during the earlier 'euthanasia' program directed at the physically disabled. Insights gained from laboratory studies of obedience and conformity are used to obtain an understanding of the circumstances under which seemingly normal individuals were led to commit mass murder. The aggression and violence exhibited by perpetrators do not require special explanations. The learning processes involved were the same as those that are involved in the acquisition of other behaviors (e.g., modeling by admired and powerful leaders, environmental cues to elicit violent behavior, and rewards for violence).[50]

Adolf Hitler took advantage of the German people's resentment for the loss of World War I and desperate economic conditions in Germany to gain support for the National Socialist movement. He blamed 'Jewish Financing' for the defeat of Germany and linked the Jews with Bolshevism. Hitler believed that Germany needed territory, given its growing population. He looked to the Eastern territories of Poland, Ukraine, and greater Russia to resettle. For this resettlement to occur, the people living there would have to be displaced. The people in the Eastern territories were believed to be inferior. Hitler believed that the German blood had been polluted. In *Masters of Death*, Richard Rhodes describes the view of Henry Friedlander, a pre-eminent historian of Hitler's eugenic policy:

> The usual interpretation [of the Holocaust] assigns the role of racial victim exclusively to the Jews, and sees anti–Semitism as the only ideological basis for

mass murder. I do not deny that anti-Semitism was a major component of Nazi ideology. I agree that the Nazi viewed the Jews as chronic enemies, and that Hitler's preoccupation with the imagined Jewish threat placed the struggle against Jews high on the list of priorities. But I do argue that anti-Semitism was only part of a larger worldview, which divided mankind into worthy and unworthy populations. Both Nazi ideologues and race scientists believed that German blood had been polluted, and that it was the nation's primary task to purge the German gene pool. The enemies were (1) the handicapped, who were considered 'degenerate.' And (2) 'alien races,' which in Central Europe meant Jews and Gypsies, since both were considered non-European nations that could not be assimilated.[51]

This philosophy was taught to the *Einsatzgruppen* volunteers early in their training at Pretzsch and was continually reinforced while they were in the field.[52]

Many factors came together at the same time to make the Holocaust possible. Economic conditions in Germany after World War I, the quest for more territory, the belief in a German master race, and the German tradition of obedience to authority all contributed to the Holocaust. Hitler's anti-Semitism was more fundamental to his attitude toward the Jews than his imperialistic, extreme Eastern policy. The Third Reich actively worked to destroy many other groups besides the Jews. The Jews were first in line.[53]

The Tactical Situation on Germany's Eastern Front

By spring 1941, the French had collapsed and the British were limited to their own territory. The low-countries had capitulated and Germany held absolute dominion over the whole of the European mainland. There was some substance to Hitler's argument that an invasion of Russia would not be a second front. He believed the Army was ready. In the spring of 1941, the Wehrmacht stood victorious and hardly blooded. They were trained and equipped to perfection. The army was a balanced and coordinated fighting machine at the pinnacle of military achievement. The German officer corps prided itself on its doctrine, a unity of training and thought that allowed junior officers to exercise their initiative because they understood their commander's intentions and they knew how their peers in adjacent units would react to the same situation.[54] A feeling of invincibility surely permeated the army and the national leadership. In light of this mood, it is no wonder that Hitler believed he could accomplish what Napoleon could not in the vast territory of Russia. In many ways, the German Army of 1941 was at the height of its power. I cannot imagine feeling any different than those involved with the many German victories.

In the summer of 1941, the Red Army offered a mystery to intelligence services in Germany. Its equipment, by all accounts, was plentiful. It possessed more tanks and as many aircraft as the rest of the world put together. The question for intelligence services was how much of this machinery was up to date, and how capable were the Soviet commanders of handling it. Its reserve manpower seemed inexhaustible, but sheer mass was valueless without proper leadership and German intelligence struggled to understand Soviet leadership.[55]

The Red Army of 1941 was in serious disorder. Although its strategy was now defensive, its official operational concepts remained the offensive, deep-operational theory. The Soviets has neglected the development of detailed defensive concepts and procedures. Purges by Stalin had produced a severe shortage of trained commanders and staff officers able to implement official concepts. The army contained a few qualified leaders from the Japanese and Finnish campaigns, but lacked both the experience and the self-confidence of the veteran Wehrmacht officer corps. The troops felt handicapped by the political requirement to defend every inch of the existing frontier.[64] Discipline had broken down during the war with Finland and the Soviet government was determined to restore it drastically. Penalties were increased for voluntary absence and desertion. Obedience was to be unconditional and the execution of orders prompt and precise.[56] Disagreements among the Red Army leadership and Stalin over the disposition of forces lead to the improper placements of units along the front. Stalin was so fearful of provoking an attack that he prevented any movements that could be interpreted as provocative by the Germans. It was a fearful time for most who served in the military. The political commissars were always listening for any sign of dissent. Everyone was cautious about offering any suggestions that seemed to differ with the party line.

The Germans believed that the Russians had not expected an attack. After midnight on 21 June, the Berlin–Moscow express train cleared and checked without any deviation from normal practice. It passed over the border and on to Brest-Litovsk without a hitch. To the north, nothing disturbed the calm of the East Prussian frontier. Southwards, in Army Group South's attack area, the Russians manned their fully illuminated posts.[57] Shortly after 3 a.m. on the morning of 22 June 1941, thirty specially selected Luftwaffe bomber crews crossed the Soviet frontier. In groups of three, these bombers struck ten major Soviet air bases precisely at 3.15 a.m., the time when a brief artillery bombardment signaled the start of the ground war. As soon as the sun rose, the Luftwaffe followed up this attack with a force of 500 bombers, 270 dive bombers, and 480 fighters to hit sixty-six Soviet airfields in the forward areas. The Red Air Force lost over 1,200 aircraft in the first morning of the war.

Throughout the next few days, the Luftwaffe had undisputed air supremacy, and all Soviet troop and rail movements received relentless bombardment. The initial ground advance met little resistance in most areas. Some border posts were overrun almost before the Soviet border guards could assemble.[58] In addition to the advantage of surprise, the Germans had secured an overwhelming superiority of numbers and firepower at the points selected for their armored penetration. The German plan had put the entire tank strength of the army into opening attacks dividing it into four Panzer groups whose purpose was to break through the Russian defensives at the first blow, then to wheel inward, isolate, and cut to pieces the mass of Soviet army as it stood on the frontier.[68] While some in Moscow anticipated the German attack, the soldiers on the front line were kept in the dark. It is doubtful the average soldier could have done anything differently given the information they had at the time.

In June 1941, overall control of the German Eastern Theater lay with the Army High Command led by General Franz Halder. Their forces were divided into Army of Norway, commanded by Colonial General Nikolaus von Falkenhorst; Army Group North, commanded by Field Marshal Wilhelm von Leeb; Army Group Center, commanded by Field Marshal Fedor von Bock; and Army Group South, commanded by Field Marshal Gerd von Rundstedt. Organized against the Germans were the Russian Army formations. Their forces, led by General Zhukov, were divided into Northern Front, commanded by Colonial General M. M. Popov; Northwestern Front, commanded by Colonial General F. I. Kuznetsov; Western Front, commanded by General D. G. Pavlov; Southwestern Front, commanded by Colonial General M. P. Kirponos; and Southern Front (formed 25 June), commanded by General I. V. Tiulenev.[59]

North of the Pripiat Marches, the initial German thrusts succeeded rapidly. Led by Fourth Panzer Group, Army Group North swept rapidly through Lithuania and into Latvia. They bypassed the tank divisions of Soviet 3rd and 12th Mechanized Corps, who were defeated by lack of coordination, fuel, and ammunition more than by Germany action. Virtually all of the Soviet mechanized corps lost 90 percent of their strength during the first week of war.[60] Fourth Panzer Group's other spearhead encountered little organized opposition, reached the Dvina River and seized several bridges intact. In Army Group Center, Third Panzer Group pressed eastward along the vulnerable boundary line between the Northwestern and Western Fronts and reached Vilnius by the evening of 23 June. The Germans had much less initial success south of the Pripiat Marshes. The River Bug ran along much of the common border in this area, hampering the initial attack and giving the Red Army troops precious minutes to react.[61] The retreating Soviet armies, their communications in chaos, also choked in their own traffic jams since all movement control had gone. The departure of the Baltic district armies stripped the Baltic Fleet's advanced naval bases of their landward protection.[62] The initial successes of the German Army surprised the Russian leadership and some of the German leadership.

By all accounts, the German invasion of the Soviet Union 22 June 1941 was a major success as the Russians were completely surprised and many of the Soviet Forces were crushed in the initial attacks. Sixteen hours after the opening of Operation Barbarossa, the German Army in the east had virtually unhinged two Soviet Fronts, the Northwestern, and the Western. At their junction, the Soviet 11th Army had been battered to pieces. The left flank of the Russian 8th Army and the right flank of the 3rd Army had been similarly devastated. North of the Kaunas, German armor was over the river Dubissa and south of the city, German tanks were astride the Nieman.

On the left flank of the Western Front of the Soviet 4th Army was in no position to offer and effective defense. The Russian Front commanders struggled desperately to maintain the cohesion of their forces.[63] The German operations in the south were dazzlingly successful. All of the objectives Hitler had outlined were achieved: the Pripet Marshes were cleared; the Dnieper bend was occupied; the Donetz basin; and the industrial complex of the Ukraine were denied to the enemy, through either dispersal or seizure. Above all, the mass of the Red Army in the south was battered to pieces in a battle that cost the Russians a million causalities.[64]

The Soviet Union went to war without a commander-in-chief; the post had been abolished seventeen years before during the military reforms of the 1920s and never revived. On the second day of the war, the Soviet government and the Central Committee hurriedly authorized the establishment of an improvised high command. The rapid breakdown in communications between the front and its formations and between the front command and the high command occurred. The evening situation reports presented by the General Staff for the information of the heads of arms and services scarcely corresponded in these early days to the map deployments at the front. The high command discussions ground to an operational-administrative bog; while trying to formulate strategic-operational assignments, Stalin and his officers busied themselves with minutiae, which devoured valuable time. They discussed the type of rifle to be issued to the infantry units, or whether bayonets were needed, and if so, should they be triple-edged? Stalin appeared to have no grasp of the scale or operations and the vastness of the war into which he had been hurled. On 25 June, the Russians organized four armies of their reserve to take up defensive positions to block the Germans advance. The speed of the German progress, however, and the disasters that unfolded on the flanks, north and southwest, ruined these plans and embroiled the Red Army in a catastrophe, tearing out huge chunks of fronts and severing military, economic, and political centers from the central government control.[65] It appeared as though the Soviet military was about to collapse.

At the end of September 1941, as the Germans had secured Kiev and were taking account of the Russian losses. The Germans estimated Russian losses of 2½ million men, 22,000 guns, 18,000 tanks, and 14,000 aircraft. It appeared, by all estimates, that the Red Army was dead. The strategic objectives, which the German Army had begun, were largely fulfilled. Leningrad had been isolated and neutralized. The Ukraine had been opened to the German economy as far as the Donetz River. Work had already begun on a draft occupation and planning study, which forecast the withdrawal to German of about eighty divisions. The victory at Kiev had encouraged many of the German Staff to believe that one more encirclement battle would finish the Russians off, and the Germans would winter in Moscow.[66]

By 14 October, the hinge of the Russian front cracked. German tanks broke through and rolled down the headwaters of the Volga River toward Moscow. The news that government offices were being transferred prompted a mass flight by all those who were capable of movement. Stalin himself remained in the city. On 19 October, Moscow was declared to be under a state siege, and special reinforcements of security forces were brought in to restore order. From that time, the momentary flickers of panic died away. The Germans were closest to Moscow in the north and center. At Mozhaisk, they could see anti-aircraft fire over Moscow on a clear night. The real danger to the Red Army was farther south, where the country was more open and where, almost without tanks, General Zhukov was faced by the whole of the 2nd Panzer Army. At this stage of the battle, Zhukov had the only independent tank force left. It was equipped with the new T34 tank. They were able to inflict casualties and stop the German 4th Panzer Group advancing to Tula, south of Moscow. The German Army had enjoyed tank superiority up to this point. From this point on, the situation was reversed. The plight of the German soldier was one of trudging through the mud and freezing temperatures at night. The advance to Moscow was slow. During the last three weeks in October, weather conditions, which included heavy rain, snow showers, and damp and penetrating mist, made movement almost impossible on two days out of three. There were over 100,000 cases of frostbite with over 14,357 requiring amputation. The Russian withdrew into Moscow. Zhukov had fixed the bounds, which were to be defended until the last, and until these were reached, he did not intend to risk any more encirclement. By the end of October, the two armies had fought each other to a standstill.[67]

The transfer of troops from the Far East had begun in the first days of November, and by the time the German push on Moscow began on 15 November, the Russians had doubled their strength. During the night of 4–5 December, the whole of the northwestern front went over to the offensive, by the 6 December, German Army Group Center was under violent pressure along its entire length, and Moscow was never again threatened.[68]

In February 1942, the Russian offensive petered out. Both sides tried to interpret each other's intentions. A number of German Generals declared that a resumption of the offensive in 1942 was impossible, and that it was wiser to make sure of holding what they had gained. Hitler's idea was to smash the Russians finally by breaking the power of their army in the south, capturing the seat of their economy, and taking the option of either wheeling up behind Moscow or down tops the oil fields of Baku. In April, a more ambitious scheme was worked out. This involved the seizure of Stalingrad, and the isthmus between the Don River and the Volga River. For Hitler, Stalingrad was to be the first step. His intention was to wheel north, along the line of the Volga River, and to cut communications of the Russians armies defending Moscow while sending scouting groups still farther east, toward the Ural Mountains.[69]

Contrary to German expectations, Stalingrad did not fall into their hands rapidly nor did the Soviet armies fall back entirely to the eastern bank of the Volga River. The attempt to storm into the center of the city and onto the Volga itself was being held. Each building in Stalingrad became its own battleground, with fortresses fashioned out of factories, railway stations, separate streets or small squares, and finally single walls. Throughout August and well into September, German success flowed one after another, but none brought the attainment of the major objective. To the north of the Soviet-German front the offensive in the Leningrad area had died away. Repeated attacks by the Germans meet stiff resistance by the Red Army. During the first week in November, Soviet units began moving into their start positions for an offensive on three fronts.[70]

No German soldier who fought on the Russian Front could forget the many seasons and faces of war. The most elemental of natural conditions (rain, mud, cold, snow, heat, and dust) formed a recurring theme of the entire war for many soldiers. Many slept day and night in the same uniform, on a plank bed, wrapped in a wool blanket. In the rainy season, the mud was so thick that it was a chore just to move. In winter, the bitter cold and snow slowed everything down. No soldier could escape the unpleasant business of living rough, of coping with a harsh environment under conditions of extreme physical and mental exhaustion. For many, the real enemy was the weather, the effects of living in the open, and the stresses and strains endemic to a group forced into proximity with an often-unfamiliar natural environment.[71]

Throughout long hours of boredom and loneliness, deprivation and hardship, horror and agony, the German soldier soon became familiar with many of the myriad faces of war. Fear was the real enemy of most soldiers: the fear of death or of cowardice, fear of the conflict within the spirit, or a simple fear of showing fear. Moreover, this fear could surface at any time. Additionally, the stark realization that his comrade lay dead or wounded forced many soldiers to confront his doubt and fear.[72] *Einsatzgruppen* men were told of Joseph Stalin's order of 3 July 1941 calling on the entire Soviet civilian population to conduct a campaign of terror, sabotage, and guerrilla warfare against the Germans. The soldiers knew that Jews were especially active in this campaign, as numerous Jewish historians have proudly acknowledged.

Living Conditions of the *Einsatzgruppen* on the Eastern Front

On the Russian front, air superiority was never such a problem, but the extremes of climate and the vast distances handicapped the German army. The *Einsatzgruppen*, for the most part, rode around comfortably in trucks, well behind the front lines and the fighting. They had a priority for supplies from the army units they followed. However, the road net of European Russia at the time was sparse and, except for a few well-built roads, was not equal to sustained use by heavy vehicles. The effect of the muddy season on roads and highways was so devastating that movement slowed to a snail's pace and eventually came to a complete standstill at times. Most hard-surfaced roads lacked good foundations and became so waterlogged that they caved in under the smallest load. Roads needed continuous maintenance, a job that required thousands of laborers. Most of the bridges on main roads and all those on secondary roads were very weak, and the Germans had to replace them with more adequate structures. The peak of road and bridge construction and maintenance occurred during the muddy seasons.[73]

Perhaps one of the more influential factors contributing to the state of mind of the *Einsatzgruppen* soldiers—and the German Army in general—was mud. The Germans had no conception of mud as it existed in European Russia. In the autumn of 1941, when front-line troops were already stuck fast, the German High Command still believed that mud could be conquered by main force, an idea that led to serious losses of vehicles and equipment. At the height of the muddy season tractors and wreckers normally capable of traversing difficult terrain were helpless, and attempts to plow through the muddy mass made roads even more impassable. Tanks, heavy wreckers, and even vehicles with good ground clearance simply pushed an ever-growing wall of mud before them until they finally stopped, half buried by their own motion. A sudden frost in the autumn of 1941 cemented a cripple, buried column into a state of complete uselessness, and it never moved again. As it could not be reached in any other way, gasoline, towropes, and food supplies were airdropped along the line of stranded armor, but all attempts to move were futile. Often, when drivers found themselves bogged down far from any habitation, they abandoned their vehicles and set out on foot to contact friendly troops in the nearest village or sought food and shelter from local civilians in order to remain alive until the worst of the muddy season passed.[74]

While the living conditions of the *Einsatzgruppen* were considerably better than the average German soldier in the Eastern Front, they had to deal with partisan activity and resentment from the civilian population, in addition to the physiological effect of their actions. Regardless of the individual's thoughts and beliefs, it mattered very little, for the killing of even suspected Jews in even the most anti-Semitic region only fanned the flames of resistance among the civilian population. In *German Anti-Partisan Warfare in Europe*, Colin Heaton writes: 'The conditions facing the German soldier in the Soviet Union have become legendary.' The partisan cells swelled not only through the masses of the disaffected civilian population, but also from large numbers of Soviet soldiers who joined their ranks after being encircled and cut off, unable to join their units. These partisans continually harassed the *Einsatzgruppen* and German Army soldiers.[75]

Another detrimental factor was the propaganda issues facing the German, as well as the fact that the primitive living conditions of the average peasant and the seemingly endless numbers of non-European races impressed upon the Germans their own sense on cultural and ethnic superiority.[76] The German was also psychologically unprepared for what awaited him. He was subjected to many varieties of friendly propaganda, although all forms continued to purport his racial superiority.

One day, he may hear that all of the sub-humans must be relocated further east, especially Jews. Later, he would hear that they must be eradicated, eliminated from potentially poisoning the pure German blood supply—that they were deemed to be a biological threat to the German people. He would also be told that not all Russians were Communists, and that the German crusade was established to free the Russians from Bolshevism, while at the same time condemning all Russians for supporting the Bolsheviks, while the Jews supported and assisted the powers in Moscow.[77] Perhaps the greatest debilitating factor with regard to morale was the witnessing and participation in combat, but even more pointedly the killing of civilians who were obviously non-combatants. These acts preyed upon the minds of many soldiers, even those who committed themselves to the extermination of the Jews.

During the summer, the woods and swamplands of Russia teemed with mosquitoes, including malaria carriers, which for weeks scourged man and beast. Even mosquito nets did not furnish complete protection against bites on the head and neck. Flies tormented men and animals in hot weather. Many of the wooden huts the soldiers used for shelter were infested with vermin such as bedbugs, fleas, head lice, and body lice. The mud huts of the south were cleaner, but the dust storms of the area caused inflammation of the eyes and respiratory system.[78]

Diarrhea was frequent during the mid-summer fly plague, but it seldom required hospitalization. In the swamp regions, there were cases of malaria and, occasionally, cases of cadaveric poisoning were experienced. Volhynia fever appeared and some cases required long convalescence. Many soldiers contracted jaundice diseases, which lasted two or three weeks and sometimes required hospitalization. Gas gangrene was not infrequent. The evacuation of the sick and wounded during summer months was often handicapped by bad road conditions, heat, and dust. Moreover, when roads were being used for sizable troop or convoy movements, delays made evacuation trips a torture.[79]

During the German advance of 1941, the German higher and lower commands revealed a tendency toward bypassing the large forests and skirting around swamps. In a country as rich in forests and swamps as western European Russia, however, such tactics were possible only to a limited extent. The lack of open space forced the troops to engage in forest fighting. The spearheading armored divisions hugged the improved roads in breaking through the forest and sought battle in open terrain. The result was that, having been outflanked and his lines having been pierced, the Russians retired laterally into the depth of the woods. While the immediate vicinity of trails and improved roads had thus been cleared of hostile forces, the German armor had no sooner surged past than the Russians once more emerged from the forests and reformed their lines. The infantry divisions and the *Einsatzgruppen,* which trailed a considerable distance behind the tanks, subsequently came up against the same, at times quite sizeable, Soviet forces. In the haste of their advance the infantry divisions were likewise unable to do a thorough job of mopping up the enemy in the extensive woodlands.[80]

Documents in *The Nuremberg Indictment, Nazi Conspiracy and Aggression, Vol. II* stated that, after trying to dynamite the victims and burn them alive in their homes and barns proved unproductive, the RSHA in Berlin, in August 1941, began to look for an alternative method of execution. It was found in the form of gas vans (heavy trucks with hermetically sealed vans into which the trucks' exhaust fumes were piped). Within a short time, these trucks were supplied to all the *Einsatzgruppen*. The carbon monoxide from the car's exhaust would be channeled into the sealed cabin, in which the victims stood. The gassing process took between fifteen and thirty minutes. During this time, the van was driven from the loading site to prepared graves. The shootings continued, augmented with the gas vans. The gas vans lead to the construction of the gas chambers at the concentration camps. With the construction of the camps with gassing facilities, the *Einsatzgruppen* would soon be out of the business of killing Jews. From the beginning of 1942 onward, the *Einsatzgruppen* increasingly turned to fighting Soviet partisans.[81]

Causing or witnessing the deaths of scores of people, including women and children, took its toll on the men of the *Einsatzgruppen*. Not all posted to *Einsatzgruppen* units were capable of carrying out their work; there were several recorded cases of men breaking down, refusing orders, or being hastily transferred. *Einsatzgruppen* officers, aware of the difficulties faced by their men, tended to be more tolerant of occasional breaches of discipline. Many unit leaders dispensed extra rations of alcohol as an incentive or reward. In comparison to other SS and Wehrmacht divisions, the *Einsatzgruppen* recorded much higher rates of alcoholism, desertion, and suicide. Yet despite this moral uncertainty and internal unrest, the *Einsatzgruppen* was able to continue its deadly campaign. It would last until the summer of 1943, by which time transportation to the death camps became the preferred method of mass killing.[82]

In 1941, SS-*General* Erich von dem Bach-Zelewski told his superior Heinrich Himmler that the Nazis had been murdering Jews, including women and children, at close range and in cold blood all summer. Bach-Zelewski was worried about this method's traumatizing effects on his men. Himmler recorded in his diary the *General*'s concerns: '...and he said to me, *Reichsfuhrer*, these men are finished for the rest of their lives. What kind of followers are we producing here—either neurotics or brutes?'[83]

The Russian Army in Germany: 1945

In *The Fall of Berlin*, historian Antony Beevor has revealed the truly staggering extent of rape by the Soviet Red Army as it advanced at the end of the Second World War; between 95,000 and 130,000 rape victims were treated at Berlin's two hospitals, while the number of German women who were victims of soldiers may have reached 2 million. Beevor quoted a playwright, Zakhar Agranenko, who wrote in his diary:

> 'Red Army soldiers don't believe in "individual liaisons" with German women,' wrote the playwright Zakhar Agranenko in his diary when serving as an officer of marine infantry in East Prussia. 'Nine, ten, twelve men at a time—they rape them on a collective basis.'[1]

The long columns of Russians advancing towards Germany in 1945 were a bizarre blend of both medieval and modern soldiers. They consisted of cavalrymen on shaggy horses and tank troopers. Light field guns were towed by Dodges and Studebakers from the lend-lease program. Others rode horse-drawn carts. The soldier's diversity was almost as great as the equipment they tended. Some were lawless adventures who drank and raped shamelessly. Some were idealistic communists who did approve of the adventures' behaviour.[2] The Russian government knew what was happening from the detailed reports of their commanders. One report stated that 'many Germans declare that all German women in East Prussia who stayed behind were raped by Red Army soldiers.' Numerous examples of gang rape were given: 'girls under 18 and old women included.'[3]

While orders were issued by the high command to exert some authority over the behaviour of the rowdy soldiers, it had little effect. Marshal Rokossovsky issued order Number 006 in an effort to direct 'the feelings of hatred at fighting the enemy on the battlefield.' It appears to have had little consequence. There were also a few random attempts to exert authority. The commander of one rifle division is said to have 'personally shot a lieutenant who was lining up a group of his men before a German woman spread-eagled on the ground.' Either the officers were involved themselves or the lack of discipline made it too risky to re-establish order over drunken soldiers equipped with submachine guns.[4]

There was a sense among the Russian soldiers that the 'Motherland' had been violated by the invasion of the Germany army. This sense was promoted by the government. The government's calls for revenge had given the idea that almost any cruelty would be allowed. Many young Russian female soldiers did not disapprove of the rape of German women. Some even found it amusing. A twenty-one-year-old girl from a reconnaissance element commented: 'Our soldiers' behaviour towards Germans, particularly German women, is absolutely correct!' Natalya Gesse, a Soviet war correspondent, commented: 'The Russian soldiers were raping every German female from eight to eighty. It was an army of rapists.'[5] Beevor writes about the use of drugs and alcohol by the soldiers:

> Drink of every variety, including dangerous chemicals seized from laboratories and workshops, was a major factor in the violence. It seems as if Soviet soldiers needed alcoholic courage to attack a woman. But then, all too often, they drank too much and, unable to complete the act, used the bottle instead with appalling effect. A number of victims were mutilated obscenely.[6]

Russian government would not permit any discussion of the rape of Germany women. Many veterans, even today, are reluctant to talk about it. Those who have spoken openly are completely unrepentant. One leader of a tank company said, 'They all lifted their skirts for us and lay on the bed.' He even went on to boast that 'two million of our children were born' in Germany. A Soviet major told a British journalist at the time: 'They often raped old women of sixty, seventy or even eighty— much to these grandmothers' surprise, if not downright delight.'

The Red Army seemed to have adopted an attitude that they had the moral mission to liberate Europe of Nazism and that it could behave as it wished. Dominion and disgrace pervaded most soldiers' treatment of women in Germany. The victims not only bore the brunt of reprisal for Wehrmacht crimes, they also represented an ancient target as old as war itself. It seemed as though rape was the act of the conqueror, perhaps to emphasize victory. In Berlin, many women were simply not ready for the shock of Russian retribution, however much horror propaganda they had heard from Nazi regime. Many reassured themselves that, while the danger must be great out in the countryside, mass rapes could hardly take place in the city in front of everyone.

In Dahlem, Soviet officers visited Sister Kunigunde, the mother superior of Haus Dahlem, a maternity clinic and orphanage. The officers and their men behaved impeccably. In fact, the officers even warned Sister Kunigunde about the second-line troops following on behind. Their prediction proved entirely accurate. Nuns, young girls, old women, pregnant women, and mothers who had just given birth were all raped without pity.[7] At the end of World War II, Red Army soldiers are estimated to have raped around 2 million German women and girls. In *The Russians in Germany: A History of the Soviet Zone of Occupation, 1945–1949*, Norman Naimark commented:

> … although the exact number of women and girls who were raped by members of the Red Army in the months preceding and years following the capitulation will never be known, their numbers are likely in the hundreds of thousands, quite possibly as high as the 2,000,000 victims estimate made by Barbara Johr, in *Befreier und Befreite*.[8]

Anthony Beevor estimates that as many as half of the victims experienced gang rape and many were repeatedly raped. Naimark states that not only did each victim have to carry the trauma with her for the rest of her days; it inflicted a massive collective trauma on the East German nation. Naimark concluded:

> The social psychology of women and men in the soviet zone of occupation was marked by the crime of rape from the first days of occupation, through the founding of the GDR (German Democratic Republic) in the fall of 1949, until— one could argue—the present.[9]

Beevor writes that approximately 90 percent of the women raped in Berlin in 1945 contracted venereal diseases and 3.7 percent of all children born in Germany from 1945 to 1946 had Russian fathers.

As the Russians entered Germany in 1945, any means of degradation and humiliation was applied to the German people. They were treated as monsters and women bore the brunt on the treatment through torture and rape. German soldiers were imprisoned, tortured, robbed, and denied any human dignity. Very few officers resisted this lack of discipline and very few seldom interfered. The call 'women come' became a feared word.[10]

Berlin was a city without men in 1945 as the Russian army advanced on the city. Women numbered 2 million out of an estimated population of 2.7 million. Doctors were besieged by women looking for information on the quickest way to commit suicide, and poison was in large demand. On 24 March 1945, the Red Army entered Danzig. A fifty-year-old Danzig teacher reported that her niece, aged fifteen, was raped seven times, and her other niece, aged twenty-two, was raped fifteen times. A Soviet officer told a group of women to seek safety in the Cathedral. Once they were securely locked inside, the soldiers entered, and ringing the bells and playing the organ, raped all the women, some more than thirty times. A Catholic pastor in Danzig declared, 'They violated even eight-year-old girls and shot boys who tried to shield their mothers.'[11]

Aleksandr Solzhenitsyn, then a young captain in the Red Army, describes the entry of his regiment into East Prussia in January 1945: 'Yes! For three weeks the war had been going on inside Germany and all of us knew very well that if the girls were German they could be raped and then shot. This was almost a combat distinction.' In his epic poem *Prussian Nights*, Solzhenitsyn gives a more persuasive description of the willful arson and murder:

> *We've hit him good and hard, the foe!*
> *Everything's aflame.—Night quarters?*
> *We'll have to spend it in the snow.*
> *Oh, well, that's bad. But all the same,*
> *We've given them a tougher time:*
> *The whole district sees a dawn*
> *The like of which it's never known! …*
> *To flame the work of centuries turns,*
> *Fire is weaving, fire is lashing,*
> *Above my head it burns and burns…*
> *In Neidenburg conflagrations shiver*
> *To shards old masonry's good stone.*
> *The town's a chaos; in a fever*
> *Of acquisition our pursuit takes it…*
> *Twenty-two Hoeringstrasse.*
> *It's not been burned, just looted, rifled.*
> *A moaning, by the walls half muffled:*
> *The mother's wounded, still alive.*
> *The little daughter's on the mattress,*
> *Dead. How many have been on it?*
> *A platoon, a company perhaps?*
> *A girl's been turned into a woman,*
> *A woman turned into a corpse.*
> *It's all come down to simple phrases:*
> *Do not forget! Do not forgive!*
> *Blood for blood! tooth for a tooth!*
> *The mother begs, 'Soldier, kill me!'*
> *Her eyes are hazy and bloodshot.*
> *The dark's upon her. She can't see.*
> *Am I one of theirs? Or whose? …*
> *A pram that's been abandoned,*
> *Blue, Lace trimmings, too:*
> *'Look, a little 'un.*
> *Still, he's a German!*
> *He'll grow and put a helmet on.*

Deal with him now, d'you think?
The order from Supreme Command
Is Blood for Blood! Give no quarter!'...
And then they shot the housewife first,
Spattering with blood the carpet's pile.
The husband was bedridden, ill:
They cured him with a carbine burst.
Only the nephew, a young boy,
In a flash managed to escape
—Out of the window and away
Over the fence with a leap! With a leap!
Like a wild creature,
Like a little hare,
Across the field toward the wood
Running, ducking, dodging aside.
The whole troop, nearly, rushed from the road,
Firing anyhow, in pursuit:
'I'll get him'. 'Winged him!' 'He's down!'
'He's away!' '—Shoot! Shoot!'
'Ah, the brute,
He's got away. Well, when he's grown...'[12]

In *The Blond Knight of Germany: A Biography of Erich Hartmann*, Raymond Toliver and Trevor Constable wrote:

> ... half-drunk Red Army soldiers, armed with rifles and machine guns, made unarmed Germans stand in rows. Other Russians forced women and girls to lie on the ground, tore off their clothes and began raping them. The male Germans could only silently clench their fists. U.S. soldiers from their truck looked on at all this with eyes wide open.[13]

A young German woman, a little over thirty, mother of a twelve-year-old girl, knelt at the feet of a Russian corporal and prayed to God that the Soviet soldiers take her and not the girl. Yet her prayers went unanswered. Tears streamed down her cheeks as she kept praying.[21] The Russian corporal walked away from the woman, his face contorted into a mocking grin. One of the soldiers hit the woman on the face with his boot. 'Damned fascist pig!' he yelled. The young mother fell on her back. The soldier who had hit her, shot her in the head and killed her. The Russians seized all the German women who were visible. The little daughter of the murdered woman was dragged behind a tank by the killer of her mother. He was joined by other Russians. Wild screams and moans rang out for half an hour; then, completely naked, the girl, unable to stand on her feet, crept back.[14]

A new pattern seemed to develop once the Russians reached Berlin. They would flash torches in the face of women huddled in bunkers to choose their victims. This process of selection, as opposed to the immediate violence shown in East Prussia, indicates a definite change. By this stage, Soviet soldiers treated German women much more as sexual spoils of war as substitutes for the Wehrmacht on which to vent their rage.[15] The soldiers appear to have felt that they were satisfying a sexual need after all their time at the front. In this, most soldier rapists did not demonstrate gratuitous violence, provided the woman did not resist.[16]

Indoctrination and Training of the Russian Army

The balance between patriotism and vengeance tipped in 1944. As the Red Army drew close to its own border, many soldiers began to complain that their job was done. Stalin needed a way to force them on—he used hatred. The soldiers were told that vengeance was theirs, and Stalin implored them 'to destroy the beast in his liar.'[17] His words were reflected in letters written by his soldiers in 1945 as they crossed onto Prussian soil. One man wrote to his parents: 'Happy is the heart as you drive through the burning German town. We are taking revenge for everything, and our revenge is just. Fire for fire, blood for blood, death for death.'[18] Violence would soon become an end in itself, as there was no shortage of men in the Red Army whose lives had been marked by state violence. German atrocities on Soviet soil compounded images that had been part of life for twenty years. These soldiers had learned to survive in a lawless, brutal world. Both vengeance and personal survival were high on their list of goals.[19] David Samoilov wrote:

> The soldier of 1941 fought for his land, he was defending his own soil. It was enough for him to know just this, and that knowledge itself made him strong. The rot set in, he added, when the war of self-defence became a war of aggression. Like many others, he was nostalgic for Stalingrad. Back then, Soviet troops had been fighting a true, just war. Now they seemed capable of outrages that looked uncannily like those that the Germans had perpetrated in 1941. They also seemed far too keen to amass personal wealth. The wristwatches and bicycles and schnapps that brightened the road towards Berlin are well-documented, but in fact looting and private gain in general, had featured while the army was on Soviet soil. Hundreds of tons of goods went missing every year, from army food supplies to livestock, home-brewed alcohol, black market guns and even boots. After decades of Soviet poverty, after the enforced collectivization of agriculture, the chance to amass real wealth, and also make sense of miserable army life by turning it to advantage, was too attractive to resist.[20]

In *World War Two: Behind Closed Doors*, the historian Laurence Rees points out that although rape was officially a crime in the Red Army, Stalin had in fact explicitly condoned it as a method of rewarding the soldiers and terrorizing German civilians.[21]

Stalin said people should 'understand it if a soldier who has crossed thousands of kilometers through blood and fire and death has fun with a woman or takes some trifle.' On another occasion, when told that Red Army soldiers sexually maltreated German refugees, he said: 'We lecture our soldiers too much; let them have their initiative.'[22] There are no surviving records to prove it, but it was apparent to survivors that rape was not only condoned but legally sanctioned by representatives of the Soviet government.[23] 'It's absolutely clear that if we don't really scare them now, there will be no way of avoiding another war in future,' one Red Army soldier wrote at the time.[24]

Economic and Political Conditions in Russia

When war broke out the Soviet Union had already engaged insubstantial rearmament. In 1940, the last year of less than total war (the Soviet Union had used military force only in Finland and the Baltic region), the Red Army comprised between 4 and 5 million soldiers; the military budget consumed one-third of government out lays and 15 per cent of the net material product at prevailing prices. One-third of the military budget was allocated to procurement of weapons, and Soviet industry produced thousands of tanks and combat aircraft, tens of thousands of guns and mortars, and millions of infantry weapons.[25]

Under the pressure of a deep invasion, Soviet GNP (Gross National Product) fell by one-third, while the resources allocated to defense increased both relatively and absolutely. The pressure on resources was somewhat alleviated by foreign aid, which added approximately 5 percent to Soviet resources in 1942 and 10 percent in 1943 and 1944. The net import of Allied resources allowed the Soviet Union to use more resources than it produced in 1942, 1943, and 1944. Wartime changes in the uses of output were accompanied by changes in both employment and productivity. Total employment fell by more than one-third, while numbers engaged in military service and war production rose. The biggest shift was out of agriculture; there were smaller movements out of civilian industry, transport, construction, and services. A considerable efficiency gain in defense industry pushed output per worker far above peacetime levels. When the war was at its most intense, the resources available to civilian producers and consumers were reduced below the minimum required to replace stocks of physical and human capital. Household consumption was already being squeezed a little by rearmament in 1940; it was squeezed ferociously in 1941–42 by the cut in overall resources and the ballooning defense budget, and squeezed even further in 1943 by the recovery of capital formation. At the low point, living standards were roughly 40 percent below the pre-war level. Millions were overworked and malnourished, and there was substantial excess mortality among the civilian population.[26]

Various experiences of 1941–42 testify both to the risks of destabilization and the importance of the Soviet countermeasures taken to strengthen the stable equilibrium.[27] For example, in 1941, expectations were widespread that Soviet resistance to German invasion would follow the same course of unraveling and collapse as that already followed by Poland, Netherlands, Belgium, France, Norway, Greece, and Yugoslavia. These forecasts were reinforced by the ease with which the Wehrmacht moved into the Baltic and the western Ukraine and the warmth of its reception there. No single episode illustrates this more clearly than the Moscow 'panic' of mid-October 1941: with the enemy a few kilometers distant, wrongly believing Stalin had left the city, crowds rioted and looted public property. The authorities took determined steps to counter such perceptions of likely defeat. Stalin suppressed information about Red Army setbacks and casualties. Many were executed for spreading defeatist rumors about events on the front line that might simply have been the truth. Moscow and Leningrad were closed to refugees from the occupied areas in the autumn of 1941 to prevent the spread of information about Soviet defeats. Evacuation of civilians from both Leningrad and Stalingrad was delayed by the authorities' desire to conceal the real military situation.

Despite this, millions implemented or contemplated strategies for defeat. Huge numbers of Red Army soldiers rejected orders that prohibited surrender or retreat. Against orders, millions of encircled soldiers surrendered to the invader in the autumn and winter of 1941 and the spring of 1942. Some prisoners who survived the winter of 1942 subsequently went over to the German side and fought alongside the Wehrmacht (for example, General A. A. Vlasov's 'Russian Liberation Army') and the Germans also recruited national 'legions' from ethnic groups in the occupied areas. At the end of July 1942, when the Germans' summer offensive reached Rostov on Don, significant numbers of Red Army troops ran away from the front line. The risks arising from such behaviors led Stalin to impose the most severe penalties. His Order No. 270 of 16 August 1941 stigmatized the behavior of Soviet soldiers who allowed themselves to fall into captivity as 'betrayal of the Motherland' and inflicted social and financial penalties on the families of the prisoners of war. His Order No. 227 of 28 July 1942 ('not a step back') combated defeatism in the retreating Red Army by deploying military police behind the lines to shoot stragglers and men retreating without orders and officers who allowed their units to disintegrate.[28]

While the war continued, Stalin singled out several national minorities suspected of collaboration—for example, the Chechens—for mass deportation to Siberia. Wartime 'deserters' from war work on the industrial front were doggedly pursued and hundreds of thousands were sentenced to terms in prisons and labor camps while the war continued. Regardless of the prospects of defeat or victory, food crimes became widespread.

People stole food from the state and stole from each other. Military and civilian food administrators stole rations for own consumption and for sideline trade. Civilians forged and traded ration cards. In the winter of 1942, Red Army units in the Caucasus began helping themselves to local food supplies.[29] Food crimes reached the extreme of cannibalism in Leningrad in the winter of 1941, but when millions lived on the edge, even quite trivial violations of food regulations could have lethal consequences for individuals who suffered losses as a result, and food crimes in general were harshly punished—not infrequently by shooting. In short, it is apparent that the stability of the Soviet war effort was seriously at risk in 1941 and 1942. Millions of Soviet citizens faced desperately hard choices between serving the state and serving their own interests and the interests of those around them with whom they identified. Strategies for victory and defeat diverged. However, beyond a certain point the danger that citizens might choose defeat in ever increasing numbers was not realized. Both Stalin and Hitler played their part in stabilizing the Soviet war effort by closing off the options of honorable surrender and the restoration of private property under German occupation.[30]

Roosevelt also contributed to Soviet stabilization. The first installment of wartime Allied aid that reached the Soviet Union in 1942, although small by later standards, amounted to some 5 percent of Soviet GNP in that year. Although Allied aid was used directly to supply the armed forces with both durable goods and consumables, indirectly it probably released resources to households. By improving the balance of overall resources, it brought about a *ceteris paribus* increase in the payoff to patriotic citizens. In other words, lend-lease was stabilizing. We cannot measure the distance of the Soviet economy from the point of collapse in 1942, but it seems beyond doubt that collapse was near. Without lend-lease, it would have been nearer.[31]

The following speech given by Joseph V. Stalin at the Red Army Parade on the Red Square, Moscow, 7 November 1941, illustrates the government's position:

COMRADES, men of the Red Army and Red Navy, commanders and political instructors, working men and working women, collective farmers-men and women, workers in the intellectual professions, brothers and sisters in the rear of our enemy who have temporarily fallen under the yoke of the German brigands, and our valiant men and women guerillas who are destroying the rear of the German invaders!

On behalf of the Soviet Government and our Bolshevik Party I am greeting you and congratulating you on the twenty-fourth anniversary of the Great October Socialist Revolution.

Comrades, it is in strenuous circumstances that we are to-day celebrating the twenty-fourth anniversary of the October Revolution. The perfidious attack of the German brigands and the war which has been forced upon us have created a threat to our country. We have temporarily lost a number of regions, the enemy has appeared at the gates of Leningrad and Moscow. The enemy reckoned that after the very first blow our army would be dispersed, and our country would be forced to her knees. But the enemy gravely miscalculated. In spite of temporary reverses, our Army and Navy are heroically repulsing the enemy's attacks along the entire front and inflicting heavy losses upon him, while our country—our entire country—has organized itself into one fighting camp in order, together with our Army and our Navy, to encompass the rout of the German invaders.

There were times when our country was in a still more difficult position. Remember the year 1918, when we celebrated the first anniversary of the October Revolution. Three-quarters of our country was at that time in the hands of foreign interventionists. The Ukraine, the Caucasus, Central Asia, the Urals, Siberia and the Far East were temporarily lost to us. We had no allies, we had no Red Army— we had only just begun to create it; there was a shortage of food, of armaments, of clothing for the Army. Fourteen states were pressing against our country. But we did not become despondent, we did not lose heart. In the fire of war we forged the Red Army and converted our country into a military camp. The spirit of the great Lenin animated us at that time for the war against the interventionists. And what happened? We routed the interventionists, recovered all our lost territory, and achieved victory.

To-day the position of our country is far better than twenty-three years ago. Our country is now many times richer than it was twenty-three years ago as regards industry, food and raw materials. We now have allies, who together with us are maintaining a united front against the German invaders. We now enjoy the sympathy and support of all the nations of Europe who have fallen under the yoke of Hitler's tyranny. We now have a splendid Army and a splendid Navy, who are defending with their lives the liberty and independence of our country. We experience no serious shortage of either food, or armaments or army clothing. Our entire country, all the peoples of our country, support our Army and our Navy, helping them to smash the invading hordes of German fascists. Our reserves of man-power are inexhaustible. The spirit of the great Lenin and his victorious banner animate us now in this patriotic war just as they did twenty-three years ago.

Can there be any doubt that we can, and are bound to, defeat the German invaders?

The enemy is not so strong as some frightened little intellectuals picture him. The devil is not so terrible as he is painted. Who can deny that our Red Army has more than once put the vaunted German troops to panic flight? If one judges, not by the boastful assertions of the German propagandists, but by the actual position of Germany, it will not be difficult to understand that the German-fascist invaders are facing disaster. Hunger and impoverishment reign in Germany to-day; in four months of war Germany has lost four and a half million men; Germany is bleeding, her reserves of man-power are giving out, the spirit of indignation is spreading not only among the peoples of Europe who have fallen under the yoke of the German invaders but also among the German people themselves, who see no end to war. The German invaders are straining their last efforts. There is no doubt that Germany cannot sustain such a strain for long. Another few months, another half-year, perhaps another year, and Hitlerite Germany must burst under the pressure of her crimes.

Comrades, men of the Red Army and Red Navy, commanders and political instructors, men and women guerillas, the whole world is looking to you as the force capable of destroying the plundering hordes of German invaders. The enslaved peoples of Europe who have fallen under the yoke of the German invaders look to you as their liberators. A great liberating mission has fallen to your lot. Be worthy of this mission! The war you are waging is a war of liberation, a just war. Let the manly images of our great ancestors—Alexander Nevsky, Dimitry Donskoy, Kuzma Minin, Dimitry Pozharsky, Alexander Suvorov and Mikhail Kutuzov—inspire you in this war!

May the victorious banner of the great Lenin be your lodestar!

For the complete destruction of the German invaders!

Death to the German invaders!

Long live our glorious Motherland, her liberty and her independence!

Under the banner of Lenin, forward to victory![32]

Characterization of the Germans

At the start of the war, there were still illusions that the Soviet Union was fighting an international class war. Moscow factory workers are reported as expressing incredulity at the Germans' rashness: 'Who do they think they're attacking? Have they gone out of their minds?... Of course, the German workers will support us, and all other peoples will rise up.... It will all be over in a week.' Even a sophisticated intellectual like Lev Kopelev was prone to such illusions. In 1979, in a conversation with the German writer Heinrich Boll, he remarked:

> When the first reports of the war came in on 22 June 1941, I must admit honestly, I was so stupid that I was delighted. I thought this is the holy war, now the German proletariat will support us, and Hitler will be overthrown immediately.[33]

Front-line soldiers also took some time to realize what had hit them. One noted in his diary on 20 July 1941, after destroying a German tank and capturing the crew:

> What naive philanthropists we were! In our interrogation we tried to get them to express class solidarity. We thought talking to us would make them see the light, and they would shout 'Rot Front!'.... But they guzzled our kasha from our mess-tins, had a smoke from our freely offered tobacco pouches, then looked at us insolently and belched in our faces 'Heil Hitler!'[34]

Once it became clear that the Nazis were waging a war of annihilation against the Soviet Union, this mood changed utterly. Even though the Soviet state remained committed in principle to inter-nationalism, most of its citizens came to see the struggle as being not between imperialists and toilers, but between Russians and Germans. The Russian-Jewish novelist and war correspondent Ilya Ehrenburg, who had kept the Soviet public informed about the struggle of the International Brigade in the Spanish Civil War, realized in the first days that this was going to be a wholly different kind of war:

> I suddenly felt that there was something very important and tenacious—the soil. I was sitting on a Moscow boulevard. Beside me sat a sad, unattractive woman with a child. Her features seemed infinitely familiar to me, as she said 'Peten'ka, don't be naughty, take pity on me!' I realized that she was a member of my family, that one could die for Peten'ka.[35]

This feeling of being a large family, not divided by class origins, was articulated by Stalin in his first broadcast to the Soviet peoples, on 3 July 1941, when he supplemented the accustomed Communist mode of address, 'Comrades!', and the neutral civic term, 'Citizens!', with the words 'Brothers and sisters!'[36] There was even perhaps here an echo of the greeting given by the Orthodox priest to his parishioners. Ehrenburg became the most vehement exponent of the new view of the war as a national struggle to the death between Russians and Germans. He wrote in Pravda: 'If you haven't killed a German in the course of a day, then your day has been wasted.... If you have killed one German, kill another. Nothing gives us so much joy as the sight of German corpses.'[37] As a Jew, Ehrenburg had twice as many reasons for hating the Germans, but the Russian poet Konstantin Simonov expressed very similar sentiments in his poem 'Kill him!', published in Pravda in 1942.

> If your home is dear to you where you were nursed as a Russian.... If your mother is dear to you, and you cannot bear the thought of a German slapping her wrinkled face.... If you do not want to give away all that you call your Homeland, Then kill a German, so that he, Not you, should lie in the earth.... Kill a German every time you see one![38]

Ethnic hatred became the dominant sentiment among soldiers and officers, especially as they moved westwards from the spring of 1943 and saw with their own eyes the destruction the Germans had wrought on their villages and people. When Soviet troops reached German territory early in 1945, Lev Kopelev as a political officer did his best to revive the party's internationalist ideals and to restrain his men from looting, raping, and killing among the civilian population. He was pursuing the line approved by the party leaders; G. F. Aleksandrov, head of Agitprop, wrote in Pravda on 14 April 1945: 'Hitlers come and go, but the German people are here to stay.'[39] Most Soviet officers shared the same attitude: 'First let's send Germany up in smoke, then we'll go back to writing good theoretically correct books on humanism and internationalism. But now we must see to it that the soldier will want to go on fighting. That's the main thing'.[40] Hating the Germans generated stronger attachment to the Soviet Union. It took some time, though, at the beginning of the war before this feeling took hold.

In *Stalingrad to Berlin: The German Defeat in the East*, Earl Ziemke describes how under the shock of invasion, the Soviet Government responded predictably with a series of decisions aimed at centralizing military and political controls and strengthening the influence of the Communist Party. Secret police units were organized to set up blocking detachments behind the front to catch stragglers and prevent unauthorized retreats. On the frontier, surprise soon turned to confusion and, in not a few instances, panic. To hold with the first echelon until a counterattack could be prepared remained the whole basis of the initial Soviet strategy. A reserve front of four armies created on the third day of the invasion in the most endangered sector due west of Moscow was first ordered to be ready to counterattack. Still trying to halt the retreat, Stalin had the Commanding General of the West Front and his staff shot. Henceforth, an officer who permitted a retreat forfeited his life.[41]

In seeking support from the population, Stalin dropped distinctions between proletarian and peasant, communist and nationalist. Effective resistance by the population helped bolster the efforts of the Soviet forces at the front. They were stirred by the heroic music of the finest Soviet composers that was written expressly for the war effort. The battle against the Germans became a struggle for Mother Russia, and was called the 'Great Patriotic War.'

Living Conditions of the Russian Soldiers

Life, as the Red Army soldier quickly came to understand, was cheap at the front. With the costly failure of the Soviets to break German resistance at Rzhev, the front during the winter of 1942–43 settled into a dreary trench warfare reminiscent of World War I. As men in the ranks increasingly despaired at the huge losses and the distant prospect of victory, they sought escape in other ways. In *Through the Maelstrom: A Red Army Soldier's War on the Eastern Front, 1942–1945*, Boris Gorbachevsky writes about being wounded in the late-summer fighting that had already been stunned by the high incidence of self-inflicted wounds being treated in the field hospitals. Now, back at the front and a company commander, he had to confront another dilemma: the shockingly high rate of desertion and the savage measures taken against front officers to stop it. In one of the most interesting chapters in the book, Gorbachevsky details the assiduous German efforts to entice Soviet soldiers to desert and the astonishing number who did just that—some 500,000 in 1942 alone. A combination of better food and living conditions trumpeted by the Germans with severe morale problems on the Soviet side fueled the nightly forays across no-man's-land.[42] For Soviet front officers, though, these desertions were more than just a drain on manpower, since the Red Army sought to stem the flow by imposing draconian punishments on them, including sentences to penal battalions and prison camps. Political officers also stepped up their indoctrination efforts, but faced the unremitting hostility of peasant soldiers toward the regime in the wake of the collectivization measures sponsored by the party in the 1930s. Interestingly, although he mentions efforts to build bonds between men and officers, the notion of camaraderie as a primal force binding front soldiers together is conspicuously absent from Gorbachevsky's account, especially in comparison with German memoirs. Despite his efforts, even Gorbachevsky cannot overcome the deep suspicion that Ivan has for his officers: Stalinist terror and oppression have insured a nearly unbridgeable gulf. Two things, not necessarily independent of each other, eventually began to stanch the flow of desertions: front propaganda increasingly substituted 'fatherland' for 'party,' and a string of Soviet victories touched off by the great triumph at Stalingrad finally persuaded men in the front ranks that they might yet win the war for Russia, not Stalin. Still, as Gorbachevsky notes, in 1943, the triumphs at Rzhev and in Belorussia came largely as a result of the application of brute force, with the front troops paying an awful price.[43]

The combination of continuing sacrifices on the part of the average soldiers and the increasing prospect of victory now raised a frightening prospect to Stalin. According to Gorbachevsky, a new spirit, a new mood, and a new sense of freedom (if that term is not an oxymoron when used in conjunction with Stalin's Russia) now infused the front ranks. War was changing attitudes, as among themselves, front soldiers increasingly expressed the expectation that they would return to a freer and more democratic society and that they would be rewarded for their sacrifices and hardships with a better way of life.

As the Red Army surged westward into Germany, the danger, from Stalin's point of view, grew ever greater, as peasant soldiers began to see how things might be different and better. Red soldiers, amazed at the wealth of their enemy, struggled to understand why Adolf Hitler had coveted Soviet territory. 'Now tell us, Captain,' one inquired of Gorbachevsky, 'why did the stinking German come crawling into Russia with war, especially when his pigs live better than our peasants? It makes a man furious to see the wealthy way they live.'[44] Gorbachevsky tried to convince his men that the German people were not responsible for Hitler's crimes, but they knew better, having seen evidence of German atrocities spread over countless villages and hundreds of miles.

These two emotions, resentment and revenge, were now mingled in an explosive brew. As Soviet troops scrambled to send packages filled with German goods home, plundering everything in their path, they also began exacting an understandable, if no less brutal vengeance. Was this retribution fanned deliberately by Stalin to distract Soviet troops from their troublesome questions? The answer from the front, as Gorbachevsky notes, is inconclusive.

4

The My Lai Massacre in Vietnam: 1968

The men of 'C' Company were angry, frightened, and struggling to stay alive in March 1968. Since the members of 'C' Company arrived three months earlier in Vietnam, thirty-eight of their members were wounded, mostly by snipers, booby traps, or mines. Four of their friends were killed.[1] The enemy continued to deny them a chance to fight and retaliate by avoiding open battle. This was very frustrating for the members of 'C' Company. A popular sergeant was killed when he stepped on a mine two days before the soldiers entered My Lai village. At a memorial service for the sergeant on 15 March, Captain Ernest Medina, 'C' Company commander, told the men that they would be outnumbered during the impending operation and they should expect a fierce battle. He told them the operation would be a chance to avenge the loss of their friend. Several members of the company later testified that they thought Captain Medina had ordered them to destroy the village and its residents. Documents in the Quang Ngai Museum illustrate the attitudes of the American soldiers:

> Compounding that situation were the racist ideas internalized by many American soldiers: that Vietnamese were 'gooks,' 'dinks,' and 'slopes,' 'sub-humans,' who deserved to be 'greased,' 'wasted,' or 'hosed down.'[2]

According to Army intelligence, the Viet Cong 48th Battalion was located on the South China Sea about mid-way between Saigon and Hanoi, in the Son My district of Quang Ngai province.[3] Son My, where My Lai is located, was known as a Viet Cong stronghold, and its people were considered Viet Cong guerrillas or sympathizers. Americans called My Lai 'Pinkville,' at first because of its color on military maps, but soon as shorthand for Communist territory. Intelligence reports said that because it was a Saturday morning, all civilians would have left for market by 7 a.m. Lieutenant Colonel Frank Barker ordered Charlie Company to attack My Lai, Bravo Company to attack My Khe, and Alpha Company to intercept fleeing Viet Cong. At 7.24 a.m., artillery launched the attack by bombarding My Lai. Between 7.30 a.m. and 7.45 a.m., helicopters dropped Charlie Company northwest of the village.[4]

No enemy fire challenged the Americans as they came into the landing zone. Contrary to intelligence, there were no guerrilla fighters and the villagers were not at market. My Lai was full of civilians, many still cooking their breakfast rice. As the barrage began, they hid in underground bunkers. When it ended, they emerged to encounter 'C' Company. The soldiers shot any villager who tried to run and herded the others into groups. Lieutenant William Calley, the First Platoon leader, ordered his men to shoot them at point-blank range. When some refused, Calley set his rifle on automatic and executed many of the villagers himself. American soldiers tossed hand grenades and dynamite into the bunkers, killing villagers who remained inside. Soldiers killed a Buddhist monk, threw his body into a well, and tossed in grenades to contaminate the water. They set houses afire and shot the residents as they tried to escape. They killed water buffalo, pigs, and ducks. They raped women and teenage girls and then killed them. Specialist Varnado Simpson admitted killing and mutilating at least twenty-five people in My Lai. 'From shooting them to cutting their throats to scalping them to cutting off their hands and cutting out their tongue,' he said, 'I did that.'[5] Haeberle described the callousness of one killing:

> There was a little boy walking toward us in a daze. He'd been shot in the arm and leg. He wasn't crying or making any noise. As he knelt down to make a picture, 'a GI fired three shots into the child,' Haeberle said. 'The first shot knocked him back, the second shot lifted him into the air. The third shot put him down and the body fluids came out. The GI just simply got up and walked away.'[6]

Writing for the Human Rights Program, School of the Americas, Fort Benning, Georgia, Major Tony Raimondo, JA, provides a timeline of the My Lai events of 16 March 1968:

> 0530 The soldiers of 'C' Co. are instructed to gather their gear, and prepare for boarding the aircrafts. More than a hundred soldiers and several tons of equipment were to be transported from LZ Dottie to the landing field, a trip of approximately 11 miles.
>
> Nine (9) liftships (radio callsign 'Dolphins') and gunships (radio callsign 'Sharks') from the 174th Helicopter Assault Co. were to provide support.
>
> The 'Slicks,' the troop-carrying helicopters, were to move 'C' Co. in two lifts. First, they would take CPT Medina's command group, the 1st PLT, and as many soldiers from 2nd PLT as possible (a total of approximately fifty troops). The plan called for this element to secure the landing field for the remainder of the company. The remainder of 2nd PLT, and 3rd PLT, along with a few additional elements from other brigade units temporarily assigned to 'C' Co. for the Pinkville operation, were to be transported on the second lift.

0730 An artillery barrage from four 105-mm guns began. It lasted approximately three minutes, and landed about 120 rounds around the landing area near the My Lai hamlet. The purpose was to clear it of enemy presence/prepare it for landing. Eventually some of the rounds strayed over into the inhabited part of the hamlet itself, creating flying shrapnel and causing terror and panic amongst the civilian population. The artillery barrage degenerated to blind firing since no spotter was close enough to adjust the fire away from the village. Nevertheless, only one villager was killed by it.

The first lift (again, carrying CPT Medina's command group, 1st PLT, and some members of 2nd PLT), took a circuitous route to keep the element of surprise. The VC may have known that an attack was imminent because of the leaflets, but they did not know where the attack would originate. The aircrafts, as they drew near the landing field, poured down a heavy fusillade of machine gun fire, with tracer rounds, on the landing area. These approximately 50 troops, once on the ground, immediately spread out to take defensive positions at the bank of a near-by irrigation ditch. They held their defensive positions, and provided covering fire while waiting for the rest of the 2nd and 3rd PLTs to join them. These soldiers, and the aircrafts that transported them, received no enemy fire.

The 'Dolphins' took off again and the lead ship announced over the air that the landing field was 'cold'—i.e., that there had been absolutely no enemy fire. Nevertheless, the 'Sharks' continued pouring all kinds of fire on the outskirts of the hamlet with machine guns, grenade launchers, and rockets. LTC Barker acknowledged the message from 'Dolphin Lead,' and relayed it back to the operations center at LZ Dottie. LTC Barker was in his command-and-control aircraft, the 'Charlie Charlie' ship, manning a console of radios that allowed him to be in contact with his ground troops and the several aircrafts, the gunships in particular. Task Force Barker's tactical operations center was located at LZ Dottie; whereas, operations for brigade headquarters were located at Duc Pho, in the southernmost part of Quang Ngai Province, to the south of LZ Dottie.

There was intense aerial activity for the next twenty minutes, as the aircrafts continued searching for signs of enemy positions. None were found. A farmer standing in one of the many paddy fields surrounding the hamlet, frantically raised his hands so as to show that he had no weapons. Nevertheless, he was immediately struck by a burst of machine gun fire. This may very well have been the first casualty and unlawful killing of the day.

The second lift did not require a circuitous route, since the element of surprise was no longer a factor (after the first lift), and therefore had a much shorter journey cross country to the landing field. These soldiers as well, shortly after the second lift reached the landing field, quickly spread out to take up defensive positions with the others. They too engaged in covering fire even in the continued absence of enemy fire.

A squad from 3rd PLT was tasked to retrieve a VC weapon spotted, and marked with a smoke canister, by one of the aero scouts. A woman carrying a small child in the brush some distance away was shot at by a soldier from 3rd PLT, with his weapon on full automatic, shortly after being spotted. His squad leader angrily reprimanded him for firing in the direction of the soldiers searching for the VC weapon. The rampage was about to begin.

At this time, while still having received no enemy fire whatsoever, almost everyone in the 1st, 2nd, and 3rd PLTs was firing their weapons, along with the gunships. The moment a Vietnamese was spotted, and regardless of status, volleys of fire were sprayed off, and the 'enemy' felled either wounded or dead.

0750 1st and 2nd PLTs started moving into the hamlet in separate groups. Spread out 'on line' (a then typical infantry formation under such circumstances), they moved forward, over a dike, through another rice paddy, and entered the village firing methodically from the hip. Again, many soldiers had their M-16s on full automatic. CPT Medina's command group, along with 3rd PLT, in accordance with the operational plan, remained behind in a defensive perimeter on the western edge of the hamlet, approximately 150 meters from the tree line that separated the hamlet from the rice paddies.

0800 CPT Medina radioed the operations center via the 'Charlie Charlie' ship of the task force commander and reported that they had fifteen confirmed 'VC' kills. Apparently, the soldiers of 'C' Co. viewed every single Vietnamese villager in My Lai as a VC combatant and therefore a lawful target, regardless of their actions or behavior on the field.

1LT Calley's 1st PLT entered the southern portion of My Lai 4 in three separate squads, line abreast. Part of the plan was for prisoners or Viet Cong suspects to be sent back to the PLT commanders, including 1LT Calley, for screening.

Soldiers soon began firing on anything that moved (including farm animals, such as pigs, chickens, ducks, and cows). Troops yelled inside small dwellings for its inhabitants to come out, using hand signals to direct them if they appeared outside. If there was no answer, they threw grenades into the shelters and bunkers. Many soldiers did not bother to use this procedure and threw hand grenades inside the hootches regardless of human presence. Small clusters of people were being gathered, in one part of the hamlet, into one larger group of fifty or sixty old men, women, and children. Some were mothers with babies in their arms, and some so badly wounded they could hardly walk.

Minutes after entering My Lai, a soldier came across a hut which had been strafed with bullets. Inside, he discovered three children, a woman with a flesh wound in her side, and an old man squatting down, hardly able to move because of serious injuries he had sustained to both legs. The soldier aimed his .45 pistol at the old man's head and pulled the trigger, causing the top of his skull to be severed. The soldier later claimed to have shot the old man as an act of mercy.

Two soldiers were taken by surprise when a woman, carrying an infant in her arms and with a toddler barely able to walk not far behind, came running out of a bamboo hut. One of them fired and injured her. An elderly woman, with an unexploded M-79 grenade lodged inside her open stomach, was spotted staggering down the path.

An old man with a straw coolie hat and no shirt (making it obvious that he was unarmed) was with a water buffalo in a paddy 50 meters away. He was shot, immediately after placing his arms up, by members of 1st PLT as 1LT Calley watched.

One soldier stabbed a middle aged Vietnamese farmer with his bayonet for no apparent reason. Then, while the victim was on the ground gasping for breath, the soldier killed him. This same soldier then grabbed another man that was being detained, shot him in the neck, threw him inside a well, and lobbed an M-26 grenade after him.

The shooting, once it began, created almost a chain reaction. Inside the hamlet, soldiers appeared out of control. Families who had huddled together for safety inside houses, in their yards, and in bunkers, were mercilessly mowed down with automatic weapon fire or blown apart by fragmentation grenades. Some women along with their children were forced inside bunkers and grenades thrown in after them.

One soldier who had wandered off on his own, found a woman about age 20 with a four-year-old child. He forced her to perform oral sex on him while he held a gun at the child's head, threatening to kill the child. When 1LT Calley happened along, he angrily told this soldier to pull up his pants and get over to where he was supposed to be.

At one point, amid all the mayhem, the 1st and 2nd PLTs overlapped when the right flank of 2nd PLT crossed paths with the left flank of 1st PLT. Troops from 1st PLT who were walking back a small group of villagers for screening were accosted by a soldier from 2nd PLT who angrily insisted that the villagers be killed on the spot. He solicited an M-16 in exchange for his M-79 so that he could initiate the executions. When this was refused, he grabbed an M-16 from a soldier and shot a Vietnamese farmer in the head. He was later calmed down.

0830 COL Henderson and LTC Barker flew back to the area of operation briefly in their respective helicopters. LTC Barker checked once more with CPT Medina to find out how the operation was going. CPT Medina reports 84 enemy killed, and LTC Barker then relayed the additional 69 KIA to the tactical operations center (SEE ENTRY AT 0800 ABOVE.) The death toll turned out to be far higher. Bear in mind that still no shots had been fired at any
member of 'C' Co., and they had yet to kill a single enemy soldier.

Three squads of 2nd PLT soldiers approached line abreast emptying dwellings and then tossing fragmentation grenades inside. Homes were also sprayed with automatic fire. A group of children aged only 6 or 7 who came towards them were quickly mowed down. Another group of Vietnamese was killed (by machine gun fire, and M-16s on full automatic) in front of a hut, after they had huddled together for safety. One squad leader told his men that he didn't like what they were doing, but that he had to follow orders.

A soldier shot at a woman with a baby at a distance of approximately 25 meters. Her right arm almost came off. A fragile piece of flesh was all that held it. She ran into a hootch while still clutching her baby; someone yelled for both of them to be killed.

A middle aged woman while attempting to climb out of a tunnel using both hands (thereby clearly revealing that she was unarmed), was shot by a machine gun team. This same machine gun team opened fire on any Vietnamese they came across. The scene continued to be one of chaos and confusion, with people running and screaming. Some of the troops became concerned that they would be shot by their fellow soldiers.

In a clearing near a small hootch, a group of fifteen Vietnamese had been gathered, four women in their thirties, three in their fifties, three girls in their late teens, and five children with ages of 3 to 14. A soldier yelled out a warning for anyone behind the group of Vietnamese to take cover because they were going to open fire. The very first shot that was fired at this group penetrated the head of a young child being carried by its mother, blowing out the back of the skull. Others then began firing as well; no one stopped until the entire group was dead.

One soldier fired two grenades, from his M-79 grenade launcher, at a number of Vietnamese sitting on the ground. The first bomblet missed, the second landed among them with devastating impact. Nevertheless, some of them managed to survive the blast. Another soldier finished off those left alive. A third soldier stooped over a tunnel and yelled for its occupants to come out. The people were about to comply when he threw in a grenade anyway.

Behind the 1st and 2nd PLTs, CPT Medina's command group had formed a security line out in the paddy fields beyond the western perimeter of My Lai 4. Some forty-five minutes had elapsed since the first troops entered the village and CPT Medina was waiting to send in 3rd PLT.

1st PLT collected a large group of about fifty to sixty Vietnamese. Among the squatting Vietnamese were ten to fifteen men with beards and ten women, as well as a handful of very elderly, gray-haired women who could hardly walk. The rest were children of all ages—from babies up to early teens.

By this time (from the time his PLT entered the hamlet), 1LT Calley had already received two radio calls from an anxious CPT Medina, who demanded to know what was happening with his platoon and challenging their slow progress through the hamlet. 1LT Calley replied that a large group of Vietnamese they had gathered was slowing down the platoon. CPT Medina instructed him to 'get rid of them.' 1LT Calley approached the two soldiers guarding the group of civilians and told them to 'take care of them.' The two soldiers responded 'OK.'

When 1LT Calley returned, several minutes later, he said to the two soldiers: 'I thought I told you to take care of them.' One of them responded: 'We are. We're watching over them.' 1LT Calley retorted that that was not what he had meant, and that he wanted them killed. 'We'll get on line and fire into them. Fire when I say fire.' One of the soldiers refused by offering the excuse that he was carrying a grenade launcher and did not want to waste ammunition. (By the way, this is the same soldier that 1LT Calley had caught with his pants down; the same one that had earlier threatened the life of a child at gun point if the mother did not perform oral sex on him.)

The other soldier participated in the killing with 1LT Calley, but could not take any more and stopped shooting towards the end, with tears streaming down his face. At this point the soldier who had not participated saw that only a few children remained alive. Mothers had thrown themselves on top of the young children in a last desperate attempt to shield them with their own bodies from the constant shower of bullets. The young children were trying to stand up. 1LT Calley opened fire killing them one by one. 1LT Calley then said 'OK, let's go.'

Ten members of 1st PLT were guarding forty to fifty Vietnamese at an irrigation ditch. While 1LT Calley was questioning a Buddhist monk through an interpreter, a child approximately two years of age somehow managed to crawl out of the ditch unnoticed by the soldiers. 1LT Calley walked over, picked up the child, shoved the child back into the ditch, and then fired at the child, before returning to question the monk. Tired of questioning the monk, 1LT Calley pulled him round, hurled him into the paddy, and opened fire with an M-16.

In the meantime, soldiers continued to escort and force the Vietnamese villagers into the irrigation ditch. Some were pushed, while others were butted; some Vietnamese jumped in by themselves; and yet others remained sitting at the edge, wailing because it was clear to them that, once inside the ditch, disaster was imminent. After 1LT Calley shoved a wounded woman into the ditch, he turned to one soldier and ordered: 'Load your machine gun and shoot these people.' When the soldier responded 'I'm not going to do that,' 1LT Calley pointed his M-16 on the soldier as if threatening to shoot him on the spot. The standstill came to an end when 1LT Calley backed off after some other soldiers intervened.

1LT Calley and other soldiers, one of whom was the same soldier that had earlier broken down and cried, after participating in the first large scale atrocity in the village, fired into the irrigation ditch. The Vietnamese tried frantically to hide under one another, mothers once again desperately attempted to protect their young children (and babies) by covering or shielding them with their bodies. The remnants of shredded human flesh and pieces of broken bone flew through the air, as magazine after magazine was emptied into the shallow ravine.

0845 CPT Medina heard all the shooting and was briefly concerned that his soldiers had encountered heavy enemy resistance. However, this was not the case, it had never been the case, and was never to be the case, in the hamlet of My Lai.

Again, members of 'C' Co. never received any enemy fire whatsoever. The 3rd PLT was sent in, according to plan, to mop up. They killed every animal they found— sometimes deliberately wounding pigs and water buffaloes, for the pleasure of watching them writhe in agony. Hootches were set on fire, and grenades thrown into holes in the ground.

Two wounded children, with an estimated age of five and eight, were seeing running while crying. One soldier shot them both in the chest and shoulders. When asked why he had killed them, the soldier replied: 'Because they were already half-dead.' A man and woman were also shot dead while running down the trail from the village. Some soldiers went around finishing off the wounded; it took three shots to kill one wounded victim with two bullet holes in her back.

After 3rd PLT moved out of their defensive positions around the landing zone, CPT Medina's command group moved across a paddy field and an irrigation gully toward the southernmost portion of the village. At one point CPT Medina fired twice and wounded a woman holding a small wicker basket in a paddy. CPT Medina approached the injured woman, searched the wicker basket, found syringes and other medical supplies, and then proceeded to shoot her twice in the head.

CPT Medina entered the hamlet and shortly thereafter was confronted, near a pile of bodies, by a Vietnamese SGT (an interpreter). The Vietnamese SGT confronted CPT Medina as to why so many civilians had been killed. CPT Medina replied: 'Sergeant Minh, don't ask anything—those were the orders.' It was evident that CPT Medina's control over his soldiers had been negligible from the time he first landed.

1100 LTC Barker was notified by his tactical operations center that several pilots had reported to their company commander that innocent civilians were being murdered. LTC Barker quickly notified by radio his executive officer, who had been flying over the battle zone, with instructions to find out what was happening, and that if the reports were true to get it stopped immediately. LTC Barker wanted assurances from CPT Medina that nothing of the kind had happened. Shortly thereafter, the cease-fire order was issued to 'C' Co.

The dead and dying were seen everywhere. The vast majority of the bodies presented extremely gruesome scenes. In one such scene, a group of seven women aged between 18 and 35, were found lying naked with tiny dark holes dotted all over their bodies.

The My Lai Massacre occurred over a span of four hours. There were from 400 to 500 Vietnamese victims. To this day we do not have an exact figure because of the inadequate investigation(s) initially conducted by the chain of command. Official KIA reported by 'C' Co. = 128. Absolutely no enemy fire had been taken by the soldiers of 'C' Co. The only casualty suffered by 'C' Co. was a self-inflicted accidental wound to the foot (a soldier was attempting to fix a jammed pistol, belonging to another soldier, when it went off). Only three enemy weapons were recovered during the entire operation. The heavy radio traffic that always accompanied a heavy firefight was nowhere to be heard that day.[7]

See Appendix II for the transcript of 1Lt Calley's Court Martial Appeal.

Indoctrination and Training of the American Army

The American way of war in Vietnam, or 'Expend Shells Not Men,' caused a lack of proportionality, as well as violated other targeting principles of The Hague Convention (i.e., unnecessary suffering and military necessity). From the beginning of our involvement in the Vietnam conflict, it had become common practice for patrols, whenever they received sniper fire, to call in artillery strike or air strikes, if available, regardless of the proximity of civilians. More bombs were dropped on Vietnam than on the entire continent of Europe during World War II. Fighter bombers, who were making 400 sorties a day by the end of 1966, along with B–52 raids in the country, dropped around 825 tons of explosives every day.[8]

General DePuy, 1st Infantry Division commander, explained to a visiting emissary from the Pentagon that 'the solution in Vietnam is more bombs, more shells, more napalm … 'til the other side cracks and gives up.' Then Secretary of Defense Robert McNamara is reputed to have claimed that Vietnam was costly in dollars but cheap in American lives. In 1967, an article in *Life* reported that killing a single Viet Cong guerrilla cost the American taxpayer $400,000 (this amount included the price for seventy-five bombs and 150 artillery shells).[9]

Our lavish use of immense firepower, especially from aerial and artillery bombardment, caused indiscriminate killing of civilians. This created an atmosphere where civilian casualties—deemed inevitable and necessary from the conditions of modern warfare—were placed outside moral consideration. Richard Falk, professor of international law at Princeton, stated that My Lai was the logical culmination of the policy that was being pursued: 'It was perhaps an exaggeration and an extreme case, but not discontinuous with the way war was being waged and the climate that was created in the minds of the soldiers as to what was permissible and what was not permissible.'[10]

One journalist reported that 'there can be no doubt that such an atrocity was possible only because a number of other methods of killing civilians and destroying their villages had come to be the rule, and not the exception, in our conduct of the war.'[11]

While many theories were put forth at the time, characterization of the Vietnamese people as 'gooks' and 'slants' during training was a popular theory. Instructors spent many hours during their combat training learning to hate the Vietnamese.[12]

The goal of American strategy in Vietnam was to kill the Viet Cong in such large numbers that they could no longer be replaced. An author-veteran of the Vietnam conflict wrote:

General Westmoreland's strategy of attrition also had an important effect on our behavior. Our mission was not to win terrain or seize positions, but simply to kill: to kill Communists and kill as many of them as possible. Stack 'em up like cordwood. Victory was a high body count, defeat a low kill ratio, war a matter of arithmetic. The pressure on unit commanders to produce enemy corpses was intense, and they in turn communicated it to their troops.... It is not surprising, therefore, that some men acquired a contempt for human life and a predilection for taking it.[13]

General Westmoreland's war of attrition was referred to as the 'meat grinder' in the Pentagon. The logic this policy of attrition required that Viet Cong be flushed out into the open, and in large numbers, so that they could be engaged by American troops. Essentially, the tactical solution to this requirement was the traditional attack mission of the infantry—'search and destroy.' As outlined in the Pentagon Papers, the idea was 'to take the war to the enemy, denying him freedom of movement anywhere in the country ... and deal him the heaviest possible blows.' Given the environment of Vietnam, this often pitted the US armed forces against the Vietnamese civilians. Lieutenant Calley, along with every other officer, quickly grasped 'the protocol of body count culture.' When asked how he arrived at a body count his court martial, Lieutenant Calley replied:

You just make an estimate off the top of your head. There is no way to really figure out exact body count.... As long as it was high, that was all they wanted.... I generally knew that if I lost a troop, I'd better come back with a body count of ten, say I shot at least ten of the enemy, which was pretty hard when you are only fighting one sniper.[14]

Although members of the armed forces were instructed on the Law of Land Warfare, virtually no one received instruction on unlawful or illegal orders, or on when not to obey orders. The instruction on The Hague and Geneva Conventions was minimal, and was about one hour in length. Every soldier received such instruction stateside as part of basic/advanced training. This was supplemented in Vietnam through the inclusion of the more important provisions of the Geneva Conventions in the ROEs, distributed by MACV (Military Assistance Command, Vietnam) in pocket-sized cards, which the Peers Commission ruled as 'nothing short of ludicrous.'[15]

Economic and Political Conditions in the United States

The Vietnam War had a major impact on everyday life in America, and the Johnson administration was forced to consider domestic consequences of its decisions daily. Since there were not enough volunteers to continue to fight a protracted war, the government instituted a draft. As the deaths mounted and Americans continued to leave for Southeast Asia, the Johnson administration was met with the full weight of American anti-war sentiments.[16]

Protests erupted on college campuses and in major cities at first, but by 1968, every corner of the country seemed to have felt the war's impact. One of the most famous incidents in the anti-war movement was the police riot in Chicago during the 1968 Democratic National Convention. Hundreds of thousands of people came to Chicago in August 1968 to protest American intervention in Vietnam and the leaders of the Democratic Party who continued to prosecute the war.

By 1968, things had gone from bad to worse for the Johnson administration. In late January, North Vietnam and the NLF launched coordinated attacks against major southern cities. These attacks, known as the Tet Offensive, were designed to force the Johnson administration to the bargaining table.

The nation's reaction to My Lai mirrored its attitudes toward a war that, by November 1969, had become markedly unpopular. The press properly expressed horror at the revelations, but it also treated My Lai ethnocentrically as an American story. Some blamed the war itself rather than the men of 'C' Company. Many newspapers that opposed the war saw in My Lai added reason to end it as soon as possible. Some also questioned why it took so long for the story to come out. The public judged My Lai similarly. Some of those who still backed the war questioned whether My Lai had happened at all or blamed the media for publicizing it. Others pointed out that the enemy committed atrocities as a matter of policy. Those who wanted the war to end were appalled at the horror and pressed for its termination.[17]

Characterization of the Vietnamese People

The Vietnamese, whether friend or foe, were referred to as 'gooks,' a disparaging term on a par with 'niggers, spics, kikes, etc.' The use of 'gooks,' 'dinks,' 'dopes,' 'slants,' 'slant-eyes,' and 'slopes' was not only systemic, but endemic. U.S. forces of all ranks in Vietnam reflected this casual and unthinking racism. The recorded use of the word 'gook,' the word most commonly used in the Vietnam conflict, can be traced all the way back to U.S. involvement in Nicaragua in 1912. It may have derived from 'gugu,' a term used disparagingly by soldiers and marines for Filipinos during the Philippine Insurrection at the turn of the century. It was widely used in the Pacific during World War II, and again in Korea.[18]

These terms categorized and depersonalized the enemy, and soon they were thought of as something not quite human. The 'Mere Gook Rule' soon developed to rationalize unsoldierly behavior: 'It was no crime to kill or torture or rob or maim a Vietnamese because he was a mere gook.' One soldier captured the pervasive view: 'They're lost. The trouble is, no one sees the Vietnamese as people. They're not people. Therefore it doesn't matter what you do to them.' The psychiatric report indicated that Lieutenant Calley felt he was not killing human beings but 'rather that they were animals with whom one could not speak or reason.' Ironically, Lieutenant Calley's Charge Sheet, which expressed our collective values in the form of law, spoke not of the murder of 'people,' 'persons,' or 'human beings,' but of 'Oriental human beings.' Racism in Vietnam, along with hatred, fear, and revenge, quickly turned into beatings, torture, rape, and murder.[19]

The Peers Commission reported: 'The most disturbing factor we encountered was the low regard in which some of the men held the Vietnamese … considering them subhuman, on the level of dogs.… Some of the men never referred to Vietnamese as anything but "gooks."' Two sociologists wrote:

> When victims are dehumanized … the moral restraints against killing or harming them become less effective. Groups of people who are systematically demonized, assigned to inferior or dangerous categories, and identified by derogatory labels are readily excluded from the bonds of human empathy and the protection of moral and legal precepts.[20]

Captain Medina's dislike for the Vietnamese was obvious, and many times openly displayed. He openly rebuked soldiers who showed any form of kindness. Several soldiers witnessed him beat suspects during interrogations. One soldier reported that Captain Medina once told 1st Platoon that they would have to guard and share their food with any prisoner that they captured and failed to kill. The intent was clear. Lieutenant Calley, who never pretended to like the Vietnamese, absorbed his commander's sentiments like a sponge.[21]

The Tactical Situation in Vietnam

Major Raimondo writes that 'C' Company was fully deployed in Vietnam by the second week of December 1967. Task Force Barker was activated on 1 January 1968 to take over military operations in the Quang Ngai Province (a province that is overwhelmingly sympathetic to the Viet Cong). 'C' Company's first casualty comes from a booby trap on 28 January 1968. The following month, on 25 February 1968, 'C' Company walked into a minefield. Captain Medina kept his head and, after three died and twelve suffered serious injuries, managed to lead his soldiers out. The soldiers of 'C' Company blamed the Vietnamese villagers nearby who failed to warn them of the minefield and booby traps.[22]

Lieutenant Calley, who had just returned from leave, saw the helicopters transporting the dead and wounded. Lieutenant Calley also noticed that, from that point on, the attitude of his soldiers towards Vietnamese children had changed— they no longer gave them candy and kicked them away. According to one account, Lieutenant Calley could hardly restrain his satisfaction when he said, 'Well, I told you so.'[23] Prior to the minefield incident, Task Force Barker had failed on two separate attempts to trap the 48th Local Force Battalion in the Quang Ngai Province. During the second attempt, 'A' Company came under heavy automatic and mortar fire coming from My Lai, the second time in a month that Task Force Barker had encountered resistance from around the hamlet of My Lai. Its company commander is among the fifteen wounded, five other soldiers died.

After the minefield incident, 'C' Company's *esprit de corps* and morale sagged and eventually vanished, and they went down to 105 soldiers. To make matters even worse, on 14 March 1968, Sergeant George Cox—an NCO well-liked and respected by the soldiers of 'C' Company, with a reputation for looking after his soldiers— was killed by a booby trap while on patrol. According to Major Raimondo: 'Since arriving in Vietnam three months earlier, 'C' Company had suffered twenty-eight casualties, including five killed. All the casualties were caused by mines, booby traps, and snipers.'[24]

Both the commissioned and non-commissioned officers of 'C' Company, with the exception of Captain Medina, did not always insist that their orders be carried out. Yet although Captain Medina insisted that his orders be obeyed, many times he acted like one of the boys. Outsiders noticed that relations between officers and soldiers were much more informal and personal than in other companies. Captain Medina did not like Lieutenant Calley and made no effort to hide it; on the contrary, he would at times openly ridicule Lieutenant Calley in front of the soldiers, and regularly called him 'Lieutenant Shithead.' When Lieutenant Calley's point of view was contrary to his, or suggested a different course of action, Captain Medina would sarcastically retort with 'Listen, sweetheart...' Many soldiers in 'C' Company regarded Lieutenant Calley as a joke, and in particular resented his barking and shouting one minute and contrived feelings of concern for them the next.[25]

Living Conditions of the American Soldiers in Vietnam

Food, water, clothing, and personal hygiene functions were not available in the jungles of Vietnam. All meals consisted of canned 'C' rations. The menu and amount of food depended upon how much the soldiers carried on their back. It was the same for water; soldiers had what they carried. During the dry season, water sources were not readily available and each soldier had to carry a minimum of six one-quart canteens to get them through to the next resupply—three to four days later. Without water, personal hygiene was a rare occurrence. During the monsoon season, it rained daily for months and water was plentiful. Bomb craters would fill with water, and the water had to be treated with iodine tablets to make it safe to drink. It was not uncommon for soldiers to water the same fatigues for three weeks or longer. By that time, most are a whitish color from evaporating sweat, stiff and brown from dried mud, and torn throughout. To the young soldiers in the Vietnam jungle, this was a way of life. These conditions contributed to a malady of skin diseases such as boils, ringworm, jungle rot, severe rashes, and infected cuts and lesions. Nobody was spared.[26]

The normal tour of duty in Vietnam was one year. This sensible policy had its disadvantages, one of which was that soldiers were being sent back home just as they were beginning to acquire experience. The result of this rotation policy was that inexperienced soldiers were prevalent, and many times represented the majority in units. Soldiers learn what acceptable behavior is or what actions are appropriate from other soldiers; very few had the experience to set the example that others could follow or to induce others to follow a certain type of behavior. As soldiers did not know each other, group identification was lacking, and behavioral norms broke down more easily and rapidly.

In every type of environment, including combat, group dynamic overshadows individual judgment and causes the individual members of a group to conform to behavior that is deemed acceptable by the group. Individual behavior then mirrors group behavior. Group's standards of behavior become those of the individual. An individual soldier can better influence the group and limit what is their acceptable behavior if he or she has the credibility of experience. This was normally not the case in Vietnam. Units became a collection of troops experiencing constant departures and arrivals. Morale and cohesion suffered because bonding decreased. This rotation policy challenged the universally truism that soldiers fight and die for each other. One author-veteran of Vietnam wrote: 'Personnel were rotated into and out of Vietnam like so many shift workers.'[27]

Abuse of Prisoners at Abu Ghraib Prison in Iraq: 2004

Abu Ghraib was placed on spectacular display when photographs of American GIs proudly humiliating and torturing Iraqi detainees suddenly and surprisingly achieved worldwide media coverage.[1] The shock value of the Abu Ghraib photos lies not in their images of torture during wartime or in prison, but in the apparent patriotic delight of the torturers.[2] In them, we are presented with a seemingly unsustainable contradiction: an image of liberators engaged in torture, and of a democracy acting sadistically in a totalitarian setting. We are confronted with America decentered publicly and unavoidably, its 'imagined community' disrupted by way of a hyper-aggressive patriotism. Simultaneously, we are not surprised at all. Mark Danner identifies the soldiers' actions at Abu Ghraib as 'a logical extension of treatment they have seen every day under a military occupation that began harshly and has grown, under the stress of the insurgency, more brutal.'[3] Slavoj Zizek insists that 'in the photos of the humiliated Iraqi prisoners, what we get is, precisely, an insight into American values,' a 'flipside' to public morality, premised in the obscene, where soldiers perceive torture and humiliation as acceptable.[4] In other contexts, some neo-conservatives express outrage at the outrage itself: war is war after all and prisons house 'dangerous' people.[5]

Washington Post staff writers Scott Higham and Joe Stephens provide details about what happened in 21 May 2004 article titled, 'Abu Ghraib Detainees' Statements Describe Sexual Humiliation and Savage Beatings':

Previously secret sworn statements by detainees at the Abu Ghraib prison in Iraq describe in raw detail abuse that goes well beyond what has been made public, adding allegations of prisoners being ridden like animals, sexually fondled by female soldiers and forced to retrieve their food from toilets.

The fresh allegations of prison abuse are contained in statements taken from 13 detainees shortly after a soldier reported the incidents to military investigators in mid-January. The detainees said they were savagely beaten and repeatedly humiliated sexually by American soldiers working on the night shift at Tier 1A in Abu Ghraib during the holy month of Ramadan, according to copies of the statements obtained by *The Washington Post.*

The statements provide the most detailed picture yet of what took place on the cellblock. Some of the detainees described being abused as punishment or discipline after they were caught fighting or with a prohibited item. Some said they were pressed to denounce Islam or were force-fed pork and liquor. Many provided graphic details of how they were sexually humiliated and assaulted, threatened with rape, and forced to masturbate in front of female soldiers.

'They forced us to walk like dogs on our hands and knees,' said Hiadar Sabar Abed Miktub al-Aboodi, detainee No. 13077. 'And we had to bark like a dog, and if we didn't do that they started hitting us hard on our face and chest with no mercy. After that, they took us to our cells, took the mattresses out and dropped water on the floor and they made us sleep on our stomachs on the floor with the bags on our head and they took pictures of everything.'

The prisoners also provided accounts of how some of the now-famous photographs were staged, including the pyramid of hooded, naked prisoners. Eight of the detainees identified by name one particular soldier at the center of the abuse investigation, Spec. Charles A. Graner Jr., a member of the 372nd Military Police Company from Cresaptown, Md. Five others described abuse at the hands of a soldier who matches Graner's description.

'They said we will make you wish to die and it will not happen,' said Ameen Saeed Al-Sheik, detainee No. 151362. 'They stripped me naked. One of them told me he would rape me. He drew a picture of a woman to my back and makes me stand in shameful position holding my buttocks.'

The Pentagon is investigating the allegations, a spokesman said last night.

'There are a number of lines of inquiry that are being taken with respect to allegations of abuse of detainees in U.S. custody,' Bryan Whitman said. 'There is still more to know and to be learned and new things to be discovered.'

The disclosures come from a new cache of documents, photographs and videos obtained by *The Post* that are part of evidence assembled by Army investigators putting together criminal cases against soldiers at Abu Ghraib. So far, seven MPs have been charged with brutalizing detainees at the prison, and one pleaded guilty Wednesday.

The sworn statements, taken in Baghdad between Jan. 16 and Jan. 21, span 65 pages. Each statement begins with a handwritten account in Arabic that is signed by the detainee, followed by a typewritten translation by U.S. military contractors. The shortest statement is a single paragraph; the longest exceeds two single-spaced typewritten pages.

While military investigators interviewed the detainees separately, many of them recalled the same event or pattern of events and procedures in Tier 1A—a block reserved for prisoners who were thought to possess intelligence that could help thwart the insurgency in Iraq, find Saddam Hussein or locate weapons of mass destruction. Military intelligence officers took over the cellblock last October and were using MPs to help 'set the conditions' for interrogations, according to an investigative report compiled by Maj. Gen. Antonio M. Taguba. Several MPs have since said in statements and through their attorneys that they were roughing up detainees at the direction of U.S. military intelligence officers.

Most of the detainees said in the statements that they were stripped upon their arrival to Tier 1A, forced to wear women's underwear, and repeatedly humiliated in front of one another and American soldiers. They also described beatings and threats of death and sexual assault if they did not cooperate with U.S. interrogators.

Kasim Mehaddi Hilas, detainee No. 151108, told investigators that when he first arrived at Abu Ghraib last year, he was forced to strip, put on a hood and wear rose-colored panties with flowers on them. 'Most of the days I was wearing nothing else,' he said in his statement.

Hilas also said he witnessed an Army translator having sex with a boy at the prison. He said the boy was between 15 and 18 years old. Someone hung sheets to block the view, but Hilas said he heard the boy's screams and climbed a door to get a better look. Hilas said he watched the assault and told investigators that it was documented by a female soldier taking pictures.

'The kid was hurting very bad,' Hilas said.

Hilas, like other detainees interviewed by the military, said he could not identify some of the soldiers because they either covered their name patches or did not wear uniforms. But he and other detainees did know the names of three, including Graner and Sgt. Javal S. Davis, both of whom have been charged and now face court-martial. Some of the detainees described a short female MP with dark hair and a blond female MP of medium height who watched and took part in some of the abuses. Three female MPs have been charged in the case so far.

Hilas told investigators that he asked Graner for the time one day because he wanted to pray. He said Graner cuffed him to the bars of a cell window and left him there for close to five hours, his feet dangling off the floor. Hilas also said he watched as Graner and others sodomized a detainee with a phosphoric light. 'They tied him to the bed,' Hilas said.

Graner's attorney, Guy L. Womack, did not return phone messages yesterday. In previous interviews, he has said that his client was following the lead of military intelligence officers.

Mustafa Jassim Mustafa, detainee No. 150542, told military investigators he also witnessed the phosphoric-light assault. He said it was around the time of Ramadan, the holiest period of the Muslim year, when he heard screams coming from a cell below. Mustafa said he looked down to see a group of soldiers holding the detainee down and sodomizing him with the light.

Graner was sodomizing him with the phosphoric light, Mustafa said. The detainee 'was screaming for help. There was another tall white man who was with

Graner—he was helping him. There was also a white female soldier, short, she was taking pictures.'

Another detainee told military investigators that American soldiers sodomized and beat him. The detainee, whose name is being withheld by *The Post* because he is an alleged victim of a sexual assault, said he was kept naked for five days when he first arrived at Abu Ghraib and was forced to kneel for four hours with a hood over his head. He said he was beaten so badly one day that the hood flew off his head. 'The police was telling me to crawl in Arabic, so I crawled on my stomach and the police were spitting on me when I was crawling, and hitting me on my back, my head and my feet,' he said in his sworn statement.

One day, the detainee said, American soldiers held him down and spread his legs as another soldier prepared to open his pants. 'I started screaming,' he said. A soldier stepped on his head, he said, and someone broke a phosphoric light and spilled the chemicals on him.

'I was glowing and they were laughing,' he said.

The detainee said the soldiers eventually brought him to a room and sodomized him with a nightstick. 'They were taking pictures of me during all these instances,' he told the investigators.

Mohanded Juma Juma, detainee No. 152307, said he was stripped and kept naked for six days when he arrived at Abu Ghraib. One day, he said, American soldiers brought a father and his son into the cellblock. He said the soldiers put hoods over their heads and removed their clothes.

Then, they removed the hoods.

'When the son saw his father naked he was crying,' Juma told the investigators. 'He was crying because of seeing his father.'

He also said Graner repeatedly threw the detainees' meals into the toilets and said, 'Eat it.'

Hussein Mohssein Mata Al-Zayiadi, detainee No. 19446, told investigators that he was one of the hooded prisoners shown in photographs masturbating before American soldiers. 'They told my friend to masturbate and told me to masturbate also, while they were taking pictures,' he said.

Al-Zayiadi also said he and other detainees were beaten and tossed into separate cells.

'They opened the water in the cell and told us to lay face down in the water and we stayed like that until the morning, in the water, naked, without clothes,' he said in his statement.

He also said soldiers forced him and others to perform like animals.

'Did the guards force you to crawl on your hands and knees on the ground?' a military investigator asked.

'Yes, they forced us to do this thing,' Al-Zayiadi said.

'What were the guards doing while you were crawling on your hands and knees?'

'They were sitting on our backs like riding animals,' Al-Zayiadi said.

He said the guards took pictures of the incident.

Al-Zayiadi also described what has become one of the iconic photographs in the prison abuse scandal.

'They brought my friends, Haidar, Ahmed, Nouri, Ahzem, Hashiem, Mustafa, and I, and they put us two on the bottom, two on top of them, and two on top of those and one on top,' he said.

'They took pictures of us and we were naked.'

Another publicized photograph—that of a hooded detainee hooked up to wires and standing on a box—is also described in the statements.

'On the third day, after five o'clock, Mr. Graner came and took me to room Number 37, which is the shower room, and he started punishing me,' said Abdou Hussain Saad Faleh, detainee No. 18170. 'Then he brought a box of food and he made me stand on it with no clothing, except a blanket. Then a tall black soldier came and put electrical wires on my fingers and toes and on my penis, and I had a bag over my head.'

Al-Sheik said he was arrested on Oct. 7, and brought to Abu Ghraib, where he was put in a tent for one night. The next day, he was transferred to the 'hard site,' the two-story building that held about 200 prisoners and contained Tiers 1A and 1B.

He said a bag was put over his head and he was made to strip. He said American soldiers started to taunt him.

'Do you pray to Allah?' one asked. 'I said yes. They said, 'Fuck you. And Fuck him.'' One of them said, "You are not getting out of here health[y], you are getting out of here handicapped." And he said to me, "Are you married?" I said, "Yes." They said, "If your wife saw you like this, she will be disappointed." One of them said, "But if I saw her now she would not be disappointed now because I would rape her."'

He said the soldiers told him that if he cooperated with interrogators they would release him in time for Ramadan. He said he did, but still was not released. He said one soldier continued to abuse him by striking his broken leg and ordered him to curse Islam. 'Because they started to hit my broken leg, I cursed my religion,' he said. 'They ordered me to thank Jesus that I'm alive.'

The detainee said the soldiers handcuffed him to a bed.

'Do you believe in anything?' he said the soldier asked. 'I said to him, "I believe in Allah." So he said, "But I believe in torture and I will torture you."'[6]

See Appendix III for the transcript of Sergeant Graner's court martial.

Indoctrination and Training of the American Army

The motivations that propelled them into the Army recruiter's office were as varied as their backgrounds. Some joined the reserves knowing little about the military except that it could be a ticket to college. Others enlisted for adventure, knowing that duty on the front lines was possible.

The seven members of the Maryland-based 372nd Military Police Company implicated in the abuse of Iraqi prisoners are a diverse band of soldiers: Four men and three women who come from small coal-mining towns and big-city suburbs.

Several of the reservists at the center of the prisoner abuse scandal were assigned to Abu Ghraib precisely because they had experience working in prisons. Ivan Frederick was described by Dan Rather as 'well suited' for his job at Abu Ghraib as a former Virginia corrections officer (along with his wife), described by his warden as 'one of the best.' Charles Graner worked as a guard at a high-security prison in Waynesburg, a former Pennsylvania mining town, home to most of the state's death row inmates (including Mumia Abu-Jamal) and subject to numerous complaints of human rights violations and prisoner abuse. Sgt. Joseph Darby, the Abu Ghraib whistle-blower, testified in Article 32 hearings that Graner had said of the abuse at Abu Ghraib: 'The Christian in me knows it was wrong, but the corrections officer in me can't help but want to make a grown man piss himself.' Specialist Sabrina Harman, a former pizzeria manager, had no explicit ties with prisons, but had hoped to follow her father and brother into law enforcement. She is now charged with taking photographs of naked detainees while they were abused and of having attached electrodes to the fingers, toes, and penis of a hooded prisoner who was then threatened with electrocution.[7]

When soldiers from a Western Maryland military police unit arrived at Abu Ghraib prison outside Baghdad last fall to take up guard duties, there was a problem: they had never been trained in handling prisoners or running a corrections facility. A blistering Army report that details abuse and humiliation of Iraqi detainees also points to training flaws among the soldiers of the 372nd Military Police Company, an Army Reserve unit from Cresaptown, outside Cumberland, and the battalion that they became part of when they reached Iraq.

'I find that prior to its deployment to Iraq for Operation Iraqi Freedom, the 320th MP Battalion and the 372nd MP Company had received no training in detention/internee operations,' wrote Maj. Gen. Antonio M. Taguba, who was assigned to investigate the prison when reports of abuse surfaced. 'The soldiers also were not instructed in the Geneva Conventions, which governs treatment of prisoners,' Taguba wrote in his report. Taguba does not say that inadequate training and poor leadership absolves those he accuses of 'egregious acts and grave breaches of international law.' He also asserts that other soldiers in similar circumstances managed to deal with the alleged shortcomings of their leaders and their training.

'Many individual soldiers,' the general wrote, 'overcame significant obstacles, persevered in extremely poor conditions and upheld Army values.' He also singled out for praise Specialist Joseph M. Darby, a member of the 372nd, for alerting his superiors to the activities at the prison.

When the soldiers mobilized for Iraq, the only training they received amounted to 'common tasks and law enforcement training,' and there was no indication that the 800th Military Police Brigade, which oversaw the 372nd and the 320th, was aware of the deficiencies or asked for more detailed training from military corrections commanders in the Army, the report said. Taguba's details about the lack of training jibe with the comments of family members of the 372nd soldiers.

'He never had any training dealing with POWs,' said Martha Frederick, the wife of Staff Sergeant Ivan H. 'Chip' Frederick, one of the six facing criminal charges. She said that her husband, although a corrections officer at a Virginia prison, had no experience taking part in interrogations. As for military training before going to Baghdad, she said her husband spent about a year on active duty in Pennsylvania, mostly patrolling a base as a military police officer, stopping speeding vehicles, for example, or chasing after kids out past their curfew. Then, several years ago, he had two weeks of drills in Egypt that focused mostly on highway stops, patrolling, and the use of radio equipment, she said.

Among the other soldiers in 372nd was Captain Donald J. Reese, a window-blind salesman before being called to active duty and becoming essentially the warden of the Iraq prison. Private Jeremy C. Sivits, who was charged with conspiracy and dereliction of duty, worked at a McDonald's restaurant in civilian life and was trained by the Army to repair military police vehicles. As a result, the brigade 'relied heavily' on those soldiers who had civilian corrections experience, said the report, with Frederick being among the most prominent.[8]

Economic and Political Conditions in the United States

Since late April 2004, when the first photographs appeared of U.S. military personnel humiliating, torturing, and otherwise mistreating detainees at Abu Ghraib prison in Iraq, the United States government has repeatedly sought to portray the abuse as an isolated incident, the work of a few 'bad apples' acting without orders. On 4 May, U.S. Secretary of Defense Donald H. Rumsfeld, in a formulation that would be used over and over again by U.S. officials, described the abuses at Abu Ghraib as 'an exceptional, isolated' case. In a nationally televised address on 24 May, President George W. Bush spoke of 'disgraceful conduct by a few American troops who dishonored [the] country and disregarded [its] values.'[9]

In the aftermath of the 11 September 2001 attacks on the United States, the Bush administration seemingly determined that winning the war on terror required that the United States circumvent international law. Senior administration lawyers in a series of internal memos argued over the objections of career military and State Department counsel that the new war against terrorism rendered 'obsolete' long-standing legal restrictions on the treatment and interrogation of detainees.[10]

The administration effectively sought to re-write the Geneva Conventions of 1949 to eviscerate many of their most important protections. These include the rights of all detainees in an armed conflict to be free from humiliating and degrading treatment, as well as from torture and other forms of coercive interrogation.[11] The Pentagon and the Justice Department developed the breathtaking legal argument that the president, as commander-in-chief of the armed forces, was not bound by U.S. or international laws prohibiting torture when acting to protect national security and that such law might even be unconstitutional if they hampered the war on terror. The United States began to create offshore, off-limits prisons, such as Guantanamo Bay, Cuba, and maintained other detainees in 'undisclosed locations' and sent terrorism suspects without legal process to countries where information was beaten out of them.[12]

The United States began to employ coercive methods designed to 'soften up' detainees for interrogation. These methods included holding detainees in painful stress positions, depriving them of sleep and light for prolonged periods, exposing them to extremes of heat, cold, noise, and light, hooding, and depriving them of all clothing. News reports describe a case where U.S. personnel with official approval tortured a detainee held in an 'undisclosed location' by submerging him in water until he believed he would drown. These techniques, familiar to victims of torture in many of the world's most repressive dictatorships, are forbidden by prohibitions against torture and other cruel, inhuman, or degrading treatment not only by the Geneva Conventions, but by other international instruments to which the U.S. is a party and by the U.S. military's own long-standing regulations.[13]

Characterization of the Iraqi People

During 2004, the mainstream media consistently reported the war in Iraq in a way that represented the American presence as a democratizing, humanitarian agent, and framed resistance fighters as foreign, malicious, fanatical, and repressive. Under this archetype, those who attack U.S. occupying forces are viewed as 'one of the biggest thorns in the side of the Americans,' as the *New York Times* aptly puts it.[14] Media condemnations of anti-occupation groups take many forms, some implied and others more overt. Some of the main negative and condescending labels used to refer to resistance fighters include 'rebels,' 'militants,' 'terrorists,' 'insurgents,' 'militiamen,' 'anti-American insurgents,' 'rebel militias,' 'radical Shiite clerics,' 'foreign guerillas,' 'redial insurgents,' and 'Saddam Loyalists.'

Soldiers were immersed in the Islamic culture, a culture that many were encountering for a first time. Clearly there are major differences in worship and beliefs, and there is the association of Muslims with terrorism. All these causes exaggerate differences and create misperceptions that can lead to fear or devaluation of a people.[15]

Veterans said the culture of this counterinsurgency war, in which most Iraqi civilians were assumed to be hostile, made it difficult for soldiers to sympathize with their victims, at least until they returned home and had a chance to reflect. 'I guess while I was there, the general attitude was, a dead Iraqi is just another dead Iraqi,' said Specialist Jeff Englehart, aged twenty-six, of Grand Junction, Colorado. Specialist Englehart served with the Third Brigade, First Infantry Division, in Baquba, about 35 miles northeast of Baghdad, for a year beginning in February 2004:

> You know, so what? The soldiers honestly thought we were trying to help the people and they were mad because it was almost like a betrayal. Like here we are trying to help you, here I am, you know, thousands of miles away from home and my family, and I have to be here for a year and work every day on these missions. Well, we're trying to help you and you just turn around and try to kill us.[16]

Much of the resentment toward Iraqis described to *The Nation* by veterans was confirmed in a report released 4 May 2007 by the Pentagon. According to the survey, conducted by the Office of the Surgeon General of the U.S. Army Medical Command, just 47 percent of soldiers and 38 percent of marines agreed that civilians should be treated with dignity and respect. Only 55 percent of soldiers and 40 percent of marines said they would report a unit member who had killed or injured 'an innocent noncombatant.'[17]

American troops in Iraq lacked the training and support to communicate with or even understand Iraqi civilians, according to nineteen interviewees. Few spoke or read Arabic. They were offered little or no cultural or historical education about the country they controlled. Translators were either in short supply or unqualified. Any stereotypes about Islam and Arabs that soldiers and marines arrived with tended to solidify rapidly in the close confines of the military and the risky streets of Iraqi cities into a crude racism.[18] Iraqi culture, identity and customs were, according to at least a dozen soldiers and marines interviewed by *The Nation*, openly ridiculed in racist terms, with troops deriding 'haji food,' 'haji music,' and 'haji homes.' In the Muslim world, the word 'haji' denotes someone who has made the pilgrimage to Mecca, but it is now used by American troops in the same way 'gook' was used in Vietnam or 'raghead' in Afghanistan. 'You can honestly see how the Iraqis in general or even Arabs in general are being, you know, kind of like dehumanized,' said Specialist Englehart. 'Like it was very common for United States soldiers to call them derogatory terms, like camel jockeys or Jihad Johnny or, you know, sand nigger.'[19]

According to Sergeant Millard and several others interviewed, 'It becomes this radicalized hatred towards Iraqis.' This racist language, as Specialist Harmon pointed out, likely played a role in the level of violence directed at Iraqi civilians. 'By calling them names,' he said, 'they're not people anymore. They're just objects.'[20]

The Tactical Situation in Iraq

With attacks on both civilians and American troops occurring almost daily and demands building from Washington to round up insurgents, soldiers at Abu Ghraib were under enormous pressure to produce information that could be used on the battlefield. Yet their sources were dubious—a collection of Iraqi prisoners who did not seem to have much information and who frequently arrived in huge numbers without documentation showing why they had been detained or even who they were.

Interrogators began working in round-the-clock shifts. Many interrogations were held in tents, makeshift wooden structures, and, later, in shipping containers. 'There were interrogations on Christmas Day,' said Sgt. First Class Steven Roberts, a reservist who screened prisoners through the last quarter of the year at Abu Ghraib and is now back home in Utah. 'There was no letting up.' However, despite the arrival of two teams of interrogation experts, special training by interrogators from the U.S. facility for detainees at Guantanamo Bay, Cuba, and a crack-the-whip command, the Abu Ghraib intelligence operation appears to have produced little useful information.[21]

Living Conditions of the American Soldiers in Iraq

Reserve component units do not have an individual replacement system to mitigate medical or other losses. Over time, the 800th MP Brigade clearly suffered from personnel shortages through release from active duty actions, medical evacuation, and demobilization. In addition to being severely undermanned, the quality of life for soldiers assigned to Abu Ghraib was extremely poor. There was no dining facility, PX, barbershop, or MWR (morale, welfare, recreation) facilities. There were numerous mortar attacks, random rifle and RPG (rocket-propelled grenade) attacks, and a serious threat to Soldiers and detainees in the facility. The prison complex was also severely overcrowded and the Brigade lacked adequate resources and personnel to resolve serious logistical problems. Finally, because of past associations and familiarity of Soldiers within the Brigade, it appears that friendship often took precedence over appropriate leader and subordinate relationships.[22] With temperatures rising to 45–48°C (113–118°F) from late June through early September, the lack of enough water and electricity for air conditioning and food storage took a toll on the soldiers.

In addition to poor morale and staff inefficiencies, it appears that the 800th MP Brigade did not articulate or enforce clear and basic soldier and Army standards. The Abu Ghraib and Camp Bucca detention facilities are significantly over their intended maximum capacity, while the guard force is undermanned and under resourced. This imbalance has contributed to the poor living conditions, escapes, and accountability lapses at the various facilities. The overcrowding of the facilities also limits the ability to identify and segregate leaders in the detainee population who maybe organizing escapes and riots within the facility.

6

The Process of Becoming Violent

Since violence, official or private, is learned through violent experience, such parallels are to be expected and should not be surprising. The violent socialization process, Athens found, divides into four stages, which he calls brutalization, belligerency, violent performances, and virulency—the stages are sequential. According to Athens, each stage has to be fully experienced before the subject advances to the next one, a process that can occur cataclysmically in a short period of time or across a period of years. That violence is a choice rather than a compulsion or a release is taken for granted in the military and among police.[1]

Brutalization, the first stage of violent socialization, Athens found to consist of three distinct, but related significant experiences that might occur in any order and at differing times and places:

(a) Violent subjugation: an authority figure from one of the novice's primary groups uses violence or threat of violence to force the novice to submit to his authority by showing obedience and respect.
(b) Personal horrification: the novice witnesses people close to him undergoing violent subjugation.
(c) Violent coaching: to prompt violent conduct, people whom the novice perceives to be or to have been authentically violent instruct the novice in how to conduct himself when confronted with conflict, emphasizing that he has an inescapable personal responsibility to physically attack people who provoke him.[2]

Japanese military recruits began to be subjected to intensive indoctrination in the tenets of *bushido* and Shinto. The tenets of *bushido* and Shinto were used to indoctrinate Japanese military recruits. A culture of extreme brutality was also encouraged within the military itself. If a Japanese colonel was displeased with one of his majors, it would not be unusual for the colonel to strike the offending major a blow across the face to reinforce his reprimand. The major chastised in this way would be expected to strike one of his captains who had incurred his displeasure. This brutality would be passed down the line from the Japanese officers to their own enlisted men who would then be expected to beat each other up. At the end of this chain of brutality were the men perceived by the Japanese to be the lowest of the low, their enlisted Koreans and Taiwanese, who received the worst beatings. The disgruntled Korean and Taiwanese camp guards had no one but the prisoners of war to beat up, and they were viewed by many prisoners as being the most brutal of their guards. The apparent aim of this indoctrination and brutality was to produce fanatics who would sacrifice their lives without hesitation for the emperor. It was also calculated to produce brutal and racist soldiers.

Harsh military discipline had a long tradition in Germany. SS training, as Himmler organized it, was known for its brutality. Even ordinary police training before the war was brutalizing. This was in keeping in the Prussian tradition. All of the *Einsatzgruppen* members who came together in Pretzsch had had intense and brutal training.

The Russian was accustomed to getting along with a minimum of comfort and equipment under climatic conditions that imposed severe hardship. Many units were thrown together with little training. Survival on the battlefield often required luck. Violence would soon become an end in itself for the Russian soldier advancing on Germany. There was no shortage of men in the Red Army those lives had been marked by state violence, whose consciousness was formed in the brutality of civil war. German atrocities on Soviet soil compounded images that had been part of life for twenty years. A kind of wild amorality prevailed along the front, especially among the huge numbers conscripted in the last year of the war. Most of these came from regions that had survived not just German occupation but also the horrors of Soviet invasion back in 1939. These recruits had learned how to survive in an anarchic, brutal world.

U.S. Army training for men during the Vietnam War consisted of approximately eight weeks of basic training (boot camp) in which the soldier were taught 'basic training'—how to shine his boots, fix his bed, perform proper hygiene, shoot and maintain his M-14 rifle (after 1970, it was the M-16 rifle), throw hand grenades, utilize his C-Rations, perform first aid, operate a map and compass (land navigation), how to salute, the rules of war (Uniform Code of Military Justice), how to stand at attention, how to march, in ranks inspection, marching in parade, and graduation. Then, onto his AIT (Advanced Individual Training), usually another eight weeks for infantry. Each MOS (Military Occupational Specialty) was a different length of time. Medical school at Fort Sam Houston might be a six-month AIT course. After his AIT is completed, then two weeks of RVN (Republic of Vietnam) training took place. Shooting his (live rounds) rifle from the hip without bringing it to the shoulder and aiming, running and jumping into and out of the back of an army truck (2½ ton), and firing blanks from his rifle. After arrival 'in country' (South Vietnam), there was another two weeks of RVN orientation, largely consisting of the same type of training. While not as brutal as the training experienced by the Japanese or German soldiers, many Americans were drafted and thrown into an environment that was designed to make them killers. Drill Sergeants constantly reminded the young recruits who the enemy was—the Vietnamese.

The continuous rotations of troops into Iraq began to take a toll on the active force in 2004. National Guard and Reserve units were increasingly be used to supplement the active duty units in combat. Such is the case of the 800th MP Brigade deployed to Abu Ghraib prison. Their lack of proper training and the conditions they experienced at Abu Ghraib contributed to the use of violence by some and the brutalization experience by others. Reviewing the results of the Stanford prison experiment may give us some insight into the performance of the Abu Ghraib guards:

Results: Overview

Although it is difficult to anticipate exactly what the influence of incarceration will be upon the individuals who are subjected to it and those charged with its maintenance, especially in a simulated reproduction, the results of the present experiment support many commonly held conceptions of prison life and validate anecdotal evidence supplied by articulate ex-convicts. The environment of arbitrary custody had great impact upon the affective states of both guards and prisoners as well as upon the interpersonal processes taking place between and within those role-groups.

In general, guards and prisoners showed a marked tendency toward increased negativity of affect, and their overall outlook became increasingly negative. As the experiment progressed, prisoners expressed intentions to do harm to others more frequently. For both prisoners and guards, self-evaluations were more deprecating as the experience of the prison environment became internalized.

Overt behavior was generally consistent with the subjective self reports and affective expressions of the subjects. Despite the fact that guards and prisoners were essentially free to engage in any form of interaction (positive or negative, supportive or affrontive, etc.), the characteristic nature of their encounters tended to be negative, hostile, affrontive and dehumanizing. Prisoners immediately adopted a generally passive response mode while guards assumed a very active initiative role in all interactions. Throughout the experiment, commands were the most frequent form of verbal behavior and, generally, verbal exchanges were strikingly impersonal, with few references to individual identity. Although it was clear to all subjects that the experimenters would not permit physical violence to take place, varieties of less direct aggressive behavior were observed frequently (especially on the part of guards). In lieu of physical violence, verbal affronts were used as one of the most frequent forms of interpersonal contact between guards and prisoners.

The most dramatic evidence of the impact of this situation upon the participants was seen in the gross reactions of five prisoners who had to be released because of extreme emotional depression, crying, rage and acute anxiety. The pattern of symptoms was quite similar in four of the subjects and began as early as the second day of imprisonment. The fifth subject was released after being treated for a psychosomatic rash which covered portions of his body. Of the remaining prisoners, only two said they were not willing to forfeit the money they had earned in return for being 'paroled.' When the experiment was terminated prematurely after only six days, all the remaining prisoners were delighted by their unexpected good fortune. In contrast, most of the guards seemed to be distressed by the decision to stop the experiment and it appeared to us that they had become sufficiently involved in their roles that they now enjoyed the extreme control and power which they exercised and were reluctant to give it up. One guard did report being personally upset at the suffering of the prisoners, and claimed to have considered asking to change his role to become one of them—but never did so. None of the guards ever failed to come to work on time for their shift, and indeed, on several occasions guards remained on duty voluntarily and uncomplaining for extra hours-without additional pay.

The extremely pathological reactions which emerged in both groups of subjects testify to the power of the social forces operating, but still there were individual differences seen in styles of coping with this novel experience and in degrees of successful adaptation to it. Half the prisoners did endure the oppressive atmosphere, and not all the guards resorted to hostility. Some guards were tough but fair ('played by the rules'), some went far beyond their roles to engage in creative cruelty and harassment, while a few were passive and rarely instigated any coercive control over the prisoners.

Results: Reality of the Simulation

At this point it seems necessary to confront the critical question of 'reality' in the simulated prison environment: were the behaviors observed more than the mere acting out assigned roles convincingly? To be sure, ethical, legal and practical considerations set limits upon the degree to which this situation could approach the conditions existing in actual prisons and penitentiaries. Necessarily absent were some of the most salient aspects of prison life reported by criminologists and documented in the writing of prisoners. There was no involuntary homosexuality, no racism, no physical beatings, no threat to life by prisoners against each other or the guards. Moreover, the maximum anticipated 'sentence' was only two weeks and, unlike some prison systems, could not be extended indefinitely for infractions of the internal operating rules of the prison.

In one sense, the profound psychological effects we observed under the relatively minimal prison-like conditions which existed in our mock prison made the results even more significant, and force us to wonder about the devastating impact of chronic incarceration in real prisons. Nevertheless, we must contend with the criticism that our conditions were too minimal to provide a meaningful analogue to existing prisons. It is necessary to demonstrate that the participants in this experiment transcended the conscious limits of their preconceived stereotyped roles and their awareness of the artificiality and limited duration of imprisonment. We feel there is abundant evidence that virtually all of the subjects at one time or another experienced reactions which went well beyond the surface demands of role-playing and penetrated the deep structure of the psychology of imprisonment.

Although instructions about how to behave in the roles of guard or prisoner were not explicitly defined, demand characteristics in the experiment obviously exerted some directing influence. Therefore, it is enlightening to look to circumstances where role demands were minimal, where the subjects believed they were not being observed, or where they should not have been behaving under the constraints imposed by their roles (as in 'private' situations), in order to assess whether the role behaviors reflected anything more than public conformity or good acting.

When the private conversations of the prisoners were monitored, we learned that almost all (a full 90 per cent) of what they talked about was directly related to immediate prison conditions, that is, food, privileges, punishment, guard harassment, etc. Only one-tenth of the time did their conversations deal with their life outside the prison. Consequently, although they had lived together under such intense conditions, the prisoners knew surprisingly little about each other's past history or future plans. This excessive concentration on the vicissitudes of their current situation helped to make the prison experience more oppressive for the prisoners because, instead of escaping from it when they had a chance to do so in the privacy of their cells, the prisoners continued to allow it to dominate their thoughts and social relations. The guards too, rarely exchanged personal information during their relaxation breaks. They either talked about 'problem prisoners,' other prison topics, or did not talk at all. There were few instances of any personal communication across the two role groups. Moreover, when prisoners referred to other prisoners during interviews, they typically deprecated each other, seemingly adopting the guards' negative attitude.

From post experimental data, we discovered that when individual guards were alone with solitary prisoners and out of range of any recording equipment, as on the way to or in the toilet, harassment often was greater than it was on the 'Yard.' Similarly, video-taped analyses of total guard aggression showed a daily escalation even after most prisoners had ceased resisting and prisoner deterioration had become visibly obvious to them. Thus, guard aggression was no longer elicited as it was initially in response to perceived threats, but was emitted simply as a 'natural' consequence of being in the uniform of a 'guard' and asserting the power inherent in that role. In specific instances we noted cases of a guard (who did not know he was being observed) in the early morning hours pacing the Yard as the prisoners slept—vigorously pounding his night stick into his hand while he 'kept watch' over his captives. Or another guard who detained an 'incorrigible' prisoner in solitary confinement beyond the duration set by the guards' own rules, and then he conspired to keep him in the hole all night while attempting to conceal this information from the experimenters who were thought to be too soft on the prisoners.

In passing we may note an additional point about the nature of role playing and the extent to which actual behavior is 'explained away' by reference to it. It will be recalled that many guards continued to intensify their harassment and aggressive behavior even after the second day of the study, when prisoner deterioration became marked and visible and emotional breakdowns began to occur (in the presence of the guards). When questioned after the study about their persistent affrontive and harassing behavior in the face of prisoner emotional trauma, most guards replied that they were 'just playing the role' of a tough guard, although none ever doubted the magnitude or validity of the prisoners' emotional response. The reader may wish to consider to what extremes an individual may go, how great must be the consequences of his behavior for others, before he can no longer rightfully attribute his actions to 'playing a role' and thereby abdicate responsibility.

When introduced to a Catholic priest, many of the role-playing prisoners referred to themselves by their prison number rather than their Christian names. Some even asked him to get a lawyer to help them get out. When a public defender was summoned to interview those prisoners who had not yet been released, almost all of them strenuously demanded that he 'bail' them out immediately.

One of the most remarkable incidents of the study occurred during a parole board hearing when each of five prisoners eligible for parole was asked by the senior author whether he would be willing to forfeit all the money earned as a prisoner if he were to be paroled (released from the study). Three of the five prisoners said, 'yes,' they would be willing to do this. Notice that the original incentive for participating in the study had been the promise of money, and they were, after only four days, prepared to give this up completely. And, more surprisingly, when told that this possibility would have to be discussed with the members of the staff before a decision could be made, each prisoner got up quietly and was escorted by a guard back to his cell. If they regarded themselves simply as 'subjects' participating in an experiment for money, there was no longer any incentive to remain in the study and they could have easily escaped this situation which had so clearly become aversive for them by quitting. Yet, so powerful was the control which the situation had come to have over them, so much a reality had this simulated environment become, that they were unable to see that their original and singular motive for remaining no longer obtained, and they returned to their cells to await a 'parole' decision by their captors.

The reality of the prison was also attested to by our prison consultant who had spent over 16 years in prison, as well as the priest who had been a prison chaplain and the public defender, all of whom were brought into direct contact with our simulated prison environment. Further, the depressed effect of the prisoners, the guards' willingness to work overtime for no additional pay. the spontaneous use of prison titles and I.D. numbers in non-role-related situations all point to a level of reality as real as any other in the lives of all those who shared this experience.

To understand how an illusion of imprisonment could have become so real we need now to consider the uses of power by the guards as well as the effects of such power in shaping the prisoner mentality.

Results: Pathology of Power

Being a guard carried with it social status within the prison, a group identity (when wearing the uniform), and above all, the freedom to exercise an unprecedented degree of control over the lives of other human beings. This control was invariably expressed in terms of sanctions, punishment, demands, and with the threat of manifest physical power. There was no need for the guards to rationally justify a request as they did their ordinary life, and merely to make a demand was sufficient to have it carried out. Many of the guards showed in their behavior and revealed in post-experimental statements that this sense of power was exhilarating.

The use of power was self-aggrandizing and self-perpetuating. The guard power, derived initially from an arbitrary and randomly assigned label, was intensified whenever there was any perceived threat by the prisoners and this new level subsequently became the baseline from which further hostility and harassment would begin. The most hostile guards on each shift moved spontaneously into the leadership roles of giving orders and deciding on punishments. They became role models whose behavior was emulated by other members of the shift. Despite minimal contact between the three separate guard shifts and nearly 16 hours a day spent away from the prison, the absolute level of aggression, as well as more subtle and 'creative' forms of aggression manifested, increased in a spiraling function. Not to be tough and arrogant was to be seen as a sign of weakness by the guards, and even those 'good' guards who did not get as drawn into the power syndrome as the others respected the implicit norm of never contradicting or even interfering with an action of a more hostile guard on their shift.

After the first day of the study, practically all prisoner rights (even such things as the time and conditions of sleeping and eating) came to be redefined by the guards as 'privileges' which were to be earned by obedient behavior. Constructive activities such as watching movies or reading (previously planned and suggested by the experimenters) were arbitrarily cancelled until further notice by the guards—and were subsequently never allowed. 'Reward,' then became granting approval for prisoners to eat, sleep, go to the toilet, talk, smoke a cigarette, wear eyeglasses, or the temporary diminution of harassment. One wonders about the conceptual nature of 'positive' reinforcement when subjects are in such conditions of deprivation, and the extent to which even minimally acceptable conditions become rewarding when experienced in the context of such an impoverished environment.

We might also question whether there are meaningful non-violent alternatives as models for behavior modification in real prisons. In a world where men are either powerful or powerless, everyone learns to despise the lack of power in others and in oneself. It seems to us, that prisoners learn to admire power for its own sake—power becoming the ultimate reward. Real prisoners soon learn the means to gain power whether through ingratiation, informing, and sexual control of other prisoners or development of powerful cliques. When they are released from prison, it is likely they will never want to feel so powerless again and will take action to establish and assert a sense of power.

The Pathological Prisoner Syndrome

Various coping strategies were employed by our prisoners as they began to react to their perceived loss of personal identity and the arbitrary control of their lives. At first they exhibited disbelief at the total invasion of their privacy, constant surveillance, and atmosphere of oppression in which they were living. Their next response was rebellion, first by the use of direct force, and later with subtle divisive tactics designed to foster distrust among the prisoners. They then tried to work within the system by setting up an elected grievance committee. When that collective action failed to produce meaningful changes in their existence, individual self-interests emerged. The breakdown in prisoner cohesion was the start of social disintegration which gave rise not only to feelings of isolation, but deprecation of other prisoners as well. As noted before, half the prisoners coped with the prison situation by becoming 'sick' extremely disturbed emotionally— as a passive way of demanding attention and help. Others became excessively obedient in trying to be 'good' prisoners. They sided with the guards against a solitary fellow prisoner who coped with his situation by refusing to eat. Instead of supporting this final and major act of rebellion, the prisoners treated him as a trouble-maker who deserved to be punished for his disobedience. It is likely that the negative self-regard among the prisoners noted by the end of the study was the product of their coming to believe that the continued hostility toward all of them was justified because they 'deserved it.' As the days wore on, the model prisoner reaction was one of passivity, dependence, and flattened affect.

Let us briefly consider some of the relevant processes involved in bringing about these reactions.

Loss of Personal Identity

For most people identity is conferred by social recognition of one's uniqueness, and established through one's name, dress, appearance, behavior style and history.

Living among strangers who do not know your name or history (who refer to you only by number), dressed in a uniform exactly like all other prisoners, not wanting to call attention to one's self because of the unpredictable consequences it might provoke—all led to a weakening of self-identity among the prisoners. As they began to lose initiative and emotional responsively, while acting ever more compliantly, indeed, the prisoners became de-individuated not only to the guards and the observers, but also to themselves.

Arbitrary Control

On post-experimental questionnaires, the most frequently mentioned aversive aspect of the prison experience was that of being subjugated to the patently arbitrary, capricious decisions and rules of the guards. A question by a prisoner as often elicited derogation and aggression as it did a rational answer. Smiling at a joke could be punished in the same way that failing to smile might be. An individual acting in defiance of the rules could bring punishment to innocent cell partners (who became, in effect, 'mutually yoked controls'), to himself, or to all.

As the environment became more unpredictable and previously learned assumptions about a just and orderly world were no longer functional, prisoners ceased to initiate any action. They moved about on orders and when in their cells rarely engaged in any purposeful activity. Their zombie-like reaction was the functional equivalent of the learned helplessness phenomenon reported by Seligman & Grove (1970). Since their behavior did not seem to have any contingent relationship to environmental consequences, the prisoners essentially gave up and stopped behaving. Thus the subjective magnitude of aversiveness was manipulated by the guards not in terms of physical punishment but rather by controlling the psychological dimension of environmental predictability (Singer & Glass, 1972).

Dependency and Emasculation

The network of dependency relations established by the guards not only promoted helplessness in the prisoners but served to emasculate them as well. The arbitrary control by the guards put the prisoners at their mercy for even the daily, commonplace functions like going to the toilet. To do so, required publicly obtained permission (not always granted) and then a personal escort to the toilet while blindfolded and handcuffed. The same was true for many other activities ordinarily practiced spontaneously without thought, such as lighting a cigarette, reading a novel, writing a letter, drinking a glass of water, or brushing one's teeth. These were all privileged activities requiring permission and necessitating a prior show of good behavior. These low level dependencies engendered a regressive orientation in the prisoners. Their dependency was defined in terms of the extent of the domain of control over all aspects of their lives which they allowed other individuals (the guards and prison stall) to exercise.

As in real prisons, the assertive, independent, aggressive nature of male prisoners posed a threat which was overcome by a variety of tactics. The prisoner uniforms resembled smocks or dresses, which made them look silly and enabled the guards to refer to them as 'sissies' or 'girls.' Wearing these uniforms without any underclothes forced the prisoners to move and sit in unfamiliar, feminine postures. Any sign of individual rebellion was labeled as indicative of 'incorrigibility' and resulted in loss of privileges, solitary confinement, humiliation or punishment of cell mates. Physically smaller guards were able to induce stronger prisoners to act foolishly and obediently. Prisoners were encouraged to belittle each other publicly during the counts. These and other tactics all served to engender in the prisoners a lessened sense of their masculinity (as defined by their external culture). It followed then, that although the prisoners usually outnumbered the guards during line-ups and counts (nine vs. three) there never was an attempt to directly overpower them. (Interestingly, after the study was terminated, the prisoners expressed the belief that the basis for assignment to guard and prisoner groups was physical size. They perceived the guards were 'bigger,' when, in fact, there was no difference in average height or weight between these randomly determined groups.)

In conclusion, we believe this demonstration reveals new dimensions in the social psychology of imprisonment worth pursuing in future research. In addition, this research provides a paradigm and information base for studying alternatives to existing guard training, as well as for questioning the basic operating principles on which penal institutions rest. If our mock prison could generate the extent of pathology it did in such a short time, then the punishment of being imprisoned in a real prison does not 'fit the crime' for most prisoners-indeed, it far exceeds it! Moreover, since both prisoners and guards are locked into a dynamic, symbiotic relationship which is destructive to their human nature, guards are also society's prisoners.[3]

Brutalization is an obvious and traumatic experience, Athens observes. It leaves the novice shaken, deeply troubled, and confused. Breaking down a recruit's identity is the purpose of military basic training. Moving into belligerency, the second stage of violent socialization, the novice questions his previous values. Brooding over his brutalization experiences, he comes to focus on his personal performance and responsibly, finally identifying the specific question he has to answer: what can I do to stop other people from violently subjugating me and people I value? When people have undergone social trauma and fragmentation, they seek guidance from others who successfully overcome comparable experiences.

The members of all the military organizations studied had plenty of violence coaches to provide guidance. From national policy, basic training instructors through their unit leaders, violence against the enemy was a prevalent theme with all the organizations studied. Struck by his insight, which takes on the force of personal revelation, and convinced of its correctness, the new belligerent subject

Japanese army recruits at a bayonet drill, practicing on Chinese prisoners. (*Look Magazine*)

Chinese women raped by Japanese soldiers. (*U.S. Army Signal Corps*)

Left: Japanese soldier prepares to cut off the head of a Chinese soldier. (*David McCormack*)

Below: Japanese soldiers bayoneting Chinese soldiers. (*David McCormack*)

The execution of Polish hostages in retaliation for an attack on a Nazi police station by the underground organization. (*U.S. Holocaust Memorial Museum Photo Archives*)

Einsatzgruppen soldiers execute Jews on the Eastern Front. (*Bundesarchiv*)

Execution of Jews from Kiev near Ivangorod in 1942. (*Historiek.net*)

Einsatzgruppen soldier executes a prisoner in Ukraine. (*The Jewish Chronicle*)

Captured prisoners on the Eastern Front. (*U.S. National Archives and Records Administration*)

Questioning Jewish leaders. (*U.S. National Archives and Records Administration*)

German women collecting potatoes. (*Keystone/Getty images*)

A German woman
raped and killed.
(*Images in History*)

A Soviet soldier out walking with his German girlfriend, watched by American GIs, Berlin, 1945. (*Hulton-Deutsch Collection/CORBIS*)

Russian troops pose in front of the Reichstag. (*Evgeny Khaldel TASS*)

Soldiers and civilians on the move in Berlin. (*U.S. National Archives and Records Administration*)

German women raped and killed by Russian soldiers.
(*U.S. National Archives and Records Administration*)

Russian soldiers bothering women in Berlin. (*Bildarchiv Preussischer Kulturbesitz*)

Russian soldiers looking for women hiding in train station. (*Russian State Archives*)

Unidentified Vietnamese bodies on road after My Lai massacre.
(*Library of Congress, Military Legal Resources*)

Vietnamese women and children in My Lai before being killed, 16 March 1968. (*Library of Congress, Military Legal Resources*)

An American soldier burning down a hut in My Lai village. (*Vietnam War Memories*)

My Lai villagers being questioned.
(*Boston Globe*)

Above: 'C' Company arrives near My Lai village. (*AP Photo/Horst Faas*)

Left: Soldier looks on at dead My Lai villagers. (*U.S. Army Photo*)

Specialist Sabrina Harman posing over the body of detainee Manadel s-Jamadi in Abu Ghraib prison. (*ABC News*)

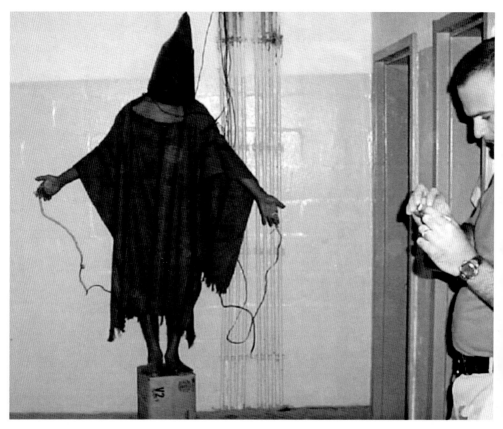

An unidentified Abu Ghraib detainee seen in a 2003 photo. (*Associated Press*)

Soldiers relax under the thin cover of bamboo in Vietnam. (*Boston Globe*)

Charles Graner, American guard, abusing prisoners at Abu Ghraib prison. (*New York Daily News*)

Prisoner being threatened with dog at Abu Ghraib. (*Associated Press*)

A prisoner, forced to wear a bag over his head, stands with guard John Loftus during the Stanford Prison Experiment. (*Duke Downey, The Chronicle*)

now firmly resolves to resort to violence in his future relations with people. The subject is prepared to use violence defensively, to protect himself or the people he values against imminent danger.[4] This can be actual or perceived danger.

The final components of violent socialization constitute stage four, virulency. However personally satisfied a violent performer may be with his defensive victories, they will not change this fundamental view of himself, his self-conception, his identity, unless other people acknowledge them and demonstrate their full significance to him by their actions. Athens explains.

> When people learn of a successful violent performance by someone whom they previously judged not to be violent, they act differently toward him. They begin treating him as if he were dangerous. For the first time, the subject keenly senses genuine trepidation when he approaches people. These heady experiences of violent notoriety, especially when combined with his painful memories of feeling powerless and inadequate during the brutalization and belligerency stages, encourage the subject to believe that violence works.[5]

Once the members reached this point, they were firmly resolved to attack people physically for the slightest or no provocation whatsoever.

One factor must be made clear regarding the average soldier studied and his participation in what may be deemed atrocities. Men who are fighting for their lives, especially against a cloaked enemy hiding among the local population, uncertain as to their duty and without proper leadership and guidance seldom take the time to disseminate between friendly and hostile indigenous personnel. Regardless of the individual's thoughts and beliefs, it mattered very little.

For example, some detrimental factors facing the *Einsatzgruppen* soldier were the propaganda issues, as well as the fact that the primitive living conditions of the average peasant and the seemingly endless numbers of non-European races impressed upon the Germans their own sense on cultural and ethnic superiority.[6] The German was also psychologically unprepared for what awaited him. He was subjected to many varieties of friendly propaganda, although all forms continued to purport his racial superiority. One day, he may hear that all of the sub-humans must be relocated further east, especially Jews. Later he would hear that they must be eradicated, eliminated from potentially poisoning the pure German blood supply that they were deemed to be a biological threat to the German people. He would also be told that not all Russians were Communists, and that the German crusade was established to free the Russians from Bolshevism, while at the same time condemning all Russians for supporting the Bolsheviks, while the Jews supported and assisted the powers in Moscow.[7]

The Japanese soldiers in China, German soldiers in Russia, American soldiers in Vietnam and Abu Ghraib, and the Russian soldiers in Germany faced an enemy they also deemed to be sub-human. Many of these soldiers progressed through the stages necessary to become a violent criminal, capable of committing an atrocity. Some made the transition quickly while others took longer to become violent actors. Fortunately, most soldiers in these groups did not completely transition into the violent criminals described herein. Lonnie Athens notes:

> Although this new theory explains the creation of dangerous violent criminals as taking place through the passage of these four stages, the mere entrance into any one stage does not guarantee the completion of that stage, much less the completion of the process as a whole.[8]

7

Conclusion

The stories of the five military units, in one respect, are not unique in the study of man's treatment of his fellow man during war. Soldiers, as individuals or in small groups, have committed atrocities in all conflicts, down through the ages. What happened in Nanking was a spontaneous outbreak of incredible violence and brutality, and it says a great deal about the Japanese military and culture at the time that it was allowed to go on for so long. The Germans, by contrast, embarked on a deliberate policy of mass murder, and recruited volunteers to do it. The Russians desire for revenge manifested in the rape and killing of innocent women and children. As the Viet Cong and the North Vietnamese Army grew only in power, the American soldiers grew to hate the Vietnamese more vehemently; this hatred was exhibited through the destruction of their villages, and the rape of their women. Psychological stressors, lack of discipline, and lack of training all came together in the 'perfect storm' that resulted in the actions of the Abu Ghraib prison guards.

While these groups operated in completely different circumstances, what is unique about these groups is the degree of brutality and the similar factors the groups were exposed to. There are empirical reasons that can be attributed to the behavior of these groups. The soldiers that committed atrocities each progressed through Athens' four stages: brutalization, belligerency, violent performances, and virulency.

Indoctrination and training of these groups set up a psychological state in which aggression flowed downward along a hierarchy, with those on the very bottom bearing the full brunt of accumulated anger, anxieties, and frustrations. Within the ranks of the army, of course, those at the bottom were the ordinary foot soldiers. No matter what army the members belonged, there was nothing they could do but suffer the abuse heaped upon them in silence. As members of a conquering army abroad, however, these soldiers were then in a position of superiority over defeated enemy soldiers and civilians. Just as the guards in the Stanford prison experiment, they soon relished their position of power.

The economic and political conditions in each of the group's countries helped foster the attitudes of the respective soldiers. The position of governments and the support for the causes that the soldiers fought for undoubtedly provided, the soldier's mind, the justification for their actions. Most believed they were on the 'right side' of the fight.

The characterization of the enemy and the civilians the soldiers faced as 'sub-human' made it easy for some to carry out the atrocities. By treating a person as an object, rather than a human being, it became easy to become desensitized to the actions. As Specialist Harmon pointed out, 'By calling them names, they're not people anymore. They're just objects.'

The tactical military situation on the ground for these soldiers, often, in very stressful condition, under fire and with little sleeps or food provided the environment for belligerent attitudes to develop. This naturally created contempt for the enemy and for the civilian population who, in many cases, supported the enemy.

The living conditions of some of the common soldier were austere at best. For example, while the *Einsatzgruppen* had it better than the average Army soldier, they were often infected with lice and were exposed to partisan snipers. After Shanghai, the Japanese were on the constant forage for food and water, and were lacking proper clothing. Their miserable existence fostered resentment for the civilian populace, who, in their judgment, were to blame for their condition. The Red Army suffered from shortages of food and ammunition while always under the eyes of their leaders who would just as quickly shot them if they did not push forward. The Vietnam soldiers lived with jungle rot, supply shortages, and the constant fear of attack from a determined and capable enemy. The Abu Ghraib guards felt the pressures of overcrowding, long hours, lack of training, and the demands of interrogation assignments.

It seems clear that, after examining these five military groups, the five factors described permitted the participants to develop into violent criminals and a faster rate than might otherwise take place in general society. Athens talks about a process of violentization that takes place over a period of time and by one entering and completing various stages. While violent criminals are obviously created in any society or any group, the military provides a unique structure in which those who may have a propensity for violence can flourish. It may be that the factors inherent in military training, and especially in combat, can compress the time necessary for a soldier to travel through Athens' stages. Clearly, the soldiers in the groups examined transformed and became the dangerous violent criminal that committed horrific acts. While not all of the soldiers in these groups participated in the rape, abuse, and killing, many did. It may be that if some of the five factors discussed can be mitigated or eliminated; that atrocities can be minimized or even eliminated.

Perhaps one can predict similar behavior from soldiers who are exposed and influenced by these five factors, regardless of the policy of their government.

One cannot help but think that the atrocities of these groups were inevitable, given the combination of the five factors.

Some Policy Implications

I believe that first line of defense against violent acts committed by soldiers is better physiological screenings of potential recruits. Those with a violent past or those with a propensity for violence should be eliminated from consideration for service. While the military has been focused on numbers, equal or greater emphasis must be placed on the quality of the individual. Militaries train people to kill—that is the business of the military. However, the character of the soldier must be an important consideration for service.

The tactical situation and the living conditions of the soldier must be considered when deploying them. Support must be given to providing the necessary supplies and guidance for successful operations. Training must be adequate for the tasks.

The economic and political factors on the soldier's country contribute to the overall narrative. However, when that narrative becomes a consorted effort to promote a country's political views or a specific religion over that of another country or its people, it supports the soldier's negative views of that country and its people.

Of the five factors discussed, perhaps the characterization of the civilian populace as morally deficient is the one factor that, if changed, can have the largest impact on the creation of a soldier capable of violence. Of course, war, by its very nature, is violent. However, by teaching and fostering the idea that the enemy's civilians are somehow less than human or not deserving of protections under the same moral guidance as our own people can only support the idea of treating people as objects. Military trainers, government officials, and the media must differentiate between genuine combatants and innocent citizens or insurgents. Trainers must insure that proper cultural and language training is provided to the soldiers who are sent to strange lands. The media must actively participate in fair and proper characterization of the people who soldiers will be dealing with.

While wars will continue and while atrocities will continue to occur, by understanding the factors that contribute to soldiers' violent actions, policies and procedures can be developed to minimize the creation of violent, dangerous soldiers.

Judgment International Military Tribunal for the Far East, Chapter VIII, Conventional War Crimes (Atrocities) Excerpt

Murder of Captured Aviators

Japanese leaders feared that aerial warfare might be waged against the cities and towns of Japan. One of the reasons given by the Japanese Military for opposing ratification of the Geneva Prisoner of War Convention of 1929 was that such ratification would double the range of enemy planes making raids on Japan in that the crews could land on Japanese territory after completing their mission and be secure in the knowledge that they would be treated as prisoners of war.

The fear that Japan would be bombed was realized on 18 April 1942, when American planes under the command of Colonel Doolittle bombed Tokyo and other cities in Japan. This was the first time Japan had been subjected to a bombing raid, and in the words of Tōjō, it was an awful 'shock' to the Japanese. Sugiyama, the Chief of the Japanese General Staff, demanded the death penalty for all aviators who bombed Japan. Although there had been no law or regulation of the Japanese Government prior to this raid under which the death penalty could be administered, Prime Minister Tōjō ordered regulations issued to be retroactive to the time of the raid which would permit the death penalty to be imposed upon the Doolittle fliers. Tōjō later admitted that he took this action as a deterrent to prevent future raids.

These regulations, which were dated 13 August 1942, were made applicable to 'enemy fliers who have raided' Japan, Manchukuo, or Japanese operational areas 'and have come within the jurisdiction of the Japanese Expeditionary Forces in China.' Thus they were directly and retrospectively aimed at the United States airmen already in the hands of the Japanese in China.

The offenses were air attacks:

1. Upon ordinary people.
2. Upon private property of a non-military nature.

3. Against other than military objectives.

4. 'Violations of war time international law.'

The punishment prescribed was death or imprisonment for ten years or more. Conduct defined as offences 1, 2, and 3 were such as the Japanese themselves had regularly practiced in China. It will be remembered that in July 1939 the Chief-of-Staff of the Central China Expeditionary Force reported to War Minister ITAGAKI that a policy of indiscriminate bombing in order to terrorize the Chinese had been adopted. The fourth, violations of the laws of war, required no such regulations. Their breach was punishable in any event, but, of course, only upon proper trial and within the limits of punishment permitted by international law.

The crews of two of the Doolittle planes, which had been forced to land in China, were taken prisoner by the Japanese occupation forces under the command of Hata. These eight fliers composing the crews were treated as common criminals, being handcuffed and bound. The members of one crew were taken to Shanghai and the members of the other crew were taken to Nanking; at each place, they were interrogated under torture. On 25 April 1942, the fliers were taken to Tokyo and were kept blindfolded and handcuffed until they were inside the Military Police Headquarters in Tokyo. They were then placed in solitary confinement, from which they were taken out and questioned again under torture for eighteen days. At the end of this period, the fliers, to avoid further torture, signed statements written in Japanese, the contents of which were unknown to them.

The fliers were returned to Shanghai on 17 June 1942, where they were incarcerated, starved, and otherwise ill-treated. On 28 July 1942, Vice-Minister of War Kimura transmitted Tōjō's orders to Hata, who was the Supreme Commander of all Japanese Force in China at that time. Tōjō's orders were to the effect that the fliers were to be punished under the new regulations. On orders from the Chief of the General Staff, Hata instructed that the fliers be put on trial. At this 'trial', some of the airmen were too ill to take part in the proceedings, there was no translation of the matters charged, and they were given no opportunity to defend themselves. The trial was a mere mockery. This trial was held on 20 August 1942, when all of the fliers were sentenced to death. Upon review in Tokyo, and on the recommendation of Tōjō, five of the sentences were reduced to life imprisonment and the remaining three death sentences were approved. On 10 October 1942, Hata ordered the sentences to be executed, and reported his action to the Army Chief of Staff. The death sentences were carried out as ordered.

In this manner was begun the policy of killing Allied fliers who fell into the hands of the Japanese. This was done not only in Japan, but in occupied territories during the remainder of the Pacific War. The usual practice was to starve and torture captured aviators before their murder. Even the formality of a trial was often omitted. Where a court-martial was held prior to their being killed, it appears that the court-martial was a mere formality.

As an illustration, we cite the case of two American B-29 fliers at Osaka on 18 July 1945, who were charged with violation of the regulations. Prior to the trial, their case was investigated by an officer appointed to perform that duty, who recommended the death penalty. The recommendation was approved by the Commander of the central Military District and by General Hata, who was at that time the Commander of the Second Army Corps at Hiroshima. The recommendation of the Investigating Officer, with the approval of the Military Commanders, was sent to the War Ministry for final approval; and that approval was obtained. At the trial, the report and recommendation of the Investigating Officer and the approval of General Hata and others were read to the court-martial by the prosecutor, who demanded the death penalty based upon those documents. The accused were asked a few routine questions and the death penalty was imposed. They were executed the same day.

In the Tokai Military District, prior to May 1945, eleven Allied airmen were subjected to trials in which their interests were not safeguarded, sentenced to death, and executed. However, the Commandant of Military Police for Japan considered this procedure imposed an unnecessary delay in the killing of captured Allied fliers; consequently, in June 1945, he sent a letter to each of the Military Police Headquarters Commandants of the several military districts in Japan, complaining of the delay in the disposition of captured Allied airmen, stating that it was impossible to dispose of them immediately by courts-martial and recommending that the Military Police in the military districts dispense with courts-martial after securing the approval of the Commander of the Military District. In the Tokai Military District, twenty-seven Allied fliers were killed without trial after this letter was received. In the Central Military District, over which Hata exercised administrative command, forty-three Allied airmen were killed without having been tried by courts-martial or otherwise. At Fukuoka, eight Allied airmen were killed without trial on 20 June 1945, eight more in the same manner on 12 August 1945, and three days later, on 15 August 1945, the third group of eight. This made a total of twenty-four Allied airmen killed at Fukuoka without being given a trial, after the above-mentioned letter recommending this procedure was sent out from Tokyo by the Commandant of Military Police.

The killing of Allied airmen in the Tokai, Central, and Western Districts of Japan was done by firing squads; in the Eastern District, which embraced Tokyo, more inhumane methods were used. Allied airmen captured in that district were detained in the Military Police Headquarters Guard House, pending a so-called investigation to determine whether they had violated the regulations. This investigation consisted of interrogation under torture in an effort to coerce the victim into confessing to facts that would subject him to the death penalty under the regulations. No less than seventeen airmen died in this guard house as a result of torture, starvation, and lack of medical care. Those who survived this torture were victims of a more dreadful death. The Tokyo Army Prison was located on the edge of the

Yoyogi Military Parade Ground. This prison was a disciplinary barracks, in which were confined Japanese soldiers serving sentences. The prison grounds were small and surrounded by a brick wall approximately 12 feet high. The prison buildings were of wood and were constructed so close together as to occupy all of the ground available within the brick wall except for necessary alleyways and courts. One of the cell blocks was set apart by a wooden wall 7 feet high. On 25 April 1945, five Allied fliers were placed in that cell block; on 9 May, twenty more were added; and on 10 May, twenty-eight others were confined there. On the night of 25 May 1945, Tokyo was heavily bombed. On that night, there were sixty-two Allied fliers confined in this cell block. There were 464 Japanese Army prisoners confined in other buildings within the prison. The wooden buildings of the prison, as well as the highly inflammable dwellings surrounding it, were hit and set on fire by incendiary bombs. The prison was completely demolished; after the fire, it was found that all of the sixty-two Allied fliers had perished. It is significant that none of the 464 Japanese, or any of their jailors, suffered a similar fate. The evidence shows that the fate of the Allied airmen was deliberately planned.

In the occupied territories, one of the methods of killing captured airmen was by decapitation with a sword—at the hands of a Japanese officer. Captured airmen were killed this way at the following locations:

Singapore, Malaya (June–July 1945)
Samarinda, Borneo (January 1945)
Palembang Sumatra (March 1942)
Batavia, Java (April 1942)
Menada, Celebes (June 1945)
Tomohon, Celebes (September 1944)
Toli Toli, Celebes (October 1944)
Kendari, Celebes (November 1944, January 1945, February 1945)
Beo, Talaud Islands (March 1945)
Rainis, Talaud Islands (January 1945)
Singkang, Celebes (July 1945)
Carara, Ambon Island (August 1944)
New Guinea (October 1944)
Totabil, New Britain (November 1944)
Porton Island (December 1943)
Kwajalein Island (October 1942)
Cebu City, Philippines (March 1945)

Another method of murdering Allied fliers was used at Hankow, China, in December 1944. Three American fliers, who had been forced down and captured sometime before, were paraded through the streets and subjected to ridicule, beating, and torture by the populace. When they had been weakened by the beatings and torture, they were saturated with gasoline and burned alive. Permission for this atrocity was granted by the Commander of the 34th Japanese Army.

The cruelty of the Japanese is further illustrated by the treatment of an Allied airman, who was captured at Rabaul on the island of New Britain. He was bound with a rope on which fishhooks had been attached so that when he moved the hooks dug into his flesh. He ultimately died of malnutrition and dysentery.

Massacres

Massacres of prisoners of war, civilian internees, sick and wounded, patients and medical staffs of hospitals, and civilian populations were common throughout the Pacific War. Prisoners of war and civilian internees were massacred in some instances shortly after capture.

A massacre at Balikpapan in Borneo occurred in the following circumstances: on 20 January 1942, two Dutch POW officers were ordered by the Japanese to Balikpapan to transmit an ultimatum to the Dutch commandant in which it was demanded to surrender Balikpapan intact. In case of noncompliance, all European were to be killed. The ultimatum was read in the presence of a Japanese major general and five other Japanese officers to the Dutch officers, who had to deliver it to the commander at Balikpapan. Reply was sent by the Commander of Balikpapan to the Japanese to the effect that the Commander at Balikpapan had had from the Dutch authorities the necessary instructions with regard to demolition, which, therefore, had to be carried out.

When the Japanese approached Balikpapan, the oil fields were set on fire. In an affidavit of an eyewitness, the Tribunal was given a description of the massacre of the white population of Balikpapan, numbering between eighty and 100, who were executed in a cruel manner on 24 February 1942, by being driven into the sea and subsequently shot after some had been killed by having arms and legs lopped off with swords, as is described later.

In this relation, it is interesting to note that there was produced, in this trial, a Foreign Affairs document marked 'Very Secret', containing a 'tentative draft of Japan's policies toward the Southern Regions', dated 4 October 1940, In this draft, it states with regard to the Dutch East Indies: if any of the important natural resources should be destroyed, all the persons connected with the raw material, ten government officials concerned, shall be severely punished as being the responsible persons.

It was of vital importance for Japan to take the NEI oil fields intact. The oil question was a decisive element in the move to the South and the Japanese Government was very much afraid lest, in case of war, the oil fields would be set on fire. Matsuoka gave expression to this fear to von Ribbentrop on 29 March 1941, when he stated: 'If at all avoidable, he would not touch the Netherlands East Indies, since he was afraid that in the event of a Japanese attack on this area the oil fields would be set on fire. They could be brought into operation again only after one or two years.'

In view of this, and remembering the fact that the Japanese Government officially ordered the destruction of all harmful documents, this Foreign Office draft obtains a special significance. Yamamoto, a former high official in the Foreign Office, when asked for the reason why most of the things planned in the 'tentative draft' actually did occur, in spite of the fact that this draft was, according to him, made only by a junior secretary, cynically replied that 'these secretaries were very good students.'

Taking all these facts together, the result justifies the inference that the plan proposed in the draft of 4 October 1940 was accepted as government policy, the more so because a massacre of male personnel also occurred at Blora, apparently in relation to the demolition of the oil fields at Tjepu, Java. Women in this place were not killed, but were all raped several times in the presence of the commanding officer.

Instances of such massacres occurred at the following locations:

Hong Kong, China (December 1941)
Opoh, Malaya (December 1941)
Between Port Sulong and Maur, Malaya (January 1942)
Perit Sulong, Malaya (January 1942)
Katonga, Malaya (January 1942)
Alexander Hospital, Malaya (January 1942)
Singapore, Malaya (February–March 1942)
Pangang, Malaya (February 1942)
Maur, Malaya (February 1942)
Jampong Job, Thailand (December 1941)
Longnawa, Borneo (August 1942)
Tarakan, Borneo (January 1942)
Banka Island, Netherlands East Indies (February 1942)
Kota Radja, Sumatra (March 1942)
Remban, Java (March 1942)
Lembang, Java (March 1942)
Soeban, Java (March 1942)
Tjiatar Pass, Java (March 1942)
Bandoeng, Java (March 1942)
Laha, Ambon Island, Moluccas (February 1942)
Okabeti, Dutch Timor (February 1942)
Oesapa Besar, Dutch Timor (April 1942)
Tatuu Mewta, Portuguese Timor (February 1942)
Milne Bay, British New Guinea (August 1942)
Buna, British New Guinea (August 1942)
Tol, New Britain (February 1942)

Tarawa Island (October 1942)
Camp O'Donnell, Philippines (April 1942)
Santa Cruz, Manila, Philippines (April 1942)

Massacres occurred in this manner in French Indochina in the hostilities against the Free French organizations there. Prisoners of war and detained civilians were massacred at such places as Longson (March 1945); Dinh Lap (March 1945); Thaikhek (March 1945); Tong (March 1945); Tan Qui (March 1945); Loas (March 1945); Dong Dang (March 1945); Hagiang (March 1945); and Tonkin (March 1945).

Citizens of the U.S.S.R. at Hailar in Manchuria were massacred on 9 August 1945. This was done at the instance of the Commander of the Kwantung Army. Those murdered were not charged with any offense, but the reason given for the murders was that they might carry on espionage or sabotage against the Japanese Army.

After the Japanese forces had occupied territory and fighting had ceased, massacres were freely committed as a means of terrorizing the civilian population and subjecting them to the domination of the Japanese. Massacres of this type were committed against the civilian population at the following places:

Shanywa, Burma (1945)
Tharrawaddy, Burma (May 1945)
Ongun, Burma (May 1945)
Ebaing, Burma (June 1945)
Kalagon, Burma (July 1945)
Mantanani Island (February 1944)
Sulug Island (October 1943)
Udar Island (Early 1944)
Dinawan Island (July 1944)
Pontianak, Borneo (October 1943–June 1944)
Singkawang, Borneo (August 1944)
Buitenzorg, Java (1943)
Kava (The 'Koo' Incident) (July 1943–March 1944)
Lautem, Portuguese Timor (January 1943)
Moa Island (September 1944)
Semata Island (September 1944)
Aileu, Portuguese Timor (September 1942)
Nauru Island (March 1943)
Hopevale, Philippines (December 1943)
Alaminos, Philippines (March 1944)
San Carlos, Philippines (February 1943)
Barrio Angad, Philippines (November 1944)
Palo Beach, Philippines (July 1943)
Tigbuan, Philippines (August 1943)

Calbayog, Philippines (July 1943)
Ranao-Pilayan, Philippines (June 1944)
Bogo, Philippines (October 1944)
Barrio Umagos, Philippines (October 1944)
Lipa Airport, Philippines (1944)
Santa Catalina, Philippines (August 1944)
Sitio Canugkay, Pilor, Philippines (December 1944).

There were massacres of prisoners of war and civilian internees or conscripted laborers during the occupation that were committed because they had become starved, diseased, or otherwise disabled and were no longer of use, or for other reasons had become a burden to the Japanese occupation force. Such massacres were committed at the following places:

Chaymoga Labor Camp, Siam (February 1944)
Hsipaw, Burma (January 1945)
Port Blair, Andaman Islands (August 1945)
Kot Tjane, Sumatra (May 1943)
Sibolga, Sumatra (April 1942)
Djombang, Java (April 1942)
Amboina, Ambon Island (July 1943)
Wewak, British New Guinea (May 1944)
Aitape, New Guinea (October 1943)
But, New Guinea (June 1944)
Rabaul, New Britain (January 1943)
Bougainville (August 1944)
Wake Island (October 1943)
In the labor camps along the Burma–Siam Railroad Project (1943–1944)

There were some massacres that were intended to discourage general violation of regulations, such as that at the labor camp on Hainan Island (May 1943) in an effort to prevent smuggling; that at Saigon, French Indochina (December 1943), intended to prevent illegal use of the radio; and that of civilians and prisoners of war at Amboina, Ambon Island (July 1943), where the civilians were killed for giving, and the prisoners for receiving food. In addition those referred to were other massacres and murders, such as that aboard the *Nitta Maru* (December 1941), where American prisoners of war were beheaded, and that on New Guinea, which involved the killing of two American prisoners of war (October 1944). In the latter case, the Japanese officer responsible said, 'I asked if I could get an American prisoner of war and kill him.' The Commander of the 36th Japanese Division promptly granted the request and delivered two prisoners to be killed. They were blindfolded, tied, and stabbed in the back with bayonets, and then decapitated with shovels.

There were massacres perpetrated in anticipation of a Japanese withdrawal or of an Allied attack. These were not limited to prisoners of war, although many prisoners were massacred under these circumstances, apparently to prevent them from being liberated by the Allied forces. Civilian internees and members of the civilian population were also massacred under such circumstances. Massacres of this type occurred in the following places:

Hailar, China (August 1945)
Malacca, Nicobar Islands (July 1945)
Sandakan, British Borneo (June–July 1945)
Ranau, British Borneo (August 1945)
Kuala Belat, British Borneo (July 1945)
Miri, British Borneo (June 1945)
Labuan, British Borneo (June 1945)
Leeluta, Portuguese Timor (September 1945)
Ballah Island (January 1943)
Ocean Island (September 1943)
Puerto Princesa, Philippines (December 1944)
Irisan Area, Philippines (April 1945)
Calambya, Philippines (February 1945)
Panghulo, Philippines (February 1945)
Tapel, Philippines (July 1945)
Barrio Dinwiddie, Philippines (August 1945)

Massacres of this kind were very numerous in Batangas Province of the Philippines. They were committed, among others, at the following places:

Barrio San Indres (January 1945)
Bauan (February 1945)
Santo Tomas (February 1945)
Lippa (February and March 1945)
Taal (February 1945)
Tanauan (February 1945)
Rosario (March 1945)

When it became apparent that Manila would be liberated, massacres of this type were committed all over the city, as well as rape and arson.

We have not mentioned massacres of prisoners of war at sea, to be discussed later, nor those that occurred in 'death marches.' These also we shall mention later. Apart from the massacres already mentioned, there were many individual murders. Many of them were committed in horrible fashion; many were committed in connection with other crimes such as rape, robbery, and arson, while others were committed apparently for no other purpose than to gratify the cruel instincts of the perpetrators.

Some of the massacres call for further description, especially those of patients and medical personnel in military hospitals that were clearly marked with the Geneva insignia and entitled to protection under that convention as well as the general laws of war. During the massacres at Hong Kong, Japanese troops entered the Military Hospital at St. Stephens College and bayoneted the sick and wounded in their beds, and raped and murdered nurses who were on duty there. During the Battle of Northwestern Jehore in Malay (January 1942), an ambulance convoy containing sick and wounded was captured by Japanese soldiers. The personnel and wounded were removed from the ambulances and killed by shooting, bayoneting, and burning alive after being saturated with oil. At Katonga, in Malay (January 1942), an ambulance convoy was fired upon by Japanese machine-gunners. The personnel and wounded were taken from the convoy, tied together, and shot in the back. The Alexandra Hospital at Singapore, Malaya, was captured by the Japanese forces on 13 February 1942. The Japanese troops went through the first floor of the hospital and bayoneted everyone on that floor. They entered the operating room where a soldier was under chloroform undergoing an operation, and bayoneted the patient, the surgeon, and the anesthetist. They then went to the second floor and other parts of the building and removed the patients and medical personnel and massacred them. When the Japanese troops entered Soebang, Java, in March 1942, they removed a nurse and her patients from the Military Hospital and massacred them with women and children of the civilian population. These massacres, in disregard of the laws of war respecting the treatment to be accorded to military hospitals and their personnel and patients, illustrate the attitude of Japanese soldiers and their officers towards the laws of war.

There is a similarity of method to be found in most of the massacres. The victims were first bound and then shot, bayoneted, or decapitated with swords. In most instances, the victims were shot and then bayoneted by Japanese soldiers, who went among the wounded killing those who still lived. In a number of cases, they were gathered on a beach with the water to their backs, or on the edge of a cliff, and there killed.

In some places, even more dreadful methods were employed. At the Manila German Club and at Fort Santiago, the victims were gathered together in a building, which was set on fire, and those who attempted to escape were shot or bayoneted as they emerged from the flames.

In evidence upon the atrocity committed at the German Club in Manila in February 1945, it was disclosed that fugitives took shelter under the club from bombardment and shellfire then proceeding. Japanese soldiers surrounded the club by a barricade of inflammable material, then poured gasoline over this barricade and ignited it. Thus, the fugitives were forced to attempt to escape through the flaming barricade. Most of them were bayoneted and shot by the waiting Japanese soldiers. Some of the women were raped and their infants bayoneted in their arms. After raping the women, the Japanese poured gasoline on their hair and ignited it. The breasts of some of the women were cut off by Japanese soldiers.

A massacre took place at St. Paul's College in Manila in the following manner: approximately 250 people were placed in the building and the doors and windows solidly shut and barred. While so confined, it was noticed that the three hanging chandeliers were wrapped in blackout paper and that strings of light wires ran from inside these wrappings to the outside of the building. Later, the Japanese brought in biscuits, candy, and liquor of some sort, placed them in the center of the room and told the captives that they were safe where they were and that they might have the food and drink that had been brought to them. Accordingly, they went to the food as deposited and within a matter of moments there were three explosions. The covered chandeliers had contained explosives. Many were thrown to the floor and a panic ensued. Japanese outside the building began firing machine guns into it and threw grenades. The explosions had blown out the windows and a portion of the wall, through which those who were able endeavored to escape. Many of these were killed as they tried to do so.

At a prisoner of war camp above Puerto Princesa Bay, on the Philippine island of Palawan, there occurred a particularly cruel and premeditated massacre of American prisoners. There were some 150 prisoners in this camp. They had been told previously by their captors that if Japan won the war they would be returned to America, but that they would be killed if Japan were defeated. Before the massacre, there had been some raiding of the island by American aircraft. In the camp, a number of shallow and lightly covered air raid shelters had been dug. At about 2 p.m. on 14 December 1944, the prisoners were ordered to go to these shelters. Japanese soldiers armed with rifles and machine guns were posted around the camp. When the prisoners were all in the shelters, gasoline was thrown into them from buckets and then this was followed by lighted torches. Explosions followed and those prisoners who were not too badly burnt struggled to escape. These were killed by fire from the rifles and machine guns placed in position for the purpose. In some cases, they were killed by bayonet thrusts. Five only of the 150 survived this dreadful experience. They did so by swimming out into the bay whence, after nightfall, they escaped into the jungle and eventually joined up with Philippine guerillas.

Mass drowning was used at Port Blair, Andaman Islands (August 1945), where the civilian internees were placed aboard ship, then to sea and forced into the water. A combination of drowning and shooting, similar to that employed at Hankow, was used at Kota Radja (March 1942), where Dutch prisoners of war were placed in sloops, towed to sea, shot, and thrown into the water. At Tarakan, Borneo (January 1942), Dutch prisoners of war were taken aboard a Japanese light cruiser, taken to the spot where a Japanese destroyer had been fired upon by them, decapitated, and thrown into the sea.

Massacres Were Ordered

The evidence shows that most of these massacres were ordered by commissioned officers, that some of them were ordered by high-ranking generals and admirals, and that, in many cases, commissioned officers were actually present during their commission—observing, directing, or actually doing the killing. Japanese orders were captured that gave directions for killing Filipinos. The file of orders issued by the Manila Navy Defense Force between December 1944 and February 1945 was captured. It contained this order: 'Be careful to make no mistake in the time of exploding and burning when the enemy invades. When killing Filipinos, assemble them together in one place as far as possible thereby saving ammunition and labor.' Diaries of Japanese soldiers were captured indicating that their owners had been ordered to massacre, and had done so pursuant to such orders. Battle reports of military units and police reports of military police, which were captured, contained reports to superior authorities relating to massacres which had been committed, together with the number of rounds of ammunition expended and the number of victims killed. Prisoners of war from many camps in Japan and the occupied areas have testified that they were informed by their Japanese, Formosan, and Korean guards that they would be killed in case the Allies invaded the locality or if Japan should lose the war. We have referred to cases where these threats were carried out. In one camp, at least, written evidence of an order from higher authority to kill the prisoners of war was found. The captured journal from a camp in Formosa contained an entry showing that a reply had been sent to an inquiry from the Chief-of-Staff of the 11th Military Police Unit of the Kiirun Fortified Area Headquarters regarding 'extreme measures' for prisoners of war. The method to be employed in carrying out these 'extreme measures' was detailed as follows: 'Whether they are destroyed individually or in groups, or however it is done, with mass bombing, poisonous smoke, poisons, drowning, decapitation, or what, dispose of them as the situation dictates. In any case, it is the aim not to allow the escape of a single one, to annihilate them all, and not to leave any traces.' This annihilation was, *inter alia*, prescribed in all cases 'where escapees from the camp may turn into a hostile fighting force.'

A general order was issued by Vice-Minister of War Shibayama on 11 March 1945. The order stated: 'The handling of prisoners of war in these times when the state of things is becoming more and more pressing and the evils of war extend to the Imperial Domain, Manchuria and other places, is in the enclosed summary. We hope you follow it, making no mistakes.' The enclosed summary to which reference was made began: 'The Policy: With the greatest efforts prevent the prisoners of war falling into the hands of the enemy. Further for this purpose carry out a transfer of the place of confinement for those prisoners of war for whom it is necessary.' The Ranau Death Marches, which began at about this time between Sandakan and Ranau in Borneo, to which we will refer presently, conformed of the policy indicated by the order just quoted.

Death Marches

The Japanese Army did not observe the laws of war in the movement of prisoners of war from one place to another. Prisoners were forced to march long distances without sufficient food and water and without rest. Sick and wounded were forced to march in the same manner as the able. Prisoners who fell behind on such marches were beaten, tortured and murdered. We have been furnished evidence of many such marches.

The Bataan March is a conspicuous example. When General King surrendered his forces on Bataan on 9 April 1942, he was assured by Japanese General Homma's Chief-of-Staff that his soldiers would be treated humanely. General King had saved sufficient trucks from demolition to move his men from Bataan to the prisoner of war camp. The American and Filipino soldiers on Bataan had been on short rations and the sick and wounded were numerous. However, when General King suggested the use of the trucks, he was forbidden to do so. The prisoners were marched in intense heat along the highway to San Fernando, Pampanga, which is a distance of 120 kilometers (or 75 miles). The sick and wounded were forced to march. Those who fell by the roadside and were unable to continue were shot or bayoneted. Others were taken from the ranks, beaten, tortured, and killed. The march continued for nine days, with the Japanese guards being relieved at 5 kilometer intervals by fresh guards who had been transported in the American trucks. During the first five days, the prisoners received little or no food or water. Thereafter, the only water available was that from an occasional artesian well or caribou wallow. When the prisoners grouped around a well in an attempt to get water, the Japanese fired upon them. Shooting and bayoneting of prisoners were commonplace. Dead bodies littered the side of the road. Murata, who had been sent to the Philippines in February 1942 by War Minister Tōjō as a civilian advisor to General Homma, drove along this highway and saw the dead bodies along the highway in such great numbers that he was prompted to ask General Homma about the situation. Murata testified that he 'merely saw it; [he] did not complain about it; [he] just asked questions.' At San Fernando, the prisoners were crowded into railway freight cars to be transported to Camp O'Donnell. They were forced to stand through lack of space and many died in the cars from exhaustion and lack of ventilation. It is not clear how many died in this movement from Bataan to Camp O'Donnell. The evidence indicates that there were approximately 8,000 deaths of American and Filipino prisoners. At Camp O'Donnell, the evidence shows that from April to December 1942, no less than 27,500 Americans and Filipinos died.

Tōjō admitted that he heard of this march in 1942 from many different sources. He said that his information was to the effect that the prisoners had been forced to march long distances in the heat and that many deaths had occurred. Tōjō also admitted that the United States Government's protest against the unlawful treatment of these prisoners had been received and discussed at the biweekly meetings of the

Bureau Chiefs in the War Ministry soon after the death march occurred, but that he left the matter to the discretion of the Bureau Chiefs. Tōjō said that the Japanese forces in the Philippines were not called upon for a report on the incident and that he did not even discuss the matter with General Homma when that General visited Japan in early 1943. Tōjō said that he first inquired into this subject when he visited the Philippines in May 1943; at that time, he discussed it with General Homma's Chief-of-Staff, who informed him of the details. Tōjō explained his failure to take action to prevent a repetition of similar atrocities as follows: 'It is Japanese custom for a commander of an expeditionary army in the field to be given a mission in the performance of which he is not subject to specific orders from Tokyo, but has considerable autonomy.' This can mean only that under the Japanese method of warfare, such atrocities were expected to occur or were at least permitted and that the Government was not concerned to prevent them.

Such atrocities were repeated during the Pacific War, which it is reasonable to assume resulted from the condonation of General Homma's conduct at Bataan.

Other Forced Marches

On the march from the port to Koepang prisoner of war camp on Dutch Timor in February 1942, the prisoners suffering from wounds, hunger, malaria, and dysentery were marched for five days with their hands tied behind their backs and were driven and beaten along by their Japanese and Korean guards like a herd of cattle. Similar marches were imposed upon Indian prisoners between Wewak, But, and Aitape in British New Guinea during 1943 and 1944. On those marches, the prisoners who became ill and were unable to keep up with the main body were shot. There was evidence of other similar happenings. Those mentioned show the accepted and common practice followed by the Japanese Army and Prisoner of War Administration when moving prisoners of war from one place to another under harsh conditions enforced by the beating and murdering of stragglers.

The Ranau marches are in a different category. They began early in 1945, when the Japanese feared that the Allies were preparing a landing at Kuching; the purpose of these marches was to remove the prisoners to prevent their liberation. The village of Ranau is in a jungle over 100 miles west of Sandakan in Borneo, on the eastern slope of Mt. Kinabalu. The trail from Sandakan to Renau lies through dense jungle and is too narrow for vehicles. The first 30 miles are marshy and heavy with mud and slush. The next 40 miles are in higher country over short, steep hills. The next 20 miles are over a mountain. The last 26 miles are all uphill and mountainous. Australian prisoners of war were moved along this jungle trail in a series of marches. The prisoners were suffering from malaria, dysentery, beriberi, and malnutrition before they were taken from the camp at Sandakan. The test to determine whether a prisoner was fit to make the march was to beat and torture him to make him stand;

if he did stand, he was considered fit for the march. The prisoners were forced to carry food and ammunition for their guards as well as their own scanty rations. One party of forty prisoners was forced to subsist for three days on this march upon six cucumbers divided among them. Those who fell out of the marching column were shot or bayoneted to death. The marches continued until the first part of April 1945. The trail was littered with the corpses of those who perished along the way. Less than one-third of the prisoners of war who began these marches at Sandakan ever reached Ranau. Those who did reach Ranau were starved and tortured to death, died of disease, or were murdered. Only six out of more than 2,000 who were prisoners at Sandakan are known to have survived. These did so by escaping from the camp at Ranau. Those who were too sick to begin the marches at Sandakan died of disease or were murdered by their guards.

Burma–Siam Railway

A flagrant example of atrocities over an extended period in one area is found in the treatment of prisoners of war and native workmen employed in the construction of the Burma–Siam Railway. Prior to and during the work, prisoners were constantly subjected to ill-treatment, torture, and privation of all kinds, commencing with a forced march of 200 miles to the area under almost indescribable hardships. As a result, in eighteen months, 16,000 prisoners out of 46,000 died.

To further their strategic plans in Burma and India, Japanese Imperial General Headquarters early in 1942 considered the question of communications. The shortest convenient line of communications at that time was through Thailand. It was decided to link the railroad running from Bangkok in Siam with that from Moulmein in Burma, the distance of the gap being about 250 miles (400 km). Thus, communication with the Japanese armies in Burma would be facilitated.

For that purpose, on the advice of Tōjō, it was decided to use prisoners of war, and orders were issued to the Southern Army, then stationed in Malaya, to proceed with the work with all possible speed—November 1943 being fixed as the completion date. Pursuant to these orders, two groups of prisoners were sent from the Singapore area commencing in August 1942; one group, known as 'A' Force, being sent by sea, and the second group, composed of 'F' and 'H' forces, by rail to Bangpong. From Bangpong, they were made to march to the various camps along the line of the projected construction.

Before 'F' and 'H' forces left Singapore, the Japanese general in charge of the prisoner of war administration informed the prisoners that they were being sent to rest camps in the mountains, where the food situation was better, because so many of them were sick and suffering from malnutrition, caused by lack of food and unsanitary conditions in the Singapore camps. He therefore insisted that the sick be included in those to be sent to the labor camps. The prisoners were crowded into railway freight cars without sufficient space to lie down. They had been told that it would not be necessary to carry along their cooking utensils as they would be replaced. However, they were not replaced. Furthermore, the only food furnished the prisoners was thin vegetable stew, and for the last twenty-four hours of the trip by rail, no food or water was available.

After four days and four nights, the prisoners were de-trained and required to surrender their baggage and what cooking gear they had brought, as well as all drugs and medical equipment. They were then required to march 200 miles on foot in two and a half weeks. The march would have taxed fit soldiers, as the route lay over rough jungle tracks in mountainous country. The march was accomplished in fifteen night stages in the rain and mud of the monsoon. The weakened condition of the prisoners, together with the necessity of carrying some 2,000 non-walking sick, made this march almost beyond human endurance. Some of those who became sick or too weak to march were beaten and driven by their guards.

In the camps established along the projected railway, which lay in virgin jungle, no cover was provided; sanitary facilities were almost non-existent, medical care and drugs were not provided, clothing was not furnished, rations were completely inadequate, while the constant driving and daily beating of the prisoners added to the ever-mounting toll of dead and disabled. Those who tried to escape were killed. Other groups of prisoners of war from Singapore followed 'F' and 'H' forces and were accorded similar treatment.

Tōjō told the Tribunal that he had received reports of the poor condition of the prisoners employed on this project, and that he sent the Chief of the Prisoner of War Information Bureau to investigate in May 1943. He admits that the only action that he took as a result of that investigation was to court-martial a certain company commander who had dealt unfairly with the prisoners of war, and to relieve from duty the Commanding General of Railway Construction. However, we find from other evidence that the Commanding General was not removed because of the ill-treatment of prisoners of war. The first Commanding General of Railway Construction, who was in charge of this project, was killed by an Allied air raid. The second Commanding General in charge of the project was transferred because he was too sick to attend to his duties, and because the work was not progressing fast enough for the Imperial General Headquarters. The inspector, who recommended the removal of the second Commanding General, was not, as stated by Tōjō, the Chief of the Prisoner of War Information bureau, but Wakamatsu, the Director of the Third Division of the Army General Staff in charge of transportation and communication. He reported to the Chief of the Army general Staff that the work was not making sufficient progress and recommended that the General in command of the railroad units in Malaya be placed in charge of the construction, and that he be allowed a two-month extension of the date set for the completion of the road.

The court-martial of one company commander was so insignificant and inadequate as a corrective measure—in view of the general disregard of the laws of war by those in charge of prisoners of war on this project and the inhumane treatment to which they were subjecting the prisoners—as to amount to condonation of their conduct. One of the principal concerns of the Government and the Japanese Imperial General Staff in 1943 was that the railway should be completed in time to use it in resisting the advance of the Allied forces, which was making progress in Burma. No concern appears to have been shown for the cost in sick, wounded, and dead Allied prisoners of war caused by the constant driving, beating, torturing, and murdering at the hands of their Japanese and Korean guards and the unsanitary conditions in which the prisoners were required to live and work, and the failure of the Japanese government to furnish the barest necessities of life and medical care.

The lack of proper accommodation, the treatment of the sick, and the inhumane treatment of prisoners engaged in connection with construction of the railway, which is typical of Japanese treatment of prisoners of war, is described by the witness Colonel Wild, who was kept on this project until November 1943. Colonel Wild, who, by reason of his knowledge of Japanese, acted as liaison officer between the prisoners of war and the Japanese officers, visited many of the camps in which the prisoners were kept and had first-hand knowledge of the treatment accorded them. The following extract from his evidence graphically describes conditions:

Q: Substantially, was there any difference between the living conditions and treatment of Prisoners of war in these various camps?
A: None.

Q: Will you describe one of them as an example?
A: When I entered Songkrei camp on the third of August 1943, I went first to a very large hut accommodating about 700 men. The hut was of the usual pattern. On each side of an earthen gangway there was a 12-foot wide sleeping platform made of split bamboo. The roof was inadequately made with an insufficient quantity of palm leaves. which let the rain through almost everywhere. There were no walls, and a stream of water was running down the earthen gangway. The framework of the hut was bamboo tied with creeper.

In this hut were 700 sick men. They were lying two deep along each side of the hut on the split bamboo platform. Their bodies were touching one another down the whole length of the hut. They were all very thin and practically naked. In the middle of the hut were about 150 men suffering from tropical ulcers. These commonly stripped the whole of the flesh from a man's leg from the knee to the ankle. There was an almost overwhelming smell of putrefaction. The only dressings available were banana leaves tied around with puttees, and the only medicine was hot water. There was another hut further up the hill of similar design in which so-called fit men were kept, and one well-roofed and better constructed hut occupied by the Japanese guards.

Q: Was any bedding supplied?
A: None whatever.

Q: What did they have to cover them from the rain?
A: When we first entered these working camps, none of them were roofed at all for the first few weeks. The monsoon had already broken, and during those weeks the men had nothing whatever to cover themselves from the rain except banana leaves. If they were strong enough, each man cut a couple of banana leaves and put them over his own body.

Q: Was any roofing material ever received?
A: In my own camp, if which I was in command, Lower Niki, we got a lorry load of atap palm, which was enough to roof, half the hut in which the worst of the sick were lying. In Niki Camp no atap palm was ever received, but we got some rotten, leaking canvas. In the other four camps, after a few weeks, about enough atap palm was supplied to roof all the huts with about half the amount that was necessary. Again, this does not apply to the Japanese and Korean guards, who always had a proper roof over them.

Q: By the middle of July 1943, that is, ten weeks after you had left Singapore, what was the state of 'F' Force as a whole?
A: We had 1700 deaths by that time, and 700 men out of the 7,000 were going out to work. Of these 700, we British officers considered that 350 should have been lying down sick. The account of the construction of this railway would be incomplete without reference to the treatment of the conscripted native labour employed.

   To supplement the prisoners of war employed on the work, native labourers, Burmese, Tamils, Javanese, Malayans and Chinese were recruited, sometimes on promises of varying kinds, and at others, by force, for labour in occupied areas. In all, about 150,000 of these labourers were employed on the railway work. The treatment given them and the conditions under which they existed were, if anything, worse than those already described. At least 60,000 of the 150,000 died during the period of construction.

We shall deal later in some detail with protests made by the Allies against ill-treatment of prisoners, and shall refer to knowledge of atrocities on the part of the General Staff and the Government. It is, however, pertinent at this stage to refer to the evidence establishing that, before the railway project was begun, the Army was advised of the terrible conditions under which the work would be done, and that the Government had knowledge of the casualties and failed to remedy these conditions.

   In 1942, before the work began, the Southern Army Headquarters was advised of the danger of prisoners contracting the various tropical diseases, and from time to time, the death rate was reported. Confirmation of the knowledge of the danger to the health of the prisoners and the insufficiency of food, shelter and medical supplies is found in a report dated 6 October 1944 from the Chief-of-Staff of the Southern Army to the Chief of the Prisoner of War Information Bureau, reading in part: 'For strategic reasons the completion of the railway was most urgent. Since the proposed site of this railway line was a virgin jungle, shelter, food, provisions and medical supplies were far from adequate and much different from normal conditions for prisoners of war.'

In July 1943, when thousands of prisoners had died or were incapacitated by disease, Foreign Minister Shigemitsu, in reply to a protest, said that the prisoners were equitably treated and that all sick received medical attention. Yet, even according to Japanese figures, within a month of the sending of Shigemitsu's message, the total of prisoners who had died in Thailand alone was 2,909. According to the same source, the death rate had increased enormously month by month, from fifty-four in November 1942 to 800 in August 1943.

In the summer of 1943, Wakamatsu, on his return to Tokyo from his inspection of the area, previously referred to, reported personally to Sugiyama, Chief of the General Staff, that he had seen many cases of beriberi and dysentery and that the quality of the food was not of the required standard.

It is claimed that many of the deaths occurred because the Allied Forces interfered with the regular supply of food and drugs. However, for the very reason of this interference with shipping, the order was given in February 1943 to shorten the terms by which the work had to be finished, by four months. Since that order, the commanders became reckless. POWs were told: men are of no importance, the railroad has to be built irrespective of any suffering or death, or 'the construction of the railway had to go on without delay as it was required for operational purposes, and had to be finished within a certain time at all costs, irrespective of the loss of lives of British and Australian prisoners.'

Finally, we refer to one of the monthly reports, dated 3 September 1943, received by the Prisoner of War Information Bureau from the Prisoner of War Commandant in Thailand, which stated that of a total of 40,314 Prisoners, 15,064 were sick. In view of the practice of forcing beriberi and dysentery cases to continue to work, the number of sick, if these had been included, would have been much greater.

Torture and Other Inhumane Treatment

The practice of torturing prisoners of war and civilian internees prevailed at practically all places occupied by Japanese troops, both in the occupied territories and in Japan. The Japanese indulged in this practice during the entire period of the Pacific War. Methods of torture were employed in all areas so uniformly as to indicate policy both in training and execution. Among these tortures were the water treatment, burning, electric shocks, the knee spread, suspension, kneeling on sharp instruments, and flogging.

The Japanese Military Police, the Kempeitai, was most active in inflicting these tortures. Other Army and Navy units, however, used the same methods as the Kempeitai. Camp guards also employed similar methods. Local police forces organized by the Kempeitai in the occupied territories also applied the same methods of torture.

We will show how the Chiefs of Camps were instructed in Tokyo before assuming their duties. We will also show that these Chiefs of Camps were under the administrative control and supervision of the Prisoner of War Administration Section of the Military Affairs Bureau of the War Ministry to which they rendered monthly reports. The Kempeitai were administered by the War Ministry. A Kempeitai training school was maintained and operated by the War Ministry in Japan. It is a reasonable inference that the conduct of the Kempeitai and the camp guards reflected the policy of the War Ministry.

To indicate the prevalence of torture and the uniformity of the methods employed we give a brief summary of these methods.

The so-called 'water treatment' was commonly applied. The victim was bound or otherwise secured in a prone position, and water was forced through his mouth and nostrils into his lungs and stomach until he lost consciousness. Pressure was then applied, sometimes by jumping upon his abdomen to force the water out. The usual practice was to revive the victim and successively repeat the process. There was evidence that this torture was used in the following places: China, at Shanghai, Peiping, and Nanking; French Indochina, at Hanoi and Saigon; Malaya, at Singapore; Burma, at Kyaikto; Thailand, at Chumporn; Andaman Islands, at Port Blair; Borneo, at Jesselton; Sumatra, at Medan, Tadjong Karang and Palembank; Java, at Batavia, Bandung, Soerabaja, and Buitennzong; Celebes, at Makassar; Portuguese Timor, at Ossu and Dilli; Philippines, at Manila, Nichols Field, Palo Beach, and Dumaguete; Formosa, at Camp Haito; and in Japan, at Tokyo.

Torture by burning was practiced extensively. This torture was generally inflicted by burning the body of the victim with lighted cigarettes, but in some instances burning candles, hot irons, burning oil, and scalding water were used. In many of these cases, the heat was applied to sensitive parts of the body, such as the nostrils, ears, abdomen, sexual organs, and, in the case of women, to the breasts. We have evidence of specific instances in which this form of torture was employed in the following places: China, at Hankow, Peiping, Shanghai, and Nomonhan; French Indochina, at Haiphong, Hanoi, Vinh, and Saigon; Malaya, at Singapore, Victoria Point, Ipoh, and Muala Lumpur; Burma, at Kyaikto; Thailand, at Chumporn; Andaman Islands, at Port Blair; Nicobar Islands, at Kakana; Borneo, at Jesselton; Sumatra, at Palambang and Pakan Baru; Java, at Batavia, Bandung, and Semarang; Moluccas Islands, at Amboina; Portuguese Timor, at Ossu; Solomon Islands, at Buin; Philippine Islands, at Manila, Iloilo City, Palo, Bataan, and Dumaguete; and in Japan, at Kawasaki.

The electric shock method was also common. Electric current was applied to a part of the victim's body so as to produce a shock. The point of application was generally a sensitive part of the body such as the nose, ears, sexual organs or breasts. The evidence shows specific instances of the use of this method of torture at the following places: China, at Peiping and Shanghai; French Indo–China, at Hanoi and Mytho; Malaya, at Singapore; Thailand, at Chumporn; Java, at Bandung, Buitenzorg and Semarang; and in the Philippines Islands, at Davao.

The so-called knee spread was a frequent method of torture. The victim, with his hands tied behind his back, was forced to kneel with a pole (sometimes as much as 3 inches in diameter) inserted behind both knee joints so as to spread those joints as pressure was applied to his thighs, at times by jumping on his thighs. The result of this torture was to separate the knee joints and so cause intense pain. The evidence shows specific instances of this torture being used at the following places: China, at Shanghai and Nanking; Burma, at Tavoy; Andaman Islands, at Port Blair; Borneo, at Sandakan; Sumatra, at Pakan Baru; Moluccas Islands, at Halmahera Island; Portuguese Timor, at Dilli; Philippine Islands, at Manila, Nichols field, and Pasay Camp; and in Japan, at Tokyo.

Suspension was another common form of torture. The body of the victim was suspended by the wrists, arms, legs, or neck, and at time in such manner as to strangle the victim or pull joints from their sockets. This method was at times combined with flogging during suspension. Specific instances of the employment of this method of torture occurred in the following places: China, at Shanghai and Nanking; French Indochina, at Hanoi; Malaya, at Singapore, Victoria Point, Ipoh, and Kuala Lumpur; Thailand, at Chumporn; Burma, at Kyaikto; Borneo, at Sandakan; Sumatra, at Brastagi; Java, at Bandung, Soerabaja and Buitenzorg; Moluccas Islands, at Amboina; Portuguese Timor, at Dilli; Philippine Islands, at Manila, Nichols Field, Palo, Iloilo City, and Dumaguete; and in Japan, at Tokyo and Yokkaichi.

Kneeling on sharp instruments was another form of torture. The edges of square blocks were mostly used as the sharp instruments; the victim was forced to kneel on these sharp edges for hours without relief; if he moved, he was flogged. Specific instances of the use of this method have been shown to us to have occurred at the following places: French Indochina, at Hanoi; Malaya, at Singapore; Andaman Islands, at Port Blair; Moluccas Islands, on Halmahera Island; Philippine Islands, at Davao; and in Japan, at Fukuoka and Omuta.

Removal of the nails of the fingers and toes also occurred. Instances of this method of torture are found at the following places: China, at Shanghai; Celebes, at Menado; Philippines, at Manila, Iloilo City; and in Japan, at Yamani.

Underground dungeons were used as torture chambers at the following places: French Indochina, at Hanoi; Malaya, at Singapore; and in Java, at Bandung.

Flogging was the most common of the cruelties of the Japanese. It was commonly used at all prisoner of war and internee camps, prisons, Kempeitai headquarters, and at all work camps and on all work projects, as well as aboard prison ships. It was indulged in freely by the guards with the approval and often at the direction of the Camp Commandant or some other officer. Special instruments were issued for use in flogging at camps; some of these were billets of wood the size of a baseball bat. On occasions, prisoners were forced to beat their fellow prisoners under the supervision of the guards. Prisoners suffered internal injuries, broken bones, and lacerations from these beatings. In many instances, they were beaten into unconsciousness only to be revived in order to suffer a further beating. The evidence shows that on occasions prisoners were beaten to death.

Mental torture was commonly employed. An illustration of this form of torture is to be found in the treatment to which the Doolittle filers were subjected. After having been subjected to the various other forms of torture, they were taken one at a time and marched blindfolded a considerable distance. The victim could hear voices and marching feet, then the noise of a squad halting and lowering their rifles as if being formed to act as a firing squad. A Japanese officer then came up to the victim and said: 'We are Knights of the Bushido of the Order of the Rising Sun; we do not execute at sundown; we execute at sunrise.' The victim was then taken back to his cell and informed that unless he talked before sunrise, he would be executed.

On 5 December 1944, the Swiss Legation in Tokyo delivered to Foreign Minister Shigemitsu a Note of Protest from the British Government. In that note, Shigemitsu was informed that a copy of a book entitled *Notes for the Interrogation of Prisoners of War*, and issued by the Japanese Hayashi Division in Burma on 6 August 1943, had been captured. The note gave Shigemitsu direct quotations from that book as follows:

Care must be exercised when making use of rebukes, invectives or torture as it will result in his telling falsehood and making a fool of you. The following are the methods normally to be adopted; (a) Torture which includes kicking, beating and anything connected with physical suffering. This method to be used only when everything else fails as it is the most clumsyone. [This passage was specially marked in the copy captured.] Change the interrogating officer when using violent torture and good results can be had if the new officer questions in a sympathetic manner. (b) Threats. (1) Hints of future physical discomforts, for instance: torture, murder, starving, solitary confinement, deprivation of sleep. (2) Hints of future mental discomforts, for instance; he will not be allowed to send letters, he will not be given the same treatment as the other prisoners of war, he will be kept till the last in the event of an exchange of prisoners, etc.… The Government of the United Kingdom has requested that the attention of the Japanese Government be drawn to the foregoing. It recalls that the Japanese Government has recently strongly denied that Imperial Japanese authorities make use of torture. See the letter from SHIGEMITSU to the Swiss Minister of 1 July 1944.

We have no evidence that any caution was taken to stop this practice of torturing Allied prisoners of war; on the other hand, the practice continued to the time of the surrender of Japan, and when the surrender came, orders were issued to assist the criminals in avoiding just punishment for their crimes. In addition to ordering all incriminating evidence in the form of documents to be destroyed, the following order as issued by the Chief of Prisoner of War Camps at the Prisoner of War Administration Section of the Military Affairs Bureau on 20 August 1945: 'Personnel who mistreated prisoners of war and internees or are held in extremely bad sentiment by them are permitted to take care of it by immediately transferring or by fleeing without trace.' This order was sent to various prisoner of war camps, including those in Formosa, Korea, Manchuria, North China, Hong Kong, Borneo, Thailand, Malaya, and Java.

Vivisection and Cannibalism

Vivisection was practiced by Japanese Medical Officers upon prisoners in their hands. There were also cases of dismemberment of prisoners by Japanese who were not medical officers. In addition to the incidents stated below, other dismembered bodies of dead captives were found in circumstances indicating that the mutilation had occurred before death.

There was evidence that at Khandok, a prisoner of war described as 'healthy, unwounded' was treated as follows: 'The man was tied to a tree outside the Hikari Kiken Office. A Japanese doctor and four Japanese medical students stood around him. They first removed the finger nails, then cutting open his chest removed his heart, on which the doctor gave a practical demonstration.'

The captured diary of Japanese, apparently an officer, recorded an incident on Guadalcanal:

26 September
Discovered and captured the two prisoners who escaped last night in the jungle, and let the Guard Company guard them. To prevent their escaping a second time, pistols were fired at their feet, but it was difficult to hit them. The two prisoners were dissected while still alive by Medical Officer Yamaji and their livers were taken out, and for the first time I saw the internal organs of a human being. It was very informative.

A case of mutilation of a living captive—this time not by a medical, but by a combatant Japanese officer—was deposed to from Canagay, in the Philippines:

… A young woman … about 24 years old, was caught hiding in the grass. The officer in charge of the entire patrol tore off her clothes, while two soldiers held her. He then had her taken to a small nipa hut, without walls … and there the officer in charge of the patrol used his saber to cut her breasts and womb. Soldiers held her while the officer did this. At first, the girl was screaming. She finally lay still and silent. The Japanese then set fire to the nipa hut…

At Manila, an eye witness described how his house boy was tied to a pillar. The Japanese then cut off his genitals and thrust his severed penis in his mouth.

Other instances of the mutilation of prisoners in the hands of Japanese soldiers occurred at Balikpapan in Borneo. The incident was related by an eye witness as follows:

I saw a district-officer in uniform and a Police Inspector in uniform. A Japanese officer started a conversation with that district-officer.… I saw that during that conversation that officer was ill-treating the district-officer by blows in his face with the hand, and further with the scabbard over his body.… The Japanese officer, who had started the talk with the (Dutch) district-officer, drew his sword and hewed off both the district-officer's arms, a little above his elbows, and then his two legs at the height of the knees. The district-officer was also taken to a cocoanut tree, bound to it and stabbed to death with the bayonet.… After this, the same officer went over to the Policeman in uniform;… he was kicked and beaten with the hand and with the sword in the scabbard. After this that (Japanese) officer hewed off his arms under the elbow and his legs near the knees; I heard him shout once more 'Gove save the Queen'. With bayonet thrusts and kicks the Policeman was made to stand up, and standing on his leg stumps, he was stabbed to death with a bayonet.

Towards the end of the Pacific War the Japanese Army and Navy descended to cannibalism, eating parts of the bodies of Allied prisoners whom they had unlawfully killed. This practice was not unnoticed nor even disapproved by the Japanese Army. A Japanese prisoner upon interrogation stated: 'On 10 December 1944 an order was issued from 18 Army Headquarters that troops were permitted to eat the flesh of Allied dead but must not eat their own dead.' This statement was confirmed by a captured memorandum upon discipline found in the possession of a major general. In this memorandum occurs the passage: 'Although it is not prescribed in the criminal code, those who eat human flesh (except that of the enemy) knowing it to be so, shall be sentenced to death as the worst kind of criminal against mankind.'

At times, this consumption of the flesh of their enemies was made into something of a festive occasion at officers' quarters. Even officers of the rank of general and rear-admiral took part. Flesh of murdered prisoners or soup made from such flesh was served at meals of Japanese below the rank of officers. The evidence indicates that this cannibalism occurred when there was other food available. That is to say, on such occasions, this horrible practice was indulged in from choice and not of necessity.

Prison Ships Were Subjected to Attack

The Japanese practices in the movement of prisoners of war by sea was in line with equally unlawful and inhumane methods of movement by land. The prisoners were crowded into holds and coal bunkers of ships with inadequate sanitary facilities and insufficient ventilation, and were given no medical service. They were forced to remain below decks during long voyages and to subsist on meager rations of food and water. These prison ships were unmarked and subjected to Allied attack in which thousands of prisoners perished.

The method employed to conserve space was generally as follows; wooden stages or temporary decks were built in empty coal bunkers and holds with a vertical distance of 3 feet between them. The space allotted to prisoners on these temporary decks was an area 6 feet by 6 feet for fifteen prisoners. They were compelled to sit cross-legged during the entire voyage. Space was conserved also by the elimination of proper sanitary facilities. The sanitary facilities provided consisted of buckets or boxes which were lowered into the hold or bunker with ropes and were removed in the same manner for emptying over the side. Drippings from these containers added to the general unsanitary conditions. Many prisoners were suffering from dysentery when taken on board; and their excreta fell freely through the cracks of the wooden stages upon the prisoners below. To save space for the preparation of food, the prisoners were served uncooked food or food that had been prepared before sailing. For the same reason, an inadequate supply of water was carried. To add to the horrible conditions that prevailed, prisoners were not allowed on deck. This method of transportation by sea of prisoners of war prevailed generally during the entire period of the Pacific War. It has been defended as necessary because of a shortage of tonnage possessed by Japan. This is not a good defense, for the Japanese Government was not entitled to move prisoners if it was unable to do so under the conditions prescribed by the laws of war.

This method of transportation was used in August 1942 in moving the first group of British prisoners from Singapore to Moulmein to labor on the Burma–Siam Railroad. It occurred again when the *Nitta Maru* called at Wake Island in January 1942 to remove 1,235 American prisoners of war and civilian internees to Yokohama and Shanghai. In this case, as in others, the prisoners and internees were forced to run the gauntlet of Japanese soldiers in which they were beaten and kicked as they went aboard. It was on connection with this voyage that our attention was first called to the 'Regulations for Prisoners', which were in force aboard prison ships. Those regulations, among other things, provided as follows:

The prisoners disobeying the following orders will be punished with immediate death: (a) those disobeying orders and instructions; (b) those showing a motion of antagonism and raising a sign of opposition;... (d) those talking without permission and raising loud voices; (e) those walking and moving without order;... (i) those climbing ladder without order;... the Navy of the Great Japanese Empire will not try to punish you all with death. Those obeying all the rules of the Japanese Navy, cooperating with Japan in constructing the 'New Order of Great Asia' will be well treated.

On some voyages, the prisoners were crowded into bunkers not fitted with temporary decks and forced to range themselves around the coal so long as standing room remained. On other voyages, highly inflammable cargo was packed into the hold with the prisoners. In addition to the many obvious discomforts and dangers to health to which this method of packing prison ships subjected the prisoners, it made their escape from the ship in case of sinking almost impossible.

The prison ships were often attacked in the same manner as other Japanese ships by the Allied forces who could not distinguish them from other ships. A large number of sinkings resulted and thousands of Allied prisoners of war were lost. It was the practice, in some cases when these attacks occurred, to fasten down the hatches to prevent the escape of the prisoners and to station Japanese soldiers armed with rifles and machine guns with orders to kill those prisoners who might overcome these obstacles and escape from the sinking ship. This happened on the *Lisbon Maru*, which was sunk in October 1942 on a voyage out of Hong Kong with British prisoners aboard. In other cases, the prisoners were shot or otherwise murdered after the sinking and while in the water. This was done in the case of the *Oryoku Maru*, which was sunk on a voyage from Manila in December 1944 with American prisoners of war aboard. The same thing occurred in the case of the sinking of the *Van Waerwyck* in the Malacca Straits in June 1944. This occurred again in the sinking of the *Junior Maru* in September 1944 off the east coast of Sumatra with large numbers of Ambonese prisoners of war and conscripted Indonesian laborers aboard.

Many prisoners of war died on these voyages from suffocation, disease, or starvation; those who survived were so weakened from the ordeal of the voyage that they were unable to labor upon arriving at their destination. This impairment of the ability of the prisoners of war to perform labor caused the War Ministry to issue 'Despatch, Army Asia Secret Order No. 1504' dated 10 December 1942. In that order, it was stated: 'Recently during the transportation of the prisoners of war to Japan many of them have taken ill or have died and quite a few of them have been incapacitated for further work due to the treatment on the way, which at times was inadequate.' Instructions were then given to insure the arrival of the prisoners at their destination in condition to perform labor. The condition of the prisoners transported by sea was not materially improved by the issuance of this order, however; on 3 March 1944, Tōjō's Vice-Minister of War, Tominaga, issued another order to 'the Units concerned,' in which, among other things, he said:

> In the Prisoner of War Administration, the use of prisoners for labor has been stressed heretofore. Although this has directly helped to increase our fighting strength, the average prisoner of war's health condition is hardly satisfactory. Their high death rate must be brought to our attention. In the light of the recent intensified enemy propaganda warfare, if the present condition continues to exist, it will be impossible for us to expect the world opinion to be what we wish it to be. Such will cause an obstacle to our prosecution of moral warfare. Not only that, it is absolutely necessary to improve the health condition of prisoners of war from the standpoint of using them satisfactorily to increase our fighting strength. It should be added that, although efforts must be exerted to utilize spaces on ships in transporting war prisoners, it is necessary that the purport of the Despatch, Army Asia Secret No. 1504 of 1942 be thoroughly understood in handling war prisoners at this juncture.

Members of the Government and many government officials were aware of the effect of these methods upon the prisoners. Such corrective measures as were taken by them, which were totally inadequate, were designed to preserve the ability of the prisoners to perform labor for use in the prosecution of the war, not to insure the enforcement of the laws of war relating to the movement of prisoners of war.

Submarine Warfare

Inhumane, illegal warfare at sea was waged by the Japanese Navy in 1943 and 1944. Survivors of passengers and crews of torpedoed ships were murdered.

Ambassador Ōshima was empowered by the Tōjō Cabinet to discuss the prosecution of the war with the Reich Foreign Minister; although technical questions were to be discussed directly by members of the Mixed Commission, it was Ōshima's expressed opinion that it was of the greatest importance that questions of policy should be discussed exclusively by Ōshima and Ribbentrop, the German Foreign Minister. Ōshima had a conference with Hitler on 3 January 1942. Hitler explained his policy of submarine warfare, which he was conducting against Allied shipping, and said that although the United States might build ships very quickly, her chief problem would be the personnel shortage since the training of seafaring personnel took a long time. Hitler explained that he had given orders for his submarines to surface after torpedoing merchant ships and to shoot up the lifeboats, so that the word would get about that most seamen were lost in torpedoing and the United States would have difficulty in recruiting new crews. Ōshima, in replying to Hitler, approved this statement of policy and stated that the Japanese, too, would follow this method of waging submarine warfare.

An order issued by the Commander of the First Submarine Force at Truk on 20 March 1943, contained this command:

All submarines shall act together in order to concentrate their attacks against enemy convoys and shall totally destroy them. Do not stop with the sinking of enemy ships and cargoes; at the same time, you will carry out the complete destruction of the crews of the enemy's ships; if possible, seize part of the crew and endeavor to secure information about the enemy.

This order for inhumane warfare at sea was followed by the Japanese submarine commanders. Between 13 December 1943 and 29 October 1944, Japanese submarines, after sinking eight British, American, and Dutch merchant vessels in the Indian Ocean and one American vessel in the Pacific Ocean, surfaced after firing their torpedoes, attempted to or did take on board the master of the ship and then proceeded to destroy the lifeboats and murder the survivors.

Repeated protests were made by the Allied governments in which they stated the exact date and position of the sinkings and the details of the atrocities committed upon the passengers and crews of the torpedoed vessels. No satisfactory answer was made to these protests and the sinkings continued without modification of the treatment of survivors.

The action taken by the Japanese Navy in the sinking of the British merchant ship *Behar* by gunfire on 9 March 1944 is illustrative. The cruiser *Tone* picked up 115 survivors. Later in the day, the *Tone* reported the sinking and capture to the flagship *Aoba*. Orders were immediately signaled to the *Tone* from the *Aoba* to kill the survivors. It was later decided to place fifteen of the survivors, including two women and one Chinese, in a civilian internee camp and to kill the remaining 100. On orders of the captain of the *Tone*, these 100 survivors were killed aboard the *Tone*.

The massacre of survivors of the American ship *Jean Nicolet* is another example of methods employed by the Japanese Navy. This ship was travelling from Australia to Ceylon in July 1944, when she was torpedoed at night by a Japanese submarine some 600 miles from land. Her ship's company was about 100, of whom about ninety were taken aboard the submarine. The ship was sunk and her boats were also smashed by gunfire, although all did not sink. The hands of the survivors were tied behind their backs. A few of the officers were taken below and their fate is not known to the Tribunal. The remainders were made to sit on the forward deck of the submarine as she cruised searched for survivors. During this time, some were washed overboard and others were beaten with wooden and metal bludgeons and robbed of personal property such as watches and rings. Then they were required to proceed singly towards the stern between lines of Japanese who beat them as they passed between their ranks. Thus, they were forced into the water to drown. Before all the prisoners had been forced to run the gauntlet, the vessel submerged, leaving the remaining prisoners on her deck to their fate. Some, however, did survive by swimming. These and their comrades whom they kept afloat were discovered the next day by aircraft, which directed a rescuing ship to them. Thus, twenty-two survived this terrible experience, from some of whom this Tribunal received testimony of this inhumane conduct of the Japanese Navy.

Illegal Employment, Starvation and Neglect of Prisoners and Internees

General Uemura, Director of the Prisoner of War Administration Section of the Military Affairs Bureau of the War Ministry, only a few weeks after the agreement with the Allies to apply the provisions of the Geneva Prisoner of War Convention to prisoners of war and civilian internees, advised the Chief-of-Staff of the Japanese Army in Formosa on 2 April 1942 that 'plans [were] being pushed for the use of prisoners of war in production,' and requested an immediate report upon the number that might be utilized for that purpose in Formosa.

On 6 May 1942, the Vice-Minister of War informed the Chief-of-Staff of the Army in Formosa of the policy governing employment of prisoners of war. He stated:

> [It has been decided that] prisoners of war can be used for the enlargement of our production and as military labor, white prisoners of war will be confined successively in Korea, Formosa and Manchuria. Superior technicians and high ranking officers—Colonels and above—will be included among the prisoners of war confined in Formosa. Those who are not suitable for use in enlargement of our production will be confined in prisoner of war camps which will be built immediately on the spot.

On 5 June 1942, General Uemura directed the Chief-of-Staff of the Army in Formosa as follows:

> Although the working of prisoner of war officers and warrant officers is forbidden by the Regulations of 1903, the policy of the control authorities is that under the situation of our country where not one person now eats without working they want them to set to work. It is desired that you give proper orders on this.

These instructions were also sent to all other Army units concerned. This directive originated within the Cabinet, for on 30 May 1942, Prime Minister Tōjō issued instructions to the commander of a division, which had a prisoner of war camp under its jurisdiction. He said: 'The present situation of affairs in this country does not permit anyone to lie idle doing nothing but eating freely. With that in view, in dealing with prisoners of war, I hope you will see that they may be usefully employed.' On 25 June 1942, Tōjō issued his instructions to newly appointed Chiefs of Prisoner of War camps. He said:

> In Japan, we have our own ideology concerning prisoners of war, which should naturally make their treatment more or less different from that in Europe and America. In dealing with them, you should, of course, observe the various Regulations concerned, aim at an adequate application of them. At the same time, you must not allow them to lie idle doing nothing but eating freely for even a single day. Their labor and technical skill should be fully utilized for the replenishment of production, and contribution rendered toward the prosecution of the Greater East Asiatic War for which no effort ought to be spared.

The application of these instructions account, at least in part, for the constant driving, beating, and prodding of the sick and wounded prisoners and those suffering from malnutrition to force them to labor upon military works until they died from disease, malnutrition, or exhaustion. These instructions were repeated on 26 June 1942 by Tōjō to another group of newly appointed prisoner of war camp chiefs and again to another such group on 7 July 1942.

That the Cabinet supported Tōjō in his program to employ prisoners of war to aid in the prosecution of the war is shown by the 'Foreign Affairs Monthly Report' of the Foreign Section of the Police Bureau of the Home Ministry issued for the month of September 1942. The report showed that, due to the labor shortage in Japan, the Cabinet Planning Board, with the concurrence of the Prisoner of War Administration Section of the Military Affairs Bureau of the War Ministry, held a conference on 15 August 1942 at which it was decided to transfer prisoners of war to Japan and employ them to mitigate the labor shortage in the industries in the National Mobilization Plan. According to the report, it had been decided to employ the prisoners of war in mining, stevedoring, and on engineering and construction works for national defense. A complete plan had been agreed upon whereby the prefectural governors, cooperating with the Welfare Ministry and the Army, would take charge of the supervision of the prisoners of war and their employment. With members of the Government, Hoshino and Suzuki participated in this decision. Hoshino had been selected as Chief Secretary of the Cabinet by Tōjō because of his long experience in economic planning and had been charged by Tōjō to devote his main efforts to such activities in cooperation with Suzuki, who he had selected to head the Cabinet Planning Bureau. Hoshino became Chief Secretary of the Cabinet on 18 October 1941 and served until the fall of the Tōjō Cabinet on 19 July 1944. Suzuki became a Councilor of the Planning Bureau on 30 May 1939, and when Hoshino was relieved as President of the Cabinet Planning Bureau and as Minister without Portfolio on 4 April 1941, Suzuki succeeded him and continued to serve as minister without Portfolio and President of the Cabinet Planning Bureau in the Third Konoye Cabinet and the Tōjō Cabinet until the Tōjō Cabinet resigned on 19 July 1944.

Consideration for Racial Needs: Food and Clothing

The Japanese Government promised early in 1942 to take into consideration the national customs and racial habits of the prisoners of war and civilian internees in supplying them with food and clothing. This was never done. Regulations in force at the time this promise was made required that camp commandants in supplying prisoners of war and internees with food and clothing should be guided by the Table of Basic Allowances governing the supply of the Army. The commandants were authorized to determine the amount of the allowance to be made to the inmates of the camps, but were directed to make such determination within the limits prescribed in the Table of Allowances. These regulations, insofar as they affected diet, were interpreted as forbidding the prisoners and internees sufficient food, even when other food existed in the vicinity of the camps. This rule was followed even when the inmates of the camps were dying in large numbers from malnutrition. The amount and kind of food prescribed by the Table of Allowances was not materially changed during the war, except to reduce the amount prescribed, although it soon became apparent to those in command that, due to different national dietary customs and habits, the prisoners and internees could not subsist on the food supplied. On 29 October 1942, orders were issued to all camp commandants that 'in view of the consumption of rice and barley by workers in heavy industries in Japan,' the ration for prisoners of war and civilian internees who were officers or civil officials should be cut so as not to exceed 420 grams per day. In January 1944, this ration of rice was further cut to a maximum of 390 grams per day. As the inmates of the camps began to suffer from malnutrition, they fell easy prey to disease and were quickly exhausted by the heavy labor forced upon them. Regardless of this, the commandants of the camps enforced Tōjō's instructions that those who did not labor should not eat, and still further reduced the ration—in some cases, they withdrew it entirely from those who were unable to labor because of illness or injury.

The regulations provided that the prisoners of war and civilian internees should war the clothing formerly worn by them—that is to say, the clothing they were wearing when captured or interned. This regulation was enforced by the camp commandants with the result that in many of the camps the inmates were in rags before the war ended. It is true that the regulation allowed the camp commandants to lend certain items of clothing in cases where the clothing formerly worn by the prisoners or internees was unfit, but this appears to have been used only in rare cases.

Consideration for Racial Needs: Medical Supplies

The Japanese Army and Navy were required by their regulations to keep on hand and in storage a supply of medicine and medical equipment sufficient for one year's use. This was done in many instances by confiscating Red Cross drugs and medical supplies, but the supplies were kept in storage or used mostly for the benefit of Japanese troops and camp guards. The prisoners of war and civilian internees were rarely furnished medicines and equipment from these warehouses. At the time of surrender, large quantities of these supplies were found stored in and around prisoner of war and civilian internee camps in which prisoners and internees had been dying at an alarming rate for lack of such supplies.

Suzuki, Kunki (who served as a staff officer of the Eastern Military district on Honshu Island under Doihara), and other commanders testified before this Tribunal. Suzuki admitted that he authorized chiefs of camps and guards at the detention camps in his district to confiscate Red Cross parcels intended for prisoners of war. The evidence shows that this was common practice at the camps located in Japan as well as in Japan's overseas possessions and in the occupied territories. Incidentally, Suzuki also admitted that he knew that his guards were beating and otherwise ill-treating the prisoners.

Failure to afford adequate or any medical supplies to the prisoners of war and civilian internees was common in all theatres of war and contributed to the deaths of thousands of prisoners and internees.

Consideration for Racial Needs: Housing

The regulations provided that Army buildings, temples, and other existing buildings should be used as prisoner of war and internee camps. The regulations also provided that employers using prisoner of war and civilian internees in war production should furnish necessary shelter for them. Nevertheless, the housing provided was in many instances inadequate as cover or insanitary or both. The Japanese adjutant at the Kanburi camp in Siam opened a hospital for the sick prisoners of war in a group of approximately twenty empty huts, which had been evacuated shortly before by a Japanese cavalry regiment that had been using the huts as stables. Atap huts with dirt floors furnished the only shelter available in most of the camps located on islands in the Pacific and along the Burma–Siam Railway. It was common practice to build these camps with the labor of the prisoners of war who were to occupy them and to force the prisoners to live in the open, exposed to the weather until the huts were completed. However, in some instances, the prisoners were spared the labor of construction by moving them into atap huts camps, which had been depopulated by epidemics; this was the case at the 60-kilometer camp on the Burma–Siam Railway project, where approximately 800 Australian prisoners of war were quartered in the huts recently occupied by Burmese laborers who had died of cholera. A former Javanese labor camp at Lahat, Molucca Islands, was converted into a prisoner of war camp in August 1944. When the Dutch and British prisoners of war arrived at the camp, they found it filled with dead bodies of Javanese. Kimura, as Vice-Minister of War, when informed that Itagaki was planning to quarter 1,000 British and 1,000 American prisoners of war in three theological schools in Korea, inquired if the buildings scheduled for accommodation of the prisoners of war were not too good for them.

Consideration for Racial Needs: Work

The policy of the Japanese Government was to use prisoners of war and civilian internees to do work directly related to war operations. In the theater of operations they were used to construct military air fields, roads, railroads, docks, and other military works, and as stevedores to load and unload military supplies. In the overseas possessions and in Japan, they were forced, in addition to the foregoing work, to labor in mines, in munitions and aircraft factories, and in other projects bearing a direct relation to war operations. As a general rule, the camps in which the prisoners of war and civilian internees were detained were located near the place of employment without regard to their safety; in consequence, they were subjected to unnecessary danger from air raids, both on and off their work. There is evidence that in some instances the camps were so located deliberately with the intention of deterring the Allies from raiding the military works or factories concerned.

Consideration for Racial Needs: Native Labor

Having decided upon a policy of employing prisoner of war and civilian internees on work directly contributing to the prosecution of the war, and having established a system to carry that policy into execution, the Japanese went further and supplemented this source of manpower by recruiting laborers from the native population of the occupied territories. This recruiting of laborers was accomplished by false promises, and by force. After being recruited, the laborers were transported to and confined in camps. Little or no distinction appears to have been made between these conscripted laborers on the one hand, and prisoners of war and civilian internees on the other hand. They were all regarded as slave laborers to be used to the limit of their endurance. For this reason, we have included these conscripted laborers in the term 'civilian internees' whenever that term is used in this chapter. The lot of these conscripted laborers was made worse by the fact that generally they were ignorant of the principles of hygiene applicable to their unusual and crowded conditions, and succumbed more readily to the diseases resulting from the insanitary conditions of confinement and work forced upon them by their Japanese captors.

Prisoners and Internees Forced to Sign Parole

To reduce the number of guards necessary for prisoners of war and civilian internees, regulations in defiance of the Rules of War were issued by the War Ministry early in 1943: 'As soon as prisoners of war have been imprisoned, they shall be administered an oath forbidding them from making an escape. Prisoners of war who refuse to take the oath mentioned in this paragraph shall be deemed to have intentions of escaping and shall be placed under strict surveillance.' This 'strict surveillance' in practice meant solitary confinement on reduced rations or subjection to torture until they took the oath required. At Singapore in August 1942, 16,000 prisoners who had refused to give the parole demanded were herded into a barrack square and kept there without food or latrine facilities for four days, in an attempt to force them to sign the parole—the resulting conditions are too disgusting to describe. Some of the prisoners of war at Hong Kong who refused to sign the parole were confined in a prison without food and forced to kneel all day. If they moved, they were beaten. The senior prisoner of war at the camp at Sandakan, who, with his men, refused to sign was immediately seized and beaten. A firing squad paraded. He was saved from death only when his men agreed to sign. Prisoners of war in camps in Batavia and Java were beaten and deprived of food until they signed the parole. At Zentsuji Camp on Shikoku Island, forty-one prisoners were kept in confinement from 14 June 1942 until 23 September 1942 for refusing to take the oath, and they were finally threatened with death if they persisted in their refusal. As already stated, the Prisoner of War Regulations also applied to civilian internees by virtue of another regulation, which we have quoted. To enforce this parole, which was obtained by coercion, the regulations further stated that 'persons on parole, who break the parole, [would] be subject to either the death penalty, or hard labor, or imprisonment for life or for a minimum of seven years. When the persons mentioned offer armed resistance, they [would] be subject to the death penalty.'

The regulations also stated: 'The persons, who violate any other oath, shall be subject to a maximum of ten years imprisonment.' This latter provision is explained by still another article in the regulations as follows:

> Before a commandant of a prisoner of war camp dispatches prisoners of war (i.e., sends prisoners of war to work details or to work camps from the prisoner of war camp), he shall endeavor to prevent escapes and unexpected disturbances, investigating thoroughly the characters, mental attitudes, past histories, as well as the abilities of the prisoners of war, and in addition he shall administer a solemn oath on other matters of importance.

Itagaki, as Commander of the Korean Army, informed War Minister Tōjō by a message dated 4 September 1942, that he intended to force all prisoners of war, including officers and warrant officers, under his jurisdiction to work; he stated:

'Not one prisoner of war must be left time in idleness.' One of the regulations he had issued stated: 'It is important to guard against destruction by the prisoners of war; if necessary, make them give an oath and establish severe penalties.' On 1 September 1942, Tōjō received a message from the Commander of the Formosa Army:

> 399 prisoners of war, including Lt. General Percival, 6 Major-Generals, or Rear-Admirals, 27 Brigadier Generals, or Commodores, 25 Colonels, or Navy Captains, 130 officers of the rank of Lt. Colonel, or Commander or below, and 210 non-commissioned officers together with 6 civil officials, who had been transferred from the Tomi group, were interned on 31 August 1942 in the Formosa Prisoner of War Camp. At first, Lt. General Percival and others refused to make an oath, but finally all but three (1 Brigadier–General, 1 Navy Captain and Engineering Lieutenant) signed their names.

This system of regulations issued and enforced by the Japanese Government to compel prisoners of war and civilian internees by duress to give an oath not to escape and not to violate other regulations and orders of the Japanese Government violated the general laws of war. The system was devised, instituted, and maintained as part of the policy of the Japanese Government in disregard and violation of the laws of war.

Excessive and Unlawful Punishment Was Imposed

Tōjō, in his instructions to chiefs of prisoner of war and civilian internee camps, told those officials to tighten their control over their subordinates and to supervise the prisoners rigidly; he said: 'It is necessary to put them under strict discipline.' He repeated this charge in his instructions to the Commander of the Zentsūji Division on 30 May 1942, when he said:

> Prisoners of war must be placed under strict discipline as far as it does not contravene the law of humanity. It is necessary to take care not to be obsessed with the mistaken idea of humanitarianism or swayed by personal feelings toward those prisoners of war which may grow in the long time of their imprisonment.

The Geneva Prisoner of War Convention of 1929 provided with respect to punishment of prisoners of war for offenses committed while they were prisoners: 'Any corporal punishment, any imprisonment in quarters without daylight, and, in general any form whatever of cruelty is forbidden [and…] Collective punishment for individual acts is also forbidden.' Other important limitations upon punishments that might be inflicted upon prisoners of war were included. All of them were designed to insure humane treatment of the prisoners. One of these limitations was contained in a provision of the Convention that dealt with escapes and attempts to escape. That provision reads:

> Escaped prisoners of war who are retaken before being able to rejoin their own army or to leave the territory occupied by the army which captured them shall be liable only to disciplinary punishment. After an attempted or accomplished escape, the comrades of the person escaping who assisted in the escape may incur only disciplinary punishment on this account. Arrest is the most severe summary punishment which may be imposed on a prisoner of war. The duration of a single punishment may not exceed 30 days.

In this connection, disciplinary punishment and summary punishment were used as synonymous terms. It was also detailed: 'Attempted escape, even if it is not a first offense, shall not be considered as an aggravating circumstance in case the prisoner of war should be given over to the courts on account of crimes or offenses against persons or property committed in the course of that attempt.'

That the Japanese truly understood the Convention is shown by their objection in 1934 to its ratification. They said that under the Convention, 'prisoners of war could not be so severely punished as Japanese soldiers and this would involve a revision of Japanese Military and Naval Disciplinary Codes to put them on an equal footing, a revision which was undesirable in the interests of discipline.' The real objection to the ratification of the Convention was that the Military desired to avoid any express commitments that would hinder their policy of ill-treatment of prisoners of war.

Early in the Pacific War, and after the Japanese Government had given its promise to apply the provisions of the Convention to Allied prisoners of war and civilian internees, ordinances, and regulations were made contrary to that promise. In 1943, this regulation was published: 'In case a prisoner of war is guilty of an act of insubordination, he shall be subject to imprisonment or arrest; and any other measures deemed necessary for the purpose of discipline may be added.' Under this regulation, corporal punishment as well as torture and mass punishment was administered. It was common practice in all areas in which prisoner of war and civilian internee camps were located to inflict corporal punishment for the slightest offence or for no offence. This punishment in its mildest forms was beating and kicking the victim. The victim, if he became unconscious, was often revived with cold water or by other means, only to have the process repeated. Thousands died as a result of this punishment. In some cases, death was hastened by weakness due to starvation and disease. Other forms of cruel punishments frequently employed included exposing the victim to the hot tropical sun for long hours without headdress or other protection; suspension of the victim by his arms in such a manner as at times to force the arms from their sockets; binding the victim where he would be attacked by insects; confining the victim in a cramped cage for days without food; confining the victim in an underground cell without food, light, or fresh air for weeks; and forcing the victim to kneel on sharp objects in a cramped position for long periods of time.

In direct defiance of the rules of war, mass punishments were commonly employed as punishment for individual acts, especially when the Japanese were unable to discover the offender. The usual form of mass punishment was to force all members of the group involved to assume a strained position such as sitting with the legs folded under the body and the hands on the knees with the palm turned upward or kneeling, and to remain in that position during daylight hours for days. Other forms of mass punishment were also employed, such as that used at Havelock Road Camp in Malaya, where the prisoners were forced to run in a circle without shoes over broken glass while being spurred on by Japanese soldiers who beat them with rifle butts. On 9 March 1943, an ordinance was issued providing the death penalty, life imprisonment, or confinement for ten years or more for a number of offences; the novel feature of this ordinance was that, in the case of each offence, it provided for the death penalty or other severe penalty to be imposed upon the so-called 'leader' of any group action resulting in the commission of the offence named, and the same punishment, or a slightly less severe penalty, for all others who might be involved. Under this ordinance, mass punishment was often inflicted upon groups of prisoners of war or civilian internees for what, at the most, amounted to no more than an individual act. This ordinance also provided the death penalty for 'prisoners of war who defy or disobey the orders of persons supervising, guarding, or escorting them'; it also provided imprisonment for five years for 'prisoners of war who privately or publicly insult persons supervising, guarding or escorting them.' This is an example, of which there are a number, where the Japanese Government departed from its undertaking in respect of the Geneva Convention by altering its laws concerning prisoners of war.

During the Pacific War, contrary to its undertaking already referred to, the Japanese Prisoner of War regulations were amended to permit an escaping prisoner to be punished in the same way as a deserter from the Japanese Army. The ordinance of 9 March 1943 contained the following provision: 'The leader of a group of persons, who have acted together in effecting an escape, shall be subject to either death or to hard labor or to imprisonment for life or for a minimum of ten years. The other persons involved shall be subject to either the death penalty, or to hard labor or to imprisonment for life or for a minimum of one year.' This provision, taken together with the regulations governing paroles not to escape, which prisoners of war were forced to give, constituted the regulations governing escapes that were enforced in all camps. These regulations were in direct violation of international law and, as we have just pointed out, were contrary to the Convention that Japan had promised to apply. Under these regulations, the death penalty was imposed almost without exception upon all prisoners who attempted to escape or escaped and were recaptured. Also, under these regulations, those comrades who assisted a prisoner to escape were also punished, frequently by the death penalty. In some camps, the prisoners were divided into groups, and the practice was to kill all members of the group if one member attempted to escape or was successful in escaping. Even the formality of a trial was dispensed with in many instances. The death penalty is proved to have been imposed for attempt to escape at the following camps: Mukden in Liaoning Province of China (July 1943); Hong Kong, China (July 1943); Singapore, Malaya (March 1942); Mergui, Burma (1942); Tarakan, Borneo (1942 and 1945); Pontianak, Borneo (June 1942); Bandjermasin, Borneo (July 1942); Samarinda, Borneo (January 1945); Palembang, Sumatra (March 1942); Djati Nanggor, Java (March 1942); Bandung, Java (April 1942); Batavia, Java (April 1942); Soekaboemi, Java (May 1942); Jogjakarta, Java (May 1942); Thimahi, Java (May 1942); Makassar, Celebes (September 1942); Amboina, Moluccas Islands (November 1942, April 1945); Oesapa Besar, Dutch Timor (February 1942); Cabanatuan, Philippines (June 1942); Motoyama, Japan (November 1942); Fukuoka, Japan (May 1944); Wake Island (October 1943); and Ranau, Borneo (August 1945).

Prisoners of War Humiliated

The Japanese maintained a policy of submitting Allied prisoners of war to violence, insults, and public humiliation to impress other peoples of Asia with the superiority of the Japanese race.

On 4 March 1942, Vice-Minister of War Kimura received a telegram from the Chief-of-Staff of the Korean Army, of which Itagaki was commander; it stated: 'As it would be very effective in stamping out the respect and admiration of the Korean people for Britain and America, and also in establishing in them a strong faith in victory, and as the Governor-General and the Army are both strongly desirous of it, we wish you would intern 1,000 British and 1,000 American prisoners of war in Korea. We wish you would give us special consideration regarding this matter.' The Governor-General of Korea at that time was Minami. On 5 March 1942, Kimmura replied at about 1,000 white prisoners of war were to be sent to Fusan, Korea. On 23 March 1942, Itagaki sent a message to War Minister Tōjō informing him of the plans to use the prisoners of war in Korea to make the Koreans realize positively the true might of our Empire as well as to contribute to psychological propaganda work for stamping out any ideas of worship of Europe and America which the greater part of Korea still retains at bottom. Itagaki went on to say that the first camp would be located at Seoul, Korea, in the abandoned Iwamura Silk Reeling Warehouse; his former plan to confine the prisoners in the theological school in Fusan having been abandoned with Kimura objected that those buildings were too good for prisoners of war. Among the main points of his plan, Itagaki stated that the prisoners of war would be used on various works in the principal cities of Korea, especially where psychological conditions were not good, in order to achieve his purpose stated at the beginning of his message. He also stated that the equipment of the camps would be cut to a minimum and that the internment, supervision, and guarding of the prisoners would be carried out so as to leave nothing to be desired in the accomplishment of the purpose for which the prisoners of war were being transported to Korea.

On 2 April 1942, the Chief-of-Staff of the Army in Formosa informed the Prisoner of War Information Bureau that he planned to use prisoners of war not only for labor to increase production for war, but also 'as material for education and guidance.'

Thus was applied the plan to use prisoners in violation of the laws of war as pro-Japanese propaganda. On 6 May 1942, the Vice-Minister of War informed the Chief-of-Staff of the Formosa Army that 'white prisoners of war will be confined successively in Korea, Formosa, and Manchuria.' He added, 'for the purpose of control and security it is planned to assign special units organized of Koreans and Formosans.' The psychological effect was to be attained by allowing Koreans and Formosans to take part in the plan to submit Allied prisoners of war to insult and public curiosity.

On 16 May 1942, Vice-Minister of War Kimura notified the Commander-in-Chief of the Southern Area Army (whose headquarters were at Singapore) that between May and August, the white prisoners of war at Singapore should be handed over to the Formosan and Korean Armies.

The white prisoners of war were handed over and sent to Korea. About 1,000 prisoners captured in the fighting in Malaya arrived in Korea and were marched through the streets of Seoul, Fusan, and Jinsen, where they were paraded before 120,000 Koreans and 57,000 Japanese. These prisoners had previously been subjected to malnutrition, ill-treatment, and neglect so that their physical condition would elicit contempt from those who saw them. Itagaki's Chief-of-Staff in reporting to Kimura on what he considered the great success of this demonstration of Japanese superiority quoted a Korean bystander, who had remarked: 'When we look at their frail and unsteady appearance, it is no wonder that they lost to the Japanese forces.' He also quoted another Korean bystander, who remarked: 'When I saw young Korean soldiers, members of the Imperial Army, guarding the prisoners, I shed tears of joy!' Itagaki's Chief-of-Staff concluded his message with the observation: 'As a whole, it seems that the idea was very successful in driving all admiration for the British out of the Koreans' minds and in driving into them an understanding of the situation.'

As far away as in Moulmein, in Burma, this practice of parading prisoners of war was followed. In February 1944, twenty-five Allied prisoners of war were paraded through the streets of that city. They were in an emaciated condition and were forced to carry notices in Burmese, falsely stating that they had been recently captured on the Arakan front. They were ridiculed and held up to contempt by a Japanese officer who accompanied the parade.

The System

Certain changes made regarding the enforcement of the laws of war and the administration of prisoners of war and civilian internees by Japan after the outbreak of the Pacific War were nominal only; they did not secure the enforcement of the laws of war. The attitude of the Japanese Government toward the enforcement of the laws of war, as demonstrated in its prosecution of the China War, did not really change with the commencement of the Pacific War. Certain changes in governmental organizations and methods of procedure were made, but no real effort was made to secure the enforcement of the laws of war. In fact, as has been shown in the regulations affecting attempts to escape, changes were made that enjoined the commission of grave breaches of the laws of war. During the China War, no special agency had been created by the Japanese Government for the administration of prisoners of war and civilian internees, and no Prisoner of War Information Bureau was maintained as required by The Hague and Geneva Conventions. Mutō said that 'the question of whether Chinese captives would be treated as prisoners of war or not was quite a problem, and it was finally decided in 1938 that because the Chinese conflict was officially known as an "incident" although it was really a war, that Chinese captives would not be regarded as prisoners of war.' Tōjō said that this was true, and that after the commencement of hostilities in the Pacific War, he considered that Japan was bound to abide by The Hague and Geneva Conventions. For that reason, he caused a Prisoner of War Information Bureau to be created. This statement by Tōjō that he considered that Japan was bound to abide by The Hague and Geneva Conventions in the prosecution of the Pacific War must be interpreted in the light of his statement made during a meeting of the Investigation Committee of the Privy Council on 18 August 1943. He then said: 'International Law should be interpreted from the view point of executing the war according to our own opinions.' This idea was the basis upon which the policy of the Japanese Government for its treatment of prisoners of war and civilian internees was developed.

Japan Agreed to Apply the Geneva Convention, 1929

On 18 December 1941, the Secretary of State of the United States directed the American Legation in Switzerland to request the Government of Switzerland to inform the Japanese Government that the Government of the United States intended to abide by the Geneva Prisoner of War Convention and the Geneva Red Cross Convention (both of which had been signed on 27 July 1929); that it further intended to extend and apply the provisions of the Geneva Prisoner of War Convention on any civilian enemy aliens that it might intern; that it hoped that the Japanese Government would apply the provisions of these conventions reciprocally as indicated; and that the Government of the United States would appreciate an expression of intention by the Japanese Government in that respect. The inquiry was delivered to the Japanese Foreign Minister Tōgō on 27 December 1941 by the Minister for Switzerland.

The governments of Great Britain and the Dominions of Canada, Australia, and New Zealand also inquired through the Argentine Ambassador in Tokyo on 3 January 1942. In that inquiry, those governments said that they would observe the terms of the Geneva Prisoner of War Convention of 1929 towards Japan and asked if the Japanese Government was prepared to make a similar declaration.

On 5 January 1942, the Argentine Ambassador delivered another note on behalf of Great Britain, Canada, Australia, and New Zealand, proposing that in the application of Articles 11 and 12 of the Convention relating to the provision of food and clothing to prisoners, both parties take into consideration the national and racial customs of the prisoners.

Upon receipt of these inquiries, Tōgō called upon the War Ministry, Navy Ministry, Ministry for Home Affairs, and Ministry of Overseas Affairs for their opinion. At that time, Tōjō was concurrently Prime Minister and War Minister; Mutō was Chief of the Military Affairs Bureau of the War Ministry; Satō was Mutō's assistant in the Military Affairs Bureau, Kimura was Vice-Minister of War; Shimada was Navy Minister; Oka was Chief of the Naval Affairs Bureau in the Naval Ministry; and Hoshino was Chief Secretary of the Cabinet.

Tōgō was concerned for the safety of the Japanese living in Allied countries, and for that reason desired to give a favorable answer to the inquiries and so instructed the Bureau of Treaties, pointing out that the fate of Japanese residents amounting to 700,000s, in the enemy countries would be affected by the treatment by Japan of the prisoners of war and civilian internees who might be in her power. The War Ministry agreed with Tōgō. On 23 January 1942, Kimura told Tōgō:

> In view of the fact that the Geneva Convention relating to prisoners of war was not ratified by His Majesty, we can hardly announce our observance of the same. But it would be safe to notify the world that we have no objection to acting in accordance with the Convention in the treatment of prisoners of war. As regards providing prisoners of war with food and clothing, we have no objection to giving due consideration to the national or racial habits and customs of the prisoners.

Tōgō answered the American and British inquiries on 29 January 1942. His note to the Government of the United States read as follows:

> Japan strictly observes the Geneva Convention of July 27, 1929, relative to the Red Cross, as a signatory of that Convention. The Imperial Government has not yet ratified the Convention relating to treatment of prisoners of war of 27 July 1929. It is therefore not bound by the said Convention. Nevertheless, it will apply 'mutatis mutandis' the provisions of that Convention to American prisoners of war in its power.

The note addressed to the Governments of Great Britain, Canada, Australia, and New Zealand on the same date was as follows:

> The Imperial Government has not ratified the agreement concerning the treatment of prisoners of war dated 27 July 1929, and therefore, it would not be bound to any extent by the said agreement, but would apply '*mutatis mutandis*' the provisions of the said agreement toward the British, Canadian, Australian and New Zealand prisoners of war under Japanese control. The Imperial Government would consider the national and racial manners and customs under reciprocal conditions when supplying clothing and provisions to prisoners of war.

The same assurances were given to the other Allied Powers.

As the War Ministry had not agreed to extend these provisions to civilian internees, Tōgō, through his Vice-Minister, inquired of the War Ministry on 27 January 1942, regarding the application of the Prisoner of War Convention to non-combatant internees. After conferences, the War Ministry acquiesced further in Tōgō's plan to protect Japanese nationals in Allied countries, and on 6 February 1942, Kimura told Tōgō:

> The 1929 Convention relating to prisoners of war has no binding power whatsoever on Japan. But this Ministry has no objection to applying the principles of the Convention to non-combatant internees within such limits as it is applicable, provided, however, that no person be subjected to labor against his will.

Tōgō informed the Government of the United States on 13 February 1942 that 'the Imperial Government will apply for the duration of the war under conditions of reciprocity the provisions of the Convention relating to treatment of prisoners of war of 27 July 1929 to enemy civilian internees, in so far as they are applicable and provided that they are not made to work without their consent.

Taking note of the assurance Tōgō had addressed the British countries on 29 January 1942 that Japan would take into consideration the national and racial customs of the prisoners of war in supplying them with clothing and provisions, the United States addressed another inquiry on that subject. That inquiry was dated 20 February 1942, and stated that the Government of the United States would be bound by the same provisions for prisoners of war as for civilian internees in conformity with Articles 11 and 12 of the Geneva Convention and expected in consequence that the Japanese Government would equally conform to those provisions in the treatment of prisoners of war and civilian internees. On 2 March 1942, Tōgō answered this inquiry in the following manner: 'The Imperial Government intends to take into consideration, with regard to provisions and clothing to be distributed, the racial and national customs of American prisoners of war and civilian internees placed under Japanese power.'

This exchange of assurances constituted a solemn agreement binding the Government of Japan as well as the governments of the other combatants to apply the provisions of the Geneva Prisoner of War Convention of 27 July 1929 to prisoners of war and civilian internees alike, to take into consideration the national and racial customs of those prisoners and internees when supplying them with food and clothing as required by that Convention, and not to force internees to work. The agreement provided that the Convention was to be applied in a spirit of reciprocity—that is to say equally by both sides, each performing in kind and in return for that done by the other. The only exception to this rule established by the agreement were such as might be justified under the reservation '*mutatis mutandis*.' That the agreement did not allow an exception to be made by reason of conflict with the municipal law of Japan is plain upon construction and is shown by Tōgō's testimony: 'The inquiries from the United States and Britain were therefore referred in the normal course by the Foreign Ministry Treaty Bureau, which managed such matters, to the War Ministry, as the ministry empowered to decide the question. The answer which came back was that we should undertake to apply the terms of the Geneva Convention *mutatis mutandis*', and it was therefore so replied to the Governments inquiring.'

'Although the prosecution seems to consider that by the giving of this answer Japan became bound by the Convention to the same extent as if she had ratified it, I assumed (and still assume) that we were binding ourselves only to apply to Convention so far as circumstances permitted. '*Mutatis mutandis*', then, I supposed to imply that in the absence of serious hindrances the Convention would be applied; I assumed also (although this was only assumption on my part) that where the requirements of the Convention came into conflict with the provisions of domestic law, the former would prevail.' The Director of the Bureau of Treaties, who conducted the conferences with the other Ministries regarding the answer to be given the Allied inquiries, further confirmed this.

Although when it was made, the members of the Tōjō Cabinet intended that the Allied Powers should understand the agreement as we have interpreted it, they did not abide by the agreement. Instead, it was used as a means to secure good treatment for Japanese who might become prisoners of war or be interned by the Allied Powers. When Vice-Minister Kimura answered Tōgō's request for his opinion regarding the answer to be made to the Allied inquiries, he said that 'it would be safe to notify the world' that Japan would observe the Convention, but he prefaced that statement with the remark that the Government could hardly afford to announce an intention to observe the Convention in view of the fact that the Emperor had not ratified it. The successive Japanese governments did not enforce the Convention, for although the Ministers of State considered these assurances to the Allies to be a promise to perform new and additional duties for the benefit of prisoners of war and internees, they never issued any new orders or instructions to their officers in charge of prisoners of war and internees to carry this new promise into execution and never set up any system which secured performance of the promise. Instead of making an effort to perform this agreement, they made efforts to conceal from the Allies their guilty non-performance by denying access to the prisoner of war and internee camps; by limiting the length, contents, and number of letters that a prisoner or internee might mail; by suppressing all news regarding such prisoners and internees; and by neglecting to answer or by making false answers to protests and inquiries addressed to them regarding the treatment of prisoners and internees.

Reference has been made in an earlier part of this judgment to the effect of the various conventions in relation to the treatment of prisoners of war and civilian internees and to the obligations of belligerents in that respect. Whatever view may be taken of the assurance or undertaking of the Japanese Government to comply with the Geneva Prisoner of War Convention '*mutatis mutandis*,' the fact remains that under the customary rules of war, acknowledged by all civilized nations, all prisoners of war, and civilian internees must be given humane treatment. It is the grossly inhumane treatment by the Japanese military forces as referred to in this part of the judgment that is particularly reprehensible and criminal. A person guilty of such inhumanities cannot escape punishment on the plea that he or his government is not bound by any particular convention. The general principles of the law exist independently of the said conventions. The conventions merely reaffirm the pre-existing law and prescribe detailed provisions for its application.

As to the effect of the undertaking by the Japanese Government to observe the convention '*mutatis mutandis*,' counsel for the defense submitted, *inter alia*, that the insufficiency of food and medical supplies in many of the instances established was due to disorganization and lack of transport facilities resulting from the Allied offensives. Whatever merit that argument has in its narrow application, it loses effect in face of the proof that the Allied Powers proposed to the Japanese Government that they should send, for distribution among prisoners of war and internees, the necessary supplies—this offer was refused by the Japanese Government.

It is not necessary to enter into a precise definition of the condition '*mutatis mutandis*,' for at no stage in the defense was anything said or even suggested to the effect that these words justified the atrocities and other grossly inhumane acts of Japanese forces, nor was it argued that these words could justify the looting, pillaging and arson that has been clearly established. On those points, the accused who gave evidence, for the most part, did no more than plead complete ignorance of the happenings deposed to.

Any interpretation placed on the condition that attempted to justify the atrocities would amount to nothing more than a submission that by the insertion of the words '*mutatis mutandis*,' the Japanese military forces would be permitted with impunity to behave with gross barbarity under the guise of complying with a Convention that prescribed humane treatment as its cardinal principle. Such a submission could not be accepted.

Ill-Treatment of Prisoners of War a Policy

The Japanese Government signed and ratified the Fourth Hague Convention of 1907 Respecting the Laws and Customs of War on Land, which provided for humane treatment of prisoners of war and condemned treacherous and inhumane conduct of war. The reason for the failure of the Japanese Government to ratify and enforce the Geneva Prisoner of War Convention that it signed at Geneva in 1929 is to be found in the fundamental training of the Japanese soldier. Long before the beginning of the period covered by the Indictment, the young men of Japan had been taught that 'the greatest honor is to die for the Emperor,' a precept that we find Araki repeating in his speeches and propaganda motion pictures. An additional precept was taught that it is an ignominy to surrender to the enemy.

The combined effect of these two precepts was to inculcate in the Japanese soldier a spirit of contempt for Allied soldiers who surrendered, which, in defiance of the rules of war, was demonstrated in their ill-treatment of prisoners. In this spirit, they made no distinction between the soldier who fought honorably and courageously up to an inevitable surrender and the soldier who surrendered without a fight. All enemy soldiers who surrendered under any circumstance were to be regarded as being disgraced and entitled to live only by the tolerance of their captors.

Ratification and enforcement of the Geneva Convention of 1929, it was thought, would involve abandonment of this view of the military. The Convention had been signed by the Japanese Plenipotentiaries at Geneva in 1929, but when the Convention came up for ratification in 1934, both the Japanese Army and Navy petitioned against ratification; by that time, they had sufficient political power to prevent ratification. They gave as some of their reasons for resisting ratification that the obligations imposed by the Convention were unilateral, that the Convention imposed new and additional burdens on Japan, and that Japan could not gain anything by ratifying it, for no Japanese soldier would ever surrender to the enemy.

In this connection, it is interesting to note that Tōjō giving instructions to chiefs of prisoner of war camps said: 'In Japan we have our own ideology concerning prisoners of war, which should naturally make their treatment more or less different from that in Europe and America.'

Japanese Purpose was to Protect Japanese Nationals

The decision to create a Prisoner of War Information Bureau was prompted by an inquiry from the International Red Cross in Geneva, which was forwarded to the War Ministry from the Foreign Ministry on 12 December 1941. The International Red Cross had telegraphed the Japanese Foreign Ministry that, in view of the fact that the war had extended to the Pacific, its Committee had placed the services of the Central Prisoner of War Bureau at the disposal of the belligerent States, and inquiring whether the Japanese Government was disposed to exchange, by the intermediary of the Central Bureau of Geneva, list of information on prisoners of war, and, insofar as possible, on civilian internees. Conferences were held by the officials in the War Ministry, and on 28 December 1941, Vice-Minister of War Kimura informed Foreign Minister Tōgō that the War Ministry was ready to exchange information, but he stated: 'It is not that we "declare that we are prepared to apply in practice" the provisions of the Prisoner of War Convention of 1929, but that we "utilize them for the convenience of transmission of information."' By 12 January 1942, the International Red Cross had received replies from Japan and the United States declaring that they were ready to proceed with the transmission of information.

Creation of the Prisoner of War Information Bureau

The Prisoner of War Information Bureau was created by Imperial Ordinance on 27 December 1941. The Bureau was charged with making investigations of the following subjects: internments, removals, releases on parole, exchanges, escapes, admissions to hospitals, and deaths of prisoners of war. It was also given the duty of maintaining records for each prisoner of war and managing the communications and correspondence regarding prisoners of war, and of collecting information pertaining to the condition of prisoners of war. The ordinance provided that the Bureau should have a director and four secretaries. This Prisoner of War Information Bureau was placed under the supervision and control of the War Minister and was organized as a section of the Military Affairs Bureau, where at different times it came under the control and supervision of Mutō and Satō. All personnel of the Prisoner of War Information Bureau were appointed on the recommendation of the War Minister. Tōjō appointed Lieutenant General Uemura as the first Director of the Bureau.

Creation of the Prisoner of War Administration Section

On 31 March 1942, regulations for the 'Treatment of Prisoners of War' were promulgated, creating what was called the 'Prisoner of War Administration Section' in the Military Affairs Bureau of the War Ministry under the supervision and control of Tōjō as War Minister. Tōjō exercised this control and supervision through Mutō as Chief of the Military Affairs Bureau. The regulations provided that the section should have a director and other personnel to be appointed upon the recommendation of the War Minister. Tōjō appointed Lieutenant General Uemura as the First Director of the Section, thereby combining in one person the administration of the Prisoner of War Information Bureau and the Prisoner of

War Administration Section. The Prisoner of War Information Bureau was only an information and records office related, as Kimura said, to use the provisions of the Prisoner of War Convention of 1929 for the purpose of gaining information; it had no power of control or supervision over prisoners of war and civilian internees. The Prisoner of War Administration Section, on the other hand, was given authority to 'conduct all affairs relative to the treatment of prisoners of war and civilian internees in the theater of war.'

The Military Affairs Bureau Retained Control

The Military Affairs Bureau of the War Ministry under Mutō, and later under Satō, retained control of the system set up for enforcement of the Laws of War during the Pacific War. Although the ordinance creating the Prisoner of War Information Bureau stated that 'in regard to matters falling within his jurisdiction, the Director may demand information from any military or naval unit concerned,' General Uemura and the directors following him were required to transmit all inquiries and other communications through the office of the Chief of the Military Affairs Bureau. They had no power to take any action without the approval of the Chief of the Military Affairs Bureau.

According to Tōjō, all orders and directives relating to prisoners of war and civilian internees were issued by the War Minister. He also says that those orders and directives were drafted by the Military Affairs Bureau after the Chief of that bureau had held conferences with the General Staff and other agencies of the Government concerned.

As we will discuss presently, biweekly conferences of all Bureau Chiefs in the War Ministry were held and attended by the War Minister and Vice-Minister of War; Tōjō and Kimura attended most of these conferences. Kimura was Vice-Minister of War from 10 April 1941 to 11 March 1943. Matters relating to prisoners of war and civilian internees were discussed at these conferences, with Tōjō and Kimura at times attending. Orders and regulations were formulated and forwarded to all agencies of the Government concerned with the treatment of prisoners of war and civilian internees.

Detention Camps and Their Administration

Detention camps for prisoners of war were authorized by Imperial Ordinances and Regulations issued by the War Ministry on 23 December 1941. These regulations provided that prisoner of war camps were to be administered by a commander of an Army or a commander of a garrison under the general supervision of the Minister of War. As we have stated, however, all these camps were not under the

Army commanders; in those areas under the jurisdiction of the Navy, the camps were administered by Navy officers of corresponding rank and authority.

Detention camps for civilian internees were authorized by regulations issued by the War Ministry on 7 November 1943. The regulations stated: 'When the commander of an army, which term shall herein include persons of the equivalent status as a commander of an army, has interned enemy nationals or neutrals at the front, he shall establish an army internment camp as soon as possible. The commander of an army that establishes the army internment camp shall administer the same.'

General regulations were issued providing for the administration of civilian internees, which were not materially different from those providing for the administration of prisoners of war. All regulations applicable to prisoners of war were made applicable to civilian internees, except in those cases where specific regulations were issued applicable to civilian internees alone. These regulations also provided that 'the commander of an army that establishes the army internment camp shall administer the same.'

The following accused administered detention camps as military commanders during the Pacific War, namely: Doihara as Commander of the Eastern Military District in Japan and as Commander of the 7th Area Army at Singapore; Hata as Commander of all Japanese Expeditionary Forces in China and as Commander of the military districts in Central and Western Honshu in Japan; Itagaki as Commander of the Korean Army and as Commander of the 7th Area Army at Singapore; Kimura as Commander of the Army in Burma; Mutō as Commander of the Japanese Army in Northern Sumatra; Satō as Commander of the Army in French Indochina; and Umezu as Commander of the Kwantung Army in Manchuria.

The regulations provided that 'a commander of an army or a commander of a garrison may, whenever necessary, delegate his subordinates to assist in the management of a prisoner of war or civilian internee camp. Persons delegated according to these provisions shall be under the supervision and command of the Commandant.' Special supervisors or chiefs were selected and trained in Tokyo to manage prisoner of war and civilian internee camps; and after careful and detailed instruction, which was completed by a personal message from Prime Minister Tōjō, these chiefs of camps were sent out from Japan to all places where prisoner of war and civilian internee camps were located to take charge of those camps and manage them under the command of the Army and Navy commanders. These chiefs of camps were required by regulations to make monthly reports to the Prisoner of War Administration Section in the Military Affairs Bureau of the War Ministry. These reports were discussed at the biweekly conferences of the Bureau Chiefs in the War Ministry, which were usually attended by the War Minister and Vice-Minister of War. These reports included statistics relative to the high death rate in the camps due to malnutrition and other causes. Tōjō said that this item received his particular attention. A summary of the monthly reports from the chiefs of camps was filed in the office of the Prisoner of War Information Bureau, which was under the same director as the Prisoner of War Administration Section.

The Navy Participated in the System

It was contemplated that the Navy would deliver to the Army for detention and administration all prisoners of war taken and civilian internees interned by it, but in many cases, this was not done or was delayed for a long time. Also, in some areas, the Navy exercised jurisdiction for administration of occupied areas. For instance, the Navy occupied such islands as Borneo, the Celebes, the Moluccas, Timor, and other islands east of a line through Bali. It also occupied other islands, such as Wake Island. In those areas occupied by the Navy, the prisoners of war and civilian internees were administered by the Navy Minister, and the enforcement of the laws of war in those areas became the responsibility of the Navy, under the direction of Shimada and Oka.

Administration of the System in Japan Proper

Prisoners of war detained in Japan were under the War Ministry in the same manner as prisoners in other areas, but it is said that the Home Ministry was in charge of the police in Japan, and was therefore considered to be the proper ministry to administer all matters relating to civilian internees in Japan proper. It will be noted that Tōjō served as Home Minister from 18 October 1941 to 17 February 1942 and from 25 November 1942 to 6 January 1943. Tōjō said that 'there was a separate body under the Home Ministry to deal with civilian internees, but [he did not] know what the name of that was.'

For the purpose of defense and military administration, Japan was divided into eight military districts. Each military district was occupied by an army, the commander of which was also the military administrator of the district and in charge of all prisoner of war camps within his district. The Eastern District embraced the Tokyo–Yokohama Area and was occupied by the 12th Area Army. Doihara commanded that army and administered the district from 1 May 1943 to 22 March 1944, and again from 25 August 1945 to the time of the surrender on 2 September 1945. The Chugoku Military District embraced the Hiroshima Area and the western tip of Honshu Island, and was garrisoned by the Second Army Corps. Hata commanded that Corps from 7 April 1945 until the surrender on 2 September 1945.

Administration of the System in Formosa, Korea, and Sakhalin

In the overseas possessions of Japan, which were not in a theater of operations, such as Formosa, Korea, and Sakhalin, civilian internees were under the administration of the Ministry of Overseas Affairs, but prisoners of war in those possessions were under the administration of the War Ministry in the same manner as prisoners in other areas. The Ministry of Overseas Affairs was established by Imperial Ordinance of 10 June 1929. That Ordinance provided that this Ministry was to control all affairs relating to the Korea Governor-General's Office, the Formosa Governor-General's Office, the Kwantung Administration Office, and the South Seas Administration Office. To provide for the major wartime reorganization of the Japanese Government, this Ministry was abolished in 1943 and its functions divided and transferred to the Ministry of Home Affairs, and the Ministry of Greater East Asia. Tōgō was Minister of overseas Affairs from 18 October 1941 to 2 December 1941.

Administration of the System in the Occupied Territories

The Ministry of Greater East Asia was created by Imperial Ordinance on 1 November 1942. That Ordinance directed that 'the Minister of Greater East Asiatic Affairs shall administer the execution of various political affairs, excepting purely diplomatic affairs, concerning Greater East Asia, which is hereinafter defined as excluding Japan proper, Korea, Formosa and Sakhalin. The Minister of Greater East Asiatic Affairs shall superintend affairs concerning the Kwantung Bureau and of the South Seas Government Office. There shall be instituted in the Ministry of Greater East Asiatic Affairs the following four Bureau: The General Affairs Bureau the Manchurian Affairs Bureau, The Chinese Affairs Bureau and the Southern Area Affairs Bureau.'

This ministry was organized to govern all areas that had fallen or might fall under the military power of Japan, except Korea, Formosa, and Sakhalin. The Ordinance further provided 'to extend cooperation to the Army and the Navy, the Ministry of Greater East Asiatic Affairs shall conduct affairs concerning administration of the occupied areas within the Greater East Asia Area.' The first Minister was Aoki, who was followed by Shigemitsu, who took over this Ministry on 20 July 1944 and served in that capacity until 7 April 1945, when he was succeeded by Tōgō, who held the office until 16 August 1945.

Accused who Administered the System in the Occupied Territories

Umezu became Commander-in-Chief of the Kwantung Army on 7 September 1939, and served in that capacity until 18 July 1944. He was the virtual ruler of Manchukuo and was directly responsible for the treatment of prisoners of war and civilian internees in Manchuria. Hata was Commander-in-Chief of the Japanese

Expeditionary Force in China from 1 March 1941 to 22 November 1944. On 11 March 1943, Kimura resigned as Vice-Minister of War; he was appointed Commander-in-Chief of the Japanese Army in Burma on 30 August 1944 and served in that position until the surrender. During his tour of duty in Burma, he put into practice the policies that he helped to develop during his term of office as Vice-Minister of War. He first established his headquarters at Rangoon. At this time, atrocities occurred in that area—at Hsipaw, Moksokwin Reserve Forest, Henzada, Ongun Cemetery, Tharrawaddy, and at the Kempeitai Jail in Rangoon. At the end of April 1945, Kimura moved his headquarters to Moulmein. Thereafter, atrocities occurred at or near Moulmein. The entire population of Kalagon, a village 10 miles from Kimura's headquarters, was massacred on 7 July 1945 under order of his field officers. Massacres occurred in Moulmein after Kimura's arrival; the Kempeitai became more inhumane in their treatment of Burmese, and the internees in the camp at Tavoy were starved and beaten.

Mutō made an inspection trip to the southern Regions from 20 March 1942 to 12 April 1942; he visited Formosa, Saigon, Bangkok, Rangoon, Singapore, Palembang, Java, Manila, and other places. He returned to Tokyo and was appointed Commander of the Imperial Guards Division on 20 April 1942, and was stationed in Northern Sumatra. He was the Japanese military commander in Northern Sumatra, with his headquarters at Medan until 12 October 1944, when he was transferred to the Philippine Islands. During his term of office as such commander, he put into practice the policies that he advocated as Chief of the Military Affairs Bureau of the War Ministry in Tokyo. In the area occupied by his troops in Northern Sumatra, some of the most disgraceful atrocities of the war were committed. Prisoners of war and civilian internees were starved, neglected, tortured, murdered, and otherwise mistreated, and civilians were massacred. The laws of war were ignored. Mutō further demonstrated his disregard for the laws of war upon his transfer on 12 October 1944 to become Chief-of-Staff of the 14th Japanese Army in the Philippines Islands under General Yamashita. On the night of 20 October 1944, Mutō arrived at Fort McKinley in the Philippines to assume his duties as Chief-of-Staff to General Yamashita. He held that assignment until the Japanese surrender in September 1945. During his tenure as such Chief-of-Staff, a campaign of massacre, torture, and other atrocities was waged by the troops under Yamashita and Mutō on the civilian population of the Philippines, including the massacres in Batangas and massacres and other atrocities at Manila. These bore the same features and followed the same pattern set eight years earlier at Nanking when Mutō was a member of Matsui's staff. During this period, prisoners of war and civilian internees were starved, tortured and murdered.

Doihara commanded the 7th Area Army at Singapore from 22 March 1944 until he was relieved by Itagaki on 7 April 1945 to become Inspector-General of Military Education. During his period of command, prisoners of war were treated as common criminals, starved, tortured, and otherwise ill-treated. After Itagaki assumed the command of the 7th Area Army at Singapore, there was no improvement in the condition of the prisoners of war under the jurisdiction of that Army. During June and July 1945, while he was in command, no less than seventeen Allied airmen were taken from their cells in the Outram Road Gaol and murdered.

Allied Protests

Formal and informal protests and warnings against violations of the laws of war lodged by the Allied Powers and the Protecting Power during the Pacific War were ignored or, when they were answered, the commission of the offenses was denied or untruthful explanations were given.

The procedure followed in Tokyo was described to us as follows: formal protests from the Allied Powers and the Protecting Power were regularly delivered to the Foreign Ministry. The Foreign Ministry then circulated copies of these protests to the Ministries and Bureau of the Japanese Government concerned. All protests concerning matters under the jurisdiction of the War Ministry and the Prisoner of War Information Bureau were first delivered to the Secretariat of the War Ministry. The Secretariat forwarded the protests to the Military Affairs Section of the Military Affairs Bureau. Mutō was Chief of this bureau from 30 September 1939 to 20 April 1942. Satō was Chief of this Section from 15 July 1938 until he replaced Mutō as Chief of the Military Affairs bureau in 1942. Satō served as Chief of the Military Affairs Bureau until 14 December 1944. The Military Affairs Section discussed the protest with the various sections of the Military Affairs Bureau concerned, such as the Prisoner of War Administration Section or the Prisoner of War Information Bureau. The protest was then taken up and discussed at the biweekly meetings of the Bureau Chiefs of the War ministry, which were usually attended by the War Minister and Vice-Minister of War. At these meetings, it was decided whether a reply would be made to the protest and the nature of the reply to be made. The Director of the Prisoner of War Administration Section, who was also the Director of the Prisoner of War Information Bureau, attended these discussions and received orders on important matters direct from the War Minister and the Vice-Minister; he furnished copies of the protests and the replies to be made thereto to the Prisoner of War Information Bureau for filing. This was the practice even when the copies of the protests were addressed to the War Minister or the Prisoner of War Information Bureau.

In addition to formal protests, radio broadcasts were regularly made over Allied stations detailing the atrocities and other violations of the laws of war being committed by the Japanese armed forces and warning the Japanese Government that it would be held responsible for these offenses. These broadcasts were monitored by the Japanese Foreign Ministry and distributed to all ministries, bureau and officials concerned. Lord Keeper of the Privy Seal Kido recorded in his diary on 19 March

1942: 'The Imperial Household Minister came to the office and told me about Eden's address in Parliament concerning our soldiers' atrocities at Hong Kong, and we exchanged opinions.'

The formal protests delivered were too numerous for detailed mention here. In general, it may be said that these protests related to the violations of the laws of war which we have mentioned, as well as to many others. In each case, specific and detailed facts were stated which permitted complete investigation. The same things may be said of the protests and warnings delivered over the radio.

We will mention here, by way of illustration only, some of those protests and warnings. As early as 14 February 1942, the United States Government delivered a note through the Swiss Government stating that it had received reports that the Japanese authorities in the occupied areas of the Philippines were subjecting American civilians to an extremely rigid and harsh regime involving abuse and humiliation; it also highlighted that the American Government desired assurances that immediate steps had been taken to remedy the situation and to accord to Americans in the Philippines moderate treatment similar to that being extended to Japanese nationals in the territories of the United States. Foreign Minister Tōgō replied on 24 February 1942 that 'conditions applied to American Nationals in the Philippines by the Japanese authorities are more favorable than contemplated by the Geneva Convention of 1929.' This statement was false. He denied that American nationals were being subjected to unfavorable treatment and said that the 'apprehensions of the American Government were based on unknown sources and cited no exact facts and therefore were without foundation.'

On 12 December 1942, the United States Government delivered another formal protest. It stated that it had learned of gross ill-treatment suffered by American civilians and prisoners of war in violation of the commitment of the Japanese Government to apply the provisions of the Geneva Prisoner of War Convention of 1929 to American prisoners of war and, insofar as they might be applicable, to civilian internees. The United States stated that it was evident that Japan had failed to fulfil its undertaking and that some Japanese officers and agencies had violated the principles of that Convention not only by positive ill-treatment, but by failure to provide for those American nationals the necessities of life. The United States then lodged an emphatic protest and stated that it expected this inhumane and uncivilized treatment of American prisoners of war and civilian internees to be made a matter of immediate investigation; that it expected those responsible to be disciplined immediately; and that it expected an assurance that ill-treatment of prisoners of war and civilian internees would be discontinued. Specific instances were cited, giving dates and other facts to support this protest. No reply was made to this protest until 28 May 1943, when Foreign Minister Shigemitsu replied that an investigation was being made and that he would communicate 'in due course' when the results of the investigation were known.

In the meantime, on 5 April 1943, the United States had filed another protest against the ill-treatment of the Doolittle fliers. The United States Government warned:

> The American Government also solemnly warns the Japanese Government that for any other violations of its undertakings as regards American prisoners of war or for any other acts of criminal barbarity inflicted upon American prisoners in violation of the laws of warfare, accepted and practiced by civilized nations, as military operations now in progress draw to their inexorable and inevitable conclusion, the American Government will visit upon the officers of the Japanese Government responsible for such uncivilized and inhumane acts the punishment they deserve.

A large number of specific protests was lodged by the United States with Foreign Minister Shigemitsu before he finally answered, on 24 April 1944, the protest of the United States that had been made on 12 December 1942. In that reply, he indicated that the investigation, which he had mentioned in his note of 28 May 1943, had been completed, and that he had a report thereon. He accused the Government of the United States of 'distorting and exaggerating the facts' and rejected the protest; he went to great length to set out what he claimed to be the facts as disclosed by the so-called investigation. The United States replied to this accusation on 1 March 1945 by a note reading:

> The United States Government cannot accept a statement by the Japanese Government impugning its veracity. The United States Government's protest concerning treatment accorded by Japanese authorities to American nationals in Japan and Japanese occupied territory is based on documentary evidence, which cannot be refuted in such an arbitrary fashion by the Japanese Government. The statements contained in the Japanese Government's reply of 24 April 1944 are so far removed from the facts as known to the United States Government that it can only conclude that the Japanese Government has permitted itself to be misled by fabricated reports of local officials and had not made in independent investigation of the matters protested in the United States Government's Note of 12 December 1942. The United States Government therefore considers the reply unsatisfactory and will continue to hold the Japanese Government answerable.

British protests were treated in the same fashion as those from the Government of the United States. An illustration is afforded by the protests and answer regarding the treatment of prisoners of war in Rangoon Gaol. On 8 July 1942, the British Government caused a protest to be delivered to Foreign Minister Tōgō in which it was stated that a photograph had appeared in the *Japan Times and Advertiser* (a newspaper published in Tokyo), which showed British prisoners of war cleaning the streets of Rangoon under the amused eyes of the public. The protest was renewed on 1 August 1942. On 15 September 1942, the British Government further protested that the prisoners in Rangoon Gaol were furnished insufficient rations, that they were forced to sleep on the bare floors of the prison, and that their boots had been confiscated. Tōjō acted as Foreign Minister from 1 September 1942 to 17 September 1942, and while occupying that office, received a note calling his attention to the foregoing protests. On 9 February 1943, Foreign Minister Tani, who had replaced Tōjō as Foreign Minister, replied: 'The competent authorities have stated after having made a full inquiry that the facts stated in said letters never happened.'

The protests of the British Government against the treatment of British prisoners of war in Burma and Siam received similar treatment. The British Government protested on 4 July 1944 in a note delivered to Shigemitsu that it had learned from postcards printed by the Japanese authorities that about 20,000 British prisoners of war had been transferred to the vicinity of Moulmein without notification. It also protested against the unfavorable conditions and ill-treatment to which these prisoners were subjected. Shigemitsu replied on 26 August 1944 that the 'majority of British and Allied prisoners of war, which were in Burma on 4 July 1944 were prisoners who had been attached to camps in Thailand and Malaya and had been provisionally transferred to Burma.' Shigemitsu replied on 3 October 1944 to further protests from the British Government relative to the health of prisoners laboring in Burma and Sima. In that reply, he said: 'The Imperial Government, by exercising great vigilance as to the health and hygiene of prisoners of war, takes added measures, such as monthly medical examination of each prisoner of war camp, to enable sickness to be treated in the first stage.' He then detailed the medical aid which he claimed had been given to the prisoners on the Burma–Siam Railway. The facts stated were entirely false as the prisoners had not received medical attention and had been dying by thousands from beriberi, cholera, malaria, and other tropical diseases. The true facts were learned when the *Rakuyo Maru* was torpedoed and sunk in the South China Sea on 12 September 1944. There had been 1,300 prisoners of war aboard that unmarked Japanese prison ship. The Japanese picked up the Japanese survivors, but deliberately left the prisoners to their fate. Approximately 100 Australian and United Kingdom survivors were later rescued and taken to Australia and Great Britain. From these prisoners, it was learned that all available prisoners of war in Singapore and Java were moved early in 1942 to Burma and Thailand to work on the Burma–Siam Railway project. We have already described the conditions under which they traveled and the terrible conditions during the construction of the railway. Shigemitsu was informed of the facts learned from these rescued prisoners of war in a note from the British Government (dated 4 December 1944), renewing the British protests. Forced at last to reply, Tōgō, who had succeeded Shigemitsu as Foreign Minister, made a belated reply to these protests on 15 May 1945. He said that it was regretted that the situation was such that 'the concerted efforts of all the sanitary services of the Japanese troops cannot prevent the spread of diseases of the digestive system, etc.' He denied that atrocities had been committed by Japanese troops in Burma, and as to the protest against the parading of British prisoners of war in Moulmein, which we have mentioned, he gave the conventional Japanese answer that it 'never happened.'

In addition to the disregard shown these formal protests, the many protests and warnings given over the radio were completely ignored—although these had been regularly recorded in the Japanese Foreign Office and distributed to the various ministries. On 24 January 1944, a report from the U.S. Government giving the details and results of the Bataan March was broadcast over the British Broadcasting Corporation's network and recorded in the Japanese Foreign Office. Again on 29 January 1944, radio station KWID at San Francisco, California, broadcast White House Secretary Stephen Early's disclosure that the Japanese would not permit the U.S. Government to send food and supplies to United States and Filipino prisoners. Early said: 'The time has come for releasing the factual reports which have been carefully investigated and authenticated because we cannot expect to get further relief to our prisoners now in the hands of the Japanese.' This broadcast was recorded in the Japanese Foreign Office. KWID again broadcast on 29 January 1944 statements by United States Secretary of State Cordell Hull and British Foreign Secretary Anthony Eden. Mr. Hull, in speaking of the treatment of prisoners of war in Japanese hands, stated: 'According to the reports of cruelty and inhumanity, it would be necessary to summon the representatives of all the demons available anywhere and combine their fiendishness with all that is bloody in order to describe the conduct of those who inflicted those unthinkable atrocities on the Americans and Filipinos.'

The vigor of this language was fully justified by the evidence given before the Tribunal. Mr. Eden had stated before the House of Commons that British protests had drawn unsatisfactory results from Japan. He said that the Japanese were violating not only international law but all human, decent civilized conduct. He warned the Japanese Government that, in time to come, the record of their military atrocities in the war would not be forgotten. Mr. Hull had closed his statement with the remark that the United States Government was assembling all possible facts concerning Japanese treatment of prisoners of war and that it intended to seek full punishment of the responsible Japanese authorities. General MacArthur's General Headquarters issued a warning on 22 October 1944 to the Japanese Commander of the 7th Area Army at Singapore, who had jurisdiction over the Philippine Islands as well as a large segment of the Pacific Area. General MacArthur warned that he would hold the enemy leaders immediately responsible for any failure to accord prisoners of war and civilian internees proper treatment. He said that although the Americans and Filipinos who surrendered in the Philippines believed they would be treated with the dignity, honor, and protection to which prisoners of war were entitled under the laws of war, unimpeachable evidence had been received of the degradation and even brutality to which they had been subjected in violation of the most sacred code of martial honor. All of these broadcasts were recorded in the Japanese Foreign office and given a wide circulation among the Japanese Ministries.

Ill–Treatment of Prisoners of War and Civilian Internees was Condoned and Concealed

The Japanese Government condoned ill-treatment of prisoners of war and civilian internees by failing and neglecting to punish those guilty of ill-treating them or by prescribing trifling and inadequate penalties for the offence. That Government also attempted to conceal the ill-treatment and murder of prisoners and internees by prohibiting the representatives of the Protecting Power from visiting camps, by restricting such visits as were allowed, by refusing to forward to the Protecting Power complete lists of prisoners taken and civilians interned, by censoring news relating to prisoners and internees, and ordering the destruction of all incriminating documents at the time of the surrender of Japan.

The following are examples of inadequate sentences imposed for ill-treatment of prisoners. For flogging, the punishment imposed was admonition or a few days confinement in quarters or a few days' extra duty. A guard guilty of torturing prisoners of war was admonished. A guard who was guilty of frequently lynching prisoners of war was admonished. Several guards were found guilty of lynching prisoners of war; the most severe punishment imposed was discharge. The penalty imposed on the officer responsible for the burning alive of sixty-two Allied fliers during an air raid on the Tokyo Army Prison was an admonition. These cases are evidence that the War Ministry knew there was ill-treatment of prisoners. The trifling nature of the punishments imposed implies condonation.

The Government actively concealed the ill-treatment to which prisoners of war and civilian internees were being subjected by refusing visits by representatives of the Protecting Power designated by the Allies. The Swiss Minister in Tokyo, as early as 12 February 1942, delivered a note to Foreign Minister Tōgō, in which he said:

> I have the honor to bring to the knowledge of Your Excellency that the Government of the United States is prepared to facilitate, at the request of the representative of the Protecting Power, their visits to Japanese subjects who are temporarily detained, interned, or at liberty on parole. I would be greatly obliged to Your Excellency if you would facilitate in part the task of my Legation so far as it concerns visits to internees.

He delivered another note to Foreign Minister Tōgō on 17 February 1942, in which he said:

> The Government of the United States of America has already informed the Spanish Ambassador, protecting Japanese interests in the United States, that he is

at liberty to visit prisoner of war camps as well as places where civilian internees are detained. The Government of the United States requests, in conformity with the Geneva Prisoner of War Convention, that the Swiss representatives in Japan and in the territories occupied by Japanese forces be authorized as soon as possible to commence their visits of inspection to places where American citizens, who are prisoners of war or civilian internees, are located.

He delivered other notes to Tōgō in March and June 1942 repeating those requests. During June 1942, he requested the same permission to visit the subjects of Great Britain and the Dominions, who were detained as prisoners or internees. Tōgō at last replied to these requests on 30 July 1942 by a note, in which he said:

I desire to inform Your Excellency that the Imperial Government having in principle refused to recognize the representation of any interests in the occupied territories comprising the Philippine Islands, Hong Kong, Malaya and the Netherlands East Indies, it follows that permission cannot be given to your delegates to visit American prisoners of war and civilian internees in the above-mentioned territories; but that in respect of Shanghai only, in occupied China, the competent authorities can give this permission.

The Governments of the United States and Great Britain protested immediately and renewed their requests. The correspondence between the Swiss Minister and Foreign Minister Tani, who succeeded Tōgō, reflects that this policy of refusing permission to visit prisoners and internees detained in the occupied territories and in Japan's overseas possessions was continued. The Swiss Minister continued to press for permission, however; and on 22 April 1943, Shigemitsu, who had become Foreign Minister, delivered a note verbal to the Swiss Minister, in which he said: 'As the Foreign Minister has communicated to the Swiss Minister by Note dated 20 July 1942, the Imperial Government shall not permit visits to prisoners of war and civilian internee camps in occupied territories.' Although the Swiss Minister had been informed by Foreign Minister Tōgō that representatives of the Protecting Power would be allowed to visit camps at Shanghai, the visits were not made because the so-called 'competent authorities,' to which Tōgō referred the Swiss Minister, refused to give permission for the visits and the permission was not forthcoming from the Tōjō Cabinet in Tokyo. Shigemitsu was informed of this in a note from the Swiss Minister dated 12 May 1943. In response to these persistent and repeated requests from the Swiss Government for permission to visit prisoners of war and civilian internees, a few selected camps, which had been prepared for the occasion, were allowed to be visited in Japan. On 2 June 1943, the Swiss Minister requested permission from Shigemitsu to visit the remaining camps in Japan as well as the camps in the occupied territories, and inquired when a second visit might be made to the camps that had been visited in Japan. Foreign Minister Shigemitsu replied on 23 July 1943:

A regards prisoner of war camps in the occupied areas, a notification will be made to Your Excellency if the time comes when permission can be granted; and as regards prisoner of war camps in Japan proper, which have not yet been visited, permission will be granted gradually at a favorable opportunity. Permission for periodic visits to those camps, that have already been visited, shall not be granted in advance; but in case a visit is desired, consideration will be given to applications made on all such occasions.

However, consideration was not given to these applications. On 12 February 1944, the Swiss Minister complained to Shigemitsu that no reply had been made to requests to visit detention camps between August 1943 and February 1944. This complaint was repeated in a note to Shigemitsu on 30 March 1944, in which the Swiss Minister said:

You know that I am not satisfied with my activities as representative of foreign interests in Japan. The results do not correspond to the efforts. I can see this in a concrete fashion as shown by the statistics of my services and requests which have been made by my Government at the request of the Governments who have confided their interests in us. I desire to confine myself for the moment to my requests to visit prisoner of war camps. Reviewing my requests made over more than two years, I find that from 1 February 1942 to 15 March 1944, I have intervened 134 times in writing. These 134 notes have brought exactly 24 replies from the Foreign Ministry. Most of these replies are either negative or forward to me decisions made by competent authorities. I have received three replies in nine months.

It was not until 13 November 1944 that he was notified by Shigemitsu's Foreign Ministry that the time had come when permission could be granted to visit prisoners of war and internees in the occupied territories, and then the visits were limited to Manila, Shonan, and Bangkok. In a note addressed to the Swiss Minister in Tokyo on 17 November 1944, Shigemitsu informed the Swiss Minister that visits would be allowed to prisoner of war camps in the occupied territories on condition of reciprocity if they did not interfere with military operations. The Swiss Minister (in a note dated 13 January 1945) asked Shigemitsu when these visits could be commenced. It was not until 7 April 1945 that Tōgō, who had succeeded Shigemitsu as Foreign Minister, replied to the many urgent requests to visit detention camps in the occupied territories. In that reply, Tōgō stated that Japan 'would lose no time' in making preparations for visits in Thailand. By the use of one excuse or another, visits were never freely allowed throughout the war.

In the few cases where the representatives of the Protecting Power were allowed to visit detention camps, the camps were prepared for the visit, and the visits were strictly supervised. Regulations issued by the Tōjō Cabinet early in the Pacific

War provided that when an interview with a prisoner of war was authorized, restrictions regarding the time and place of the interview, the range within which the conversation was to be conducted would be imposed, and that a guard would be present during the interview. These regulations were enforced notwithstanding the repeated objections of the Protecting Power. In a note to the Swiss Minister, dated 22 April 1943, Shigemitsu said: 'The Imperial Government shall not allow delegates of the Protecting Power to interview prisoners of war without the presence of a guard.' The Swiss Minister protested and Shigemitsu replied on 24 June 1943: 'The Ministry hastens to inform the Legation that Article 13 of our country's detailed regulations stipulates that a guard shall be present when prisoners of war are interviewed, and that it is not possible to modify our treatment of prisoners of war practiced in conformity with said Article.' After a visit to the prisoner of war camp at Motoyama in Japan in the spring of 1943, the senior prisoner at the camp—who had dared to complain of the working conditions to which the prisoners had been subjected—was tortured; he was forced to kneel for five hours before a Japanese guard. The next time this camp was visited, this senior prisoner was placed in confinement and was not allowed to speak to the representative, although that representative demanded to interview him.

The fate of prisoners of war and civilian internees was further concealed by refusal to forward to the Protecting Power a list of the names of prisoners of war and civilian internees detained. An example of the refusal to supply such lists is the case of the prisoners of war and civilian internees detained after the capture of Wake Island. The Swiss Minister, on 27 May 1942, requested of Tōgō the names of the prisoners of war and civilian internees captured on Wake Island and their present whereabouts. On 6 October 1942, the Swiss Minister informed the Foreign Minister (then Tani) that the U.S. Government was still without report on approximately 400 American civilians who were on Wake Island at the time of its capture.

On 8 April 1943, with the list not having been furnished, the Swiss Minister informed Foreign Minister Tani that the U.S. Government was insisting upon being furnished the names and location of the remaining 400. Foreign Minister Tani replied on 19 April 1943 that all information to be furnished had already been given. On 21 August 1943, the Swiss Minister furnished new Foreign Minister Shigemitsu a list of 432 American civilians who should have been on Wake Island at the time of its occupation by the Japanese forces, but whose names were not found on the lists given to the International Red Cross Bureau by the Japanese, and requested information regarding those civilians. On 15 May 1945, the Swiss Minister informed Foreign Minister, now Tōgō, that no answer had been received to the request for information regarding the remaining 432 civilians from Wake Island. The information was not obtained until after the surrender of Japan. In truth, all these unfortunate people were murdered by the Japanese Navy in October 1943.

News reports and mail were specially censored, no doubt to prevent disclosure of the ill-treatment to which prisoners of war were being subjected. Censorship regulations issued by the Information Bureau of the War Ministry on 20 December 1943, while Tōjō was War Minister, provided, among other things, the following:

Care should be taken to avoid issuing twisted reports of our fair attitude which might give the enemy food for evil propaganda and bring harm to our interned brothers. For this reason, any reports including photographs, pictures, etc., which come under the following categories are prohibited: anything that gives the impression that prisoners of war are too well treated or are cruelly treated; any concrete information concerning facilities, supplies, sanitary conditions, or other matters pertaining to living conditions within prisoner of war camps; any information giving the names of any location of prisoner of war camps other than the following:

Then followed twelve general names such as Tokyo, Korea, Borneo, etc. The mail which prisoners of war were allowed to send was restricted almost to the point of prohibition. Prisoners in some camps, such as those at Singapore, were told by their guards that unless they reported favorably on conditions at the camp, their cards would not be sent. This appears to have been the general rule.

When it became apparent that Japan would be forced to surrender, an organized effort was made to burn or otherwise destroy all documents and other evidence of ill-treatment of prisoners of war and civilian internees. The Japanese Minister of War issued an order on 14 August 1945 to all Army headquarters that confidential documents should be destroyed by fire immediately. On the same day, the Commandant of the Kempeitai sent out instructions to the various Kempeitai Headquarters detailing the methods of burning large quantities of documents efficiently. The Chief of the Prisoner of War Camps under the Prisoner of War Administration Section of the Military Affairs Bureau sent a circular telegram to the Chief–of–Staff of the Formosan Army on 20 August 1945, in which he said: 'Documents which would be unfavorable for us in the hands of the enemy are to be treated in the same way as secret documents and destroyed when finished with.' This telegram was sent to the Korean Army, Kwantung Army, North China Army, Hong Kong, Mukden, Borneo, Thailand, Malaya, and Java. It was in this telegram that the Chief of Prisoner of War Camps made this statement: 'Personnel who ill-treated prisoners of war and internees or who are held in extremely bad sentiment by them are permitted to take care of it by immediately transferring or by fleeing without trace.

United States, Appellee *v.* William L. Calley, Jr., First Lieutenant, U.S. Army, Appellant,

No. 26,875, United States Court of Military Appeals, 22 U.S.C.M.A. 534, 21 December 1973, Excerpt

QUINN, Judge; DUNCAN, Judge (concurring in the result); DARDEN, Chief Judge (dissenting).

QUINN, Judge:

First Lieutenant Calley stands convicted of the premeditated murder of 22 infants, children, women, and old men, and of assault with intent to murder a child of about 2 years of age. All the killings and the assault took place on March 16, 1968 in the area of the village of May Lai in the Republic of South Vietnam. The Army Court of Military Review affirmed the findings of guilty and the sentence, which, as reduced by the convening authority, includes dismissal and confinement at hard labor for 20 years. The accused petitioned this Court for further review, alleging 30 assignments of error. We granted three of these assignments.

We consider first whether the public attention given the charges was so pernicious as to prevent a fair trial for the accused. At the trial, defense counsel moved to dismiss all the charges on the ground that the pretrial publicity made it impossible for the Government to accord the accused a fair trial. The motion was denied. It is contended that the ruling was wrong.

The defense asserts, and the Government concedes, that the pretrial publicity was massive. The defense perceives the publicity as virulent and vicious. At trial, it submitted a vast array of newspaper stories, copies of national news magazines, transcripts of television interviews, and editorial comment. Counsel also referred to comments by the President in which he alluded to the deaths as a 'massacre' and to similar remarks by the Secretary of State, the Secretary of Defense, the Secretary of the Army, and various members of Congress. Before us, defense counsel contend that the decisions of the United States Supreme Court in Marshall *v.* United States, 360 US 310 (1959), Irvin *v.* Dowd, 366 US 717 (1961), and Sheppard *v.* Maxwell, 384 US 333 (1966) require reversal of this conviction. In our opinion, neither the cited cases, nor others dealing with pretrial publicity and its effect upon an accused's constitutional right to a fair trial, mandate that result.

Under our constitutional system of government and individual rights, the exercise of a constitutional right by one person can affect the constitutional right of another. Thus, the First Amendment guarantees to the public and the news media the right to comment on and discuss impending or pending criminal prosecutions. The content of the comments can pose a danger to the right of an accused to the fair trial assured by the Due Process clause of the Fifth Amendment. The accommodation of such competing rights has been, and will continue to be, a challenge to the courts. As we construe the Supreme Court's decisions in this area, the trier of the facts, and more particularly, a juror, is not disqualified just because he has been exposed to pretrial publicity or even has formulated an opinion as to the guilt or innocence of an accused on the basis of his exposure. '[I]f the juror can lay aside his impression or opinion and render a verdict based on the evidence presented in court,' he is qualified to serve. Irvin *v.* Dowd, *supra* at 723. The difficult is that sometimes the impact of the quantity and character of pretrial publicity is so patently profound that the juror's personal belief in his impartiality is not sufficient to overcome the likelihood of bias, as assessed by the court. *Id.* at 728; *see also* United States *v.* Dean, 5 USCMA 44, 17 CMR 44 (1954). Our task, therefore, is not merely to ascertain that there was widespread publicity adverse to the accused, but to judge whether it was of a kind that inevitably had to influence the court members against the accused, irrespective of their good-faith disclaimers that they could, and would, determine his guilt from the evidence presented to them in open court, fairly and impartially.

We have reviewed the material submitted to support the defense argument on the issue. In contrast to the publicity in some of the cases cited, most of the matter is factual and impersonal in the attribution of guilt. Many accounts note that the accused had not been tried and the question of his culpability remained undetermined by the standard of American law. A number of editorials appear to regard the tragedy as another reason to deplore or oppose our participation in the war in Vietnam. A considerable amount of the material is favorable to Lieutenant Calley; some stories were largely expressions of sympathy.

First official government statements were to the effect that a full investigation would be conducted to determine whether the killings took place and, if so, to establish the identity of those responsible. Later statements described what occurred at My Lai as a massacre and promised that those who perpetrated it would be brought to justice. By the time of the trial few persons in the United States who read, watched or listened to the daily news would not have been convinced that many Vietnamese civilians, including women and children, had been killed during the My Lai operation. It is by no means certain, however, that the conviction that people had died included a judgment that Lieutenant Calley was criminally responsible for those deaths. Our attention has not been called to any official statement or report that demanded Lieutenant Calley's conviction as the guilty party.

Unlike the situation in the *Sheppard* case, neither the trial judge nor government counsel ignored the potentially adverse effect of the extensive publicity. In pretrial proceedings, the prosecution labored jointly with the defense to minimize the effects of the publicity. The military judge issued special orders to prospective witnesses to curb public discussion of the case and to insulate them from the influence of possible newspaper, magazine, radio and television reports of the case. At trial, the judge was exceedingly liberal in the scope of the *voir dire* of the court members and in bases for challenge for cause, but defense counsel challenged only two members because of exposure to the pretrial publicity.

We have carefully examined the extensive *voir dire* of the court members in the light of the pretrial materials submitted to us and we are satisfied that none of the court members had formed unalterable opinions about Lieutenant Calley's guilt from the publicity to which they had been exposed and that the total impact of that publicity does not oppose the individual declaration by each member retained on the court that he could, fairly and impartially, decide whether Lieutenant Calley was guilty of any crime upon the evidence presented in open court. Irvin *v.* Dowd, *supra*; Reynolds *v.* United States, 98 US 145, 146 (1879). We conclude that this assignment of error has no merit.

In his second assignment of error the accused contends that the evidence is insufficient to establish his guilt beyond a reasonable doubt. Summarized, the pertinent evidence is as follows:

Lieutenant Calley was a platoon leader in 'C' Company, a unit that was part of an organization known as Task Force Barker, whose mission was to subdue and drive out the enemy in an area in the Republic of Vietnam known popularly as Pinkville. Before March 16, 1968, this area, which included the village of My Lai 4, was a Viet Cong stronghold. 'C' Company had operated in the area several times. Each time the unit had entered the area it suffered casualties by sniper fire, machine gun fire, mines, and other forms of attack. Lieutenant Calley had accompanied his platoon on some of the incursions.

On March 15, 1968, a memorial service for members of the company killed in the area during the preceding weeks was held. After the service Captain Ernest L. Medina, the commanding officer of 'C' Company, briefed the company on a mission in the Pinkville area set for the next day. 'C' Company was to serve as the main attack formation for Task Force Barker. In that role it would assault and neutralize May Lai 4, 5, and 6 and then mass for an assault on My Lai, 1. Intelligence reports indicated that the unit would be opposed by a veteran enemy battalion, and that all civilians would be absent from the area. The objective was to destroy the enemy. Disagreement exists as to the instructions on the specifics of destruction.

Captain Medina testified that he instructed his troops that they were to destroy My Lai 4 by 'burning the hootches, to kill the livestock, to close the wells and to destroy the food crops.' Asked if women and children were to be killed, Medina said he replied in the negative, adding that, 'You must use common sense. If they have a weapon and are trying to engage you, then you can shoot back, but you must use common sense.' However, Lieutenant Calley testified that Captain Medina informed the troops they were to kill every living thing—men, women, children, and animals—and under no circumstances were they to leave any Vietnamese behind them as they passed through the villages *en route* to their final objective. Other witnesses gave more or less support to both versions of the briefing.

On March 16, 1968, the operation began with interdicting fire. 'C' Company was then brought to the area by helicopters. Lieutenant Calley's platoon was on the first lift. This platoon formed a defense perimeter until the remainder of the force was landed. The unit received no hostile fire from the village.

Calley's platoon passed the approaches to the village with his men firing heavily. Entering the village, the platoon encountered only unarmed, unresisting men, women, and children. The villagers, including infants held in their mothers' arms, were assembled and moved in separate groups to collection points. Calley testified that during this time he was radioed twice by Captain Medina, who demanded to know what was delaying the platoon. On being told that a large number of villagers had been detained, Calley said Medina ordered him to 'waste them.' Calley further testified that he obeyed the orders because he had been taught the doctrine of obedience throughout his military career. Medina denied that he gave any such order.

One of the collection points for the villagers was in the southern part of the village. There, Private First Class Paul D. Meadlo guarded a group of between 30 to 40 old men, women, and children. Lieutenant Calley approached Meadlo and told him, 'You know what to do,' and left. He returned shortly and asked Meadlo why the people were not yet dead. Meadlo replied he did not know that Calley had meant that they should be killed. Calley declared that he wanted them dead. He and Meadlo then opened fire on the group, until all but a few children fell. Calley then personally shot these children. He expended 4 or 5 magazines from his M-16 rifle in the incident.

Lieutenant Calley and Meadlo moved from this point to an irrigation ditch on the east side of My Lai 4. There, they encountered another group of civilians being held by several soldiers. Meadlo estimated that this group contained from 75 to 100 persons. Calley stated, 'We got another job to do, Meadlo,' and he ordered the group into the ditch. When all were in the ditch, Calley and Meadlo opened fire on them. Although ordered by Calley to shoot, Private First Class James J. Dursi refused to join in the killings, and Specialist Four Robert E. Maples refused to give his machine gun to Calley for use in the killings. Lieutenant Calley admitted that he fired into the ditch, with the muzzle of his weapon within 5 feet of people in it. He expended between 10 and 15 magazines of ammunition on this occasion.

With his radio operator, Private Charles Sledge, Calley moved to the north end of the ditch. There, he found an elderly Vietnamese monk, whom he interrogated. Calley struck the man with his rifle butt and then shot him in the head. Other testimony indicates that immediately afterwards a young child was observed running toward the village. Calley seized him by the arm, threw him into the ditch, and fired at him. Calley admitted interrogating and striking the monk, but denied shooting him. He also denied the incident involving the child.

Appellate defense counsel contend that the evidence is insufficient to establish the accused's guilt. They do not dispute Calley's participation in the homicides, but they argue that he did not act with the malice or *mens rea* essential to a conviction of murder; that the orders he received to kill everyone in the village were not palpably illegal; that he was acting in ignorance of the laws of war; that since he was told that only 'the enemy' would be in the village, his honest belief that there were no innocent civilians in the village exonerates him of criminal responsibility for their deaths; and, finally, that his actions were in the heat of passion caused by reasonable provocation.

In assessing the sufficiency of the evidence to support findings of guilty, we cannot reevaluate the credibility of the witnesses or resolve conflicts in their testimony and thus decide anew whether the accused's guilt was established beyond a reasonable doubt. Our function is more limited; it is to determine whether the record contains enough evidence for the triers of the facts to find beyond a reasonable doubt each element of the offenses involved. United States *v.* Papenheim, 19 USCMA 203, 41 CMR 203 (1970); United States *v.* Wilson, 13 USCMA 670, 33 CMR 202 (1963).

The testimony of Meadlo and others provided the court members with ample evidence from which to find that Lieutenant Calley directed and personally participated in the intentional killing of men, women, and children, who were unarmed and in the custody of armed soldiers of C Company. If the prosecution's witnesses are believed, there is also ample evidence to support a finding that the accused deliberately shot the Vietnamese monk whom he interrogated, and that he seized, threw into a ditch, and fired on a child with the intent to kill.

Enemy prisoners are not subject to summary execution by their captors. Military law has long held that the killing of an unresisting prisoner is murder. Winthrop's Military Law and Precedents, 2d ed., 1920 Reprint, at 788–91.

While it is lawful to kill an enemy 'in the heat and exercise of war,' yet 'to kill such an enemy after he has laid down his arms … is murder.'

Digest of Opinions of the Judge Advocates General of the Army, 1912, at 1074–75 n. 3.

Conceding for the purposes of this assignment of error that Calley believed the villagers were part of 'the enemy,' the uncontradicted evidence is that they were under the control of armed soldiers and were offering no resistance. In his testimony, Calley admitted he was aware of the requirement that prisoners be treated with respect. He also admitted he knew that the normal practice was to interrogate villagers, release those who could satisfactorily account for themselves, and evacuate the suspect among them for further examination. Instead of proceeding in the usual way, Calley executed all, without regard to age, condition, or possibility of suspicion. On the evidence, the court-martial could reasonably find Calley guilty of the offenses before us.

At trial, Calley's principal defense was that he acted in execution of Captain Medina's order to kill everyone in My Lai 4. Appellate defense counsel urge this defense as the most important factor in assessment of the legal sufficiency of the evidence. The argument, however, is inapplicable to whether the evidence is legally sufficient. Captain Medina denied that he issued any such order, either during the previous day's briefing or on the date the killings were carried out. Resolution of the conflict between his testimony and that of the accused was for the triers of the facts. United States *v.* Guerra, 13 USCMA 463, 32 CMR 463 (1963). The general findings of guilty, with exceptions as to the number of persons killed, does not indicate whether the court members found that Captain Medina did not issue the alleged order to kill, or whether, if he did, the court members believed that the accused knew the order was illegal. For the purpose of the legal sufficiency of the evidence, the record supports the findings of guilty.

In the third assignment of error, appellate defense counsel assert gross deficiencies in the military judge's instructions to the court members. Only two assertions merit discussion. One contention is that the judge should have, but did not, advise the court members of the necessity to find the existence of 'malice aforethought' in connection with the murder charges; the second allegation is that the defense of compliance with superior orders was not properly submitted to the court members.

The existence *vel non* of malice, say appellate defense counsel, is the factor that distinguishes murder from manslaughter. *See* United States *v.* Judd, 10 USCMA 113, 27 CMR 187 (1959). They argue that malice is an indispensable element of murder and must be the subject of a specific instruction. In support, they rely upon language in our opinion in United States *v.* Roman, 1 USCMA 244, 2 CMR 150 (1952).

Roman involved a conviction of murder under Article of War 92, which provided for punishment of any person subject to military law 'found guilty of murder.' As murder was not further defined in the Article, it was necessary to refer to the common law element of malice in the instructions to the court members in order to distinguish murder from manslaughter. United States *v.* Roman, *supra*; *cf.* United States *v.* Judd, *supra*. In enactment of the Uniform

Code of Military Justice, Congress eliminated malice as an element of murder by codifying the common circumstances under which that state of mind was deemed to be present. Hearings on HR 2498 Before a Subcommittee of the House Armed Services Committee, 81st Cong., 1st Sess. 1246–1248 (1949); HR Rep No. 491, 81st Cong, 1st Sess 3 (1949). One of the stated purposes of the Code was the 'listing and definition of offenses, redrafted and rephrased in modern legislative language.' S Rep No. 486, 81st Cong, 1st Sess 2 (1949). That purpose was accomplished by defining murder as the unlawful killing of a human being, without justification or excuse. Article 118, Uniform Code of Military Justice, 10 USC § 918. Article 118 also provides that murder is committed if the person, intending to kill or inflict grievous bodily harm, was engaged in an inherently dangerous act, or was engaged in the perpetration or attempted perpetration of certain felonies. In each of these instances before enactment of the Uniform Code, malice was deemed to exist and the homicide was murder. The Code language made it unnecessary that the court members be instructed in the earlier terminology of 'malice aforethought.' Now, the conditions and states of mind that must be the subject of instructions have been declared by Congress; they do not require reference to malice itself. *Cf.* United States *v.* Craig, 2 USCMA 650, 10 CMR 148 (1953).

The trial judge delineated the elements of premeditated murder for the court members in accordance with the statutory language. He instructed them that to convict Lieutenant Calley, they must be convinced beyond a reasonable doubt that the victims were dead; that their respective deaths resulted from specified acts of the accused; that the killings were unlawful; and that Calley acted with a premeditated design to kill. The judge defined accurately the meaning of an unlawful killing and the meaning of a 'premeditated design to kill.' These instructions comported fully with requirements of existing law for the offense of premeditated murder, and neither statute nor judicial precedent requires that reference also be made to the pre-Code concept of malice.

We turn to the contention that the judge erred in his submission of the defense of superior orders to the court. After fairly summarizing the evidence, the judge gave the following instructions pertinent to the issue:

The killing of resisting or fleeing enemy forces is generally recognized as a justifiable act of war, and you may consider any such killings justifiable in this case. The law attempts to project whose persons not actually engaged in warfare, however; and limits the circumstances under which their lives may be taken.

Both combatants captured by and noncombatants detained by the opposing force, regardless of their loyalties, political views, or prior acts, have the right to be treated as prisoners until released, confined, or executed, in accordance with law and established procedures, by competent authority sitting in judgment of such detained or captured individuals. Summary execution of detainees or prisoners is forbidden by law. Further, it's clear under the evidence presented in this case, that hostile acts or support of the enemy North Vietnamese or Viet Cong forces by inhabitants of My Lai (4) at some time prior to 16 March 1968, would not justify the summary execution of all or a part of the occupants of My Lai (4) on 16 March, nor would hostile acts committed that day, if, following the hostility, the belligerents surrendered or were captured by our forces. I therefore instruct you, as a matter of law, that if unresisting human beings were killed to My Lai (4) while within the effective custody and control of our military forces, their deaths cannot be considered justified, and any order to kill such people would be, as a matter of law, an illegal order. Thus, if you find that Lieutenant Calley received an order directing him to kill unresisting Vietnamese within his control or within the control of his troops, that order would be an illegal order.

A determination that an order is illegal does not, of itself, assign criminal responsibility to the person following the order for acts done in compliance with it. Soldiers are taught to follow orders, and special attention is given to obedience of orders on the battlefield. Military effectiveness depends upon obedience to orders. On the other hand, the obedience of a soldier is not the obedience of an automaton. A soldier is a reasoning agent, obliged to respond, not as a machine, but as a person. The law takes these factors into account in assessing criminal responsibility for acts done in compliance with illegal orders.

The acts of a subordinate done in compliance with an unlawful order given him by his superior are excused and impose no criminal liability upon him unless the superior's order is one which a man of ordinary sense and understanding would, under the circumstances, know to be unlawful, or if the order in question is actually known to the accused to be unlawful.

… In determining what orders, if any, Lieutenant Calley acted under, if you find him to have acted, you should consider all of the matters which he has testified reached him and which you can infer from other evidence that he saw and heard. Then, unless you find beyond a reasonable doubt that he was not acting under orders directing him in substance and effect to kill unresisting occupants of My Lai (4), you must determine whether Lieutenant Calley actually knew those orders to be unlawful.

… In determining whether or not Lieutenant Calley had knowledge of the unlawfulness of any order found by you to have been given, you may consider all relevant facts and circumstances, including Lieutenant Calley's rank; educational background; OCS schooling; other training while in the Army, including basic training, and his training in Hawaii and Vietnam; his experience on prior operations involving contact with hostile and friendly Vietnamese; his age; and any other evidence tending to prove or disprove that on 16 March 1968, Lieutenant Calley knew the order was unlawful. If you find beyond a reasonable doubt, on the basis of all the evidence, that Lieutenant Calley actually knew the order under which he asserts he operated was unlawful, the fact that the order was given operates as no defense.

Unless you find beyond reasonable doubt that the accused acted with actual knowledge that the order was unlawful, you must proceed to determine whether, under the circumstances, a man of ordinary sense and understanding would have known the order was unlawful. You deliberations on this question do not focus on Lieutenant Calley and the manner in which he perceived the legality of the order found to have been given him. The standard is that of a man of ordinary sense and understanding under the circumstances.

Think back to the events of 15 and 16 March 1968.... Then determine, in light of all the surrounding circumstances, whether the order, which to reach this point you will have found him to be operating in accordance with, is one which a man of ordinary sense and understanding would know to be unlawful. Apply this to each charged act which you have found Lieutenant Calley to have committed. Unless you are satisfied from the evidence, beyond a reasonable doubt, that a man of ordinary sense and understanding would have known the order to be unlawful, you must acquit Lieutenant Calley for committing acts done in accordance with the order.

Appellate defense counsel contend that these instructions are prejudicially erroneous in that they require the court members to determine that Lieutenant Calley knew that an order to kill human beings in the circumstances under which he killed was illegal by the standard of whether 'a man of ordinary sense and understanding' would know the order was illegal. They urge us to adopt as the governing test whether the order is so palpably or manifestly illegal that a person of 'the commonest understanding' would be aware of its illegality. They maintain the standard stated by the judge is too strict and unjust; that it confronts members of the armed forces who are not persons of ordinary sense and understanding with the dilemma of choosing between the penalty of death for disobedience of an order in time of war on the one hand and the equally serious punishment for obedience on the other. Some thoughtful commentators on military law have presented much the same argument.

n1 In the words of one author: 'If the standard of reasonableness continues to be applied, we run the unacceptable risk of applying serious punishment to one whose only crime is the slowness of his wit or his stupidity. The soldier, who honestly believes that he must obey an order to kill and is punished for it, is convicted not of murder but of simple negligence.' Finkelstein, Duty to Obey as a Defense, March 9, 1970 (unpublished essay, Army War College). *See also* L. Norene, Obedience to Orders as a Defense to a Criminal Act, March 1971 (unpublished thesis presented to The Judge Advocate General's School, U.S. Army).

The 'ordinary sense and understanding' standard is set forth in the present Manual for Courts-Martial, United States, 1969 (Rev) and was the standard accepted by this Court in United States *v.* Schultz, 18 USCMA 133, 39 CMR 133 (1969) and United States *v.* Keenan, 18 USCMA 108, 39 CMR 108 (1969). It appeared as early as 1917. Manual for Courts-Martial, U.S. Army, 1917, paragraph 442. Apparently, it originated in a quotation from F. Wharton, Homicide § 485 (3d ed. 1907). Wharton's authority is Riggs *v.* State, 3 Coldwell 85, 91 American

Decisions 272, 273 (Tenn 1866), in which the court approved a charge to the jury as follows:

'[I]n its substance being clearly illegal, so that a man of ordinary sense and understanding would know as soon as he heard the order read or given that such order was illegal, would afford a private no protection for a crime committed under such order.'

Other courts have used other language to define the substance of the defense. Typical is McCall *v.* McDowell, 15 F Case 1235, 1240 (CCD Cal 1867), in which the court said:

But I am not satisfied that Douglas ought to be held liable to the plaintiff at all. He acted not as a volunteer, but as a subordinate in obedience to the order of his superior. Except in a plain case of excess of authority, where at first blush it is apparent and palpable to the commonest understanding that the order is illegal, I cannot but think that the law should excuse the military subordinate when acting in obedience to the orders of his commander. Otherwise he is placed in the dangerous dilemma of being liable in damages to third persons for obedience to an order, or to the loss of his commission and disgrace for disobedience thereto.... The first duty of a solider is obedience, and without this there can be neither discipline nor efficiency in an army. If every subordinate officer and solider were at liberty to question the legality of the orders of the commander, and obey them or not as they may consider them valid or invalid, the camp would be turned into a debating school, where the precious moment for action would be wasted in wordy conflicts between the advocates of conflicting opinions.

Colonel William Winthrop, the leading American commentator on military law, notes:

But for the inferior to assume to determine the question of the lawfulness of an order given him by a superior would of itself, as a general rule, amount to insubordination, and such an assumption carried into practice would subvert military discipline. Where the order is apparently regular and lawful on its face, he is not to go behind it to satisfy himself that his superior has proceeded with authority, but is to obey it according to its terms, the only exceptions recognized to the rule of obedience being cases of orders so manifestly beyond the legal power or discretion of the commander as to admit of no rational doubt of their unlawfulness...

Except in such instances of palpable illegality, which must be of rare occurrence, the inferior should presume that the order was lawful and authorized and obey it accordingly, and in obeying it can scarcely fail to be held justified by a military court.

In the stress of combat, a member of the armed forces cannot reasonably be expected to make a refined legal judgment and be held criminally responsible if he guesses wrong on a question as to which there may be considerable disagreement. But there is no disagreement as to the illegality of the order to kill in this case. For 100 years, it has been a settled rule of American law that even in war the summary killing of an enemy, who has submitted to, and is under, effective physical control, is murder. Appellate defense counsel acknowledges that rule of law and its continued viability, but they say that Lieutenant Calley should not be held accountable for the men, women and children he killed because the court-martial could have found that he was a person of 'commonest understanding' and such a person might not know what our law provides; that his Captain had ordered him to kill these unarmed and submissive people and he only carried out that order as a good disciplined soldier should.

Whether Lieutenant Calley was the most ignorant person in the United States Army in Vietnam, or the most intelligent, he must be presumed to know that he could not kill the people involved here. The United States Supreme Court has pointed out that '[t]he rule that "ignorance of the law will not excuse" [a positive act that constitutes a crime] … is deep in our law.' Lambert *v*. California, 355 US 225, 228 (1957). An order to kill infants and unarmed civilians who were so demonstrably incapable of resistance to the armed might of a military force as were those killed by Lieutenant Calley is, in my opinion, so palpably illegal that whatever conceptional difference there may be between a person of 'commonest understanding' and a person of 'common understanding,' that difference could not have had any 'impact on a court of lay members receiving the respective wordings in instructions,' as appellate defense counsel contend. In my judgment, there is no possibility of prejudice to Lieutenant Calley in the trial judge's reliance upon the established standard of excuse of criminal conduct, rather than the standard of 'commonest understanding' presented by the defense, or by the new variable test postulated in the dissent, which, with the inclusion of such factors for consideration as grade and experience, would appear to exact a higher standard of understanding from Lieutenant Calley than that of the person of ordinary understanding.

In summary, as reflected in the record, the judge was capable and fair, and dedicated to assuring the accused a trial on the merits as provided by law; his instructions on all issues were comprehensive and correct. Lieutenant Calley was given every consideration to which he was entitled, and perhaps more. We are impressed with the absence of bias or prejudice on the part of the court members. They were instructed to determine the truth according to the law and his they did with due deliberation and full consideration of the evidence. Their findings of guilty represent the truth of the facts as they determined them to be and there is substantial evidence to support those findings. No mistakes of procedure cast doubt upon them.

Consequently, the decision of the Court of Military Review is affirmed.

DUNCAN, Judge (concurring in the result):

My difference of opinion from Judge Quinn's view of the defense of obedience to orders is narrow. The issue of obedience to orders was raised in defense by the evidence. Contrary to Judge Quinn, I do not consider that a presumption arose that the appellant knew he could not kill the people involved. The Government, as I see it, is not entitled to a presumption of what the appellant knew of the illegality of an order. It is a matter for the fact finders under proper instructions.

Paragraph 216, Manual for Courts-Martial, United States, 1969 (Rev), provides for special defenses: excuse because of accident or misadventure; self-defense; entrapment; coercion or duress; physical or financial inability; and obedience to apparently lawful orders. Subparagraph *d* of paragraph 216 is as follows:

An order requiring the performance of a military duty may be inferred to be legal. An act performed manifestly beyond the scope of authority, or pursuant to an order that a man of ordinary sense and understanding would know to be illegal, or in a wanton manner in the discharge of a lawful duty, is not excusable.

The military judge clearly instructed the members pursuant to this provision of the Manual. The heart of the issue is whether, under the circumstances of this case, he should have abandoned the Manual standard and fashioned another. The defense urges a purely subjective standard; the dissent herein yet another. I suggest that there are important general as well as certain specific considerations which convince me that the standard should not be abandoned. The process of promulgating Manual provisions is geared to produce requirements for the system only after most serious reflection by knowledgeable and concerned personnel. These persons have full regard for the needs of the armed forces and genuine concern for the plight of one accused. Those who prepared the Manual provision and the President of the United States, the Commander-in-Chief, who approved and made the provision a part of our law, were aware that disobedience to orders is the anathema to an efficient military force. Judge Quinn points out that this Court has established as precedent the applicability of the special defense upon proof adduced pursuant to the Manual standard. These are important general reasons for not aborting a standard that has been long in existence and often used.

It is urged that in using the Manual test of 'a man of ordinary sense and understanding' those persons at the lowest end of the scale of intelligence and experience in the services may suffer conviction while those more intelligent and experienced would possess faculties which would cause them to abjure the order with impunity. Such an argument has some attraction but in my view falls short of that which should impel a court to replace that which is provided to us as law.

It appears to me that all tests which measure an accused's conduct by an objective standard—whether it is the test of 'palpable illegality to the commonest understanding' or whether the test establishes a set of profile considerations by which to measure the accused's ability to assess the legality of the order—are less than perfect, and they have a certain potential for injustice to the member having the slowest wit and quickest obedience. Obviously the higher the standard, the likelihood is that fewer persons will be able to measure up to it. Knowledge of the fact that there are other standards that are arguably more fair does not convince me that the standard used herein is unfair, on its face, or as applied to Lieutenant Calley.

Perhaps a new standard, such as the dissent suggests, has merit; however, I would leave that for the legislative authority or for the cause where the record demonstrates harm from the instructions given. I perceive none in this case. The general verdict in this case implies that the jury believed a man of ordinary sense and understanding would have known the order in question to be illegal. Even conceding argue do that this issue should have been resolved under instructions requiring a finding that almost every member of the armed forces would have immediately recognized that the order was unlawful, as well as a finding that as a consequence of his age, grade, intelligence, experience, and training, Lieutenant Calley should have recognized the order's illegality, I do not believe the result in this case would have been different.

This assumes that the jury found that the order the appellant contends he obeyed was given. I believe the trial judge to have been correct in his denial of the motion to dismiss the charges for the reason that pretrial publicity made it impossible for the Government to accord the accused a fair trial.

Both the principal opinion and the analysis of the Court of Military Review state that in the enactment of the Uniform Code of Military Justice Congress has, in effect, codified the requirement of malice aforethought by defining murder as the unlawful killing of a human being, without justification or excuse. Article 118 UCMJ, 10 USC § 918. It should also be noted that in the case at bar the members of the panel were charged that a finding that the homicides were without justification or excuse was necessary to convict for premeditated murder. Furthermore, I cannot say that the evidence lacks sufficiency to convict in respect to any of the charges.

DARDEN, Chief Judge (dissenting):

Although the charge the military judge gave on the defense of superior orders was not inconsistent with the Manual treatment of this subject, I believe the Manual provision is too strict in a combat environment. Among other things, this standard permits serious punishment of persons whose training and attitude incline them either to be enthusiastic about compliance with orders or not to challenge the authority of their superiors. The standard also permits conviction of members who are not persons of ordinary sense and understanding.

The principal opinion has accurately tracted the history of the current standard. Since this Manual provision is one of substantive law rather than one relating to procedure or modes of proof, the Manual rule is not binding on this Court, which has the responsibility for determining the principles that govern justification in the law of homicide. United States *v.* Smith, 13 USCMA 105, 32 CMR 105 (1962). My impression is that the weight of authority, including the commentators whose articles are mentioned in the principal opinion, supports a more liberal approach to the defense of superior orders. Under this approach, superior orders should constitute a defense except 'in a plain case of excess of authority, where at first blush it is apparent and palpable to the commonest understanding that the order is illegal.'

While this test is phrased in language that now seems 'somewhat archaic and ungrammatical,' the test recognizes that the essential ingredient of discipline in any armed force is obedience to orders and that this obedience is so important it should not be penalized unless the order would be recognized as illegal, not by what some hypothetical reasonable soldier would have known, but also by 'those persons at the lowest end of the scale of intelligence and experience in the services.' This is the real purpose in permitting superior orders to be a defense, and it ought not to be restricted by the concept of a fictional reasonable man so that, regardless of his personal characteristics, an accused judged after the fact may find himself punished for either obedience or disobedience, depending on whether the evidence will support the finding of simple negligence on his part.

It is true that the standard of a 'reasonable man' is used in other areas of military criminal law, e.g., in connection with the provocation necessary to reduce murder to voluntary manslaughter; what constitutes an honest and reasonable mistake; and, indirectly, in connection with involuntary manslaughter. But in none of these instances do we have the countervailing consideration of avoiding the subversion of obedience to discipline in combat by encouraging a member to weigh the legality of an order or whether the superior had the authority to issue it. *See* Martin *v.* Mott, 25 US 19, 30 (1827).

The preservation of human life is, of course, or surpassing importance. To accomplish such preservation, members of the armed forces must be held to standards of conduct that will permit punishment of atrocities and enable this nation to follow civilized concepts of warfare. In defending the current standard, the Army Court of Military Review expressed the view that:

Heed must be given not only to the subjective innocence-through-ignorance in the soldier, but to the consequences for his victims. Also, barbarism tends to invite reprisal to the detriment of our own force or disrepute which interferes with the achievement of war aims, even though the barbaric acts were preceded by orders for their commission. Casting the defense of obedience to orders solely in subjective terms of *mens rea* would operate practically to abrogate those objective restraints which are essential to functioning rules of war. United States *v.* Calley, 46 CMR 1131, 1184 (ACMR 1973).

I do not disagree with these comments. But while humanitarian considerations compel us to consider the impact of actions by members of our armed forces on citizens of other nations, I am also convinced that the phrasing of the defense of superior orders should have as its principal objective fairness to the unsophisticated soldier and those of somewhat limited intellect who nonetheless are doing their best to perform their duty.

The test of palpable illegality to the commonest understanding properly balances punishment for the obedience of an obviously illegal order against protection to an accused for following his elementary duty of obeying his superiors. Such a test reinforces the need for obedience as an essential element of military discipline by broadly protecting the soldier who has been effectively trained to look to his superiors for direction. It also promotes fairness by permitting the military jury to consider the particular accused's intelligence, grade, training, and other elements directly related to the issue of whether he should have known an order was illegal. Finally, that test imputes such knowledge to an accused not as a result of simple negligence but on the much stronger circumstantial concept that almost anyone in the armed forces would have immediately recognized that the order was palpably illegal.

I would adopt this standard as the correct instruction for the jury when the defense of superior orders is in issue. Because the original case language is archaic and somewhat ungrammatical, I would rephrase it to require that the military jury be instructed that, despite his asserted defense of superior orders, an accused may be held criminally accountable for his acts, allegedly committed pursuant to such orders, if the court members are convinced beyond a reasonable doubt (1) that almost every member of the armed forces would have immediately recognized that the order was unlawful, and (2) that the accused should have recognized the order's illegality as a consequence of his age, grade, intelligence, experience, and training.

The temptation is to say that even under this new formulation Lieutenant Calley would have been found guilty. No matter how such a position is phrased, essentially it means that the appellate judge rather than the military jury is functioning as a fact finder. My reaction to this has been expressed by the former chief justice of the California Supreme Court in these words:

If an erroneous instruction or an erroneous failure to give an instruction relates to a substantial element of the appellant's case, an appellate court would not find it highly probable that the error did not influence the verdict.

The same authority also expressed this thought:

The concept of fairness extends to reconsideration of the merits when a judgment has been or might have been influenced by error. In that event there should be a retrial in the trial court, time consuming or costly though it may be. The short-cut alternative of reconsidering the merits in the appellate court, because it is familiar with the evidence and aware of the error, has the appeal of saving time and money. Unfortunately, it does not measure up to accepted standards of fairness.

In the instant case, Lieutenant Calley's testimony placed the defense of superior orders in issue, even though he conceded that he knew prisoners were normally to be treated with respect and that the unit's normal practice was to interrogate Vietnamese villagers, release those who could account for themselves, and evacuate those suspected of being a part of the enemy forces. Although crucial parts of his testimony were sharply contested, according to Lieutenant Calley, (1) he had received a briefing before the assault in which he was instructed that every living thing in the village was to be killed, including women and children; (2) he was informed that speed was important in securing the village and moving forward; (3) he was ordered that under no circumstances were any Vietnamese to be allowed to stay behind the lines of his forces; (4) the residents of the village who were taken into custody were hindering the progress of his platoon in taking up the position it was to occupy; and (5) when he informed Captain Medina of this hindrance, he was ordered to kill the villagers and to move his platoon to a proper position.

In addition to the briefing, Lieutenant Calley's experience in the Pinkville area caused him to know that, in the past, when villagers had been left behind his unit, the unit had immediately received sniper fire from the rear as it pressed forward. Faulty intelligence apparently led him also to believe that those persons in the village were not innocent civilians but were either enemies or enemy sympathizers. For a participant in the My Lai operation, the circumstances that could have obtained there may have caused the illegality of alleged orders to kill civilians to be much less clear than they are in a hindsight review.

A *New York Times* Book Reviewer has noted, 'One cannot locate the exact moment in his [Calley's] narrative when one can be absolutely certain that one would have acted differently given the same circumstances.' *See* Paris ed., *New York Herald Tribune*, September 13, 1971.

Since the defense of superior orders was not submitted to the military jury under what I consider to be the proper standard, I would grant Lieutenant Calley a rehearing.

I concur in Judge Quinn's opinion on the other granted issues.

Department of the Army, Headquarters, III Corps and Fort Hood, Texas, General Court-Martial Order Number 29, 7 September 2005

Staff Sergeant Ivan L. Frederick II, U.S. Army, Headquarters and Headquarters Company, 16th Military Police Brigade (Airborne), Fort Bragg, North Carolina 28307, was arraigned at Baghdad and Victory Base, Iraq, on the following offenses at a general court-martial convened by the Commander, III Corps. The case was later transferred to the Commander, III Corps and Fort Hood, upon redeployment from Iraq.

Charge I: Article 81. Plea: Guilty. Finding: Guilty.

Specification 1: Did, at or near Baghdad Central Correctional Facility, Abu Ghraib, Iraq, on or about 24 October 2003, conspire with Corporal Charles A. Graner, Jr. and Private First Class Lynndie R. England, to commit an offense under the Uniform Code of Military Justice, to wit: maltreatment of subordinates, and in order to effect the object of the conspiracy the said Staff Sergeant Frederick handcuffed three detainees together and directed the said Private First Class England to photograph the detainees. Plea: Not Guilty. Finding: Not Guilty.

Specification 2: Did, at or near Baghdad Central Correctional Facility, Abu Ghraib, Iraq, on or about 8 November 2003, conspire with Sergeant Javal S. Davis, Corporal Charles A. Graner, Jr., Specialist Jeremy C. Sivits, Specialist Sabrina D. Harman, Specialist Megan M. Ambuhl, and Private First Class Lynndie R. England, to commit an offense under the Uniform Code of Military Justice, to wit: maltreatment of Subordinates, and in order to effect the object of the conspiracy the said Staff Sergeant Frederick did place naked detainees in a human pyramid and photographed the pyramid of naked detainees. Plea: Guilty, excepting the words 'did place naked detainees in a human pyramid and.' To the excepted words: not guilty. Finding: Guilty, excepting the words 'did place naked detainees in a human pyramid and.' To the excepted words: not guilty.

Charge II: Article 2. Plea: Guilty. Finding: Guilty.

Specification: Was, at or near Baghdad Central Correctional Facility, Abu Ghraib, Iraq, from on or about 20 October 2003 to on or about 1 December 2003, derelict in the performance of his duties in that he willfully failed to protect detainees from abuse, cruelty and maltreatment, as it was his duty to do. Plea: Guilty. Finding: Guilty.

Charge III: Article 93. Plea: Guilty. Finding: Guilty.

Specification 1: At or near Baghdad Central Correctional Facility, Abu Ghraib, Iraq, on or about 8 November 2003 did maltreat a detainee, a person subject to his orders, by participating in and allowing the placing of wires on the detainee's hands while he stood on a Meals Ready to Eat box with his head covered and allowing the detainee to be told he would be electrocuted if he fell off of the box, and allowing the detainee to be photographed. Plea: Guilty, excepting the words 'be told' and substituting the word 'believe.' To the excepted words: not guilty. To the substituted word: guilty. Finding: Guilty, excepting the words 'be told' and substituting the word 'believe.' To the excepted words: not guilty. To the substituted word: guilty.

Specification 2: At or near Baghdad Central Correctional Facility, Abu Ghraib, Iraq, on or about 8 November 2003, did maltreat several detainees, persons subject to his orders, by placing naked detainees in a human pyramid and photographing the pyramid of naked detainees. Plea: Guilty, excepting the words 'placing naked detainees in a human pyramid and.' To the excepted words: not guilty. Finding: Guilty, excepting the words 'placing naked detainees in a human pyramid and.' To the excepted words: not guilty.

Specification 3: At or near Baghdad Central Correctional Facility, Abu Ghraib, Iraq, on or about 8 November 2003, did maltreat several detainees, persons subject to his orders, by ordering the detainees to strip, and then ordering the detainees to masturbate in front of the other detainees and soldiers, and then placing one in a position so that the detainee's face was directly in front of the genitals of another detainee to simulate fellatio and photographing the detainees during these acts. Plea: Guilty, excepting the words 'and then placing one in a position so that the detainee's face was directly in front of the genitals of another detainee to simulate fellatio and photographing the detainees during these acts.' To the excepted words: not guilty. Finding: Guilty, excepting the words 'and then placing one in a position so that the detainee's face was directly in front of the genitals of another detainee to simulate fellatio and photographing the detainees during these acts.' To the excepted words: not guilty.

Specification 4: At or near Baghdad Central Correctional Facility, Abu Ghraib, Iraq, on or about 8 November 2003 did maltreat a detainee, a person subject to his orders, by posing for a photograph sitting on top of a detainee who was bound by padded material between two medical litters. Plea: Guilty. Finding: Guilty.

Specification 5: At or near Baghdad Central Correctional Facility, Abu Ghraib, Iraq, on or about 8 November 2003 did maltreat two detainees, persons subject to his orders ,by grabbing the hands and arms of the said detainees and ordering them to strike or punch each other, with the detainees then striking or punching each other. Plea: Not Guilty. Finding: Not Guilty.

Charge IV: Article 128. Plea: Guilty. Finding: Guilty.

Specification 1: Did, at or near Baghdad Central Correctional Facility, Abu Ghraib, Iraq, on or about 8 November 2003, unlawfully strike several detainees by jumping on and impacting the bodies within a pile of said detainees with his shoulder or upper part of his body. Plea: Not Guilty. Finding: Not Guilty.

Specification 2: Did, at or near Baghdad Central Correctional Facility, Abu Ghraib, Iraq, on or about 8 November 2003, unlawfully stomp on the hands and bare feet of several detainees with his shod feet. Plea: Not Guilty. Finding: Not Guilty.

Specification 3: Did, at or near Baghdad Central Correctional Facility, Abu Ghraib, Iraq, on or about 8 November 2003, commit an assault upon a detainee by striking him with a means or force likely to produce death or grievous bodily harm, to wit: by punching the detainee with a closed fist in the center of the chest with enough force to cause the detainee to have difficulty breathing and require medical attention. Plea: Not guilty, but guilty of the lesser included offense of assault consummated by a battery, excepting the words 'striking him with a means or force likely to produce death or grievous bodily harm, to wit: by punching with enough force to cause the detainee to have difficulty breathing and require medical attention' and substituting therefore the words 'unlawfully striking a detainee in the chest with a closed fist.' To the excepted words: not guilty. To the substituted words: guilty. Finding: Not guilty, but guilty of the lesser included offense of assault consummated by a battery, excepting the words 'striking him with a means or force likely to produce death or grievous bodily harm, to wit: by punching with enough force to cause the detainee to have difficulty breathing and require medical attention' and substituting therefore the words 'unlawfully striking a detainee in the chest with a closed fist.' To the excepted Words: not guilty. To the substituted words: guilty.

Charge V: Article 134. Plea: Guilty. Finding: Guilty.

Specification: Did, at or near Baghdad Central Correctional Facility, Abu Ghraib, Iraq, on or about 8 November 2003, wrongfully commit an indecent act with detainees, Corporal Charles A. Graner, Jr., Specialist Megan M. Ambuhl, and Private First Class Lynndie R. England, by observing a group of detainees masturbating, or attempting to masturbate, while they were located in a public corridor of the Baghdad Central Correctional Facility, with other soldiers who photographed or watched the detainees' actions. Plea: Guilty. Finding: Guilty.

Sentence

Sentence was adjudged on 21 October 2004. To be reduced to the grade of Private (E–1); to forfeit all pay and allowances; to be confined for ten years; and to be discharged with a dishonorable discharge.

Action

Only so much of the sentence as provides for reduction to the grade of Private (E–1); forfeiture of all pay and allowances; confinement for ninety months and a dishonorable discharge is approved and, except for the part of the sentence extending to a dishonorable discharge, will be executed. The accused will be credited with twenty days of confinement against the sentence to confinement.

By command of Lieutenant General Metz.

Article 15–6 Investigation of the 800th Military Police Brigade, 4 May 2004 (Declassified)

1. (U) On 19 January 2004, Lieutenant General (LTG) Ricardo S. Sanchez, Commander, Combined Joint Task Force Seven (CJTF-7), requested that the Commander, US Central Command, appoint an Investigating Officer (IO) in the grade of Major General (MG) or above to investigate the conduct of operations within the 800th Military Police (MP) Brigade. LTG Sanchez requested an investigation of detention and internment operations by the Brigade from 1 November 2003 to present. LTG Sanchez cited recent reports of detainee abuse, escapes from confinement facilities, and accountability lapses, which indicated systemic problems within the brigade and suggested a lack of clear standards, proficiency, and leadership. LTG Sanchez requested a comprehensive and all-encompassing inquiry to make findings and recommendations concerning the fitness and performance of the 800th MP Brigade.

2. (U) On 24 January 2003, the Chief of Staff of US Central Command (CENTCOM), MG R. Steven Whitcomb, on behalf of the CENTCOM Commander, directed that the Commander, Coalition Forces Land Component Command (CFLCC), LTG David D. McKiernan, conduct an investigation into the 800th MP Brigade's detention and internment operations from 1 November 2003 to present. CENTCOM directed that the investigation should inquire into all facts and circumstances surrounding recent reports of suspected detainee abuse in Iraq. It also directed that the investigation inquire into detainee escapes and accountability lapses as reported by CJTF-7, and to gain a more comprehensive and all-encompassing inquiry into the fitness and performance of the 800th MP Brigade.

3. (U) On 31 January 2004, the Commander, CFLCC, appointed MG Antonio M. Taguba, Deputy Commanding General Support, CFLCC, to conduct this investigation. MG Taguba was directed to conduct an informal investigation

under AR 15-6 into the 800th MP Brigade's detention and internment operations. Specifically, MG Taguba was tasked to:

a. (U) Inquire into all the facts and circumstances surrounding recent allegations of detainee abuse, specifically allegations of maltreatment at the Abu Ghraib Prison (Baghdad Central Confinement Facility (BCCF)).

b. (U) Inquire into detainee escapes and accountability lapses as reported by CJTF-7, specifically allegations concerning these events at the Abu Ghraib Prison.

c. (U) Investigate the training, standards, employment, command policies, internal procedures, and command climate in the 800th MP Brigade, as appropriate.

d. (U) Make specific findings of fact concerning all aspects of the investigation, and make any recommendations for corrective action, as appropriate.

4. (U) LTG Sanchez's request to investigate the 800th MP Brigade followed the initiation of a criminal investigation by the US Army Criminal Investigation Command (USACIDC) into specific allegations of detainee abuse committed by members of the 372nd MP Company, 320th MP Battalion in Iraq. These units are part of the 800th MP Brigade. The Brigade is an Iraq Theater asset, TACON to CJTF-7, but OPCON to CFLCC at the time this investigation was initiated. In addition, CJTF-7 had several reports of detainee escapes from U.S./Coalition Confinement Facilities in Iraq over the past several months. These include Camp Bucca, Camp Ashraf, Abu Ghraib, and the High Value Detainee (HVD) Complex/Camp Cropper. The 800th MP Brigade operated these facilities. In addition, four Soldiers from the 320th MP Battalion had been formally charged under the Uniform Code of Military Justice (UCMJ) with detainee abuse in May 2003 at the Theater Internment Facility (TIF) at Camp Bucca, Iraq.

5. (U) I began assembling my investigation team prior to the actual appointment by the CFLCC Commander. I assembled subject matter experts from the CFLCC Provost Marshal (PM) and the CFLCC Staff Judge Advocate (SJA). I selected COL Kinard J. La Fate, CFLCC Provost Marshal to be my Deputy for this investigation. I also contacted the Provost Marshal General of the Army, MG Donald J. Ryder, to enlist the support of MP subject matter experts in the areas of detention and internment operations.

6. (U) The Investigating Team also reviewed the Assessment of DoD Counter-Terrorism Interrogation and Detention Operations in Iraq conducted by MG Geoffrey D. Miller, Commander, Joint Task Force Guantanamo (JTF-GTMO). From 31 August to 9 September 2003, MG Miller led a team of personnel experienced in strategic interrogation to HQ, CJTF-7 and the Iraqi Survey Group (ISG) to review current Iraqi Theater ability to rapidly exploit internees for actionable intelligence. MG Miller's team focused on three areas: intelligence integration, synchronization, and fusion; interrogation operations;

and detention operations. MG Miller's team used JTFGTM procedures and interrogation authorities as baselines.

7. (U) The Investigating Team began its inquiry with an in-depth analysis of the Report on Detention and Corrections in Iraq, dated 5 November 2003, conducted by MG Ryder and a team of military police, legal, medical, and automation experts. The CJTF-7 Commander, LTG Sanchez, had previously requested a team of subject matter experts to assess, and make specific recommendations concerning detention and corrections operations. From 13 October to 6 November 2003, MG Ryder personally led this assessment/ assistance team in Iraq.

Assessment of Dod Counter-Terrorism Interrogation and Detention Operations in Iraq (MG Miller's Assessment)

1. (S/NF) The principal focus of MG Miller's team was on the strategic interrogation of detainees/internees in Iraq. Among its conclusions in its Executive Summary were that CJTF-7 did not have authorities and procedures in place to affect a unified strategy to detain, interrogate, and report information from detainees/internees in Iraq. The Executive Summary also stated that detention operations must act as an enabler for interrogation.

2. (S/NF) With respect to interrogation, MG Miller's Team recommended that CJTF-7 dedicate and train a detention guard force subordinate to the Joint Interrogation Debriefing Center (JIDC) Commander that 'sets the conditions for the successful interrogation and exploitation of internees/detainees.' Regarding Detention Operations, MG Miller's team stated that the function of Detention Operations is to provide a safe, secure, and humane environment that supports the expeditious collection of intelligence. However, it also stated 'it is essential that the guard force be actively engaged in setting the conditions for successful exploitation of the internees.'

3. (S/NF) MG Miller's team also concluded that Joint Strategic Interrogation Operations (within CJTF–7) are hampered by lack of active control of the internees within the detention environment. The Miller Team also stated that establishment of the Theater Joint Interrogation and Detention Center (JIDC) at Abu Ghraib (BCCF) will consolidate both detention and strategic interrogation operations and result in synergy between MP and MI resources and an integrated, synchronized, and focused strategic interrogation effort.

4. (S/NF) MG Miller's team also observed that the application of emerging strategic interrogation strategies and techniques contain new approaches and operational art. The Miller Team also concluded that a legal review and recommendations on internee interrogation operations by a dedicated Command Judge Advocate is required to maximize interrogation effectiveness.

IO Comments on MG Miller's Assessment

1. (S/NF) MG Miller's team recognized that they were using JTF-GTMO operational procedures and interrogation authorities as baselines for its observations and recommendations. There is a strong argument that the intelligence value of detainees held at JTF-Guantanamo (GTMO) is different than that of the detainees/internees held at Abu Ghraib (BCCF) and other detention facilities in Iraq. Currently, there are a large number of Iraqi criminals held at Abu Ghraib (BCCF). These are not believed to be international terrorists or members of Al Qaida, Anser Al Islam, Taliban, and other international terrorist organizations.

2. (S/NF) The recommendations of MG Miller's team that the 'guard force' be actively engaged in setting the conditions for successful exploitation of the internees would appear to be in conflict with the recommendations of MG Ryder's Team and AR 190-8 that military police 'do not participate in military intelligence supervised interrogation sessions.' The Ryder Report concluded that the OEF template whereby military police actively set the favorable conditions for subsequent interviews runs counter to the smooth operation of a detention facility.

Report on Detention and Corrections in Iraq (MG Ryder's Report)

1. (U) MG Ryder and his assessment team conducted a comprehensive review of the entire detainee and corrections system in Iraq and provided recommendations addressing each of the following areas as requested by the Commander CJTF-7:

   a. (U) Detainee and corrections system management.

   b. (U) Detainee management, including detainee movement, segregation, and accountability.

   c. (U) Means of command and control of the detention and corrections system.

   d. (U) Integration of military detention and corrections with the Coalition Provisional Authority (CPA) and adequacy of plans for transition to an Iraqi–run corrections system.

   e. (U) Detainee medical care and health management.

   f. (U) Detention facilities that meet required health, hygiene, and sanitation standards.

   g. (U) Court integration and docket management for criminal detainees.

   h. (U) Detainee legal processing.

   i. (U) Detainee databases and records, including integration with law enforcement and court databases.

2. (U) Many of the findings and recommendations of MG Ryder's team are

beyond the scope of this investigation. However, several important findings are clearly relevant to this inquiry and are summarized below (emphasis is added in certain areas):

A. (U) Detainee Management (Including Movement, Segregation, and Accountability)

1. (U) There is a wide variance in standards and approaches at the various detention facilities. Several Division/Brigade collection points and US monitored Iraqi prisons had flawed or insufficiently detailed use of force and other standing operating procedures or policies (e.g. weapons in the facility, improper restraint techniques, detainee management, etc.) Though, there were no military police units purposely applying inappropriate confinement practices.
2. (U) Currently, due to lack of adequate Iraqi facilities, Iraqi criminals (generally Iraqi-on-Iraqi crimes) are detained with security internees (generally Iraqi-on-Coalition offenses) and EPWs in the same facilities, though segregated indifferent cells/compounds.
3. (U) The management of multiple disparate groups of detained people in a single location by members of the same unit invites confusion about handling, processing, and treatment, and typically facilitates the transfer of information between different categories of detainees.
4. (U) The 800th MP (I/R) units did not receive Internment/Resettlement (I/R) and corrections specific training during their mobilization period. Corrections training is only on the METL of two MP (I/R) Confinement Battalions throughout the Army, one currently serving in Afghanistan, and elements of the other are at Camp Arifjan, Kuwait. MP units supporting JTF-GTMO received ten days of training in detention facility operations, to include two days of unarmed self-defense, training in interpersonal communication skills, forced cell moves, and correctional officer safety.

B. (U) Means of Command and Control of the Detention and Corrections System

1. (U) The 800th MP Brigade was originally task organized with eight MP(I/R) Battalions consisting of both MP Guard and Combat Support companies. Due to force rotation plans, the 800th redeployed two Battalion HHCs in December2003, the 115th MP Battalion and the 324th MP Battalion. In December 2003, the 400th MP Battalion was relieved of its mission and redeployed in January 2004. The 724th MP Battalion redeployed on

11 February 2004 and the remainder is scheduled to redeploy in March and April 2004. They are the 310th MP Battalion, 320th MP Battalion, 530th MP Battalion, and 744th MP Battalion. The units that remain are generally under strength, as Reserve Component units do not have an individual personnel replacement system to mitigate medical losses or the departure of individual Soldiers that have reached twenty-four months of Federal active duty in a five-year period.

2. (U) The 800th MP Brigade (I/R) is currently a CFLCC asset, TACON to CJTF-7 to conduct Internment/Resettlement (I/R) operations in Iraq. All detention operations are conducted in the CJTF-7 AO; Camps Ganci, Vigilant, Bucca, TSP Whitford, and a separate High Value Detention (HVD) site.

3. (U) The 800th MP Brigade has experienced challenges adapting its task organizational structure, training, and equipment resources from a unit designed to conduct standard EPW operations in the COMMZ (Kuwait). Further, the doctrinally trained MP Soldier-to-detainee population ratio and facility layout templates are predicated on a compliant, self-disciplining EPW population, and not criminals or high-risk security internees.

4. (U) EPWs and Civilian Internees should receive the full protections of the Geneva Conventions, unless the denial of these protections is due to specifically articulated military necessity (e.g., no visitation to preclude the direction of insurgency operations).

5. (U) AR 190-8, Enemy Prisoners of War, Retained Personnel, Civilian Internees, and other Detainees, FM 3-19.40, Military Police Internment and Resettlement Operations, and FM 34-52, Intelligence Interrogations, require military police to provide an area for intelligence collection efforts within EPW facilities. Military Police, though adept at passive collection of intelligence within a facility, do not participate in Military Intelligence supervised interrogation sessions. Recent intelligence collection in support of Operation Enduring Freedom posited a template whereby military police actively set favorable conditions for subsequent interviews. Such actions generally run counter to the smooth operation of a detention facility, attempting to maintain its population in a compliant and docile state. The 800th MP Brigade has not been directed to change its facility procedures to set the conditions for MI interrogations, nor participate in those interrogations.

6. MG Ryder's Report also made the following, near-term and mid-term recommendations regarding the command and control of detainees:

a. (U) Align the release process for security internees with DoD Policy. The process of screening security internees should include intelligence findings, interrogation results, and current threat assessment.

b. (U) Determine the scope of intelligence collection that will occur at Camp Vigilant. Refurbish the Northeast Compound to separate the screening operation from the Iraqi run Baghdad Central Correctional Facility. Establish procedures that define the role of military police Soldiers securing the compound, clearly separating the actions of the guards from those of the military intelligence personnel.

c. (U) Consolidate all Security Internee Operations, except the MEK security mission, under a single Military Police Brigade Headquarters for OIF 2.

d. (U) Insist that all units identified to rotate into the Iraqi Theater of Operations (ITO) to conduct internment and confinement operations in support of OIF 2 be organic to CJTF-7.

IO Comments Regarding MG Ryder's Report

1. (U) The objective of MG Ryder's Team was to observe detention and prison operations, identify potential systemic and human rights issues, and provide near-term, mid-term, and long-term recommendations to improve CJTF-7 operations and transition of the Iraqi prison system from US military control/ oversight to the Coalition Provisional Authority and eventually to the Iraqi Government. The Findings and Recommendations of MG Ryder's Team are thorough and precise and should be implemented immediately.

2. (U) Unfortunately, many of the systemic problems that surfaced during MG Ryder's Team's assessment are the very same issues that are the subject of this investigation. In fact, many of the abuses suffered by detainees occurred during, or near to, the time of that assessment. As will be pointed out in detail in subsequent portions of this report, I disagree with the conclusion of MG Ryder's Team in one critical aspect, that being its conclusion that the 800th MP Brigade had not been asked to change its facility procedures to set the conditions for MI interviews. While clearly the 800th MP Brigade and its commanders were not tasked to set conditions for detainees for subsequent MI interrogations, it is obvious from a review of comprehensive CID interviews of suspects and witnesses that this was done at lower levels.

3. (U) I concur fully with MG Ryder's conclusion regarding the effect of AR 190-8. Military Police, though adept at passive collection of intelligence within a facility, should not participate in Military Intelligence supervised interrogation sessions. Moreover, Military Police should not be involved with setting 'favorable conditions' for subsequent interviews. These actions, as will be outlined in this investigation, clearly run counter to the smooth operation of a detention facility.

Preliminary Investigative Actions

1. (U) Following our review of MG Ryder's Report and MG Miller's Report, my investigation team immediately began an in-depth review of all available

documents regarding the 800th MP Brigade. We reviewed in detail the voluminous CID investigation regarding alleged detainee abuses at detention facilities in Iraq, particularly the Abu Ghraib (BCCF) Detention Facility. We analyzed approximately fifty witness statements from military police and military intelligence personnel, potential suspects, and detainees. We reviewed numerous photos and videos of actual detainee abuse taken by detention facility personnel, which are now in the custody and control of the US Army Criminal Investigation Command and the CJTF-7 prosecution team. The photos and videos are not contained in this investigation. We obtained copies of the 800th MP Brigade roster, rating chain, and assorted internal investigations and disciplinary actions involving that command for the past several months.

2. (U) In addition to military police and legal officers from the CFLCC PMO and SJA Offices we also obtained the services of two individuals who are experts in military police detention practices and training. These were LTC Timothy Weathersbee, Commander, 705th MP Battalion, United States Disciplinary Barracks, Fort Leavenworth, and SFC Edward Baldwin, Senior Corrections Advisor, US Army Military Police School, Fort Leonard Wood. I also requested and received the services of Col. (Dr.) Henry Nelson, a trained US Air Force psychiatrist assigned to assist my investigation team.

3. (U) In addition to MG Ryder's and MG Miller's Reports, the team reviewed numerous reference materials including the 12 October 2003 CJTF-7 Interrogation and Counter-Resistance Policy, the AR 15-6 Investigation on Riot and Shootings at Abu Ghraib on24 November 2003, the 205th MI Brigade's Interrogation Rules of Engagement (IROE), facility staff logs/journals and numerous records of AR 15-6 investigations and Serious Incident Reports (SIRs) on detainee escapes/shootings and disciplinary matters from the 800th MP Brigade.

4. (U) On 2 February 2004, I took my team to Baghdad for a one-day inspection of the Abu Ghraib Prison (BCCF) and the High Value Detainee (HVD) Complex in order to become familiar with those facilities. We also met with Col. Jerry Mocello, Commander, 3rd MP Criminal Investigation Group (CID), Col. Dave Quantock, Commander, 16th MP Brigade, Col. Dave Phillips, Commander, 89th MP Brigade, and Col. Ed Sannwaldt, CJTF-7 Provost Marshal. On 7 February 2004, the team visited the Camp Bucca Detention Facility to familiarize itself with the facility and operating structure. In addition, on 6 and 7 February 2004, at Camp Doha, Kuwait, we conducted extensive training sessions on approved detention practices. We continued our preparation by reviewing the ongoing CID investigation and were briefed by the Special Agent in Charge, CW2 Paul Arthur. We refreshed ourselves on the applicable reference materials within each team member's area of expertise, and practiced investigative techniques. I met with the team on numerous occasions to

finalize appropriate witness lists, review existing witness statements, arrange logistics, and collect potential evidence. We also coordinated with CJTF-7 to arrange witness attendance, force protection measures, and general logistics for the team's move to Baghdad on 8 February 2004.

5. (U) At the same time, due to the Transfer of Authority on 1 February 2004 between III Corps and V Corps, and the upcoming demobilization of the 800th MP Brigade Command, I directed that several critical witnesses who were preparing to leave the theater remain at Camp Arifjan, Kuwait until they could be interviewed. My team deployed to Baghdad on 8 February 2004 and conducted a series of interviews with a variety of witnesses. We returned to Camp Doha, Kuwait on 13 February 2004. On 14 and 15 February we interviewed a number of witnesses from the 800th MP Brigade. On 17 February we returned to Camp Bucca, Iraq, to complete interviews of witnesses at that location. From 18 February through 28 February, we collected documents, compiled references, did follow–up interviews, and completed a detailed analysis of the volumes of materials accumulated throughout our investigation. On 29 February, we finalized our executive summary and out-briefing slides. On 9 March we submitted the AR 15-6 written report with findings and recommendations to the CFLCC Deputy SJA, LTC Mark Johnson, for a legal sufficiency review. The out-brief to the appointing authority, LTG McKiernan, took place on 3 March 2004.

Findings and Recommendations (Part One)

(U) The investigation should inquire into all of the facts and circumstances surrounding recent allegations of detainee abuse, specifically, allegations of maltreatment at the Abu Ghraib Prison (Baghdad Central Confinement Facility).

1. (U) The US Army Criminal Investigation Command (CID), led by Col. Jerry Mocello, and a team of highly trained professional agents have done a superb job of investigating several complex and extremely disturbing incidents of detainee abuse at the Abu Ghraib Prison. They conducted over fifty interviews of witnesses, potential criminal suspects, and detainees. They also uncovered numerous photos and videos portraying in graphic detail detainee abuse by Military Police personnel on numerous occasions from October to December 2003. Several potential suspects rendered full and complete confessions regarding their personal involvement and the involvement of fellow Soldiers in this abuse. Several potential suspects invoked their rights under Article 31 of the Uniform Code of Military Justice (UCMJ) and the 5th Amendment of the U.S. Constitution.

2. (U) In addition to a comprehensive and exhaustive review of all of these

statements and documentary evidence, we also interviewed numerous officers, NCOs, and junior enlisted Soldiers in the 800th MP Brigade, as well as members of the 205th Military Intelligence Brigade working at the prison. We did not believe it was necessary to re-interview all the numerous witnesses who had previously provided comprehensive statements to CID, and I have adopted those statements for the purposes of this investigation.

Regarding Part One of the Investigation, I Make the Following Specific Findings of Fact

1. (U) That Forward Operating Base (FOB) Abu Ghraib (BCCF) provides security of both criminal and security detainees at the Baghdad Central Correctional Facility, facilitates the conducting of interrogations for CJTF-7, supports other CPA operations at the prison, and enhances the force protection/quality of life of Soldiers assigned in order to ensure the success of ongoing operations to secure a free Iraq.

2. (U) That the Commander, 205th Military Intelligence Brigade, was designated by CJTF-7 as the Commander of FOB Abu Ghraib (BCCF) effective 19 November 2003. That the 205th MI Brigade conducts operational and strategic interrogations for CJTF-7. That from 19 November 2003 until Transfer of Authority (TOA) on 6 February 2004, Col. Thomas M. Pappas was the Commander of the 205th MI Brigade and the Commander of FOB Abu Ghraib (BCCF).

3. (U) That the 320th Military Police Battalion of the 800th MP Brigade is responsible for the Guard Force at Camp Ganci, Camp Vigilant, & Cellblock 1 of FOB Abu Ghraib (BCCF). That from February 2003 to until he was suspended from his duties on 17 January 2004, LTC Jerry Phillabaum served as the Battalion Commander of the 320th MP Battalion. That from December 2002 until he was suspended from his duties, on 17 January 2004, CPT Donald Reese served as the Company Commander of the 372nd MP Company, which was in charge of guarding detainees at FOB Abu Ghraib. I further find that both the 320th MP Battalion and the 372nd MP Company were located within the confines of FOB Abu Ghraib.

4. (U) That from July of 2003 to the present, BG Janis L. Karpinski was the Commander of the 800th MP Brigade.

5. (S) That between October and December 2003, at the Abu Ghraib Confinement Facility (BCCF), numerous incidents of sadistic, blatant, and wanton criminal abuses were inflicted on several detainees. This systemic and illegal abuse of detainees was intentionally perpetrated by several members of the military police guard force (372nd Military Police Company, 320th Military Police Battalion, 800th MP Brigade), in Tier (section) 1-A of the Abu Ghraib Prison (BCCF). The allegations of abuse were substantiated by detailed witness statements

and the discovery of extremely graphic photographic evidence. Due to the extremely sensitive nature of these photographs and videos, the ongoing CID investigation, and the potential for the criminal prosecution of several suspects, the photographic evidence is not included in the body of my investigation. The pictures and videos are available from the Criminal Investigative Command and the CTJF-7 prosecution team. In addition to the aforementioned crimes, there were also abuses committed by members of the 325th MI Battalion, 205th MI Brigade, and Joint Interrogation and Debriefing Center (JIDC). Specifically, on 24 November 2003, SPC Luciana Spencer, 205th MI Brigade, sought to degrade a detainee by having him strip and returned to cell naked.

6. (S) I find that the intentional abuse of detainees by military police personnel included the following acts:

a. (S) Punching, slapping, and kicking detainees; jumping on their naked feet.

b. (S) Videotaping and photographing naked male and female detainees.

c. (S) Forcibly arranging detainees in various sexually explicit positions for photographing.

d. (S) Forcing detainees to remove their clothing and keeping them naked for several days at a time.

e. (S) Forcing naked male detainees to wear women's underwear.

f. (S) Forcing groups of male detainees to masturbate themselves while being photographed and videotaped.

g. (S) Arranging naked male detainees in a pile and then jumping on them.

h. (S) Positioning a naked detainee on a MRE Box, with a sandbag on his head, and attaching wires to his fingers, toes, and penis to simulate electric torture.

i. (S) Writing 'I am a Rapist' [*sic.*] on the leg of a detainee alleged to have forcibly raped a fifteen-year old fellow detainee, and then photographing him naked.

j. (S) Placing a dog chain or strap around a naked detainee's neck and having a female Soldier pose for a picture.

k. (S) A male MP guard having sex with a female detainee.

l. (S) Using military working dogs (without muzzles) to intimidate and frighten detainees, and in at least one case biting and severely injuring a detainee.

m. (S) Taking photographs of dead Iraqi detainees.

7. (U) These findings are amply supported by written confessions provided by several of the suspects, written statements provided by detainees, and witness statements. In reaching my findings, I have carefully considered the pre-existing statements of the following witnesses and suspects:

a. (U) SPC Jeremy Sivits, 372nd MP Company—Suspect.

b. (U) SPC Sabrina Harman, 372nd MP Company—Suspect.

c. (U) SGT Javal S. Davis, 372nd MP Company—Suspect.

d. (U) PFC Lynndie R. England, 372nd MP Company—Suspect.

e. (U) Adel Nakhla, Civilian Translator, Titan Corp., Assigned to the 205th MI Brigade.

f. (U) SPC Joseph M. Darby, 372nd MP Company.

g. (U) SGT Neil A. Wallin, 109th Area Support Medical Battalion.

h. (U) SGT Samuel Jefferson Provance, 302nd MI Battalion.

i. (U) Torin S. Nelson, Contractor, Titan Corp., Assigned to the 205th MI Brigade.

j. (U) CPL Matthew Scott Bolanger, 372nd MP Company.

k. (U) SPC Mathew C. Wisdom, 372nd MP Company.

l. (U) SSG Reuben R. Layton, Medic, 109th Medical Detachment.

m. (U) SPC John V. Polak, 229th MP Company.

8. (U) In addition, several detainees also described the following acts of abuse, which under the circumstances, I find credible based on the clarity of their statements and supporting evidence provided by other witnesses:

a. (U) Breaking chemical lights and pouring the phosphoric liquid on detainees.

b. (U) Threatening detainees with a charged 9-mm pistol.

c. (U) Pouring cold water on naked detainees.

d. (U) Beating detainees with a broom handle and a chair.

e. (U) Threatening male detainees with rape.

f. (U) Allowing a military police guard to stitch the wound of a detainee who was injured after being slammed against the wall in his cell.

g. (U) Sodomizing a detainee with a chemical light and perhaps a broom stick.

h. (U) Using military working dogs to frighten and intimidate detainees with threats of attack, and in one instance actually biting a detainee.

9. (U) I have carefully considered the statements provided by the following detainees, which under the circumstances I find credible based on the clarity of their statements and supporting evidence provided by other witnesses:

a. (U) Amjed Isail Waleed, Detainee No. 151365.

b. (U) Hiadar Saber Abed Miktub-Aboodi, Detainee No. 13077.

c. (U) Huessin Mohssein Al-Zayiadi, Detainee No. 19446.

d. (U) Kasim Mehaddi Hilas, Detainee No. 151108.

e. (U) Mohanded Juma Juma [sic.], Detainee No. 152307.

f. (U) Mustafa Jassim Mustafa, Detainee No. 150542.

g. (U) Shalan Said Alsharoni, Detainee, No. 150422.

h. (U) Abd Alwhab Youss, Detainee No. 150425.

i. (U) Asad Hamza Hanfosh, Detainee No. 152529.

j. (U) Nori Samir Gunbar Al-Yasseri, Detainee No. 7787.

k. (U) Thaar Salman Dawod, Detainee No. 150427.

l. (U) Ameen Sa'eed Al-Sheikh, Detainee No. 151362.

m. (U) Abdou Hussain Saad Faleh, Detainee No. 18470

10. (U) I find that contrary to the provision of AR 190-8, and the findings found in MG Ryder's Report, Military Intelligence (MI) interrogators and Other US Government Agency's (OGA) interrogators actively requested that MP guards set physical and mental conditions for favorable interrogation of witnesses. Contrary to the findings of MG Ryder's Report, I find that personnel assigned

to the 372nd MP Company, 800th MP Brigade were directed to change facility procedures to 'set the conditions' for MI interrogations. I find no direct evidence that MP personnel actually participated in those MI interrogations.

11. (U) I reach this finding based on the actual proven abuse that I find was inflicted on detainees and by the following witness statements.

a. (U) SPC Sabrina Harman, 372nd MP Company, stated in her sworn statement regarding the incident where a detainee was placed on a box with wires attached to his fingers, toes, and penis, 'that her job was to keep detainees awake.' She stated that MI was talking to CPL Grainer. She stated: 'MI wanted to get them to talk. It is Grainer and Frederick's job to do things for MI and OGA to get these people to talk.'

b. (U) Sgt. Javal S. Davis, 372nd MP Company, stated in his sworn statement as follows: 'I witnessed prisoners in the MI hold section, wing 1A being made to do various things that I would question morally. In Wing 1A we were told that they had different rules and different SOP for treatment. I never saw a set of rules or SOP for that section just word of mouth. The Soldier in charge of 1Awas Corporal Granier. He stated that the Agents and MI Soldiers would ask him to do things, but nothing was ever in writing he would complain [*sic*].' When asked why the rules in 1A/1B were different than the rest of the wings, Sgt. Davis stated: 'The rest of the wings are regular prisoners and 1A/B are Military Intelligence (MI) holds.' When asked why he did not inform his chain of command about this abuse, Sgt. Davis stated: 'Because I assumed that if they were doing things out of the ordinary or outside the guidelines, someone would have said something. Also the wing belongs to MI and it appeared MI personnel approved of the abuse.' Sgt. Davis also stated that he had heard MI insinuate to the guards to abuse the inmates. When asked what MI said he stated: 'Loosen this guy up for us,' 'Make sure he has a bad night,' 'Make sure he gets the treatment.' He claimed these comments were made to Cpl. Granier and SSgt. Frederick. Finally, Sgt. Davis stated that [*sic*]: 'the MI staffs to my understanding have been giving Granier compliments on the way he has been handling the MI holds. Example being statements like, "Good job, they're breaking down real fast. They answer every question. They're giving out good information, Finally, and Keep up the good work. Stuff like that."'

c. (U) SPC Jason Kennel, 372nd MP Company, was asked if he were present when any detainees were abused. He stated: 'I saw them nude, but MI would tell us to take away their mattresses, sheets, and clothes.' He could not recall who in MI had instructed him to do this, but commented that 'if they wanted me to do that they needed to give me paperwork.' He was later informed that 'we could not do anything to embarrass the prisoners.'

d. (U) Mr. Adel L. Nakhla, a U.S. civilian contract translator was questioned about several detainees accused of rape. He observed [*sic*]: 'They (detainees) were all naked, a bunch of people from MI, the MP were there that night and the inmates were ordered by Sgt. Granier and Sgt. Frederick ordered the guys while questioning them to admit what they did. They made them do strange exercises by sliding on their stomach, jump up and down, throw water on them and made them some wet, called them all kinds of names such as 'gays' do they like to make love to guys, then they handcuffed their hands together and their legs with shackles and started to stack them on top of each other by insuring that the bottom guys penis will touch the guy on tops butt.

e. (U) SPC Neil A. Wallin, 109th Area Support Medical Battalion, a medic testified that: 'Cell 1A was used to house high priority detainees and cell 1B was used to house the high risk or trouble making detainees. During my tour at the prison I observed that when the male detainees were first brought to the facility, some of them were made to wear female underwear, which I think was to somehow break them down.'

12. (U) I find that prior to its deployment to Iraq for Operation Iraqi Freedom, the 320th MP Battalion and the 372nd MP Company had received no training in detention/internee operations. I also find that very little instruction or training was provided to MP personnel on the applicable rules of the Geneva Convention Relative to the Treatment of Prisoners of War, FM 27-10, AR 190-8, or FM 3-19.40. Moreover, I find that few, if any, copies of the Geneva Conventions were ever made available to MP personnel or detainees. (ANNEXES 21-24, 33, and multiple witness statements)

13. (U) Another obvious example of the Brigade Leadership not communicating with its Soldiers or ensuring their tactical proficiency concerns the incident of detainee abuse that occurred at Camp Bucca, Iraq, on 12 May 2003. Soldiers from the 223rd MP Company reported to the 800th MP Brigade Command at Camp Bucca that four Military Police Soldiers from the 320th MP Battalion had abused a number of detainees during in processing at Camp Bucca. An extensive CID investigation determined that four soldiers from the 320th MP Battalion had kicked and beaten these detainees following a transport mission from Talil Air Base.

14. (U) Formal charges under the UCMJ were preferred against these Soldiers and an Article 32 Investigation conducted by LTC Gentry. He recommended a general court martial for the four accused, which BG Karpinski supported. Despite this documented abuse, there is no evidence that BG Karpinski ever attempted to remind 800th MP Soldiers of the requirements of the Geneva Conventions regarding detainee treatment or took any steps to ensure that such abuse was not repeated. Nor is there any evidence that LTC(P) Phillabaum, the commander of the Soldiers involved in the Camp Bucca abuse incident, took any initiative to ensure his Soldiers were properly trained regarding detainee treatment.

Recommendations as to Part One of the Investigation

1. (U) Immediately deploy to the Iraq Theater an integrated multi-discipline Mobile Training Team (MTT) comprised of subject matter experts in internment/resettlement operations, international and operational law, information technology, facility management, interrogation and intelligence gathering techniques, chaplains, Arab cultural awareness, and medical practices as it pertains to I/R activities. This team needs to oversee and conduct comprehensive training in all aspects of detainee and confinement operations.

2. (U) That all military police and military intelligence personnel involved in any aspect of detainee operations or interrogation operations in CJTF-7, and subordinate units, be immediately provided with training by an international/operational law attorney on the specific provisions of The Law of Land Warfare FM 27-10, specifically the Geneva Convention Relative to the Treatment of Prisoners of War, Enemy Prisoners of War, Retained Personnel, Civilian Internees, and Other Detainees, and AR 190-8.

3. (U) That a single commander in CJTF-7 be responsible for overall detainee operations throughout the Iraq Theater of Operations. I also recommend that the Provost Marshal General of the Army assign a minimum of two (2) subject matter experts, one officer and one NCO, to assist CJTF-7 in coordinating detainee operations.

4. (U) That detention facility commanders and interrogation facility commanders ensure that appropriate copies of the Geneva Convention Relative to the Treatment of Prisoners of War and notice of protections be made available in both English and the detainees' language and be prominently displayed in all detention facilities. Detainees with questions regarding their treatment should be given the full opportunity to read the Convention.

5. (U) That each detention facility commander and interrogation facility commander publish a complete and comprehensive set of Standing Operating Procedures (SOPs) regarding treatment of detainees, and that all personnel be required to read the SOPs and sign a document indicating that they have read and understand the SOPs.

6. (U) That in accordance with the recommendations of MG Ryder's Assessment Report, and my findings and recommendations in this investigation, all units in the Iraq Theater of Operations conducting internment/confinement/detainment operations in support of Operation Iraqi Freedom be OPCON for all purposes, to include action under the UCMJ, to CJTF-7.

7. (U) Appoint the C3, CJTF as the staff proponent for detainee operations in the Iraq Joint Operations Area (JOA) (MG Tom Miller, C3, CJTF-7, has been appointed by COMCJTF-7).

8. (U) That an inquiry UP AR 381-10, Procedure 15 be conducted to determine the extent of culpability of Military Intelligence personnel, assigned to the

205th MI Brigade and the Joint Interrogation and Debriefing Center (JIDC) regarding abuse of detainees at Abu Ghraib (BCCF).

9. (U) That it is critical that the proponent for detainee operations is assigned a dedicated Senior Judge Advocate, with specialized training and knowledge of international and operational law, to assist and advise on matters of detainee operations.

Findings as to Part Two of the Investigation

(U) The Investigation enquires into detainee escapes and accountability lapses as reported by CJTF-7, specifically allegations concerning these events at the Abu Ghraib Prison: Regarding Part Two Of The Investigation, I Make The Following Specific Findings Of Fact:

1. The 800th MP Brigade was responsible for theater-wide Internment and Resettlement (I/R) operations.

2. (U) The 320th MP Battalion, 800th MP Brigade was tasked with detainee operations at the Abu Ghraib Prison Complex during the time period covered in this investigation.

3. (U) The 310th MP Battalion, 800th MP Brigade was tasked with detainee operations and Forward Operating Base (FOB) Operations at the Camp Bucca Detention Facility until TOA on 26 February 2004.

4. (U) The 744th MP Battalion, 800th MP Brigade was tasked with detainee operations and FOB Operations at the HVD Detention Facility until TOA on 4 March 2004.

5. (U) The 530th MP Battalion, 800th MP Brigade was tasked with detainee operations and FOB Operations at the MEK holding facility until TOA on 15 March 2004.

6. (U) Detainee operations include accountability, care, and wellbeing of Enemy Prisoners of War, Retained Person, Civilian Detainees, and Other Detainees, as well as Iraqi criminal prisoners.

7. (U) The accountability for detainees is doctrinally an MP task IAW FM 3-19.40.

8. (U) There is a general lack of knowledge, implementation, and emphasis of basic legal, regulatory, doctrinal, and command requirements within the 800th MP Brigade and its subordinate units.

9. (U) The handling of detainees and criminal prisoners after in-processing was inconsistent from detention facility to detention facility, compound to compound, encampment to encampment, and even shift to shift throughout the 800th MP Brigade AOR.

10. (U) Camp Bucca, operated by the 310th MP Battalion, had a 'Criminal Detainee In-Processing SOP' and a 'Training Outline' for transferring and releasing detainees, which appears to have been followed.

11. (U) Incoming and outgoing detainees are being documented in the National Detainee Reporting System (NDRS) and Biometric Automated Toolset System (BATS) as required by regulation at all detention facilities. However, it is underutilized and often does not give a 'real time' accurate picture of the detainee population due to untimely updating.

12. (U) There was a severe lapse in the accountability of detainees at the Abu Ghraib Prison Complex. The 320th MP Battalion used a self-created 'change sheet' to document the transfer of a detainee from one location to another. For proper accountability, it is imperative that these change sheets be processed and the detainee manifest be updated within twenty-four hours of movement. At Abu Ghraib, this process would often take as long as four days to complete. This lag-time resulted in inaccurate detainee Internment Serial Number (ISN) counts, gross differences in the detainee manifest and the actual occupants of an individual compound, and significant confusion of the MP Soldiers. The 320th MP Battalion S-1, CPT Theresa Delbalso, and the S-3, Maj. David DiNenna, explained that this breakdown was due to the lack of manpower to process change sheets in a timely manner.

13. (U) The 320th Battalion TACSOP requires detainee accountability at least four times daily at Abu Ghraib. However, a detailed review of their operational journals revealed that these accounts were often not done or not documented by the unit. Additionally, there is no indication that accounting errors or the loss of a detainee in the accounting process triggered any immediate corrective action by the Battalion TOC.

14. (U) There is a lack of standardization in the way the 320th MP Battalion conducted physical counts of their detainees. Each compound within a given encampment did their headcounts differently. Some compounds had detainees line up in lines of ten, some had them sit in rows, and some moved all the detainees to one end of the compound and counted them as they passed to the other end of the compound.

15. (U) FM 3-19.40 outlines the need for two roll calls (100% ISN band checks) per day. The 320th MP Battalion did this check only two times per week. Due to the lack of real-time updates to the system, these checks were regularly inaccurate.

16. (U) The 800th MP Brigade and subordinate units adopted non-doctrinal terms such as 'band checks,' 'roll-ups,' and 'call-ups,' which contributed to the lapses in accountability and confusion at the soldier level.

17. (U) Operational journals at the various compounds and the 320th Battalion TOC contained numerous unprofessional entries and flippant comments, which highlighted the lack of discipline within the unit. There was no indication that the journals were ever reviewed by anyone in their chain of command.

18. (U) Accountability SOPs were not fully developed and standing TACSOPs were widely ignored. Any SOPs that did exist were not trained on, and were

never distributed to the lowest level. Most procedures were shelved at the unit TOC, rather than at the subordinate units and guards mount sites.

19. (U) Accountability and facility operations SOPs lacked specificity, implementation measures, and a system of checks and balances to ensure compliance.

20. (U) Basic Army Doctrine was not widely referenced or utilized to develop the accountability practices throughout the 800th MP Brigade's subordinate units. Daily processing, accountability, and detainee care appears to have been made up as the operations developed with reliance on, and guidance from, junior members of the unit who had civilian corrections experience.

21. (U) Soldiers were poorly prepared and untrained to conduct I/R operations prior to deployment, at the mobilization site, upon arrival in theater, and throughout their mission.

22. (U) The documentation provided to this investigation identified twenty-seven escapes or attempted escapes from the detention facilities throughout the 800th MP Brigade's AOR. Based on my assessment and detailed analysis of the substandard accountability process maintained by the 800th MP Brigade, it is highly likely that there were several more unreported cases of escape that were probably 'written off' as administrative errors or otherwise undocumented. 1LT Lewis Raeder, Platoon Leader, 372nd MP Company, reported knowing about at least two additional escapes(one from a work detail and one from a window) from Abu Ghraib (BCCF) that were not documented. LTC Dennis Mc Glone, Commander, 744th MP Battalion, detailed the escape of one detainee at the High Value Detainee Facility who went to the latrine and then outran the guards and escaped. Lastly, BG Janis Karpinski, Commander, 800th MP Brigade, stated that there were more than thirty-two escapes from her holding facilities, which does not match the number derived from the investigation materials.

23. (U) The Abu Ghraib and Camp Bucca detention facilities are significantly over their intended maximum capacity while the guard force is undermanned and under resourced. This imbalance has contributed to the poor living conditions, escapes, and accountability lapses at the various facilities. The overcrowding of the facilities also limits the ability to identify and segregate leaders in the detainee population who maybe organizing escapes and riots within the facility.

24. (U) The screening, processing, and release of detainees who should not be in custody takes too long and contributes to the overcrowding and unrest in the detention facilities. There are currently three separate release mechanisms in the theater-wide internment operations. First, the apprehending unit can release a detainee if there is a determination that their continued detention is not warranted. Secondly, a criminal detainee can be released after it has been determined that the detainee has no intelligence value, and that their

release would not be detrimental to society. BG Karpinski had signature authority to release detainees in this second category. Lastly, detainees accused of committing 'Crimes Against the Coalition,' who are held throughout the separate facilities in the CJTF-7 AOR, can be released upon a determination that they are of no intelligence value and no longer pose a significant threat to Coalition Forces. The release process for this category of detainee is a screening by the local U.S. Forces Magistrate Cell and a review by a Detainee Release Board consisting of BG Karpinski, Col. Marc Warren, SJA, CJTF-7, and MG Barbara Fast, C-2, CJTF-7. MG Fast is the 'Detainee Release Authority' for detainees being held for committing crimes against the coalition. According to BG Karpinski, this category of detainee makes up more than 60% of the total detainee population, and is the fastest growing category. However, MG Fast, according to BG Karpinski, routinely denied the board's recommendations to release detainees in this category who were no longer deemed a threat and clearly met the requirements for release. According to BG Karpinski, the extremely slow and ineffective release process has significantly contributed to the overcrowding of the facilities.

25. (U) After Action Reviews (AARs) are not routinely being conducted after an escape or other serious incident. No lessons learned seem to have been disseminated to subordinate units to enable corrective action at the lowest level. The Investigation Team requested copies of AARs, and none were provided (Multiple Witness Statements).

26. (U) Lessons learned (i.e. Findings and Recommendations from various 15-6 Investigations concerning escapes and accountability lapses) were rubber stamped as approved and ordered implemented by BG Karpinski. There is no evidence that the majority of her orders directing the implementation of substantive changes were ever acted upon. Additionally, there was no follow-up by the command to verify the corrective actions were taken. Had the findings and recommendations contained within their own investigations been analyzed and actually implemented by BG Karpinski, many of the subsequent escapes, accountability lapses, and cases of abuse may have been prevented.

27. (U) The perimeter lighting around Abu Ghraib and the detention facility at Camp Bucca is inadequate and needs to be improved to illuminate dark areas that have routinely become avenues of escape.

28. (U) Neither the camp rules nor the provisions of the Geneva Conventions are posted in English or in the language of the detainees at any of the detention facilities in the 800th MP Brigade's AOR, even after several investigations had annotated the lack of his critical requirement (Multiple Witness Statements and the Personal Observations of the Investigation Team).

29. (U) The Iraqi guards at Abu Ghraib (BCCF) demonstrate questionable work ethics and loyalties, and are a potentially dangerous contingent within

the Hard-Site. These guards have furnished the Iraqi criminal inmates with contraband, weapons, and information. Additionally, they have facilitated the escape of at least one detainee.

30. (U) In general, U.S. civilian contract personnel (Titan Corporation, CACI, etc.), third country nationals, and local contractors do not appear to be properly supervised within the detention facility at Abu Ghraib. During our on-site inspection, they wandered about with too much unsupervised free access in the detainee area. Having civilians in various outfits (civilian and DCUs) in and about the detainee area causes confusion and may have contributed to the difficulties in the accountability process and with detecting escapes (Multiple Witness Statements and the Personal Observations of the Investigation Team).

31. (U) SGM Marc Emerson, Operations SGM, 320th MP Battalion, contended that the Detainee Rules of Engagement (DROE) and the general principles of the Geneva Convention were briefed at every guard mount and shift change on Abu Ghraib. However, none of our witnesses, nor our personal observations, support his contention. I find that SGM Emerson was not a credible witness.

32. (U) Several interviewees insisted that the MP and MI Soldiers at Abu Ghraib (BCCF) received regular training on the basics of detainee operations; however, they have been unable to produce any verifying documentation, sign-in rosters, or soldiers who can recall the content of this training.

33. (S/NF) The various detention facilities operated by the 800th MP Brigade have routinely held persons brought to them by Other Government Agencies (OGAs) without accounting for them, knowing their identities, or even the reason for their detention. The Joint Interrogation and Debriefing Center (JIDC) at Abu Ghraib called these detainees 'ghost detainees.' On at least one occasion, the 320th MP Battalion at Abu Ghraib held a handful of 'ghost detainees' (6-8) for OGAs that they moved around within the facility to hide them from a visiting International Committee of the Red Cross (ICRC) survey team. This maneuver was deceptive, contrary to Army Doctrine, and in violation of international law.

34. (U) The following riots, escapes, and shootings have been documented and reported to this Investigation Team. Although there is no data from other missions of similar size and duration to compare the number of escapes with, the most significant factors derived from these reports are twofold. First, investigations and SIRs lacked critical data needed to evaluate the details of each incident. Second, each investigation seems to have pointed to the same types of deficiencies; however, little to nothing was done to correct the problems and to implement the recommendations as was ordered by BG Karpinski, nor was there any command emphasis to ensure these deficiencies were corrected:

a. (U) 4 June '03: This escape was mentioned in the 15-6 Investigation covering the 13 June '03 escape, recapture, and shootings of detainees at Camp Vigilant

(320th MP Battalion). However, no investigation or additional information was provided as requested by this investigation team.

b. (U) 9 June '03: Riot and shootings of five detainees at Camp Cropper (115th MP Battalion). Several detainees allegedly rioted after a detainee was subdued by MPs of the 115th MP Battalion after striking a guard in compound 'B' of Camp Cropper. A 15-6 investigation by 1LT Magowan (115th MP Battalion, Platoon Leader) concluded that a detainee had acted up and hit an MP. After being subdued, one of the MPs took off his DCU top and flexed his muscles to the detainees, which further escalated the riot. The MPs were overwhelmed and the guards fired lethal rounds to protect the life of the compound MPs, whereby five detainees were wounded. Contributing factors were poor communications, no clear chain of command, facility obstructed views of posted guards, the QRF did not have non-lethal equipment, and the SOP was inadequate and outdated.

c. (U) 12 June '03: Escape and recapture of detainee No. 8399, escape and shooting of detainee No. 7166, and attempted escape of an unidentified detainee from Camp Cropper Holding Area (115th MP Battalion). Several detainees allegedly made their escape in the nighttime hours prior to 0300. A 15-6 investigation by CPT Wendlandt (115th MP Battalion, S-2) concluded that the detainees allegedly escaped by crawling under the wire at a location with inadequate lighting. One detainee was stopped prior to escape. An MP of the 115th MP Battalion search team recaptured detainee No. 8399, and detainee No. 7166 was shot and killed by a Soldier during the recapture process. Contributing factors were overcrowding, poor lighting, and the nature of the hardened criminal detainees at that location. It is of particular note that the command was informed at least twenty-four hours in advance of the upcoming escape attempt and started doing amplified announcements in Arabic stating the camp rules. The investigation pointed out that rules and guidelines were not posted in the camps in the detainees' native languages.

d. (U) 13 June '03: Escape and recapture of detainee No. 8968 and the shooting of eight detainees at Abu Ghraib (BCCF) (320th MP Battalion). Several detainees allegedly attempted to escape at about 1400 hours from the Camp Vigilant Compound, Abu Ghraib (BCCF). A 15-6 investigation by CPT Wyks (400th MP Battalion, S-1) concluded that the detainee allegedly escaped by sliding under the wire while the tower guard was turned in the other direction. This detainee was subsequently apprehended by the QRF. At about 1600 the same day, thirty to forty detainees rioted and pelted three interior MP guards with rocks. One guard was injured and the tower guards fired lethal rounds at the rioters injuring seven and killing one detainee.

e. (U) 05 November '03: Escape of detainees No. 9877 and No. 10739 from Abu Ghraib (320th MP Battalion). Several detainees allegedly escaped at 0345 from the Hard-Site, Abu Ghraib (BCCF). An SIR was initiated by SPC Warner

(320th MP Battalion, S-3 RTO). The SIR indicated that two criminal prisoners escaped through their cell window in tier 3A of the Hard-Site. No information on findings, contributing factors, or corrective action has been provided to this investigation team.

f. (U) 07 November '03: Escape of detainee No. 14239 from Abu Ghraib (320th MP Battalion). A detainee allegedly escaped at 1330 from Compound 2 of the Ganci Encampment, Abu Ghraib (BCCF). An SIR was initiated by SSgt. Hydro (320th MP Battalion, S-3 Asst. NCOIC). The SIR indicated that a detainee escaped from the North end of the compound and was discovered missing during distribution of the noon meal, but there is no method of escape listed in the SIR. No information on findings, contributing factors, or corrective action has been provided to this investigation team.

g. (U) 08 November '03: Escape of detainees No. 115089, No. 151623, No. 151624, No. 116734, No. 116735, and No. 116738 from Abu Ghraib (320th MP Battalion). Several detainees allegedly escaped at 2022 from Compound 8 of the Ganci encampment, Abu Ghraib. An SIR was initiated by Maj. DiNenna (320th MP Battalion, S-3). The SIR indicated that five to six prisoners escaped from the North end of the compound, but there is no method of escape listed in the SIR. No information on findings, contributing factors, or corrective action has been provided to this investigation team.

h. (U) 24 November '03: Riot and shooting of twelve detainees No. 150216, No. 150894, No. 153096, No. 153165, No. 153169, No. 116361, No. 153399, No. 20257, No. 150348, No. 152616, No. 116146, and No. 152156 at Abu Ghraib (320th MP Battalion). Several detainees allegedly began to riot at about 1300 in all of the compounds at the Ganci encampment. This resulted in the shooting deaths of three detainees, nine wounded detainees, and nine injured U.S. Soldiers. A 15-6 investigation by Col. Bruce Falcone (220th MP Brigade, Deputy Commander) concluded that the detainees rioted in protest of their living conditions, that the riot turned violent, the use of non-lethal force was ineffective, and, after the 320th MP Battalion CDR executed 'Golden Spike,' the emergency containment plan, the use of deadly force was authorized. Contributing factors were lack of comprehensive training of guards, poor or non-existent SOPs, no formal guard-mount conducted prior to shift, no rehearsals or ongoing training, the mix of less than lethal rounds with lethal rounds in weapons, no AARs being conducted after incidents, ROE not posted and not understood, overcrowding, uniforms not standardized, and poor communication between the command and Soldiers.

i. (U) 24 November '03: Shooting of detainee at Abu Ghraib (320th MP Battalion). A detainee allegedly had a pistol in his cell and around 1830 an extraction team shot him with less than lethal and lethal rounds in the process of recovering the weapon. A 15-6 investigation by Col. Bruce Falcone (220th Brigade, Deputy Commander) concluded that one of the detainees in tier 1A of the Hard-Site had gotten a pistol and a couple of knives from an Iraqi Guard working in the encampment. Immediately upon receipt of this information, an *ad hoc* extraction team consisting of MP and MI personnel conducted what they called a routine cell search, which resulted in the shooting of an MP and the detainee. Contributing factors were a corrupt Iraqi Guard, inadequate SOPs, the Detention ROE in place at the time was ineffective due to the numerous levels of authorization needed for use of lethal force, poorly trained MPs, unclear lanes of responsibility, and ambiguous relationship between the MI and MP assets.

j. (U) 13 December '03: Shooting by non-lethal means into crowd at Abu Ghraib (320th MP Battalion). Several detainees allegedly got into a detainee-on-detainee fight around 1030 in Compound 8 of the Ganci encampment, Abu Ghraib. An SIR was initiated by SSG Matash (320th MP Battalion, S-3 Section). The SIR indicated that there was a fight in the compound and the MPs used a non-lethal crowd-dispersing round to break up the fight, which was successful. No information on findings, contributing factors, or corrective action has been provided to this investigation team.

k. (U) 13 December '03: Shooting by non-lethal means into crowd at Abu Ghraib (320th MP Battalion). Several detainees allegedly got into a detainee-on-detainee fight around 1120 in Compound 2 of the Ganci encampment, Abu Ghraib. An SIR was initiated by SSG Matash (320th MP Battalion, S-3 Section). The SIR indicated that there was a fight in the compound and the MPs used two non-lethal shots to disperse the crowd, which was successful. No information on findings, contributing factors, or corrective action has been provided to this investigation team.

l. (U) 13 December '03: Shooting by non-lethal means into crowd at Abu Ghraib (320th MP Battalion). Approximately thirty to forty detainees allegedly got into a detainee-on-detainee fight around 1642 in Compound 3 of the Ganci encampment, Abu Ghraib (BCCF). An SIR was initiated by SSG Matash (320th MP Battalion, S-3 Section). The SIR indicates that there was a fight in the compound and the MPs used a non-lethal crowd-dispersing round to break up the fight, which was successful. No information on findings, contributing factors, or corrective action has been provided to this investigation team.

m. (U) 17 December '03: Shooting by non-lethal means of detainee from Abu Ghraib (320th MP Battalion). Several detainees allegedly assaulted an MP at 1459 inside the Ganci Encampment, Abu Ghraib (BCCF). An SIR was initiated by SSG Matash (320th MP BRIGADE, S-3 Section). The SIR indicated that three detainees assaulted an MP, which resulted in the use of a non-lethal shot that calmed the situation. No information on findings, contributing factors, or corrective action has been provided to this investigation team.

n. (U) 07 January '04: Escape of detainee No. 115032 from Camp Bucca (310th MP Battalion). A detainee allegedly escaped between the hours of 0445 and

0640 from Compound 12, of Camp Bucca. Investigation by CPT Kaires (310th MP Battalion S-3) and CPT Holsombeck (724th MP Battalion S-3) concluded that the detainee escaped through an undetected weakness in the wire. Contributing factors were inexperienced guards, lapses in accountability, complacency, lack of leadership presence, poor visibility, and lack of clear and concise communication between the guards and the leadership.

o. (U) 12 January '04: Escape of Detainees No. 115314 and No. 109950 as well as the escape and recapture of five unknown detainees at the Camp Bucca Detention Facility (310th MP Battalion). Several detainees allegedly escaped around 0300 from Compound 12, of Camp Bucca. An AR 15-6 Investigation by LTC Leigh Coulter (800th MP Brigade, OIC Camp Arifjan Detachment) concluded that three of the detainees escaped through the front holding cell during conditions of limited visibility due to fog. One of the detainees was noticed, shot with a non-lethal round, and returned to his holding compound. That same night, four detainees exited through the wire on the South side of the camp and were seen and apprehended by the QRF. Contributing factors were the lack of a coordinated effort for emplacement of MPs during implementation of the fog plan, overcrowding, and poor communications.

p. (U) 14 January '04: Escape of detainee No. 12436 and missing Iraqi guard from Hard-Site, Abu Ghraib (320th MP Battalion). A detainee allegedly escaped at 1335 from the Hard-Site at Abu Ghraib (BCCF). An SIR was initiated by SSG Hydro (320th MP Battalion, S-3 Asst. NCOIC). The SIR indicates that an Iraqi guard assisted a detainee to escape by signing him out on a work detail and disappearing with him. At the time of the second SIR, neither missing person had been located. No information on findings, contributing factors, or corrective action has been provided to this investigation team.

q. (U) 26 January '04: Escape of detainees Nos 115236, 116272, and 151933 from Camp Bucca (310th MP Battalion). Several Detainees allegedly escaped between the hours of 0440 and 0700 during a period of intense fog. Investigation by CPT Kaires (310th MP Battalion S-3) concluded that the detainees crawled under a fence when visibility was only 10–15 meters due to fog. Contributing factors were the limited visibility (darkness under foggy conditions), lack of proper accountability reporting, inadequate number of guards, commencement of detainee feeding during low visibility operations, and poorly rested MPs.

35. (U) As I have previously indicated, this investigation determined that there was virtually a complete lack of detailed SOPs at any of the detention facilities. Moreover, despite the fact that there were numerous reported escapes at detention facilities throughout Iraq (in excess of thirty-five), AR 15-6 Investigations following these escapes were simply forgotten or ignored by the Brigade Commander with no dissemination to other facilities. After-Action Reports and Lessons Learned, if done at all, remained at individual facilities

and were not shared among other commanders or soldiers throughout the Brigade. The Command never issued standard TTPs for handling escape incidents (Multiple Witness Statements and the Personal Observations of the Investigation Team).

Recommendations Regarding Part Two of the Investigation:

1. (U) ANNEX 100 of this investigation contains a detailed and referenced series of recommendations for improving the detainee accountability practices throughout the OIF area of operations.
2. (U) Accountability practices throughout any particular detention facility must be standardized and in accordance with applicable regulations and international law.
3. (U) The NDRS and BATS accounting systems must be expanded and used to their fullest extent to facilitate real time updating when detainees are moved and or transferred from one location to another.
4. (U) 'Change sheets,' or their doctrinal equivalent must be immediately processed and updated into the system to ensure accurate accountability. The detainee roll call or ISN counts must match the manifest provided to the compound guards to ensure proper accountability of detainees.
5. (U) Develop, staff, and implement comprehensive and detailed SOPs utilizing the lessons learned from this investigation as well as any previous findings, recommendations, and reports.
6. (U) SOPs must be written, disseminated, trained on, and understood at the lowest level.
7. (U) Iraqi criminal prisoners must be held in separate facilities from any other category of detainee.
8. (U) All of the compounds should be wired into the master manifest whereby MP Soldiers can account for their detainees in real time and without waiting for their change sheets to be processed. This would also have the change sheet serve as away to check up on the accuracy of the manifest as updated by each compound. The BATS and NDRS system can be utilized for this function.
9. (U) Accountability lapses, escapes, and disturbances within the detainment facilities must be immediately reported through both the operational and administrative Chain of Command via a Serious Incident Report (SIR). The SIRs must then be tracked and followed by daily SITREPs until the situation is resolved.
10. (U) Detention Rules of Engagement (DROE), Interrogation Rules of Engagement (IROE), and the principles of the Geneva Conventions need to be briefed at every shift change and guard mount.
11. (U) AARs must be conducted after serious incidents at any given facility. The observations and corrective actions that develop from the AARs must be

analyzed by the respective MP Battalion S-3 section, developed into a plan of action, shared with the other facilities, and implemented as a matter of policy.

12. (U) There must be significant structural improvements at each of the detention facilities. The needed changes include significant enhancement of perimeter lighting, additional chain link fencing, staking down of all concertina wire, hard site development, and expansion of Abu Ghraib (BCCF) .

13. (U) The Geneva Conventions and the facility rules must be prominently displayed in English and the language of the detainees at each compound and encampment at every detention facility IAW AR 190-8.

14. (U) Further restrict US civilians and other contractors' access throughout the facility. Contractors and civilians must be in an authorized and easily identifiable uniform to be more easily distinguished from the masses of detainees in civilian clothes.

15. (U) Facilities must have a stop movement/transfer period of at least one hour prior to every 100% detainee roll call and ISN counts to ensure accurate accountability.

16. (U) The method for doing head counts of detainees within a given compound must be standardized.

17. (U) Those military units conducting I/R operations must know of, train on, and constantly reference the applicable Army Doctrine and CJTF command policies. The references provided in this report cover nearly every deficiency I have enumerated. Although they do not, and cannot, make up for leadership shortfalls, all soldiers, at all levels, can use them to maintain standardized operating procedures and efficient accountability practices.

Findings as to Part Three of the Investigation

(U) Investigate the training, standards, employment, command policies, internal procedures, and command climate in the 800th MP Brigade, as appropriate: Pursuant to Part Three of the Investigation, select members of the Investigation team (Primarily Col. La Fate and I) personally interviewed the following witnesses:

1. (U) BG Janis Karpinski, Commander, 800th MP Brigade.
2. (U) COL Thomas Pappas, Commander, 205th MI Brigade.
3. (U) COL Ralph Sabatino, CFLCC Judge Advocate, CPA Ministry of Justice (Interviewed by Col. Richard Gordon, CFLCC SJA).
4. (U) LTC Gary W. Maddocks, S-5 and Executive Officer, 800th MP Brigade.
5. (U) LTC James O'Hare, Command Judge Advocate, 800th MP Brigade.
6. (U) LTC Robert P. Walters Jr., Commander, 165th MI Battalion (Tactical Exploitation).
7. (U) LTC James D. Edwards, Commander, 202nd MI Battalion.

8. (U) LTC Vincent Montera, Commander, 310th MP Battalion.

9. (U) LTC Steve Jordan, former Director, Joint Interrogation and Debriefing Center/LNO to the 205th MI Brigade.

10. (U) LTC Leigh A. Coulter, Commander, 724th MP Battalion and OIC Arifjan Detachment, 800th MP Brigade.

11. (U) LTC Dennis McGlone, Commander, 744th MP Battalion.

12. (U) MAJ David Hinzman, S-1, 800th MP Brigade.

13. (U) MAJ William D. Proietto, Deputy CJA, 800th MP Brigade.

14. (U) MAJ Stacy L. Garrity, S-1 (FWD), 800th MP Brigade.

15. (U) MAJ David W. DiNenna, S-3, 320th MP Battalion 35.

16. (U) MAJ Michael Sheridan, XO, 320th MP Battalion.

17. (U) MAJ Anthony Cavallaro, S-3, 800th MP Brigade.

18. (U) CPT Marc C. Hale, Commander, 670th MP Company.

19. (U) CPT Donald Reese, Commander, 372nd MP Company.

20. (U) CPT Darren Hampton, Assistant S-3, 320th MP Battalion.

21. (U) CPT John Kaires, S-3, 310th MP Battalion.

22. (U) CPT Ed Diamantis, S-2, 800th MP Brigade.

23. (U) CPT Marc C. Hale, Commander, 670th MP Company.

24. (U) CPT Donald Reese, Commander, 372nd MP Company.

25. (U) CPT James G. Jones, Commander, 229th MP Company.

26. (U) CPT Michael Anthony Mastrangelo, Jr., Commander, 310th MP Company.

27. (U) CPT Lawrence Bush, IG, 800th MP Brigade.

28. (U) 1LT Lewis C. Raeder, Platoon Leader, 372nd MP Company.

29. (U) 1LT Elvis Mabry, Aide-de-camp to Brigade Commander, 800th MP Brigade.

30. (U) 1LT Warren E. Ford, II, Commander, HHC 320th MP Battalion.

31. (U) 2LT David O. Sutton, Platoon Leader, 229th MP Company.

32. (U) CW2 Edward J. Rivas, 205th MI Brigade.

33. (U) CSM Joseph P. Arrington, Command Sergeant Major, 320th MP Battalion.

34. (U) SGM Pascual Cartagena, Acting Command Sergeant Major, 800th MP Brigade.

35. (U) CSM Timothy L. Woodcock, Command Sergeant Major, 310th MP Battalion.

36. (U) 1SG Dawn J. Rippelmeyer, First Sergeant, 977th MP Company.

37. (U) SGM Mark Emerson, Operations SGM, 320th MP Battalion.

38. (U) MSG Brian G. Lipinski, First Sergeant, 372nd MP Company.

39. (U) MSG Andrew J. Lombardo, Operations Sergeant, 310th MP Battalion.

40. (U) SFC Daryl J. Plude, Platoon Sergeant, 229th MP Company.

41. (U) SFC Shannon K. Snider, Platoon SGT, 372nd MP Company.

42. (U) SFC Keith A. Comer, 372nd MP Company.

43. (U) SSG Robert Elliot, Squad Leader, 372nd MP Company.

44. (U) SSG Santos A. Cardona, Army Dog Handler, 42nd MP Detachment, 16th MP Brigade.

45. (U) SGT Michael Smith, Army Dog Handler, 523rd MP Detachment, 937th Engineer Group.
46. (U) MA1 William J. Kimbro, USN Dog Handler, NAS Signal and Canine Unit.
47. (U) Mr. Steve Stephanowicz, US civilian Contract Interrogator, CACI, 205th MI Brigade.
48. (U) Mr. John Israel, US civilian Contract Interpreter, Titan Corporation, 205th MI Brigade.

Regarding Part Three of the Investigation, I Make the Following Specific Findings of Fact

1. (U) I find that BG Janis Karpinski took command of the 800th MP Brigade on 30 June 2003 from BG Paul Hill. BG Karpinski has remained in command since that date. The 800th MP Brigade is comprised of eight MP battalions in the Iraqi TOR: 115th MP Battalion, 310th MP Battalion, 320th MP Battalion, 324th MP Battalion, 400th MP Battalion, 530th MP Battalion, 724th MP Battalion, and 744th MP Battalion.

2. (U) Prior to BG Karpinski taking command, members of the 800th MP Brigade believed they would be allowed to go home when all the detainees were released from the Camp Bucca Theater Internment Facility following the cessation of major ground combat on 1 May 2003. At one point, approximately 7,000 to 8,000 detainees were held at Camp Bucca. Through Article 5 Tribunals and a screening process, several thousand detainees were released. Many in the command believed they would go home when the detainees were released. In late May to early June 2003 the 800th MP Brigade was given a new mission to manage the Iraqi penal system and several detention centers. This new mission meant Soldiers would not redeploy to CONUS when anticipated. Morale suffered, and over the next few months there did not appear to have been any attempt by the Command to mitigate this morale problem.

3. (U) There is abundant evidence in the statements of numerous witnesses that soldiers throughout the 800th MP Brigade were not proficient in their basic MOS skills, particularly regarding internment/resettlement operations. Moreover, there is no evidence that the command, although aware of these deficiencies, attempted to correct them in any systemic manner other than ad hoc training by individuals with civilian corrections experience (Multiple Witness Statements and the Personal Observations of the Investigation Team).

4. (U) I find that the 800th MP Brigade was not adequately trained for a mission that included operating a prison or penal institution at Abu Ghraib Prison Complex. As the Ryder Assessment found, I also concur that units of the 800th MP Brigade did not receive corrections-specific training during their mobilization period. MP units did not receive pinpoint assignments prior

to mobilization and during the post mobilization training, and thus could not train for specific missions. The training that was accomplished at the mobilization sites were developed and implemented at the company level with little or no direction or supervision at the Battalion and Brigade levels, and consisted primarily of common tasks and law enforcement training. However, I found no evidence that the Command, although aware of this deficiency, ever requested specific corrections training from the Commandant of the Military Police School, the U.S. Army Confinement Facility at Mannheim, Germany, the Provost Marshal General of the Army, or the U.S. Army Disciplinary Barracks at Fort Leavenworth, Kansas.

5. (U) I find that without adequate training for a civilian internee detention mission, Brigade personnel relied heavily on individuals within the Brigade who had civilian corrections experience, including many who worked as prison guards or corrections officials in their civilian jobs. Almost every witness we interviewed had no familiarity with the provisions of AR 190-8 or FM 3-19.40. It does not appear that a Mission Essential Task List (METL) based on in-theater missions was ever developed nor was a training plan implemented throughout the Brigade.

6. (U) I also find, as did MG Ryder's Team, that the 800th MP Brigade as a whole, was under strength for the mission for which it was tasked. Army Doctrine dictates that an I/R Brigade can be organized with between seven and twenty-one battalions, and that the average battalion size element should be able to handle approximately 4,000 detainees at a time. This investigation indicates that BG Karpinski and her staff did a poor job allocating resources throughout the Iraq JOA. Abu Ghraib (BCCF) normally housed between 6,000 and 7,000 detainees, yet it was operated by only one battalion. In contrast, the HVD Facility maintains only about 100 detainees, and is also run by an entire battalion.

7. (U) Reserve Component units do not have an individual replacement system to mitigate medical or other losses. Over time, the 800th MP Brigade clearly suffered from personnel shortages through release from active duty (REFRAD) actions, medical evacuation, and demobilization. In addition to being severely under manned, the quality of life for Soldiers assigned to Abu Ghraib (BCCF) was extremely poor. There was no DFAC, PX, barbershop, or MWR facilities. There were numerous mortar attacks, random rifle and RPG attacks, and a serious threat to Soldiers and detainees in the facility. The prison complex was also severely overcrowded and the Brigade lacked adequate resources and personnel to resolve serious logistical problems. Finally, because of past associations and familiarity of Soldiers within the Brigade, it appears that friendship often took precedence over appropriate leader and subordinate relationships (Multiple Witness Statements, and the Personal Observations of the Investigation Team).

8. (U) With respect to the 800th MP Brigade mission at Abu Ghraib (BCCF), I find that there was clear friction and lack of effective communication between the Commander, 205th MI Brigade, who controlled FOB Abu Ghraib (BCCF) after 19 November 2003, and the Commander, 800th MP Brigade, who controlled detainee operations inside the FOB. There was no clear delineation of responsibility between commands, little coordination at the command level, and no integration of the two functions. Coordination occurred at the lowest possible levels with little oversight by commanders.

9. (U) I find that this ambiguous command relationship was exacerbated by a CJTF-7 Fragmentary Order (FRAGO) 1108 issued on 19 November 2003. Paragraph 3.C.8, Assignment of 205th MI Brigade Commander's Responsibilities for the Baghdad Central Confinement Facility, states as follows:

3.C.8. A. (U) 205 Mi Brigade [FRAGO]

(U) Effective Immediately Commander 205 MI Brigade Assumes Responsibility for the Baghdad Confinement Facility (BCCF) and is Appointed the Fob Commander. Units Currently at Abu Ghraib (BCCF) are TACON to 205 MI Brigade for 'Security of Detainees and Fob Protection.' Although not supported by BG Karpinski, FRAGO 1108 made all of the MP units at Abu Ghraib TACON to the Commander, 205th MI Brigade. This effectively made an MI Officer, rather than an MP Officer, responsible for the MP units conducting detainee operations at that facility. This is not doctrinally sound due to the different missions and agendas assigned to each of these respective specialties.

10. (U) Joint Publication 0-2, Unified Action Armed Forces (UNAAF), 10 July 2001 defines Tactical Control (TACON) as the detailed direction and control of movements or maneuvers within the operational area necessary to accomplish assigned missions or tasks. 'TACON is the command authority over assigned or attached forces or commands or military capability made available for tasking that is limited to the detailed direction and control of movements or maneuvers within the operational area necessary to accomplish assigned missions or tasks. TACON is inherent in OPCON and may be delegated to and exercised by commanders at any echelon at or below the level of combatant commander.'

11. (U) Based on all the facts and circumstances in this investigation, I find that there was little, if any, recognition of this TACON Order by the 800th MP Brigade or the 205th MI Brigade. Further, there was no evidence if the Commander, 205th MI Brigade clearly informed the Commander, 800th MP Brigade, and specifically the Commander, 320th MP Battalion assigned at Abu Ghraib (BCCF), on the specific requirements of this TACON relationship.

12. (U) It is clear from a comprehensive review of witness statements and personal

interviews that the 320th MP Battalion and 800th MP Brigade continued to function as if they were responsible for the security, health and welfare, and overall security of detainees within Abu Ghraib (BCCF) prison. Both BG Karpinski and Col. Pappas clearly behaved as if this were still the case.

13. (U) With respect to the 320th MP Battalion, I find that the Battalion Commander, LTC (P) Jerry Phillabaum, was an extremely ineffective commander and leader. Numerous witnesses confirm that the Battalion S-3, Maj. David W. DiNenna, basically ran the battalion on a day-to-day basis. At one point, BG Karpinski sent LTC (P) Phillabaum to Camp Arifjan, Kuwait for approximately two weeks, apparently to give him some relief from the pressure he was experiencing as the 320th Battalion Commander. This movement to Camp Arifjan immediately followed a briefing provided by LTC (P) Phillabaum to the CJTF–7 Commander, LTG Sanchez, near the end of October 2003. BG Karpinski placed LTC Ronald Chew, Commander of the 115th MP Battalion, in charge of the 320th MP Battalion for a period of approximately two weeks. LTC Chew was also in command of the 115th MP Battalion assigned to Camp Cropper, BIAP, Iraq. I could find no orders, either suspending or relieving LTC (P) Phillabaum from command, nor any orders placing LTC Chew in command of the 320th. In addition, there was no indication this removal and search for a replacement was communicated to the Commander CJTF-7, the Commander 377th TSC, or to Soldiers in the 320th MP Battalion. Temporarily removing one commander and replacing him with another serving Battalion Commander without an order and without notifying superior or subordinate commands is without precedent in my military career. LTC (P) Phillabaum was also reprimanded for lapses in accountability that resulted in several escapes. The 320th MP Battalion was stigmatized as a unit due to previous detainee abuse which occurred in May 2003 at the Bucca Theater Internment Facility (TIF), while under the command of LTC (P) Phillabaum. Despite his proven deficiencies as both a commander and leader, BG Karpinski allowed LTC (P) Phillabaum to remain in command of her most troubled battalion guarding, by far, the largest number of detainees in the 800th MP Brigade. LTC (P) Phillabaum was suspended from his duties by LTG Sanchez, CJTF-7 Commander on 17 January 2004.

14. (U) During the course of this investigation I conducted a lengthy interview with BG Karpinski that lasted over four hours, and is included verbatim in the investigation Annexes. BG Karpinski was extremely emotional during much of her testimony. What I found particularly disturbing in her testimony was her complete unwillingness to either understand or accept that many of the problems inherent in the 800th MP Brigade were caused or exacerbated by poor leadership and the refusal of her command to both establish and enforce basic standards and principles among its soldiers (Personal Observations of the Interview Team).

15. (U) BG Karpinski alleged that she received no help from the Civil Affairs Command, specifically, no assistance from either BG John Kern or Col. Tim Regan. She blames much of the abuse that occurred in Abu Ghraib (BCCF) on MI personnel and stated that MI personnel had given the MPs 'ideas' that led to detainee abuse. In addition, she blamed the 372nd Company Platoon Sergeant, SFC Snider, the Company Commander, CPT Reese, and the First Sergeant, MSG Lipinski, for the abuse. She argued that problems in Abu Ghraib were the fault of Col. Pappas and LTC Jordan because Col. Pappas was in charge of FOB Abu Ghraib.

16. (U) BG Karpinski also implied during her testimony that the criminal abuses that occurred at Abu Ghraib (BCCF) might have been caused by the ultimate disposition of the detainee abuse cases that originally occurred at Camp Bucca in May 2003. She stated that 'about the same time those incidents were taking place out of Baghdad Central, the decisions were made to give the guilty people at Bucca plea bargains. So, the system communicated to the soldiers, the worst that's gonna happen is, you're gonna go home.' I think it important to point out that almost every witness testified that the serious criminal abuse of detainees at Abu Ghraib (BCCF) occurred in late October and early November 2003. The photographs and statements clearly support that the abuses occurred during this time period. The Bucca cases were set for trial in January 2004 and were not finally disposed of until 29 December 2003. There is entirely no evidence that the decision of numerous MP personnel to intentionally abuse detainees at Abu Ghraib (BCCF) was influenced in any respect by the Camp Bucca cases.

17. (U) Numerous witnesses stated that the 800th MP Brigade S-1, Maj. Hinzman and S-4, Maj. Green, were essentially dysfunctional, but that despite numerous complaints, these officers were not replaced. This had a detrimental effect on the Brigade Staff's effectiveness and morale. Moreover, the Brigade Command Judge Advocate, LTC James O'Hare, appears to lack initiative and was unwilling to accept responsibility for any of his actions. LTC Gary Maddocks, the Brigade XO did not properly supervise the Brigade staff by failing to lay out staff priorities, take overt corrective action when needed, and supervise their daily functions.

18. (U) In addition to poor morale and staff inefficiencies, I find that the 800th MP Brigade did not articulate or enforce clear and basic Soldier and Army standards. I specifically found these examples of unenforced standards:

a. There was no clear uniform standard for any MP Soldiers assigned detention duties. Despite the fact that hundreds of former Iraqi soldiers and officers were detainees, MP personnel were allowed to wear civilian clothes in the FOB after duty hours while carrying weapons.

b. Some Soldiers wrote poems and other sayings on their helmets and soft caps.

c. In addition, numerous officers and senior NCOs have been reprimanded/

disciplined for misconduct during this period. Those disciplined include;

1). (U) BG Janis Karpinski, Commander, 800th MP Brigade, Memorandum of Admonishment by LTG Sanchez, Commander, CJTF-7, on 17 January 2004.

2). (U) LTC (P) Jerry Phillabaum, Commander, 320th MP Battalion, GOMOR from BG Karpinski, Commander 800th MP Brigade, on 10 November 2003, for lack of leadership and for failing to take corrective security measures as ordered by the Brigade Commander; filed locally, Suspended by BG Karpinski, Commander 800th MP Brigade, 17 January 2004; Pending Relief for Cause, for dereliction of duty.

3). (U) LTC Dale Burtyk, Commander, 400th MP Battalion, GOMOR from BG Karpinski, Commander 800th MP Brigade, on 20 August 2003, for failure to properly train his Soldiers (Soldier had negligent discharge of M-16 while exiting his vehicle, round went into fuel tank); filed locally.

4). (U) MAJ David DiNenna, S-3, 320th MP Battalion, GOMOR from LTG McKiernan, Commander CFLCC, on 25 May 2003, for dereliction of duty for failing to report a violation of CENTCOM General Order No. 1 by a subordinate Field Grade Officer and Senior Noncommissioned Officer, which he personally observed; returned to soldier unfiled. GOMOR from BG Karpinski, Commander 800th MP Brigade, on 10 November '03, for failing to take corrective security measures as ordered by the Brigade Commander; filed locally.

5). (U) Maj. Stacy Garrity, Finance Officer, 800th MP Brigade, GOMOR from LTG McKiernan, Commander CFLCC, on 25 May 2003, for violation of CENTCOM General Order No. 1, consuming alcohol with an NCO; filed locally.

6). (U) CPT Leo Merck, Commander, 870th MP Company Court–Martial Charges Preferred, for Conduct Unbecoming an Officer and Unauthorized Use of Government Computer in that he was alleged to have taken nude pictures of his Female Soldiers without their knowledge; Trial date to be announced.

7). (U) CPT Damaris Morales, Commander, 770th MP Company, GOMOR from BG Karpinski, Commander 800th MP Brigade, on 20 August 2003, for failing to properly train his Soldiers (Soldier had negligent discharge of M-16 while exiting his vehicle, round went into fuel tank); filed locally.

8). (U) CSM Roy Clement, Command Sergeant Major, 800th MP Brigade, GOMOR and Relief for Cause from BG Janis Karpinski, Commander 800th MP Brigade, for fraternization and dereliction of duty for fraternizing with junior enlisted soldiers within his unit; GOMOR officially filed and he was removed from the CSM list.

9). (U) CSM Edward Stotts, Command Sergeant Major, 400th MP Battalion, GOMOR from BG Karpinski, Commander 800th MP Brigade, on 20 August 2003, for failing to properly train his Soldiers (Soldier had negligent discharge of M-16 while exiting his vehicle, round went into fuel tank); filed locally.

10). (U) 1SG Carlos Villanueva, First Sergeant, 770th MP Company, GOMOR from BG Karpinski, Commander 800th MP Brigade, on 20 August 2003, for failing to properly train his Soldiers(Soldier had negligent discharge of M-16 while exiting his vehicle, round went into fuel tank); filed locally.

11). (U) MSG David Maffett, NBC NCO, 800th MP Brigade, GOMOR from LTG McKiernan, Commander CFLCC, on 25 May 2003, for violation of CENTCOM General Order No. 1, consuming alcohol; filed locally.

12) (U) SGM Marc Emerson, Operations SGM, 320th MP Battalion, Two GO Letters of Concern and a verbal reprimand from BG Karpinski, Commander 800th MP Brigade, for failing to adhere to the guidance/directives given to him by BG Karpinski; filed locally.

d. (U) Saluting of officers was sporadic and not enforced. LTC Robert P. Walters, Jr., Commander of the 165th Military Intelligence Battalion (Tactical Exploitation), testified that the saluting policy was enforced by COL Pappas for all MI personnel, and that BG Karpinski approached Col. Pappas to reverse the saluting policy back to a no-saluting policy as previously existed.

19. (U) I find that individual Soldiers within the 800th MP Brigade and the 320thBattalion stationed throughout Iraq had very little contact during their tour of duty with either LTC (P) Phillabaum or BG Karpinski. BG Karpinski claimed, during her testimony, that she paid regular visits to the various detention facilities where her Soldiers were stationed. However, the detailed calendar provided by her Aide-de-Camp, 1LT Mabry, does not support her contention. Moreover, numerous witnesses stated that they rarely saw BG Karpinski or LTC (P) Phillabaum (Multiple Witness Statements).

20. (U) In addition I find that psychological factors, such as the difference in culture, the Soldiers' quality of life, the real presence of mortal danger over an extended time period, and the failure of commanders to recognize these pressures contributed to the pervasive atmosphere that existed at Abu Ghraib (BCCF) Detention Facility and throughout the 800th MP Brigade.

21. As I have documented in other parts of this investigation, I find that there was no clear emphasis by BG Karpinski to ensure that the 800th MP Brigade Staff, Commanders, and Soldiers were trained to standard in detainee operations and proficiency or that serious accountability lapses that occurred over a significant period of time, particularly at Abu Ghraib (BCCF), were corrected. AR 15-6 Investigations regarding detainee escapes were not acted upon, followed up with corrective action, or disseminated to subordinate commanders or Soldiers. Brigade and unit SOPs for dealing with detainees if they existed at all, were not read or understood by MP Soldiers assigned the difficult mission of detainee operations. Following the abuse of several detainees at Camp Bucca in May 2003, I could find no evidence that BG Karpinski ever directed corrective training for her soldiers or ensured that MP Soldiers throughout Iraq clearly understood the requirements of the

Geneva Conventions relating to the treatment of detainees (Multiple Witness Statements and the Personal Observations of the Investigation Team).

22. On 17 January 2004 BG Karpinski was formally admonished in writing by LTG Sanchez regarding the serious deficiencies in her Brigade. LTG Sanchez found that the performance of the 800th MP Brigade had not met the standards set by the Army or by CJTF-7. He found that incidents in the preceding six months had occurred that reflected a lack of clear standards, proficiency and leadership within the Brigade. LTG Sanchez also cited the recent detainee abuse at Abu Ghraib (BCCF) as the most recent example of a poor leadership climate that 'permeates the Brigade.' I totally concur with LTG Sanchez' opinion regarding the performance of BG Karpinski and the 800th MP Brigade (Personal Observations of the Investigating Officer).

Recommendations as to Part Three of the Investigation

1. (U) That BG Janis L. Karpinski, Commander, 800th MP Brigade be Relieved from Command and given a General Officer Memorandum of Reprimand for the following acts which have been previously referred to in the aforementioned findings:

a. (U) Failing to ensure that MP Soldiers at theater-level detention facilities throughout Iraq had appropriate SOPs for dealing with detainees and that Commanders and Soldiers had read, understood, and would adhere to these SOPs.

b. (U) Failing to ensure that MP Soldiers in the 800th MP Brigade knew, understood, and adhered to the protections afforded to detainees in the Geneva Convention Relative to the Treatment of Prisoners of War.

c. (U) Making material misrepresentations to the Investigation Team as to the frequency of her visits to her subordinate commands.

d. (U) Failing to obey an order from the CFLCC Commander, LTG McKiernan, regarding the withholding of disciplinary authority for Officer and Senior Noncommissioned Officer misconduct.

e. (U) Failing to take appropriate action regarding the ineffectiveness of a subordinate Commander, LTC (P) Jerry Phillabaum.

f. (U) Failing to take appropriate action regarding the ineffectiveness of numerous members of her Brigade Staff including her XO, S-1, S-3, and S-4.

g. (U) Failing to properly ensure the results and recommendations of the AARs and numerous 15-6 Investigation reports on escapes and shootings (over a period of several months) were properly disseminated to, and understood by, subordinate commanders.

h. (U) Failing to ensure and enforce basic Soldier standards throughout her command.

i. (U) Failing to establish a Brigade METL.

j. (U) Failing to establish basic proficiency in assigned tasks for Soldiers throughout the 800th MP Brigade.

k. (U) Failing to ensure that numerous and reported accountability lapses at detention facilities throughout Iraq were corrected.

2. (U) That Col. Thomas M. Pappas, Commander, 205th MI Brigade, be given a General Officer Memorandum of Reprimand and Investigated UP Procedure 15, AR381-10, US Army Intelligence Activities for the following acts which have been previously referred to in the aforementioned findings:

a. (U) Failing to ensure that Soldiers under his direct command were properly trained in and followed the IROE.

b. (U) Failing to ensure that Soldiers under his direct command knew, understood, and followed the protections afforded to detainees in the Geneva Convention Relative to the Treatment of Prisoners of War.

c. (U) Failing to properly supervise his soldiers working and 'visiting' Tier 1 of the Hard-Site at Abu Ghraib (BCCF).

3. (U) That LTC (P) Jerry L. Phillabaum, Commander, 320th MP Battalion, be Relieved from Command, be given a General Officer Memorandum of Reprimand, and be removed from the Colonel/O-6 Promotion List for the following acts which have been previously referred to in the aforementioned findings:

a. (U) Failing to properly ensure the results, recommendations, and AARs from numerous reports on escapes and shootings over a period of several months were properly disseminated to, and understood by, subordinates.

b. (U) Failing to implement the appropriate recommendations from various 15-6 Investigations as specifically directed by BG Karpinski.

c. (U) Failing to ensure that Soldiers under his direct command were properly trained in Internment and Resettlement Operations.

d. (U) Failing to ensure that Soldiers under his direct command knew and understood the protections afforded to detainees in the Geneva Convention Relative to the Treatment of Prisoners of War.

e. (U) Failing to properly supervise his soldiers working and 'visiting' Tier 1 of the Hard-Site at Abu Ghraib (BCCF).

f. (U) Failing to properly establish and enforce basic soldier standards, proficiency, and accountability.

g. (U) Failure to conduct an appropriate Mission Analysis and to task organize to accomplish his mission.

4. (U) That LTC Steven L. Jordan, Former Director, Joint Interrogation and Debriefing Center and Liaison Officer to 205th Military Intelligence Brigade, be relieved from duty and be given a General Officer Memorandum of Reprimand for the following acts which have been previously referred to in the aforementioned findings:

a. (U) Making material misrepresentations to the Investigating Team, including his leadership role at Abu Ghraib (BCCF).

b. (U) Failing to ensure that Soldiers under his direct control were properly trained in and followed the IROE.

c. (U) Failing to ensure that Soldiers under his direct control knew, understood, and followed the protections afforded to detainees in the Geneva Convention Relative to the Treatment of Prisoners of War.

d. (U) Failing to properly supervise soldiers under his direct authority working and 'visiting' Tier 1 of the Hard-Site at Abu Ghraib (BCCF).

5. (U) That MAJ David W. DiNenna, Sr., S-3, 320th MP Battalion, be Relieved from his position as the Battalion S-3 and be given a General Officer Memorandum of Reprimand for the following acts which have been previously referred to in the aforementioned findings:

a. (U) Received a GOMOR from LTG McKiernan, Commander CFLCC, on 25 May2003, for dereliction of duty for failing to report a violation of CENTCOM General Order No. 1 by a subordinate Field Grade Officer and Senior Noncommissioned Officer, which he personally observed; GOMOR was returned to Soldier and not filed.

b. (U) Failing to take corrective action and implement recommendations from various 15-6 investigations even after receiving a GOMOR from BG Karpinski, Commander 800th MP Brigade, on 10 November '03, for failing to take corrective security measures as ordered; GOMOR was filed locally.

c. (U)Failing to take appropriate action and report an incident of detainee abuse, whereby he personally witnessed a Soldier throw a detainee from the back of a truck.

6. (U) That CPT Donald J. Reese, Commander, 372nd MP Company, be Relieved from Command and be given a General Officer Memorandum of Reprimand for the following acts which have been previously referred to in the aforementioned findings:

a. (U) Failing to ensure that Soldiers under his direct command knew and understood the protections afforded to detainees in the Geneva Convention Relative to the Treatment of Prisoners of War.

b. (U) Failing to properly supervise his Soldiers working and 'visiting' Tier 1 of the Hard-Site at Abu Ghraib (BCCF).

c. (U) Failing to properly establish and enforce basic soldier standards, proficiency, and accountability.

d. (U) Failing to ensure that Soldiers under his direct command were properly trained in Internment and Resettlement Operations.

7. (U) That 1LT Lewis C. Raeder, Platoon Leader, 372nd MP Company, be Relieved from his duties as Platoon Leader and be given a General Officer Memorandum of Reprimand for the following acts which have been previously referred to in the aforementioned findings:

a. (U) Failing to ensure that Soldiers under his direct command knew and understood the protections afforded to detainees in the Geneva Convention Relative to the Treatment of Prisoners of War.

b. (U) Failing to properly supervise his soldiers working and 'visiting' Tier 1 of the Hard-Site at Abu Ghraib (BCCF).

c. (U) Failing to properly establish and enforce basic Soldier standards, proficiency, and accountability.

d. (U) Failing to ensure that Soldiers under his direct command were properly trained in Internment and Resettlement Operations.

8. (U) That SGM Marc Emerson, Operations SGM, 320th MP Battalion, be Relieved from his duties and given a General Officer Memorandum of Reprimand for the following acts which have been previously referred to in the aforementioned findings:

a. (U) Making a material misrepresentation to the Investigation Team stating that he had 'never' been admonished or reprimanded by BG Karpinski, when in fact he had been admonished for failing to obey an order from BG Karpinski to 'stay out of the towers' at the holding facility.

b. (U) Making a material misrepresentation to the Investigation Team stating that he had attended every shift change/guard-mount conducted at the 320th MP Battalion, and that he personally briefed his Soldiers on the proper treatment of detainees, when in fact numerous statements contradict this assertion.

c. (U) Failing to ensure that Soldiers in the 320th MP Battalion knew and understood the protections afforded to detainees in the Geneva Convention Relative to the Treatment of Prisoners of War.

d. (U) Failing to properly supervise his soldiers working and 'visiting' Tier 1 of the Hard-Site at Abu Ghraib (BCCF).

e. (U) Failing to properly establish and enforce basic soldier standards, proficiency, and accountability.

f. (U) Failing to ensure that his Soldiers were properly trained in Internment and Resettlement Operations.

9. (U) That 1SG Brian G. Lipinski, First Sergeant, 372nd MP Company, be Relieved from his duties as First Sergeant of the 372nd MP Company and given a General Officer Memorandum of Reprimand for the following acts which have been previously referred to in the aforementioned findings:

a. (U) Failing to ensure that Soldiers in the 372nd MP Company knew and understood the protections afforded to detainees in the Geneva Convention Relative to the Treatment of Prisoners of War.

b. (U) Failing to properly supervise his soldiers working and 'visiting' Tier 1 of the Hard-Site at Abu Ghraib (BCCF).

c. (U) Failing to properly establish and enforce basic soldier standards, proficiency, and accountability.

d. (U) Failing to ensure that his Soldiers were properly trained in Internment and Resettlement Operations.

10. (U) That SFC Shannon K. Snider, Platoon Sergeant, 372nd MP Company, be Relieved from his duties, receive a General Officer Memorandum of Reprimand, and receive action under the Uniform Code of Military Justice for the following acts which have been previously referred to in the aforementioned findings:

a. (U) Failing to ensure that Soldiers in his platoon knew and understood the protections afforded to detainees in the Geneva Convention Relative to the Treatment of Prisoners of War.

b. (U) Failing to properly supervise his soldiers working and 'visiting' Tier 1 of the Hard-Site at Abu Ghraib (BCCF).

c. (U) Failing to properly establish and enforce basic soldier standards, proficiency, and accountability.

d. (U) Failing to ensure that his Soldiers were properly trained in Internment and Resettlement Operations.

e. (U) Failing to report a Soldier, who under his direct control, abused detainees by stomping on their bare hands and feet in his presence.

11. (U) That Mr. Steven Stephanowicz, Contract U.S. Civilian Interrogator, CACI, 205th Military Intelligence Brigade, be given an Official Reprimand to be placed in his employment file, termination of employment, and generation of a derogatory report to revoke his security clearance for the following acts which have been previously referred to in the aforementioned findings:

a. (U) Made a false statement to the investigation team regarding the locations of his interrogations, the activities during his interrogations, and his knowledge of abuses.

b. Allowed and/or instructed MPs, who were not trained in interrogation techniques, to facilitate interrogations by 'setting conditions,' which were neither authorized and in accordance with applicable regulations/policy. He clearly knew his instructions equated to physical abuse.

12. (U) That Mr. John Israel, Contract U.S. Civilian Interpreter, CACI, 205th Military Intelligence Brigade, be given an Official Reprimand to be placed in his employment file and have his security clearance reviewed by competent authority for the following acts or concerns which have been previously referred to in the aforementioned findings:

a. (U) Denied ever having seen interrogation processes in violation of the IROE, which is contrary to several witness statements.

b. (U) Did not have a security clearance.

13. (U) I find that there is sufficient credible information to warrant an Inquiry UP Procedure 15, AR 381-10, US Army Intelligence Activities, be conducted to determine the extent of culpability of MI personnel, assigned to the 205th MI Brigade and the Joint Interrogation and Debriefing Center (JIDC) at Abu

Ghraib (BCCF). Specifically, I suspect that Col. Thomas M. Pappas, LTC Steve L. Jordan, Mr. Steven Stephanowicz, and Mr. John Israel were either directly or indirectly responsible for the abuses at Abu Ghraib (BCCF) and strongly recommend immediate disciplinary action as described in the preceding paragraphs as well as the initiation of a Procedure 15 Inquiry to determine the full extent of their culpability.

Other Findings/Observations

1. (U) Due to the nature and scope of this investigation, I acquired the assistance of Col. (Dr.) Henry Nelson, a USAF Psychiatrist, to analyze the investigation materials from a psychological perspective. He determined that there was evidence that the horrific abuses suffered by the detainees at Abu Ghraib (BCCF) were wanton acts of select soldiers in an unsupervised and dangerous setting. There was a complex interplay of many psychological factors and command insufficiencies. A more detailed analysis is contained in ANNEX 1of this investigation.

2. (U) During the course of this investigation I conducted a lengthy interview with BG Karpinski that lasted over four hours, and is included verbatim in the investigation Annexes. BG Karpinski was extremely emotional during much of her testimony. What I found particularly disturbing in her testimony was her complete unwillingness to either understand or accept that many of the problems inherent in the 800th MP Brigade were caused or exacerbated by poor leadership and the refusal of her command to both establish and enforce basic standards and principles among its Soldiers.

3. (U) Throughout the investigation, we observed many individual Soldiers and some subordinate units under the 800th MP Brigade that overcame significant obstacles, persevered in extremely poor conditions, and upheld the Army Values. We discovered numerous examples of Soldiers and Sailors taking the initiative in the absence of leadership and accomplishing their assigned tasks.

a. (U) The 744th MP Battalion, commanded by LTC Dennis McGlone, efficiently operated the HVD Detention Facility at Camp Cropper and met mission requirements with little to no guidance from the 800th MP Brigade. The unit was disciplined, proficient, and appeared to understand their basic tasks.

b. (U) The 530th MP Battalion, commanded by LTC Stephen J. Novotny, effectively maintained the MEK Detention Facility at Camp Ashraf. His Soldiers were proficient in their individual tasks and adapted well to this highly unique and non-doctrinal operation.

c. (U) The 165th MI Battalion excelled in providing perimeter security and force protection at Abu Ghraib (BCCF). LTC Robert P. Walters, Jr., demanded standards be enforced and worked endlessly to improve discipline throughout the FOB.

4. (U) The individual Soldiers and Sailors that we observed and believe should be favorably noted include:

a. (U) Master-at-Arms First Class William J. Kimbro, U.S. Navy Dog Handler, knew his duties and refused to participate in improper interrogations despite significant pressure from the MI personnel at Abu Ghraib.

b. (U) SPC Joseph M. Darby, 372nd MP Company discovered evidence of abuse and turned it over to military law enforcement.

c. (U) 1LT David O. Sutton, 229th MP Company, took immediate action and stopped an abuse, then reported the incident to the chain of command.

Conclusion

1. (U) Several US Army Soldiers have committed egregious acts and grave breaches of international law at Abu Ghraib/BCCF and Camp Bucca, Iraq. Furthermore, key senior leaders in both the 800th MP Brigade and the 205th MI Brigade failed to comply with established regulations, policies, and command directives in preventing detainee abuses at Abu Ghraib (BCCF) and at Camp Bucca during the period August 2003 to February 2004.

2. (U) Approval and implementation of the recommendations of this AR 15-6Investigation and those highlighted in previous assessments are essential to establish the conditions with the resources and personnel required to prevent future occurrences of detainee abuse.

Endnotes

Introduction

1. Heather, P., *The Fall of the Roman Empire: A New History*, (2005), pp. 227-229.
2. Vasiliev, A. A., *History of the Byzantine Empire Vol. I*, (1958), p. 188.
3. Chang, I., *The Rape of Nanking: The Forgotten Holocaust of World War II*, (1997), p. 6.
4. Rhodes, R., *Masters of Death: The SS–Einsatzgruppen and the Invention of the Holocaust*, (2002), p. xii.
5. *Ibid.*, p. 23.
6. *Ibid.*, p. 56.
7. Merridale, C., 'Ideology and Combat in the Red Army, 1939-45,' *Journal of Contemporary History, Vol. 41, No. 2*, (Apr., 2006), p. 319.
8. Bartone, P. T., 'Lessons of Abu Ghraib: Understanding and Preventing Prisoner Abuse in Military Operations,' *Defense Horizons, Number 64*, (Nov. 2008).
9. Athens, L., *The Creation of Dangerous Violent Criminals*, (1992), pp. 57-60.
10. Fogel, J. A., *The Nanjing Massacre in History and Historiography*, (2000), p. 17.
11. Athens, p. 82.

Chapter 1

1. *International Military Tribunal for the Far East (IMTFE) Judgment, Chapter VIII*, (1948), pp. 1011-13.
2. 'Nationalist Government, Table of Rape of Nanking Individual Victims,' *Correspondence from the Secretary's Office of the National Government's General Secretary to the Ministry of Justice*, (17 January 1946), pp. 485-507.
3. 'Rabe to Japanese Embassy,' December 17, 1937, *DNSZ, No. 9, p.17.4, NYT*, (1937), p. 10.
4. *Ibid.*, p. 12.
5. 'Directive Concerning the Operation in and Entry to Nanking,' *CCAA Command, DSKS, vol.3, NSSI*, p.540.
6. Matsui, I., *Diary*, (1937), p.1 8.
7. 'How to Fight the Chinese Military,' *Army's Infantry School*, quoted in Yoshida, *Emperor's Military and the Nanking Incident*, (1933), p. 45.

8. Grew, J., *Report from Tokyo: A Message to the American People* (New York: Simon and Schuster, 1942), pp. 29-30.

9. Kobayashi, M., ed., *Sakigake: Kyodo Butai Senki*, (1938), pp. 577-80.

10. Masao, M., *Thought and Behavior in Modern Japanese Politics*, ed. Ivan Morris, (1969), p. 19.

11. Masazumi, I., *Reflection on Strategic Planning during the China Incident*, pp. 38-39.

12. *International Military Tribunal for the Far East (IMTFE) Judgment, Chapter VIII*, (1948), pp. 1011-18.

13. Iinuma, M., *Diary*, NSS1, (1937), pp. 215-16.

14. Matsui, I., *Diary*, NSS1, (1937), pp.18-19.

15. Nakajima, K., *Diary*, NSS1, (1937), p. 328.

16. Testimony of Sakakibara Kazuein 'SNS' (11), (1985), p. 8.

17. Shoro, H., *My Observation of Nanking Before and After Its Fall*, Kaiko, June 1983, p. 19.

18. Sasaki, T., *Diary*, NSS1 (1937), p. 378.

19. Hata, I., *Nanking Incident*, pp. 143-44, and Hora, T., *Nanking Massacre: Definitive Version*, p. 34.

20. Morozumi, G., *Memoir*, NSS2, p. 339.

21. '30th Infantry Brigade Order,' 4.50 a.m., 14 December 1937, in NSS1, p. 545.

22. Unidentified source quoted in NEM, p. 273. The original Japanese phrase corresponding to 'in some way or the other.'

23. Ikuhiko, H., *The Nanking Incident: The Structure of the Massacre*, (1986), p. 139.

24. Kung-Ku, C., *Three Months in Fallen Capital*, (1981), p. 77.

25. Hamilton, V. L., and Sanders, J., *Every day Justice: Responsibility and the Individual in Japan and the United States*, (1992), pp.130, 134.

26. Lory, H., *Japan's Military Masters: The Army in Japanese Life*, (1943), pp. 153-56.

27. Kawakami, K. K., *Manchoukuo, Child of Conflict*, (1933), p. vi.

28. Young, A. M., *Imperial Japan, 1926–1938*, (1974), p. 250.

29. Lory, H., p. 99.

30. Yoshida, T., *The Emperor's Military and the Nanjing Incident*, (1986), pp. 107-10.

31. Hirotato, S., *Red Machine, No. 1193B*, (1938).

32. Masatoshi, I., *Testimony, SNS (11)*, (1985), pp. 9-10.

33. 1st Battalion of the 66th Infantry Regiment, *Battle Report, Military Historical Detachment*.

34. 10th Army [Yanagawa] Army Group Legal Department Record, pp. 16, 36.

35. Best, *Humanity in Warfare*, (1983), p. 83.

36. 'Handbook on Japanese Military Forces,' *Technical Manual E30–480*, (1944), p. 5.

37. *Ibid.*, p. 12.

38. *International Military Tribunal for the Far East (IMTFE) Judgment, Chapter VIII*, (1948), pp. 149-151.

39. Roberts, J. M., *The New History of the World*, (2003), p. 927.

40. *Ibid.*, p. 928.

41. Chang, I., p. 191.

42. *Ibid.*, p. 192.

43. Rees, L., *Horror in the East*, (2001), p. 84.

44. *Ibid.*, p. 100.

45. Chang, I., p. 65.

46. Matsuoka, Y., Japan Manchukeo Yearbook, 1938, p. 19.

47. Yamamoto, M., *Nanking: Anatomy of an Atrocity*, (2000), p. 67.

48. *Ibid.*, p. 17.

49. Chang, p. 100.

50. Rabe, J., *The Good German of Nanking: The Diaries of John Rabe*, (1998), p. 87.

51. Shaw, A. G. L., *Modern World History: Social, Political and Economic Development, 1780-1955*, (1977), p. 55.
52. *Ibid.*, p. 60.
53. Dorn, F., *The Sino-Japanese War, 1937-41: From Marco Polo Bridge to Pearl Harbor*, (1974), p. 69.
54. Honda, K., *Nanking he no Michi (The Road to Nanjing)*, (1989), pp. 41-44.
55. Toland, J., p. 5.
56. *Ibid.*, p. 7.
57. Shigeharu, M., *Shanghai Jidai: The Shanghai Age (3): A Journalist's Memoirs*, (1975), p. 242.
58. Roberts, J. M., p. 927.

Chapter 2

1. 'German Military Training,' *Military Intelligence Service, U.S. War Department, Special Series 3, MIS 461*, (1942), p. 2.
2. Rhodes, *Masters of Death: The SS-Einsatzgruppen and the Invention of the Holocaust*, (2002), p. xii.
3. *Ibid.*, pp. 3-4.
4. *Ibid.*, p. 6.
5. Arad, Y., Krakowski, S., and Spector, S., ed. *The Einsatzgruppen Reports*, (1989), p. 100.
6. *Ibid.*, p. 112.
7. *Ibid.*, p. 113.
8. *Ibid.*, p. 121
9. *Ibid.*, p. 216.
10. Clark, A., *Barbarossa: The Russian-German Conflict, 1941-45*, (1965), p. 129.
11. Gutman, I., ed., *Encyclopedia of the Holocaust, 4 vols*, (1990), p. 45.
12. Hohne, H., *The Order of the Death's Head: The Story of Hitler's SS*, (1971), pp. 407-409.
13. 'The Schutzstaffeln (SS),' *The Nuremberg Indictment, Nazi Conspiracy and Aggression. Vol. II*, (1946), pp. 173-237.
14. *Ibid.*, p. 240.
15. *Ibid.*, p. 242.
16. Heaton, *German Anti-Partisan Warfare in Europe, 1939-1945*, (2001), p. 133.
17. *Ibid.*, p. 140.
18. 'The Einsatzgruppen Case, Military Tribunal II. Case No. 9,' *Trial of the Major War Criminals. Vol. I. P. 230.* (1947), pp. 369-375.
19. 'German Military Training,' (1942), p. 2.
20. *Ibid.*, p. 7.
21. *Ibid.*, p. 22.
22. Rhodes, R., pp. 3-4.
23. *Ibid.*, p. 6.
24. Erickson, J., *The Road to Stalingrad: Stalin's War with Germany*, (1999), pp. 131-132.
25. 'Organization and Obligations of the SS and the Police,' *National Political Education of the Army, (USA 439). IV, 616*, (1937), p. 616.
26. *Ibid.*, p. 617.
27. *Ibid.*, p. 618.
28. *Ibid.*, p. 631.
29. *Ibid*, p. 633.
30. 'The Great War and the Shaping of the 20th Century,' *Public Broadcasting Service*, (www.pbs.org/greatwar/, 2004).

31. 'Germany and the Treaty of Versailles,' www.schoolshistory.org.uk/, (2004).
32. *Ibid.*
33. Carmichael, J., *The Satanizing of the Jews: Origin and Development of Mystical Anti-Semitism*, (1992), p. 55.
34. *Ibid.*, p. 57.
35. 'Germany and the Treaty of Versailles,' www.schoolshistory.org.uk/, (2004).
36. *Ibid.*
37. 'Online History Lessons,' (2004).
38. 'The Holocaust,' *Jewish Virtual Library*, www.jewishvirtuallibrary.org/jsource/Holocaust/SS.html, (2005).
39. Online History Lessons, www.schoolshistory.org.uk/, (2004).
40. *Ibid.*
41. *Ibid.*
42. *Ibid.*
43. *Ibid.*
44. 'The Holocaust,' *Jewish Virtual Library*, www.jewishvirtuallibrary.org/jsource/Holocaust/SS.html, (2005)
45. *Ibid.*
46. *Nazi Conspiracy and Aggression, Vol. II*, (1946), p. 89.
47. *Ibid.*
48. *Ibid.*
49. *Ibid.*
50. 'About the Holocaust,' *Holocaust Memorial Center*, (holocaustcenter.org/Holocaust (2003)).
51. 'The Holocaust,' *Jewish Virtual Library*, www.jewishvirtuallibrary.org/jsource/Holocaust/SS.html, (2005).
52. *Ibid.*
53. Solkoff, *Beginnings, Mass Murder, and Aftermath of the Holocaust: Where History and Psychology Interact*, (www.normansolkoff.net/holocaust.html, (2002).
54. Rhodes, p. 95.
55. *Ibid.*, p. 97.
56. *Ibid.*, p. 99.
57. Glantz, D., M., and House, J., *When Titans Clashed: How the Red Army Stopped Hitler*, (1995) pp. 26-28.
58. *Ibid.*, p. 31.
59. Clark, A., *Barbarossa: The Russian–German Conflict, 1941–45*, (1965), p. 28.
60. Glantz, p. 33.
61. Erickson, p. 21.
62. *Ibid.*, p. 107.
63. Glantz, p. 49.
64. Clark, p. 48.
65. Glantz, p. 32.
66. *Ibid.*, p. 35.
67. *Ibid.*, p. 40.
68. Erickson, pp. 131-132.
69. 'The Einsatzgruppen Case, Military Tribunal II. Case No.9,' *Trial of the Major War Criminals. Vol. I. P. 230.* (1947), p. 38.
70. Erickson, pp. 137-139.
71. Megargee, G. P., *War of Annihilation: Combat and Genocide on the Eastern Front, 1941*, (2005), p. xiv.

72. Hohne, H., *The Order of the Death's Head: The Story of Hitler's SS*, (1971), pp. 407-409.
73. 'Effects of Climate on Combat in European Russia,' *Historical Study. CMH Pub 104–6*, (1952), p. 38.
74. *Ibid.*, p. 41.
75. Heaton, C., p. 132.
76. *Ibid.*, p. 120.
77. *Ibid.*, p. 121.
78. 'Effects of Climate on Combat in European Russia,' (1952), p. 60.
79. *Ibid.*, p. 77.
80. 'Terrain Factors in the Russian Campaign,' *Historical Study. CMH Pub 104–5*, (1951), p. 31.
81. 'The Schutzstaffeln (SS),' (1946), pp. 173-237.
82. *Ibid.*, p. 241.
83. *Ibid.*, p. 243.

Chapter 3

1. Beevor, *The Fall of Berlin* (2003), p. 23.
2. *Ibid.*, p. 37.
3. *Ibid.*, p. 38.
4. *Ibid.*, p. 39.
5. *Ibid.*, p. 45.
6. *Ibid.*, p. 55.
7. *Ibid.*, pp. 57-132
10. *Ibid.*, pp. 153-155
11. *Ibid.*, p. 20.
12. Solzhenitsyn, A., *Prussian Nights: A Poem*, Trans. Robert Conquest, (1977), p. 113.
13. Toliver, R., and Constable, T., *The Blond Knight of Germany: A Biography of Erich Hartmann*, (1986), p. 6.
14. *Ibid.*
15. *Ibid.*
16. *Ibid.*
17. *Ibid.*
18. This theme became the leitmotiv of Stalin's speeches from 1 May 1944.
19. 'Captured field post,' *Bundesarchiv-Militararchiv, RH2-2688*, p. 12.
20. Samoilov, *Lyudi odnogo variant, part II, Avora, No. 3*, (1990), p. 81.
21. Rees, L., *World War Two: Behind Closed Doors*, (New York: Vintage Books, 2010)
22. Roberts, J. M., 'Stalin's Army of Rapists: The Brutal War Crime that Russia and Germany Tried to Ignore,' *Daily Mail*, www.dailymail.co.uk/news/article-1080493/Stalins-army-rapists-The-brutal-war-crime-Russia-Germany-tried-ignore.html, (2008).
23. Naimark, *The Russians in Germany: The History of the Soviet Zone of Occupation, 1945–1949*, (1995), p. 129.
24. Naimark, N. M., *About the Russians and About Us–The Question of Rape and Soviet–German Relations in the East Zone*, (1990), p. 57.
25. Harrison, M., *Accounting for War: Soviet Production, Employment, and the Defence Burden, 1940–1945*, (1996), pp. 68 and 284.
26. Overy, R. J., *War and Economy in the Third Reich*, (1994), p. 346.
27. Abelshauser, 'Germany: Guns, Butter and Economic Miracles,' in Mark Harrison, ed., *The Economics of World War II: Six Great Powers in International Comparison*, (1998), p. 155.

28. Filtzer, D., 'Labour Discipline and Criminal Law in Soviet Industry, 1945–1953,' *PERSA Working Papers No. 8*, (2000), p. 10.
29. Zolotarev, V. A., ed., 'Velikaia Otechestvennaia. Tyl Krasnoi Armii v Velikoi Otechestvennoi voiny 1941–1945 gg. Dokumenty I materialy,' *Russkii Arkhiv*, 25 (14) (1998), pp. 304-5.
30. Barber, J., *Popular Reactions in Moscow to the German Invasion of June 22, 1941*, (1991), p. 6.
31. Boll, H., and Kopelew, L., *Why We Shot Each Other (1984)*, p. 14.
32. J. V. Stalin, Speech at the Red Army Paradeon the Red Square, Moscow, 7 November 1941 www.marxists.org/reference/archive/stalin/works/1941/11/07.htm
33. Kopelev, L., *No Jail for Thought*, ed. and trans. Anthony Austin, (1977), pp. 10, 53.
34. Ziemke, E., *Stalingrad to Berlin: The German Defeat in the East*, (1968), p. 488.
35. Erickson, J., *The Road to Stalingrad: Stalin's War with Germany*, (1975), p. 245.
36. *Ibid.*, p. 300.
37. *Ibid.*, p. 361-362.
38. Simonov,K., p. 88.
39. Kopelev, L., p. 58.
40. *Ibid.*, p. 71.
41. Ziemke, p. 490.
42. Gorbachevsky, B., *Through the Maelstrom: A Red Army Soldier's War on the Eastern Front, 1942–1945* (2008), p. 374.
43. *Ibid.*, p. 380.
44. *Ibid.*, p. 381.

Chapter 4

1. 'The Vietnam War and the Korean Army, Vol. 3,' *Ministry of Defense Institute of Military History*, (2003), p. 412.
2. Quoted from Quang Ngai General Museum, *A Look Back upon Son My*, (1998), p. 12.
3. Blackburn, R. M., *Mercenaries and Lyndon Johnson's 'More Flags': The Hiring of Korean, Filipino, and Thai Soldiers in the Vietnam War* (1994), p. 140.
4. Chomsky, N., preface to John Duffett, ed., *Against the Crime of Silence*, (1970), pp. xiv-xv.
5. 'Remember My Lai,' May 23, 1989, transcript of TV show, *PBS: Frontline*, www.pbs.org/wgbh/pages/frontline/programs/transcripts/714.html
6. Eszterhas, J., *et al.*, Massacre at Mylai, Life, (1969), p. 41.
7. Raimondo, T., 'The My Lai Massacre: A Case Study,' *Human Rights Program, School of the Americas*, (undated), pp. 8-13.
8. *Ibid.*, p. 16.
9. *Ibid.*, p. 16.
10. *Ibid.*, p. 16.
11. *Ibid.*, p. 16.
12. *Ibid.*, p. 16.
13. *Ibid.*, p. 17
14. *Ibid.*, p. 17
15. *Ibid.*, p. 19
16. Brigham, *Battlefield Vietnam: A Brief History*, www.pbs.org/battlefieldvietnam/history/
17. *Ibid.*
18. Raimondo, p. 15.
19. *Ibid.*, p. 16

20. *Ibid.*, p. 16.
21. *Ibid.*, p. 16.
22. *Ibid.*, p. 20.
23. *Ibid.*, p. 20.
24. *Ibid.*, p. 20.
25. *Ibid.*, p. 20.
26. Kowalski, J., *Cherries: A Vietnam War Novel*, (2010), p. 124.
27. Raimondo, p. 17.

Chapter 5

1. *Abu Ghraib Prison Scandal*,
    www.image.cbsnews.com/images/2004/05/06image6l5902x.jpg.
2. *Ibid.*
3. Danner, T., 'Torture and Truth,' *New York Review of Books 51*, (2004), p. 4.
4. Zizek, S., 'Between Two Deaths,' *London Review of Books 26.11*, 3 June 2004, lrb.veriovps. co.uk/v26/nl 1/zizeOl_.html.
5. Limbaugh, R., 'MPs Just Blowing Off Steam,' *CBS News*, 6 May 2004, www.cbsnews.com/ news/rush-mps-just-blowing-off-steam/.
6. Higham S., and Stephens, J., 'Abu Ghraib Detainees' Statements Describe Sexual Humiliation and Savage Beatings,' *The Washington Post*, 21 May 2004, www. washingtonpost.com/wp-dyn/articles/A43783-2004May20.html
7. 'Abu Ghraib a Crime Scene Says Military Judge,' *ABC News Online*, 21 June 2004, www. abc.net.au/news/newsitems/200406/sll37076.htm.
8. Morris, N., and Rothman, D. J. 'Perfecting the Prison,' *The Oxford History of the Prison: The Practice of Punishment in Western Society*, (1995), p. 100.
9. 'Defense Secretary Donald Rumsfeld Reaction to Abuse in Iraq,' ABC News, Good Morning America, 5 May 2004, web.lexisnexis.com/universe/document?_ m=d76dc22881lec3bf0b237cfb9358758b&_docnum=2&wchP=dGLbVzz-zSkVA&_ md5=f3ed76662b03985cac5806edac98bc29 (accessed June 28, 2005). 40.
10. Ignatieff, M., *A Just Measure of Pain: The Penitentiary in the Industrial Revolution, 1750-1850*, (1978), p. 212.
11. Butler, J., *Precarious Life: The Powers of 'Mourning and Violence*, (2004), p. 53.
12. Ignatieff, M., *The Lesser Evil: Political Ethics in An Age of Terror*, (2004), p. 101.
13. Brody, R., 'The Road to Abu Ghraib,' *Human Rights Watch, June, 2004*), www.hrw.org/ reports/2004/usa0604/, (2005).
14. Dimaggio, A. R., *Mass Media, Mass Propaganda: Examining American News in the 'War on Terror,'* (2008), p. 103.
15. *Ibid.*, p. 104.
16. *Hedges and Al-Arian*, 'Confessions from U.S. Soldiers in Iraq on the Brutal Treatment of Civilians,' *The Nation*, July 12, 2007, http://www.alternet.org/story/56761/confessions_ from_u.s._soldiers_in_iraq_on_the_brutal_treatment_of_civilians.
17. *Ibid.*
18. *Ibid.*
19. *Ibid.*
20. *Ibid.*
21. Bowden, M., 'The Dark Art of Interrogation: A Survey of the Landscape of Persuasion,' *The Atlantic Monthly*, (2003), p. 56.

Chapter 6

1. Athens, L., *The Creation of Dangerous Violent Criminals.* (Urbana: University of Illinois Press, 1992), pp. 57-60.
2. *Ibid.*
3. Haney, C., Banks, C., and Zlmbardo, P., *A Study of Prisoners and Guards* in a *Simulated Prison, Stanford University,* (1973), pp. 9-17.
4. Athens, p. 56.
5. *Ibid.*
6. Heaton, pp. 120-121.
7. *Ibid.*
8. Athens, p. 80.

Bibliography

Books

'The Schutzstaffeln (SS),' *The Nuremberg Indictment, Nazi Conspiracy and Aggression, Vol. II* (Washington, D. C.: United States Government Publishing Office, 1946)

1955 (Melbourne: Longman Cheshire, 1977)

Abramsky, S., *Hard Time Blues: How Politics Built a Prison Nation* (New York: Thomas Dunne Books, 2002)

Arad, Y., Krakowski, S., and Spector, S., ed., *The Einsatzgruppen Reports*, (New York Holocaust Library, 1989)

Athens, L., *The Creation of Dangerous Violent Criminals* (Urbana: University of Illinois Press, 1992)

Barber, J., *Popular Reactions in Moscow to the German Invasion of June 22, 1941* (Soviet Union, 1991)

Beevor, A., *The Fall of Berlin* (London: Penguin Books, 2003)

Best, G., *Humanity in Warfare*, (New York: Columbia University Press, 1983)

Blackburn, R. M., *Mercenaries and Lyndon Johnson's 'More Flags': The Hiring of Korean, Filipino, and Thai Soldiers in the Vietnam War* (Jefferson: McFarland, 1994)

Boll, H., and Kopelew, L., *Why We Shot Each Other* (Munich: Deutscher Taschenbuchverlag, 1984)

Brigham, R. K., *Battlefield Vietnam: A Brief History*, www.pbs.org/battlefieldvietnam/history/ (undated)

Brook, T., *Documents on the Rape of Nanking* (Ann Arbor: University of Michigan Press, 1999)

Brooks, R., *When Sorry Isn't Enough: The Controversy over Apologies & Reparations for Human Injustice* (New York: New York University Press, 1999)

Butler, J., *Precarious Life: The Powers of 'Mourning and Violence* (London: Verso, 2004)

Carmichael, J., *The Satanizing of the Jews; Origin and Development of Mystical Anti-Semitism* (New York: Fromm International Publishing Company, 1992)

Chang, I., *The Rape of Nanking: The Forgotten Holocaust of World War II* (New York: Penguin Books, 1997)

Chomsky, N., preface to John Duffett, ed., *Against the Crime of Silence* (New York: Clarion, 1970)

Clark, A., *Barbarossa: The Russian-German Conflict, 1941–45* (New York: HarperCollins Publishers, Inc., 1965) de Tocqueville, A., *Democracy in America* (New York: Vintage Books, 1990)

Dimaggio, A. R., *Mass Media, Mass Propaganda: Examining American News in the 'War on Terror,'* (Lanham: Lexington Books, 2008)

Dorn, F., *The Sino-Japanese War, 1937–41: From Marco Polo Bridge to Pearl Harbor* (New York: Macmillan Publishing, 1974)

Economics of World War II: Six Great Powers in International Comparison, (Cambridge: Cambridge University Press, 1998)

Erickson, J., *The Road to Stalingrad: Stalin's War with Germany* (New Haven: Yale University Press, 1999)

Fogel, J. A., *The Nanjing Massacre in History and Historiography* (Berkeley: University of California Press, 2000)

Gettleman, M. E., Franklin, J., Young, M. B., and Franklin, H. B., eds., *Vietnam and America: The Most Comprehensive Documented History of the Vietnam War* (New York: Grove, 1995)

Gilbert, M., *The Holocaust: A History of the Jews of Europe During the Second World War* (New York: Henry Holt and Company, 1985)

Glantz, D. M. and House, J., *When Titans Clashed: How the Red Army Stopped Hitler* (Lawrence: University Press of Kansas, 1995)

Gorbachevsky, B., *Through the Maelstrom: A Red Army Soldier's War on the Eastern Front, 1942–1945* (University Press of Kansas, 2008)

Grew, J., *Report from Tokyo: A Message to the American People* (New York: Simon and Schuster, 1942)

Gutman, I., ed., *Encylopedia of the Holocaust, 4 vols,* (New York: Macmillan Publishing Company, 1990)

Hamilton, V. L., and Sanders, J., *Every Day Justice: Responsibility and the Individual in Japan and the United States* (New Haven: Yale University Press, 1992)

Haney, C., Banks, C., and Zlmbardo, P., *A Study of Prisoners and Guards* in a *Simulated Prison, Stanford University* (Washington: Office of Naval Research, Department of the Navy, 1973)

Harrison, M., *Accounting for War: Soviet Production, Employment, and the Defence Burden, 1940–1945* (Cambridge: Cambridge University Press, 1996)

Hata, I., *Nanking Incident* and Hora, T., *Nanking Massacre: Definitive Version*

Heather, P., *The Fall of the Roman Empire: A New History* (London: Oxford University Press, 2005)

Heaton, C., *German Anti-Partisan Warfare in Europe, 1939–1945* (Atglen: Schiffer Publishing Ltd, 2001)

Hohne, H., *The Order of the Death's Head: The Story of Hitler's SS* (New York, NY: Ballantine Books, 1971)

Honda, K., *Nanking he no Michi (The Road to Nanjing)* (Tokyo: Asahi Bunko, 1989)

Ignatieff, M., *A Just Measure of Pain: The Penitentiary in the Industrial Revolution, 1750–1850* (Prescott: Peregrine Books, 1978); *The Lesser Evil: Political Ethics in An Age of Terror* (Princeton, N.J.: Princeton University Press, 2004)

Iinuma, M., *Diary,* Nankin senshi shiryo shu, Vol. 1, IMTFE EXHIBIT No. 3399, Rg 238, Entry 14, Box 301, National Archives of USA

Ikuhiko, H., *The Nanking Incident: The Structure of the Massacre* (Toyko: Chuo Koronska, 1986)

International Military Tribunal for the Far East (IMTFE) Judgment, Chapter VIII (Christchurch, NZ: Justice Erima H. Northcroft Collection, University of Canterbury, 1948)

Kaplan, A., 'Left Alone with America: The Absence of Empire in the Study of American Culture,' *Cultures of United States Imperialism,* ed. Amy Kaplan and Donald E. Pease (Durham, N.C.: Duke University Press, 1993); *The Anarchy of Empire in the Making of U.S. Culture* (Cambridge, MA: Harvard University Press, 2002)

Kawakami, K. K., *Manchoukuo, Child of Conflict* (New York: Macmillan, 1933)

Kopelev, L., *No Jail for Thought,* ed. and trans. Anthony Austin (London, 1977)

Kowalski, J., *Cherries: A Vietnam War Novel* (CreateSpace, 2010)

Kung-Ku, C., *Three Months in Fallen Capital* (Taipei: The Central Library, 1981)

Lory, H., *Japan's Military Masters: The Army in Japanese Life* (Westport: Greenwood Press, 1943)

Morris, N., and Rothman, D. J. 'Perfecting the Prison', *The Oxford History of the Prison: The Practice of Punishment in Western Society* (1995), p. 100

Masao, M., *Thought and Behavior in Modern Japanese Politics*, ed. Ivan Morris (New York: Oxford University Press, 1969)

Masazumi, I., *Reflection on Strategic Planning during the China Incident, July 1937-December 1938* (Unknown Publisher)

Megargee, G. P., *War of Annihilation: Combat and Genocide on the Eastern Front, 1941* (Lanham: Rowman and Littlefield Publishers, Inc., 2005)

Musmanno, M. A, *The Eichmann Kommandos* (New York: MacFadden Books, 1961)

Naimark, Norman M., *The Russians in Germany: The History of the Soviet Zone of Occupation, 1945–1949* (Harvard: Harvard University Press, 1995)

Nazi Conspiracy and Aggression, Vol. II (Washington: United States Government Printing Office, 1946)

Ngai, Quang General Museum, *A Look Back upon Son My* (Quang Ngai: Quang Ngai General Museum, 1998)

Nuremberg Military Tribunals under Control Council Law No. 10, Vol. IV. (Washington, D. C.: United States Government Publishing Office, 1946)

Overy, R. J., *War and Economy in the Third Reich* (Oxford: Oxford University Press, 1994)

Rabe, J., *The Good German of Nanking: The Diaries of John Rabe* (London: Little Brown and Co., 1998)

Rees, L., *Horror in the East* (London: BBC Books, 2001); *World War Two: Behind Closed Doors* (New York: Vintage Books, 2010)

Rhodes, R., *Masters of Death: The SS-Einsatzgruppen and the Invention of the Holocaust* (New York, NY: Vintage Books, 2002)

Roberts, J. M., *The New History of the World* (New York: Oxford University Press, 2003)

Ruane, K., *The Vietnam Wars* (Manchester University Press, 2000)

Russell, L., *The Knights of Bushido: A Short History of Japanese War Crimes* (Liverpool: Greenhill Books, 2005)

Schell, J., *The Real War* (New York: Pantheon, 1987)

Seniavskaia, E. S., *The Psychology of War in the 20th Century: Russia's Historical Experience* (Moscow, 1999)

Shaw, A. G. L., *Modern World History: Social, Political and Economic Development, 1780–*

Shigeharu, M., *Shanghai Jidai: The Shanghai Age (3): A Journalist's Memoirs* (Tokyo: Chuo Koron, 1975)

Shoro, H., *My Observation of Nanking Before and After Its Fall*, Kaiko, June 1983

Simonov, K., *Stikhotvoreniia i poemy (Verses and Narrative Poems)* (Moscow, 1945)

Solzhenitsyn, A., *Prussian Nights: A Poem*, trans. Robert Conquest, (New York: Farrar, Straus and Giroux, 1977)

Taylor, T., *The Anatomy of the Nuremberg Trials* (Boston: Little Brown 1992)

Toland, J., *The Rising Sun: The Decline and Fall of the Japanese Empire, 1936–1945* (New York: Random House, Inc., 2003)

Toliver, R., and Constable, T., *The Blond Knight of Germany: A Biography of Erich Hartmann* (New York: McGraw-Hill, Inc., 1986)

Vasiliev, A. A., *History of the Byzantine Empire Vol. I* (Madison: University of Wisconsin Press, 1958)

Weiner, A., *Making Sense of War: The Second World War and the Fate of the Bolshevik Revolution* (Princeton, Princeton University Press, 2001)

Yamamoto, M., *Nanking: Anatomy of an Atrocity* (Westport: Praeger Publishing, 2000)

Yoshida, T., *Making of the Rape of Nanking: History and Memory in Japan, China, and the United States* (New York: Oxford University Press, Inc., 2006)

Yoshida, Y., *The Emperor's Military and the Nanjing Incident* (Tokyo: Aoki Shoten, 1986)

Young, A. M., *Imperial Japan, 1926–1938* (Westport: Greenwood Press, 1974)

Ziemke, E., *Stalingrad to Berlin: The German Defeat in the East* (Washington D.C.: Center of Military History, United States Army, 1968)

Online Articles

'About the Holocaust,' *Holocaust Memorial Center*, holocaustcenter.org/Holocaust.

'Abu Ghraib a Crime Scene Says Military Judge,' *ABC News Online*, 21 June 2004 www.abc.net. au/news/newsitems/200406/sll37076.htm (accessed 29 June 2005)

'Agent: England Described 'Humiliation' Techniques,' *cnn.com*, 6 August 2004, www.cnn.com/2004/LAW/08/06/lynndie.england.hearing/index.html (accessed 29 June 2005)

'Camp Delta Death Chamber Plan,' *BBC News World Edition*, 10 June 2003, news.bbc.co.uk/2/hi/americas/2979076.stm (accessed 28 June 2005)

'Defense Secretary Donald Rumsfeld Reaction to Abuse in Iraq,' *ABC News, Good Morning America, 5 May 2004*, web.lexisnexis.com/universe/document?_m=d76d c22881lec3bf0b237cfb9358758b&_docnum=2&wchP=dGLbVzz-zSkVA&_ md5=f3ed76662b03985cac5806edac98bc29 (accessed June 28, 2005).

'Einsatzgruppen,' *The Simon Wiesenthal Center*, motlc.wiesenthal.com/text/x06/xm0689.html, 1997

'Germany and the Treaty of Versailles,' *[UK] Schools History*, www.schoolshistory.org.uk/, 2004

'Humiliation and Savage Beatings,' *The Washington Post*, 21 May 2004, www.washingtonpost. com/wp-dyn/articles/A43783-2004May20.html (assessed 24 March 2016)

'Online History Lessons,' *[UK] Schools History*, www.schoolshistory.org.uk/, 2004

'The Einsatzgruppen Case, Military Tribunal II Case No. 9,' *Trials of War Criminals Before the* 'The Final Report of the Independent Panel to Review DoD Detention Operations, chaired by James R. Schlesinger, issued August 2004,' news.findlaw.com/hdocs/docs/dod/abughraibrpt.pdf

'The Great War and the Shaping of the 20th Century,' *Public Broadcasting Service*, www.pbs.org/greatwar/, 2004

'The Holocaust,' *Jewish Virtual Library*, www.jewishvirtuallibrary.org/jsource/Holocaust/SS.html, 2005

Abelshauser, W., 'Germany: Guns, Butter and Economic Miracles,' in Mark Harrison, ed., *The Abu Ghraib Prison Scandal*, wwwimage.cbsnews.com/images/2004/05/06image6l5902x.jpg (accessed 15 June 2005)

Bowman, T., 'Army Report Points to Training Flaws at Prison,' *The Baltimore Sun*, 4 May 2004, www.baltimoresun.com/news/bal-te.training04may04-story.html, (assessed 10 February 2015)

Brody, R., 'The Road to Abu Ghraib,' *Human Rights Watch, June, 2004*, www.hrw.org/reports/2004/usa0604/, (accessed 28 June 2005)

Calley, W., 'Witness for the Defense, Direct examination by George Latimer,' University of Missouri.law2.umkc.edu/.../myl_Calltest.html

Hedges, C., Al-Arian, L., 'Confessions from U.S. Soldiers in Iraq on the Brutal Treatment of Civilians,' *The Nation*, 12 July 2007, www.alternet.org/story/56761/confessions_from_u.s._soldiers_in_iraq_on_the_brutal_treatment_of_civilians, (accessed on 10 March 14)

Hochschild, A., 'What's in a Word? Torture,' *New York Times*, 23 May 2004, nytimes.com/2004/05/23/opinion/23HOCH.html (accessed 28 June 28 2005)

Limbaugh, R., 'MPs Just Blowing Off Steam,' *CBS News*, 6 May 2004, www.cbsnews.com/news/rush-mps-just-blowing-off-steam/ (assessed 15 March 2015)

Roberts, A. W., 'Stalin's Army of Rapists: The Brutal War Crime that Russia and Germany tried to Ignore,' *Daily Mail*, 24 October 2008, www.dailymail.co.uk/news/article–1080493/Stalins–army–rapists–The–brutal–war–crime–Russia–Germany–tried–ignore.html

Solkoff, N., *Beginnings, Mass Murder, and Aftermath of the Holocaust: Where History and Psychology Interact*, www.normansolkoff.net/holocaust.html, 2002

Stalin, J. V., *Speech at the Red Army Parade on the Red Square, Moscow, 7 November 1941*, www.marxists.org/reference/archive/stalin/works/1941/11/07.htm

Stein, A., 'Prison Stocks: A Secure Pick?' *Money*, 30 April 2004, web.lexis-nexis.com/universe/

The O'Reilly Factor, 'Unresolved Problem: Update on Abu Ghraib Scandal,' Bill O'Reilly, 8.21 p.m., Monday 17 January 2005, Fox News Network, web.lexis-nexis.com/universe/

Zizek, S., 'Between Two Deaths,' *London Review of Books 26.11*, 3 June 2004, online edition, lrb.veriovps.co.uk/v26/nl 1/zizeO l_.html (accessed 1 January 2005)

Publications

'Directive Concerning the Operation in and Entry to Nanking,' *CCAA Command, DSKS, Vol. 3, NSS1*

'Effects of Climate on Combat in European Russia,' *Historical Study. CMH Pub 104–6*. (Washington, D.C.: U.S. Army Center of Military History, 1952)

'German Military Training,' *Military Intelligence Service, U.S. War Department. Special Series 3, MIS 461* (Washington, D. C.: 17 September 1942)

'Handbook on Japanese Military Forces,' *Technical Manual E30-480* (U.S. War Department, 1 October 1944)

'How to Fight the Chinese Military,' *Army's Infantry School*, quoted in Yoshida, *Emperor's Military and the Nanking Incident*, (1933)

'Nationalist Government, Table of Rape of Nanking Individual Victims,' *Correspondence from the Secretary's Office of the National Government's General Secretary to the Ministry of Justice*, (1946)

'Organization and Obligations of the SS and the Police,' *National Political Education of the Army, (USA 439), IV*, January 1937

'Rabe to Japanese Embassy,' 17 December 1937, *DNSZ, N o.9, p.17.4, NYT*

'Report of the Department of the Army Review of the Preliminary Investigations into the My Lai Incident,' *Volume I: The Report of the Investigation, 29 March 1969*, Library of Congress Call Number DS557.8.M9 U54 1974 and OCLC Number 1646516

'Terrain Factors in the Russian Campaign,' *Historical Study, CMH Pub 104-5* (Washington, D.C.:U.S. Army Center of Military History, 1951)

'The Vietnam War and the Korean Army, Vol. 3,' *Ministry of Defense Institute of Military History*, (Seoul: Republic of Korea, 2003)

10th Army (Yanagawa) Army Group Legal Department Record

1st Battalion of the 66th Infantry Regiment, *Battle Report, Military Historical Detachment*

Bartone, P. T., 'Lessons of Abu Ghraib: Understanding and Preventing Prisoner Abuse in Military Operations,' *Defense Horizons, Number 64* (November 2008)

Bowden, M., 'The Dark Art of Interrogation: A Survey of the Landscape of Persuasion,' *The Atlantic Monthly*, October 2003

Captured field post, *Bundesarchiv/Militärarchiv* Freiburg Breisgau, RH2–2688.

Danner, M., 'Torture and Truth,' *New York Review of Books 51*, 10 June 2004

Eszterhas, J., *et al.*, 'The Massacre at Mylai,' *Life*, 5 December 1969

Filtzer, D., 'Labour Discipline and Criminal Law in Soviet Industry, 1945–1953,' *PERSA Working Papers No. 8, University of Warwick, Department of Economics* (2000)

Higham S., and Stephens, J., 'Abu Ghraib Detainees' Statements Describe Sexual Humiliation and Savage Beatings', *The Washington Post*, 21 May 2004, www.washingtonpost.com/wp-dyn/articles/A43783-2004May20.htmlHirotato, S., 3 January 1938, *Red Machine, no. 1193B*

Kobayashi, M., ed., *Sakigake: Kyodo Butai Senki*, 6 January 1938

Mamoru, I., *Diary*, 14–15 December 1937

Masatoshi, I., *Testimony, SNS (11)*, Kaiko, February 1985

Matsuoka, Y., Japan Manchukeo Yearbook, 1938

Matsui, I., *Diary*, 15 December 1937

Merridale, C., 'Ideology and Combat in the Red Army, 1939-45', *Journal of Contemporary History, Vol. 41, No. 2* (April 2006)

Morozumi, G., *Memoir*, NSS2

Naimark, N. M., *About the Russians and About Us–The Question of Rape and Soviet–German Relations in the East Zone*, (unpublished paper, Stanford University, January 30, 1990)

Nakajima, K., *Diary*, 15 December 1937

Raimondo, Maj. T., 'The My Lai Massacre: A Case Study', *Human Rights Program, School of the Americas* (Fort Benning, Georgia [undated])

Samoilov, D., *Lyudi odnogo variant, part II, Avora, No. 3* (1990)

Sasaki, T., *Diary*, 13 December 1937

Schlosser, E., 'The Prison-Industrial Complex', *The Atlantic Monthly 282.6* (December 1998)

Testimony of Sakakibara Kazuein 'SNS' (11) (Kaiko, February 1985)

Zolotarev, V. A., ed. (1998), 'Velikaia Otechestvennaia. Tyl Krasnoi Armii v Velikoi Otechestvennoi voiny 1941–1945 gg. Dokumenty I materialy', *Russkii Arkhiv*, 25 (14) (1998)